MONTAIGNE AND THE LIFE OF FREEDOM

More than any other early modern text, Montaigne's *Essais* have come to be associated with the emergence of a distinctively modern subjectivity, defined in opposition to the artifices of language and social performance. Felicity Green challenges this interpretation with a compelling revisionist reading of Montaigne's text, centred on one of his deepest but hitherto most neglected preoccupations: the need to secure for himself a sphere of liberty and independence that he can properly call his own, or himself. *Montaigne and the Life of Freedom* restores the *Essais* to their historical context by examining the sources, character and significance of Montaigne's project of self-study. That project, as Green shows, reactivates and reshapes ancient practices of self-awareness and self-regulation, in order to establish the self as a space of inner refuge, tranquillity and dominion, free from the inward compulsion of the passions and from subjection to external objects, forces and persons.

FELICITY GREEN is Junior Research Fellow in history at Trinity College, Cambridge. She has also held fellowships at the Swedish Collegium for Advanced Study and at the Huntington Library.

IDEAS IN CONTEXT 101

Edited by David Armitage, Jennifer Pitts, Quentin Skinner and James Tully

The books in this series will discuss the emergence of intellectual traditions and of related new disciplines. The procedures, aims and vocabularies that were generated will be set in the context of the alternatives available within the contemporary frameworks of ideas and institutions. Through detailed studies of the evolution of such traditions, and their modification by different audiences, it is hoped that a new picture will form of the development of ideas in their concrete contexts. By this means, artificial distinctions between the history of philosophy, of the various sciences, of society and politics, and of literature may be seen to dissolve.

The series is published with the support of the Exxon Foundation.

A list of books in the series will be found at the end of the volume.

MONTAIGNE AND THE LIFE OF FREEDOM

FELICITY GREEN
Trinity College, Cambridge

CAMBRIDGE
UNIVERSITY PRESS

CAMBRIDGE UNIVERSITY PRESS
Cambridge, New York, Melbourne, Madrid, Cape Town,
Singapore, São Paulo, Delhi, Mexico City

Cambridge University Press
The Edinburgh Building, Cambridge CB2 8RU, UK

Published in the United States of America by Cambridge University Press, New York

www.cambridge.org
Information on this title: www.cambridge.org/9781107024397

First published 2012

Printed in the United States of America

A catalogue record for this publication is available from the British Library.

Library of Congress Cataloguing in Publication Data

Green, Felicity, 1984–
Montaigne and the life of freedom / Felicity Green.
p. cm. – (Ideas in context ; 101)
Includes bibliographical references and index.
ISBN 978-1-107-02439-7 (hardback)
1. Montaigne, Michel de, 1533–1592 – Criticism and interpretation. 2. Liberty in literature.
3. Self in literature. I. Title.
PQ1643.G67 2012
844′.3–dc23 2012002691

ISBN 978-1-107-02439-7 Hardback

Contents

Acknowledgements

This book could not have been written without the help and support of a number of institutions and individuals, and it is a pleasure to record my gratitude to them here. My research was funded, in the first instance, by a doctoral award from the Arts and Humanities Research Council. I owe further thanks for financial and academic assistance to King's College and, since my election as a Title A (Research) Fellow in October 2009, to Trinity College Cambridge; it has been a great privilege to work under such stimulating conditions. I am also grateful to the Anglo-California Foundation for enabling me to spend an enriching semester as a visiting student at the University of California at Berkeley.

My greatest debt is to my PhD supervisor, Quentin Skinner, without whose exceptional insight, encouragement and kindness I could never have completed this work. His intellectual generosity, acuity and learning have provided me with a constant source of inspiration and support. I also wish to express particular thanks to my examiners, Annabel Brett and Terence Cave, as well as to Warren Boutcher, for their extremely perceptive comments and for their invaluable guidance about revising my work for publication. I have gained immeasurably from the learning and generosity of many other scholars, including Louis Caron, Timothy Hampton, David Hillman, Kinch Hoekstra, Victoria Kahn, Sachiko Kusukawa, Dmitri Levitin, Joseph Moshenska, Michael Moriarty, Richard Scholar, Richard Serjeantson, Sophie Smith, Michael Sonenscher and Alexandra Walsham; I am most grateful for their advice and for their interest. All remaining mistakes and faults are, of course, my responsibility alone.

Last but not least, I am deeply grateful to my friends and family for their kindness, patience and support at all stages of this project. My greatest thanks are due to Tom, for his unfailing insight, friendship and love; and to my parents, to whom I dedicate this book, with gratitude and affection.

Conventions

TEXTS

References to the *Essais* are by book, chapter and page number to the following editions:

P *Les Essais*, eds. Jean Balsamo, Michel Magnien and Catherine Magnien-Simonin. Paris: Gallimard (Bibliothèque de la Pléiade), 2007.

V *Les Essais de Michel de Montaigne*, ed. Pierre Villey, revised by V.-L. Saulnier, re-edited with a preface and supplement by Marcel Conche. Paris: Presses universitaires de France, 2004.

F *The complete Essays of Montaigne*, translated by Donald Frame. Stanford University Press, 1958.

The Pléiade edition (P) is based on the first posthumous edition of the *Essais* (1595). All quotations are taken from this text, which provides the most complete version of Montaigne's work.[1] The Villey-Saulnier edition (V), for many years the standard version of the *Essais*, is based on the 'Bordeaux Copy', a working copy of the 1588 text with extensive emendations in Montaigne's own hand. Cross-references to this edition are provided for the convenience of the reader.

The order of certain chapters in the 1595 edition differs from that of earlier editions, due to the displacement of one chapter (*That the taste of good and evil depends in large part on the opinion we have of them*) from I.14 to I.40. In what follows, then, I.25, for example, refers to *On the education of children*, and not to *On pedantry*.

TRANSCRIPTIONS

Montaigne revised the *Essais* continually and extensively over a period of two decades, inserting subtle emendations, lengthy *allongeails* and whole

[1] For a more detailed discussion, see Green 2009.

new chapters as he went along. I have therefore chosen to identify the text with the complete set of its versions and revisions, rather than with its most advanced state. This decision has led me to depart from the Pléiade edition in two important respects: by reinstating the letters conventionally used to signal successive stages in the composition of the *Essais*, and by including earlier variants rejected in the final (1595) recension of the text.

Superscript letters are used as follows: ^A refers to the text of the first edition, published in 1580; ^B to material added between 1580 and 1588; and ^C to all later additions. I have used <angle brackets> to identify those passages where the 1595 text diverges from the Bordeaux Copy. Text present in an earlier state of the work but excised or replaced in later revisions is indicated with a single line of deletion.

The original spelling, punctuation, capitalisation, italicisation and paragraphing have been preserved. However, I have expanded all contractions and changed 'i' to 'j' and 'u' to 'v' in accordance with modern typography (except when quoting from Latin). All Greek words, phrases and titles have been transliterated.

TRANSLATIONS

Donald Frame's version of the *Essais* (F) has provided the starting point for all my translations of Montaigne into English. However, I have frequently taken the liberty of modifying Frame's text to reflect Montaigne's choice of language with greater accuracy. Moreover, because Frame based his translation on the Bordeaux Copy, I have supplied my own translations for those passages added to the 1595 text. When using editions of classical texts for which facing-page translations are provided, I have used these as my starting point, while sometimes modifying them in the interests of a more literal rendering of the original text. All other translations are my own unless otherwise indicated.

When translating Montaigne, I have rendered *liberté* as 'liberty' and *franchise* as 'freedom'. I have, of course, been constrained to adopt 'free' and 'freely' as translations of *libre* and *librement*, for which there is no direct English equivalent. In addition, I have occasionally translated *franc* and *franchement* as 'frank' and 'frankly', in contexts carrying a narrower connotation of boldness or plainness in speech. It seems to be the case, more generally, that *franchise* in Montaigne's usage places slightly more emphasis on the moral character of the free man (his fearlessness, his magnanimity), whereas *liberté* tends to draw attention to the lack of dependency and attachment that makes such virtues possible. This distinction is not, however, a consistent or significant one: the terms are often used interchangeably by Montaigne – as close equivalents, if not as exact synonyms.[2] I have therefore allowed myself to use both 'freedom' and 'liberty' in my own prose – C'to diversify', as Montaigne would put it,[3] without wishing to attach great conceptual importance to the slightly different shades of meaning carried by the two terms.

The original titles of works written in languages other than English (including the *Essais*) have not been translated. The titles of individual chapters of Montaigne's text have, however, been rendered in English.

GENDER

I try to maintain gender-neutral language as far as possible. It is sometimes evident, however, that Montaigne conceives of liberty as a peculiarly masculine quality, and that he is concerned to present himself not merely as a free person but as a free man. In these cases, I have chosen to follow his gendered usage to avoid altering his sense.

[2] In *On vanity*, for example, Montaigne writes that C'idleness and freedom' ('l'oysiveté, la franchise') are his 'most favoured qualities' and that C'liberty and idleness' ('la liberté et l'oysiveté') are his 'mistress qualities'. III.9: P 1014, 1038; V 969, 992; F 741, 759.

[3] C'Pour diversifier'. II.37: P 796, V 758, F 574.

Introduction

This book explores the relationship between self-examination, self-regulation and human freedom in a late Renaissance text: the *Essais* (c. 1571–92) of Michel de Montaigne.[1] More than any other literary or philosophical work of its period, the *Essais* have come to be regarded as a landmark in the development of modern subjectivity – as an embodiment of conceptions and concerns astonishingly akin to our own. I argue that this sense of familiarity is, in certain fundamental respects, illusory – a projection of our own preoccupations and expectations on to Montaigne's text. By drawing attention to questions about the freedom of the self in the *Essais*, I hope not only to illuminate a lost dimension of Montaigne's work, but to recover something of the strangeness and fertility of a way of thinking about the self largely occluded in our own culture.[2]

One of the most striking and original features of the text is its rejection of abstract and didactic learning in favour of a dynamic portrait of the

[1] Born in 1533, Montaigne is thought to have begun work on the *Essais* in about 1571 (see Villey 1933). Books I and II were first published in 1580, in a two-volume octavo edition printed in Bordeaux by Simon Millanges (Montaigne 1580). A considerably expanded quarto edition (the fifth edition) appeared in Paris (Abel L'Angelier) in 1588, with the addition of a third volume and the insertion of much new material into the first two books of the existing text (Montaigne 1588). The margins of the 'Bordeaux Copy' – Montaigne's own working copy of the 1588 edition, now preserved at the Bibliothèque municipale in Bordeaux (Rés. 1238) – are filled with further extensive manuscript additions made in his own hand in the years before his death in 1592. This resource has recently been made available in a colour facsimile edition (Montaigne 2002a) and is also available online as part of the Montaigne Project hosted by the University of Chicago (Montaigne 2002b). The Bordeaux Copy diverges at a number of points from the first posthumous (folio) edition of 1595 (Paris: Abel L'Angelier), which was prepared by Montaigne's 'fille d'alliance' (II.17: P 70[illegible], V 661, F 502), Marie de Gournay (Montaigne 1595). For fuller bibliographical information, see Sayce and Maskell 1983. For information about the editions used in this book, see under 'Conventions'.

[2] Recent years have witnessed a surge of interest in the history of subjectivity and selfhood: see, for example, Taylor 1989, Porter 1997, Reiss 2005, Seigel 2005, Martin and Barresi 2006 and Sorabji 2006. These accounts, however, have little to say about the role of freedom in the construction of personhood and individual agency. For a stimulating exploration of the difficulties involved in studying representations of the person and the self in other periods and cultures, see Carrithers, Collins and Lukes 1985.

author's own dispositions and cogitations. Montaigne claims to [A]'examine', 'monitor' and 'sample' himself, to [B]'see' himself and 'seek for' himself 'down to the very entrails'.[3] At the heart of this groundbreaking project of self-study is a call for a symbolic retreat from the world into the seclusion of one's own home, library or *arriereboutique* – spaces in which it is possible to live for or belong to oneself ([A]'*estre à soy*').[4]

This foregrounding of the self resonates strongly with modern readers, who tend to think of themselves as individuals possessed of hidden feelings and inward depths, caught in a web of language and social performance always falling short of their essential being. From this perspective, Montaigne's efforts to distinguish all that is properly 'moy' or 'à moy' (myself, my own) from all that is not reflect a striving for sincere self-presence and self-expression in a world of alienating appearances and constructed roles.[5] Subjectivity here emerges at a point of perceived friction between artificial and authentic layers of conduct and self-understanding – between our concern to establish ourselves as the authors of our own identities and the suspicion that our 'selves' are mere performances, scripted by social and ideological forces beyond our control.[6]

My objection to this approach is that it involves the suppression of a crucial dimension of Montaigne's project: the fact that the [B]'ruling form' that he claims to discover in himself is specifically that of a *free* self.[7] [C]'Idleness and freedom', he writes in *On vanity*, are his 'most favoured qualities' – a point reiterated just a few pages later with the claim that [C]'liberty and idleness' are his 'ruling qualities'.[8] His soul, we are told in *On presumption*, is [A]'free and all its own'; he succeeds only when moved by his 'own pure and free will', having had 'neither forced governor nor master to this day'.[9] As these quotations suggest, Montaigne's self-portrait is at

3 [A]'Je me considere sans cesse, je me contrerolle, je me gouste'. II.17: P 697, V 657, F 499. [B]'Moy, qui me voy, et qui me recherche jusques aux entrailles'. III.5: P 889, V 847, F 643–4.

4 I.38: P 246, V 242, F 178.

5 See, for example, Cameron 1968, Lüthy 1987, Kushner 1993, Martin 1997, Delègue 1998, Martin 2004 and, above all, Starobinski 1993; cf. (in the context of English Renaissance drama) Maus 1995. For further examples and more extensive discussion, see Chapter 2, Section IV. For a critique of this approach in relation to seventeenth-century English 'life-writings', see Shuger 2000.

6 This dichotomy between subjectivity (understood as autonomous self-creation) and subjection to power (in the Foucauldian or Althusserian sense) is central to Greenblatt 1980; see also (again in an English context) Barker 1984 and Belsey 1985. For recent appeals to Montaigne as the exponent of an inner self ultimately irreducible to social and ideological determination, see Lee 2000 and Grady 2002.

7 [B]'Forme maistresse'. III.2: P 851, V 811, F 615.

8 [C]'Mes qualitez plus favories, l'oysiveté, la franchise'. III.9: P 1014, V 969, F 741. [C]'La liberté et l'oysiveté, qui sont mes maistresses qualitez'. III.9: P 1038, V 992, F 759.

9 [A]'Ma pure et libre volonté [. . .] J'ay une ame libre et toute sienne [. . .]. N'ayant eu jusques à cett' heure ny commandant ny maistre forcé'. II.17: P 680–1, V 642–3, F 487.

its heart that of a man who belongs to himself, in the sense that his will is his own, instead of being enslaved to someone or something other than himself. It is with the analysis of this self-image that the following study is principally concerned.

Montaigne's reflections on freedom, as this book seeks to make clear, resist incorporation into any one framework of analysis. Certain dimensions of his thinking – in particular his preoccupation with dependency, with the enslavement of the will, and with the vicissitudes of personal obligation (as opposed to legitimate subjection) – resonate unmistakably with what has come to be described, in the wake of Quentin Skinner, as a 'neo-Roman' or 'republican' understanding of freedom as nondomination.[10] Montaigne's version of that language, however, is ethical, rather than constitutional, in its orientation: freedom is to be secured not through political participation in a free state, but through a personal practice of self-regulation allowing us to preserve our will from subjection and expropriation. That project of voluntary disengagement is, in turn, indebted to ancient thought, and in particular to Stoic conceptions of independence as a state of inner tranquillity and detachment. Here again, however, that language of moral freedom and self-control appears in a heavily revised and nuanced incarnation, couched in a discourse of human frailty, vulnerability and self-protection, emphasising the limits of our voluntary power over ourselves and centred on the withdrawal or suspension of the will, rather than its assertion.

These considerations all serve to direct the question of subjectivity and interiority in the *Essais* away from conceptions of *identity* (the text as a celebration of Montaigne's unrepeatable and singular individuality) and towards the more explicitly ethical notions of agency, personhood and control. A primary aim of this book is thus to reorient critical attention to a crucial but hitherto overlooked strand in Montaigne's conception of self. The historical importance and interest of the *Essais*, I contend, lies not only in their anticipation of later forms of autobiographical and introspective writing, but in their distinctive and highly nuanced approach to the problem of personal liberty.

It is also possible, however, to give my argument a more polemical twist. I do not wish to suggest that the existence of a hidden, affective self would have been unintelligible to Montaigne; nor do I wish to imply, just as implausibly, that countless readers of the *Essais* have been mistaken in their assessment of the text as a remarkably original work, unprecedented in its attention to the inner dispositions and reflections of its author.

[10] Skinner 2008b contains the most recent and complete statement of this analysis.

When we realise, however, that Montaigne's efforts to return to and live for himself are, at least in part, an expression of his concern to preserve himself from slavery, conventional appeals to sincerity or authenticity as defining attributes of his notion of self lose much of their force. The *nature* of Montaigne's interest in the self, I suggest, has been fundamentally misrepresented and misunderstood. His book represents him as he truly is – but as a witness of his moral character as a free man, not as an expression (sincere or otherwise) of his innermost psychological being.

As the title of the work suggests, Montaigne's eclectic reflections are offered not as doctrines to be studied or learned, but as material for further evaluation and elaboration. He examines problems from a multiplicity of angles, 'trying out' and 'sampling' a variety of opinions without binding himself to any one school of thought or point of view. As one recent commentator has emphasised, this discontinuous and open-ended way of writing serves to promote a particular kind of 'free-thinking', in which both writer and reader may participate.[11] Montaigne judges matters for himself, instead of deferring to the authority of other thinkers; his text is purely his own, free of philosophical and literary debts. The freedom made possible by the *essai*, however, extends beyond his autonomy as a writer and as a thinker. For Montaigne, I argue in Chapter 1, liberty and dependency constitute ethical, as well as intellectual, concerns. His claim to own his book, and to be represented within it, embodies an appeal to moral, and not merely literary, independence.

Chapter 2 focuses on the terms in which Montaigne himself describes his project of 'self-study' and on the language that he uses to articulate what we would now call 'the self'. My analysis centres on two patterns of discourse: a rhetoric of inwardness urging us to look or withdraw *into* ourselves, and a rhetoric of self-possession calling for us to *own* or *belong to* ourselves. I am able to show, first, that these expressions reflect habits of language inherited from ancient texts, in particular the writings of Plutarch and Seneca; and, second, that the habits of thought which underpin them are far removed from our own. When Montaigne contrasts that which is inside us with what is merely external, he is not referring to the distance that separates self and mime, referent and sign, in our own culture. He is instead distinguishing that which is intrinsic to us – in the sense that it can truly be accounted as our own, that it is in our power – from all those possessions and attributes that are merely accidental or fortuitous. When he claims to belong to himself, or to be his own, he is not affirming himself

[11] Scholar 2010.

as the origin and author of his own identity, unfettered by what we would think of today as the forces of ideological subjection; nor does he mean, as some scholars have supposed, that he is his own property.[12] To belong to oneself is instead to be one's own man and master, as opposed to another man's creature.

As I seek to show in Chapter 3, liberty, and not authenticity, provides the key to Montaigne's way of thinking and writing about the self. His appeals for us to return to and reclaim ownership over ourselves emerge as an urgent and practical response to the problem of public engagement and service in a turbulent and corrupt world. Public life, Montaigne claims, should be shunned because it removes us from ourselves – not in the sense that it exposes us to the distorting gaze of others, but because it turns us into slaves by rendering us dependent on the favour of others and by encouraging us to live for the sake of that which lies beyond our powers. Solitude and privacy, in this context, are defined not in opposition to social life per se, but rather to the active pursuit of public office, advancement and reputation. Montaigne's retreat to his estate is an exile of the will, an inward refuge from slavery. Freedom here consists both in the absence of personal subjection to the will of others and in an internal disposition of the mind, achieved by turning one's efforts and will back towards oneself. To be free is to govern oneself in accordance with one's own will, and thus to belong to oneself.

This conception of liberty as a form of self-possession radically reorients our understanding of Montaigne's turn to 'self'. However, it does not quite get us, on its own, to the heart of what the *Essais* have to say about liberty: it is only one half of a complex picture. Chapter 4 considers a strand in Montaigne's reflections that appears at first sight to be entirely separate from, and at variance with, the robust language of independence and self-ownership discussed in Chapter 3. Freedom is here associated with idleness (*oysiveté*) and negligence (*nonchalance*) – with the fragility of an indolent and ill-disciplined will that recoils from occupation and strain, not because it yearns for independence, but because it seeks to be without care. Pressing further, we come to see that these two threads of discourse – self-possession and carelessness – are in fact part of a single story about liberty.

Having analysed Montaigne's composite account of freedom under its two leading aspects, it remains for us to ask how that liberty is to be achieved and defended in practice. Chapter 5 examines the nature and limits of self-discipline in the *Essais*, focusing in particular on Montaigne's use of the

[12] Schaefer 1990, esp. pp. 315–21, Van Delft 1990, Levine 2001, Jordan 2003, Jordan 2004.

language of *mesnagerie* (household management) as a metaphor for the prudent disposition of the will. Montaigne's approach to the government of his household, as it is represented in his text, offers a tacit subversion of the counsel of vigilant control and command offered by the canonical ancient treatise on the subject, Xenophon's *Oeconomicus*. In Montaigne's hands, *mesnagerie* comes to be associated with a form of strategic inattention to the affairs of the household and with the acceptance of the limited and 'impure' nature of one's authority. This emphasis on judicious compromise and restraint, I contend, provides both a mirror image and a model for his indirect and surreptitious approach to self-regulation and self-containment. Like the household, the self here emerges as a space of managed (rather than wholly controlled) freedom, sustained by a loose and measured rein.

Liberty provides the central focus of this book and of the reading of the *Essais* that it proposes. I am not claiming, however, that freedom provides the key to the text – that the work as a whole is to be understood exclusively, or even fundamentally, in the terms foregrounded in this study. Montaigne's designation of his book as an exercise in self-study provides formal coherence and retrospective unity to a sprawling and multifarious text, without fully containing or controlling it. My principal interest lies in just one of the projects pursued by this eclectic and archipelagic text: the cultivation of an art of both living and writing centred on the self. It is this aspect of the work, this strand in Montaigne's project, that freedom helps illuminate.

A few qualifications and clarifications are therefore in order before drawing this introduction to a close. I am not suggesting, in the first place, that liberty is the highest moral value adumbrated in the *Essais*. The problem of personal freedom is, as I hope to show, one of Montaigne's most persistent ethical preoccupations. There may be other principles or ideals, however, for the sake of which a free man might choose to surrender his liberty, allowing or accepting himself to fall into dependency. The [A]'true and perfect' friendship that Montaigne claims to have shared with the late Estienne de La Boétie, in particular, is implicitly presented as a form of 'voluntary servitude' – at once a pure expression of his will and a state of slavery.[13]

Unlike those friendships [A]'which law and natural obligation impose on us', and which bind fathers and sons, or husbands and wives, Montaigne's

[13] [A]'Ces vrayes et parfaictes amitiez'. I.27: P 191, V 185, F 136. *On friendship* was originally conceived as a frame for La Boétie's polemic against tyranny, the *Discours de la servitude volontaire* (see Chapter 3, Section III). See Langer 1994 and Rigolot 2005.

friendship with La Boétie is a product of his free will (*liberté volontaire*).[14] Yet this friendship, in which one gives oneself, one's soul and one's will entirely to another, unmistakably involves a form of mastery, [A]'possessing the soul, and ruling it with absolute sovereignty'.[15] Montaigne and La Boétie belong to each other, rather than to themselves:

> [A]I know not what quintessence of all this mixture, which, having seized my whole will, led it to plunge and lose itself in his; [C]which, having seized his whole will, led it to plunge and lose itself in mine: with equal hunger, equal rivalry. [A]I say lose, in truth, for it reserved nothing that was proper to us, nor was anything either his or mine.[16]

This vision of friendship as a [A]'confusion' of wills[17] probes the outer limits of freedom as self-possession. Montaigne surrenders his will and his liberty to his friend, leaving him with nothing that he can call his own.

This servitude is not only voluntary, however, but reciprocal: La Boétie's will is indistinguishable from Montaigne's. This Aristotelian construction of the friend as an *alter ego*[18] results in the dissolution of obligation both outside and within the friendship. The bond of perfect friendship is so all-encompassing as to supersede all other ties of fellowship, requiring of us that we be [C]'friends more than citizens, friends more than friends or enemies of [our] country, or friends of ambition and disturbance'.[19] In [B]'this sovereign and masterful friendship', moreover, consideration of debt and service has no place: [A]'the union of such friends, being truly perfect, makes them lose the sense of such duties, and hate and banish from between them, these words of division and difference, benefit, obligation, gratitude, prayer, thanks, and the like'.[20]

Not only can Montaigne's account of perfect friendship be read as an attempt to transcend the dichotomy between freedom and servitude that is elsewhere so fundamental to his reflections, but the ideal of liberty

14 [A]'À mesure que ce sont amitiez que la loy et l'obligation naturelle nous commande, il y a d'autant moins de nostre choix et liberté volontaire'. I.27: P 191, V 185, F 137.

15 [A]'Cette amitié, qui possede l'ame, et la regente en toute souveraineté'. I.27: P 193, V 191, F 141.

16 [A]'C'est je ne sçay quelle quinte-essence de tout ce meslange, qui ayant saisi toute ma volonté, l'amena se plonger et se perdre dans la sienne, [C]qui ayant saisi toute sa volonté, l'amena se plonger et se perdre en la mienne: d'une faim, d'une concurrence pareille. [A]Je dis perdre à la verité, ne nous reservant rien qui nous fust propre, ny qui fust ou sien ou mien'. I.27: P 195, V 189, F 139.

17 'Cette confusion si pleine de nos volontez'. I.27: P 197, V 190, F 141.

18 On this point, see Langer 1994 and Cave 1999, pp. 120–3.

19 [C]'Plus amis que citoyens, plus amis qu'amis ou que ennemis de leur païs, qu'amis d'ambition et de trouble'. I.27: P 196, V 189, F 140.

20 [A]'L'union de tels amis estant veritablement parfaicte, elle leur faict perdre le sentiment de tels devoirs, et haïr et chasser d'entre eux, ces mots de division et de difference, bien-faict, obligation, recognoissance, priere, remerciement, et leurs pareils'. I.27: P 197, V 190, F 141.

is itself tacitly subjected to significant limitations. In the first place, his representation of freedom as an unlearned, natural condition identifies self-possession and carelessness as aristocratic qualities, accessible only to a B'few souls so orderly, so strong and well-born, that they can be trusted with their own guidance'.[21] Although the focus of this book is on the intellectual and discursive contexts (rather than the social conditions) that govern Montaigne's thinking about liberty, it is important to emphasise that independence, frankness, leisure and nonchalance are all traits characteristically associated with the nobility of *ancien régime* France.[22] To this extent, Montaigne's self-presentation as a free man reflects the ideology of a particular class, defined in opposition to a servile majority of vulgar scholars and mendacious flatterers, rather than an ethics of more universal application. Contrary to those scholars who have linked the *Essais* to the morality of an emergent bourgeoisie,[23] it is hard to see how liberty, as Montaigne understands it, could be either imagined or realised in the absence of the economic self-sufficiency and freedom from occupation of the land-owning aristocracy. Freedom is intimately tied to freehold: the free man can do without the material rewards of princely service; he is not in the employ of any other man; he lives in a state of leisure; he has dominion and authority over his own household.

Liberty, in this perspective, is itself the hostage of our birth – a paradox highlighted by Montaigne in *On vanity*, where the ability to live within the limits of one's own power, instead of relying on the favour of other men, is unmasked as a product of divine grace.

> BOh, how much am I obliged to God that it was his pleasure that I should receive all I have directly from his grace: and that he has kept all my indebtedness for himself privately! CHow earnestly I beseech his holy mercy, that I may never owe thanks for essential things to anyone! Fortunate freedom: which has guided me so far. May it continue to the end![24]

Montaigne may be free from debts to any man, but for this he is indebted to God. The freedom of the self, in this light, operates within a purely human sphere, circumscribed by the soul's dependency on God. The question as to

21 B'Il est peu d'ames si reglees, si fortes et bien nées, à qui on se puisse fier de leur propre conduicte'. II.12: P 592, V 559, F 419.

22 Posner 1999.

23 In addition to the works cited in Footnote 12 above, see Desan 1992 and the more qualified claims made by Keohane 1977.

24 B'Ô combien je suis tenu à Dieu, de ce qu'il luy a pleu, que j'aye receu immediatement de sa grace, tout ce que j'ay: qu'il a retenu particulierement à soy toute sa debte! CCombien je supplie instamment sa saincte misericorde, que jamais je ne doive un essentiel grammercy à personne! Bien heureuse franchise: qui m'a conduict si loing. Qu'elle acheve'. III.9: P 1013, V 968, F 739.

what limits, if any, our duty of subjection to God imposes on the exercise of our liberty is unfortunately not one that I can hope to adequately answer here. The problem of free will, moreover, lies beyond the scope of this book, which is more particularly concerned with the self's relationship with other agents and with the inner disposition of the soul towards that which lies beyond its power.[25]

It may be helpful, however, to recall here Pascal's castigation of Montaigne's 'sot projet' of self-portrayal – a condemnation rooted in the claim that the self (*le moi*) is 'unjust because it makes itself the centre of everything', as part of that fallen 'instinct which incites one to make oneself God'.[26] The self, for Pascal, is worthy of hate as a source not merely of narcissistic *divertissement*, but of self-idolatry and rebellion against God. Montaigne's withdrawal into the self offers as a solution to human misery what is in fact the cause of our unhappiness and enslavement: our failure to acknowledge our dependency upon God and our existence, not as self-sufficient entities, but as 'members' of humanity and of Christ, in the literal sense of bodily parts that have no life on their own but only insofar as they partake of the whole.[27] Pascal's objection to Montaigne thus centres not (as is often supposed) on the immodesty of his fascination with himself, but on the sin of pride that leads him to seek contentment in, and independence for, himself.

One way, however, of understanding the argumentative arc of the final three chapters of this book – from self-possession to carelessness to 'impure' self-management – would be to insist on the precariousness and imperfection of Montaigne's freedom. One of his main concerns in writing the *Essais*, certainly, is to demonstrate that his essential and natural condition is one of liberty. He does not, however, claim always and everywhere to be in possession of his freedom; still less does he pretend to master himself. Montaigne's conception of 'self', as I hope to have made clear, hinges on a fundamental moral distinction between that which is subject to his will and that which lies beyond the limits of his power. In practice, however, that boundary is rarely clear-cut.

Finally, a few words about my approach to the text. My guiding concern has been to analyse the *Essais* as a landscape of intuitions, inclinations and preoccupations rather than as the expression of fixed assumptions or deeply

[25] But on this question, see Langer 1990 and Carraud and Marion 2004.

[26] Pascal 2004. 'Ce sot projet de se peindre' (fragment 653). 'Le moi est haïssable. [. . .] Je le hais parce qu'il est injuste, qu'il se fait centre de tout' (fragment 509). 'Qui ne hait en soi son amour-propre, et cet instinct qui le porte à se faire Dieu, est bien aveuglé' (fragment 524).

[27] Mesnard 1989.

held beliefs. One effect of my argument, as I have already intimated, is to draw attention to the persistence and depth of Montaigne's commitment to personal freedom. I have ultimately found it more helpful, however, to think of interpretation as a way of explaining what makes Montaigne's book into the particular text that it is, rather than as a way of reconstructing his patterns of belief. In other words, I have sought to understand the text not as an archival imprint of his fundamental 'views' about liberty, but as an exceptionally flexible exercise of judgment, allowing him to draw upon and confront contrasting argumentative and rhetorical strategies. My aim has been to evoke a dense tapestry of thinking habits inscribed in the text, made up of persistent preoccupations and anxieties, recurrent motifs and configurations, echoes between chapters, and traces left by other texts – to examine Montaigne's reflections on freedom as a palimpsest of discourse rather than a solid edifice of ideas.

In an effort to view that palimpsest in its full complexity, I have chosen to treat the *Essais* as a single body of discourse instead of structuring my analysis around the close, sequential reading of discrete chapters. This approach has led me to focus attention on particular passages and reflections, sometimes juxtaposing discussions situated some distance apart in the text. It is vital to stress, however, that these quotations are offered not as insights into Montaigne's 'position' or 'beliefs' on the theme of freedom, but as instances of his intricate handling of the language of liberty. Mindful of Jean-Yves Pouilloux's warnings against the temptation to anthologise Montaigne's text, I have sought to interpret these passages not as disembodied fragments of prose, but as reflections embedded within particular textual contexts, invested with a peculiarly self-reflexive and self-critical force.[28]

I have also sought, however, to carry the discussion initiated by Pouilloux one step further. Crucially, it seems to me, the *Essais* represent more than a purely formal exercise in critical thinking. They address particular problems and questions in particular ways, acting within and upon prevailing systems of discourse. To explain the *Essais*, to explain Montaigne's *manière*, is thus not only to elucidate the sceptical and self-critical dynamic of his writing (and rewriting). It is also to understand the preoccupations, presuppositions and interpretative categories that nourish and shape his fluid reflections – to reconstruct the complex horizons of understanding and expectation which it inhabits and brings into being. To explain the text, in this sense, is to read Montaigne as a *bricoleur*, appropriating and refashioning preexisting tropes,

[28] Pouilloux 1969, Pouilloux 1995.

vocabularies, arguments and other textual materials.[29] This approach helps us to move beyond a stark contrast between form and content, *manière* and *matière*, by reading Montaigne's 'dispositions' in discursive rather than purely cognitive terms, as habits of language as well as thought.

It also allows us to dispense entirely with the assumption that the *Essais* can and should be explicated in terms of a single world view, and that it is in moments of consonance that Montaigne's presence is most truthfully disclosed. Instead of scrutinizing the work for evidence of latent conceptual patterns, persisting despite its self-critical impulse, our task becomes one of analysing the *Essais* as a text in conversation both with other texts and with itself. From this perspective, questions of coherence and continuity lose much of their importance: the focus of attention shifts instead towards recomposing the supple and plural discourses deployed by the text. This approach, I contend, equips us not only for understanding Montaigne's complex exploration of freedom and self, but for seeing his own text, his *bricolage*, as an expression of his liberty.

[29] For the concept of *bricolage*, see Lévi-Strauss 1962 and Derrida 1967, esp. p. 418.

CHAPTER I

Freedom and the essai

I

Montaigne's decision to present his thoughts as disparate and eclectic reflections marked by tension and doubt, rather than work them into a systematic and controlled argument, has rightly come to be considered fundamental to any credible account of the *Essais*. His [C]'style, and [his] mind, alike go a-roaming', essaying topics from contrasting angles; indeed, he claims to have [C]'some personal obligation, to speak only by halves, to speak confusedly, to speak discordantly'.[1] The text moves restlessly from one subject to another, delighting in counter-examples, qualifications and sudden reversals of perspective, offering monstrous 'ravings', vain 'stupidities' and idle 'fancies' rather than purposive arguments or authoritative statements of position.[2]

These labyrinthine digressions and cultivated discontinuities provide the foundation for Montaigne's distinctive representation of the self as a mobile, ephemeral and fragmentary entity, defined not by [B]'being' but 'passage', in keeping with his conception of life as [B]'a material and corporeal movement: an action by its very essence imperfect, and irregular'.[3] At a still more fundamental level, his efforts to [B]'represent a continual agitation and mutation of [his] thoughts, whatever subject they light on' serve to identify the *Essais* (in Jean-Yves Pouilloux's seminal formulation) as a book concerned with *penser* rather than *pensée* – with the activity of thinking

1 [C]'Mon stile, et mon esprit, vont vagabondant de mesmes: [. . .] Joint, qu'à l'advanture ay-je quelque obligation particuliere, à ne dire qu'à demy, à dire confusement, à dire discordamment'. III.9: P 1041–2, V 994–6, F 761–2.

2 [A]'Chimeres et monstres fantasques' (I.8: P 55, V 33, F 21); [A]'crotesques et corps monstrueux' (I.27: P 189, V 183, F 135); 'resveries' (I.25: P 150, V 146, F 106[A]; II.18: P 704, V 665, F 504[C]); [A]'inepties' (I.25: P 153, V 148, F 108; II.37: P 823, V 783, F 595); [B]'fadaises' (III.1: P 829, V 790, F 599); 'fantasies' (II.10: P 428, V 407, F 296[A]; III.9: P 989, V 964, F 721[B]).

3 [B]'L'estre', 'le passage' (III.2: P 845, V 805, F 611); [B]'un mouvement materiel et corporel: action imparfaicte de sa propre essence, et desreglée' (III.9: P 1034, V 988, F 756). See Rigolot 1988, Starobinski 1993, Jeanneret 2001 and Nakam 2006.

itself rather than the construction of a system of thought.[4] As readers, our attention is carried not to the 'matter' (*matiere*) under discussion, but to the 'shape' (*façon*, *maniere*) which Montaigne gives to it.[5] The tensions, fractures and uncertainties exhibited by his writing signal his commitment to an exacting mode of sceptical enquiry, allowing the text to contest its own certainties and convey dissonant points of view in such a way that final resolution and closure are continually deferred.[6]

These qualities of openness, ambiguity and disaggregation are integral to Montaigne's conception of his text as a book of *essais*. As has often been emphasised, the title of the work should not be taken to imply that each of its constituent chapters is an 'essay' in the modern sense of the term – that *On moderation* and *On anger* are to be classed as instances of that recognizable literary genre which Montaigne is conventionally taken to have inaugurated. The term *essai* refers rather to the activity to which the writing of the book gives rise and which it purports to relate – to try (*essayer*), to weigh (*exagiare*), to taste (*assaggiare*) – as is made clear by Montaigne's description of the work as containing the 'Essais' of his judgment,[7] the [A]'essai' of his natural faculties[8] and the [B]'essais' of his life.[9] The work ought properly to be understood, then, as the 'Essais' not merely by, but *of*, Michel de Montaigne – the 'trials' or 'soundings' of which Montaigne is not only the author but the object.[10]

The concept of *essai* extends not only to the characteristic activity underlying Montaigne's project, however, but to the distinctive form of writing which that activity requires and dictates. As Graham Good has expressed it:

> With Montaigne the 'essai' is still a sketchy concept, a kind of linking medium between the established forms of the 'sentence' or quotation on one side, and the 'book' on the other [. . .]. The term 'essai' [. . .] hovers between the then established usage as 'attempt' or 'trial' and an anticipation of the generic usage.[11]

4 [B]'Representer une continuelle agitation et mutation de mes pensées, en quelque matiere qu'elles tombent'. III.9: P 990, V 946, F 721. See Pouilloux 1969, which has more recently been reissued in an expanded and revised edition (Pouilloux 1995).

5 II.10: P 428, V 408, F 296[A]; III.8: P 973, V 928, F 708[B].

6 See Demonet and Legros 2004, Sellevold 2004 and Tournon 2006.

7 I.50: P 321, V 301, F 219[A]; II.17: P 692, V 653, F 495[B].

8 I.25: P 151, V 146, F 107; II.10: P 427, V 407, F 296.

9 III.13: P 1126, V 1079, F 826.

10 For the significance of Montaigne's choice of title, see Blinkenberg 1950, Telle 1968, Gray 1982 and Mathieu-Castellani 1988.

11 Good 1988, p. 28, quoted in de Obaldia 1995, p. 29.

The *essai* is to be understood, if not as a fully fledged genre, then as a 'structural or methodological principle', a set of formal properties and procedures, a way of conducting, ordering and presenting one's reflections.[12] The concept reaches beyond its etymological resonance, while always remaining anchored in it, to encompass at once a particular mode of philosophical enquiry (a willingness to think experimentally rather than conclusively, to suspend judgment in favour of continued uncertainty and doubt, to write without the sanction of didactic authority), and the set of discursive techniques that bring that mode into being, at the level of the individual utterance or sentence, as well as on the larger scale of the paragraph or chapter (or indeed of the work as a whole).

The *essai* form, as scholars have long recognised, draws both its impetus and its urgency from practices central to the literary culture of Renaissance humanism. Foremost among these are the intertextual operations of quotation, imitation and appropriation: processes that engage both writer and reader in a careful negotiation of the authority of preexisting texts. Montaigne's rejection of systematic models of exposition is at once an extension of humanist practices of 'commonplace thinking' and an attempt to resolve the tension between repetition and reinvention inherent in them. That conflict has typically been presented as a contest between tradition and self-expression – as evidence of the author's struggle to find an authentic, personal, original voice. As I argue in Section II of this chapter, however, Montaigne's adoption of the *essai* form represents an affirmation of independence, rather than individuality.

As several scholars have recently stressed, the *essai* embodies a distinctively anti-authoritarian conception of philosophical agency, centred on the need to think for oneself (within certain limits), instead of taking opinions on trust.[13] Freedom here entails exercising one's own faculties and forming one's own judgment, instead of merely depending on, or deferring to, the ideas and writings of others. That independence, however, must be construed in ethical and not merely intellectual terms. As we shall see in Section III, the point of *thinking* freely is, above all else, to learn how to *live* freely. Intellectual liberty and moral independence are inseparably connected: freedom matters not just as a condition of truth – as an object of essentially epistemological concern – but as a central component in a wider, more properly ethical, art of existence.

The liberty of the *essai*, accordingly, is not limited to the playful subversion and reworking of existing arguments and enquiries. As I argue in Section IV, Montaigne's repudiation of intellectual tutelage is

[12] de Obaldia 1995, p. 29. [13] Boutcher 2005, Force 2009, Scholar 2010.

complemented by a further dimension of philosophical freedom – the liberty, made possible by the *essai* form, to tackle subjects under a multiplicity of guises, without surrendering to any one conclusion, and to try out ideas without binding oneself, either through assent or dissent, to the propositional content of one's discourse. Underlying this approach to thinking and writing is a form of ethical as much as epistemological scepticism, founded on a rejection of systematic and dogmatic philosophy as a source not merely of error and illusion, but of perturbation and servitude.

The fifth and final section of this chapter draws out the implications of this analysis of freedom as a defining property of the *essai* for Montaigne's insistence that his text represents or expresses him – that it yields knowledge of himself, and not merely of things, as a book 'consubstantial' with its author. This set of claims, I suggest, relies not on a mimetic conception of the text as a faithful depiction of its subject, but on the validation of its author's autonomous and self-sufficient agency. Montaigne's text represents him because it is 'exactly [his] own' ('exactement mien') – because it bears the unmistakable impression of his own intellectual and moral qualities. The language of dependency and ownership deployed by Montaigne here emerges not only as a central component of his 'accidental' philosophy,[14] but as a crucial dimension of his conception of the self.

II

For all his scepticism about our ability to draw lessons from the ancients, Montaigne remains deeply committed to the possibility of 'speaking with the dead' – to a conception of writing as a form of conversation and exchange (*conference*, *commerce*) with classical texts.[15] This appeal to the classics is at its most visible in the case of the frequent (predominantly Latin) quotations that structure the text, contrasting both typographically and linguistically with the continuous flow of Montaigne's vernacular prose.[16] His conversation with the dead is not limited, however, to these instances of conscious and visible citation. His instinct is to turn to the classics in search both of thinking matter and of an idiom or language within which to work through and articulate his ideas. As he explains in *On books*, [C] I make others

[14] On 'accidental philosophy,' see Hartle 2003, which takes as its prompt Montaigne's description of himself as a [C]'nouvelle figure: Un philosophe impremedité et fortuit'. II.12: P 578, V 546, F 409.

[15] The phrase is borrowed from Pieters 2006; see further Grafton 1997. For the *Essais* as witness to a 'crisis of exemplarity' in late Renaissance literature, see Hampton 1990.

[16] The paragraph breaks found in Pierre Villey's edition (and Donald Frame's translation) are an editorial artifice. The new Pléiade edition restores the unity of Montaigne's dense, continuous prose, interrupted only by chapter breaks and occasional, indented quotations.

say, <not before me, but after me>, what I cannot say so well', whether due to the 'weakness' of his 'language' or of his 'understanding'.[17] The text here emerges as a discursive space inhabited by the ruined fragments of other texts – as a cultural artefact constituted through the continual 'essaying' of examples, arguments and rhetorical strategies excavated from predominantly ancient sources.[18]

Montaigne's familiarity with the classics is presented as a product of nature and effortless dabbling, rather than as the fruit of erudite study. His Latin, he claims, was acquired [A]'without art, without books, with grammar or precept, without the whip, and without tears', having been received from the cradle, as his mother tongue, from a German tutor wholly ignorant of French.[19] As for his knowledge of Greek, Montaigne's unabashed profession of absolute ignorance – although almost certainly an exaggeration – further underlines the gap separating him from the figure of the scholar, devoted to the patient and painstaking study of books.[20] By his own admission, certainly, Montaigne received an expensive and first-rate humanist education at the recently established Collège de Guyenne in Bordeaux, described in the *Essais* as [A]'flourishing greatly at that time, and the best in France'.[21] He insists, however, that this training left him [A]'without any benefit that [he] can place in evidence now', other than the

[17] [C]'Je fay dire aux autres, <non à ma teste, mais à ma suite,> ce que je ne puis si bien dire, ~~tantost~~ par foiblesse de mon langage, ~~tantost~~ <ou> par foiblesse de mon sens'. II.10: P 428, V 408, F 296.

[18] 'Each essay presents a ruin and the *Essais* as a whole represent the ruins of antiquity'. Sedley 2005, p. 44. See also Boccassini 1993 and McGowan 2000.

[19] [A]'Sans art, sans livre, sans grammaire ou precepte, sans fouet, et sans larmes'. I.25: P 180, V 173–4, F 128.

[20] [A]'Je n'entens rien au Grec'. II.4: P 382, V 363, F 262. On other occasions, Montaigne is somewhat less emphatic. [A]'As for Greek, of which I have practically no knowledge at all' ('quant au Grec, duquel je n'ay quasi du tout point d'intelligence'). I.25: P 181, V 174, F 129. [A]'I do not take much [. . .] to [books] in Greek, because my judgment cannot do its work with a childish and ~~average~~ [C]apprentice [A]understanding' ('je ne me prens gueres [. . .] aux [livres] Grecs, par ce que mon jugement ne sçait pas faire ses besoignes d'une puerile et ~~moyenne~~ [C]apprantisse [A]intelligence'). II.10: P 430, V 409–10, F 297. These assertions should not, however, be taken too literally: of the 75 sentences painted on the ceiling and beams of Montaigne's library, more than half are in Greek (Legros 2000). Moreover, his Greek hand (as found in the Bordeaux Copy) suggests, at the very least, a facility in writing the language and some familiarity with its meaning (see Montaigne 2002a and 2002b, fols. 177r and 490r). Richard Sayce notes, however, that the scattered Greek quotations of the *Essais* 'seem to come almost entirely from intermediate sources', and that it is 'certain' that he read Plutarch and Herodotus in French translation, a fact proved 'by numerous verbatim transcriptions' (Sayce 1972, p. 29). On Montaigne's Greek see further Christodoulou 1992 and Legros 1999.

[21] I.25: P 180, V 175, F 129. For the 'programme d'études' at the Collège de Guyenne, see Vinet 1886; see also Gaullier 1874, Gorris Camos 2001, and, on schools in Renaissance France more generally, Huppert 1984. Trinquet 1972 remains the only extended study of Montaigne's youth and education, even though its methodology and some of its central claims have now been discredited (see Balsamo 2008).

corruption of his native Latin.[22] The same logic is applied to his plundering of classical texts, a practice that purports to be haphazard and ill-disciplined, innocent of sustained effort and learning: [C]'I have not studied one bit to make a book: but I have studied a bit, because I had made it: if it is studying a bit, to skim over and pinch, by his head, or by his feet, now one author, now another'.[23]

This emphasis on punctual, disconnected reading links the *Essais* to a practice central to humanist pedagogy and which Montaigne himself (for all his protestations of ignorance) would assuredly have encountered at school: the compilation of commonplace-books.[24] These were personal notebooks into which pupils were expected to copy quotations, arguments and examples culled from authoritative and exemplary texts. These extracts were typically arranged under thematic headings to facilitate their redeployment in the student's own compositions. Schoolboys were thus encouraged to read texts extensively rather than intensively, approaching them as resources to be exploited and appropriated – as repositories of commonplaces, offering variations on familiar topics and themes, to be put to use in new settings. Montaigne's emphasis on the spontaneity and disorder of his reading and writing certainly contrasts with the methodical, orderly habits his humanist tutors would have sought to inculcate. Nevertheless, the commonplace book provides a vital context for his conception of the *Essais* as an [C]'ill-fitted patchwork'[25] formed through the assembly and reworking of borrowed materials into new patterns of thought.

The shift from commonplace to *essai*, conversely, reflects the pressures inherent in this intellectual inheritance.[26] For even while advertising his ready recourse to intertextual material, Montaigne is anxious to distinguish his text from what he refers to disparagingly in *On physiognomy* as [C]'those concoctions of commonplaces' ('ces pastissages de lieux communs'), which 'serve to show us off, not to guide us'.[27] His [B]'borrowed ~~ornaments~~ <adornments>' are merely a concession to [B]'public opinion', [C]'the fancy

[22] [A]'Sans aucun fruit, que je peusse à present mettre en compte'. I.25: P 182, V 175, F 130.

[23] [C]'Je n'ay aucunement estudié pour faire un livre: mais j'ay aucunement estudié, pour ce que je l'avoy faict: si c'est aucunement estudier, qu'effleurer et pincer, par la teste, ou par les pieds, tantost un autheur, tantost un autre'. II.18: P 704, V 666, F 505.

[24] See Moss 2000, esp. p. 213. For an important assessment of Montaigne's debt – and departure – from this model, see Goyet 1986–7.

[25] [C]'Une marqueterie mal jointe'. III.9: P 1008, V 964, F 736.

[26] On imitation as a source of anxiety in the *Essais* and Renaissance literature more generally, see Cave 1979, Rigolot 1982 and Greene 1986. On the problem of originality and imitation in the *Essais*, see Compagnon 1979, Beaujour 1980 and Cave 1982.

[27] [C]'À nous montrer, non à nous conduire'. III.12: P 1103, V 1056, F 808–9.

of the age ~~and the exhortations of others~~ <and idleness>': they [C]'may be useful to someone else', but he himself does not set stock by them.[28] Others may accuse him of having [C]'only made a bunch of other people's flowers', a *florilegium* of borrowed quotations. Yet had he followed his own advice, instead of yielding to convention, he [C]'would at all hazards have spoken absolutely alone'.[29] The *Essais* here emerge as the antitype of the *florilegium* or *cento* for which they might otherwise be mistaken. When Montaigne hides one of his quotations by incorporating it seamlessly into his own reflections, [C]'transplanting it into [his] own soil and confounding it with [his] own', he is careful to [C]'give it some particular application with [his] own hand, so that it may be less purely someone else's'.[30] His stated [B]'design' is 'to make a show only of what is [his] own, and of what is [his] own by nature';[31] the [B]'principal end and perfection' of his work being that it is 'exactly [his] own'.[32]

This language of ownership has conventionally tended to be interpreted as an appeal to originality and individuality as markers of true authorship. Montaigne's ambivalence towards his predecessors, in this light, reflects anxieties about influence and repetition, as obstacles to authentic, spontaneous self-expression. But this is to overlook the central thrust of the *Essais*'s problematic relationship with past texts: Montaigne's account of his 'borrowings' as challenges to his authorial independence and agency, rather than to his identity.

The metaphor of ownership must in the first place be understood in the context of sixteenth-century conceptions of intellectual authorship and production. As Kathy Eden has shown, Montaigne's claim to own his text draws on Erasmian notions of both shared and private property in intellectual goods.[33] His borrowings are not, from this perspective, examples of theft because wisdom (and specifically the wisdom conveyed by the

28 [B]'Certes j'ay donné à l'opinion publique, que ces ~~ornemens~~ <parements> empruntez m'accompaignent: [...] [C]Je m'en charge de plus fort, tous les jours, outre ma proposition et ma forme premiere, sur la fantasie du siecle: et ~~enhortemens d'autruy~~ <par oisiveté>. S'il me messied à moy, comme je le croy, n'importe: il peut estre utile à quelque autre'. III.12: P 1102–3, V 1055, F 808.

29 [C]'Un amas de fleurs estrangeres'. [C]'À tout hazard, j'eusse parlé tout fin seul'. III.12: P 1102, V 1055, F 808.

30 [C]'Si j'en transplante quelcun en mon solage, et confons aux miens'. II.10: P 428, V 387, F 296. [C]'Je luy donne quelque particuliere adresse de ma main, à ce qu'il soit d'autant moins purement estranger'. III.12: P 1103, V 1056, F 809. See also I.25: P 178, V 171, F 127[C].

31 [B]'Mon dessein. Qui ne veux faire montre que du mien et de ce qui est mien par nature'. III.12: P 1102, V 1055, F 808.

32 [B]'Sa fin principale et perfection, c'est d'estre exactement mien'. III.5: P 918, V 875, F 667.

33 Eden 2008. For an exploration of these themes in Erasmus' *Adages*, see Eden 2001.

classical tradition) belongs to all. The materials upon which he draws are in fact *commune*, not *alienum*:

[A]Truth and reason are common to everyone, and no more belong to the man who first spoke them, than to the man who says them later. [C]It is no more according to Plato, than according to me: since he and I understand and see it in the same way.[34]

Not only does Montaigne share in the intellectual wealth of his predecessors, but he has *appropriated* their materials, digesting and transforming them in such a way as to make them wholly proper to him, an integral and inalienable part of himself:

[A]The bees plunder the flowers here and there, but afterward they make of them honey, which is all theirs; it is no longer thyme, or marjoram: Even so with the pieces borrowed from others, he will transform and blend them, to make a work that is all his own: to wit his judgment.[35]

By claiming the fragments that he borrows as his 'own', Montaigne is at once anchoring his text in a common intellectual inheritance and affirming his ability to reshape these materials to his own particular ends.

The relevant distinction, then, is not between pre-existing discourse that is borrowed or stolen and new material that originates with Montaigne. The claim that truth and reason belong to all itself derives from Seneca's claim in the *Epistulae* that 'any truth [. . .] is my property [*meum est*]' and that 'the best ideas are common property [*communia*]' – a *topos* reworked in the Renaissance by both Petrarch and Erasmus.[36] The metaphor of the bees, similarly, represents a familiar classical *topos*, and thus an instance of the very practice that it sets out to justify.[37] The contrast is rather between those borrowings that remain stubbornly 'estranger', and those that are successfully digested, incorporated, transplanted – between those parts of a text that merely reflect the agency of others, and those that truly testify to the author's 'ouvrage'.

The problem raised by imitation, in this perspective, has more to do with independence than with what we would now call originality. As Pierre Force

34 [A]'La verité et la raison sont communes à un chacun, et ne sont non plus à qui les a dites premierement, qu'à qui les dit après. [C]Ce n'est non plus selon Platon, que selon moy: puis que luy et moy l'entendons et voyons de mesme'. I.25: P 157, V 152, F 111.

35 [A]'Les abeilles pillotent deçà delà les fleurs, mais elles en font après le miel, qui est tout leur; ce n'est plus thin, ny marjolaine: Ainsi les pieces empruntées d'autruy, il les transformera et confondra, pour en faire un ouvrage tout sien: à sçavoir son jugement'. I.25: P 157, V 152, F 111.

36 Eden 2008, pp. 23–31. Cf. Seneca 1989, 12.11, p. 72.

37 Pigman 1980. Cf. Seneca 1989, II.84.3, p. 276.

has persuasively argued, for early modern writers such as Montaigne, 'saying something new' is valued neither as an end in itself nor as a condition of authentic speech, but for what it can tell the reader about the author's 'worth and capacity'.[38] Most men, as Montaigne explains in *On the art of conversation*, are [B]'rich with borrowed ability', whether because they hit on the truth by chance, or because they repeat the witty sayings of others without fully understanding them.[39] When judging a speaker, accordingly,

> [B]in order to judge the parts that are most his own, and most worthy, the strength and beauty of his soul: we must know what is his, and what is not: and in what is not his, how much is due him in consideration of the choice, disposition, ornament, and language that he has supplied.[40]

These parts of an interlocutor's speech (or of an author's text) are truly 'sien', truly his intellectual property, not in the sense that they are wholly new, having never been claimed before by others, but because they are bound to him by an essential, and not merely accidental, relation.

This anchoring of ownership in the exercise of one's own 'judgment', as Warren Boutcher has recently argued, involves a decisive repudiation of prevailing conventions of textual authorship and intellectual authority.

> [B]I have known books to be made out of things, never either studied or understood: the author entrusting to various of his learned friends, the search for this, and that material, to build it: contenting himself for his part, with having planned the project, and piled up by his industry, this stack of unfamiliar provisions: at least the ink, and the paper are his. That is buying, or borrowing a book, not making one. It is teaching men, not that you can make a book, but, what they might have been in doubt about, that you cannot make one.[41]

In a culture in which a book's patron was commonly identified as its author and owner, books served as 'a public index of the patron-author's moral and intellectual agency', by displaying 'the learning at the patron-author's

[38] Force 2005, p. 24. [B]'Nostre prix et capacité'. III.8: P 980, V 934, F 714.

[39] [B]'Riches d'une suffisance estrangere'. III.8: P 981, V 936, F 715.

[40] [B]'Pour juger en luy les parties plus siennes, et plus dignes, la force et beauté de son ame: il faut sçavoir ce qui est sien, et ce qui ne l'est point: et en ce qui n'est pas sien, combien on luy doibt en consideration du choix, disposition, ornement, et langage qu'il a forny'. III.8: P 986, V 940, F 718.

[41] [B]'J'ay veu faire des livres de choses, ny jamais estudiées ny entendues: l'autheur commettant à divers de ses amis sçavants, la recherche de cette-cy, et de cette autre matiere, à le bastir: se contentant pour sa part, d'en avoir projetté le dessein, et lié par son industrie, ce fagot de provisions incogneues: au moins est sien l'ancre, et le papier. Cela, c'est achetter, ou emprunter un livre, non pas le faire. C'est apprendre aux hommes, non qu'on sçait faire un livre, mais, ce dequoy il pouvoient estre en doute, qu'on ne le sçait pas faire'. III.12: P 1103, V 1056, F 808.

command'. To make a book, in this light, is to commission or sponsor it, to invest in the commodity of philosophical learning by (as Montaigne puts it) 'planning the project' and 'piling up' a 'stack of unfamiliar provisions' assembled by others on one's behalf. Montaigne rejects these norms of patron-authorship, by insisting that one cannot claim a book as one's own simply by paying others to compose it. He has not 'bought' or 'borrowed' his book: 'he has not just ordered the materials and wafted in to see how the workmen were doing'. His book (and not merely the paper and ink used to make it) is his own, in the sense that both its contents and its shape are determined at every turn by his own judgment and understanding. As Boutcher puts it, 'we see everything pass through his understanding onto the paper'. Montaigne is 'his own prototype, his own patron'; he is 'the moral and intellectual agent indexed so freely by everything in the book'.[42]

It is here that the question of freedom first becomes urgent and explicit. Montaigne marks his distance from other texts by vindicating his book as his *own*, both in the sense that he is its owner, exercising sovereign authority and jurisdiction over his borrowings, and in the sense that it is proper (or particular) to him, that it bears the indelible mark of his mind. He positions himself at once as an heir to, and as a critic of, the humanist culture of *bricolage*, writing neither for those [C]'learned men to whom it falls to pass judgment on books', who 'know no other value than that of learning, and admit no other procedure in our minds than that of erudition and art', nor for 'common, popular minds', who 'do not see the grace and the weight of a loose and subtle discourse', but for a third species, the rarest of them all, made up of 'souls regulated and strong in themselves', who rely on their own resources rather than those borrowed or acquired from others.[43]

III

Montaigne's insistence on his independence as a thinker represents a central and productive theme of much recent scholarship on the *Essais*. These accounts rightly emphasise the importance of autonomous, critical judgment to Montaigne's conception of philosophical agency. Montaigne's

[42] Boutcher 2005, pp. 36, 39.

[43] [C]'Les sçavants, à qui appartient la juridiction livresque, ne cognoissent autre prix que de la doctrine; et n'advouent autre proceder en noz esprits, que celuy de l'erudition, et de l'art: [. . .] Les ames grossieres et populaires ne voyent pas la grace d'un discours delié'. 'Ames reglées et fortes d'elles mesmes'. II.17: P 696, V 657, F 498.

legacy, Boutcher argues, was 'precisely the freedom to judge others' philosophical legacies on their own merits', 'by freely assessing the philosophical merit of the bequest and moving the discussion on unhampered by any obligations to the legator', in such a way that 'the authority of a legacy with its heirs' is no longer taken to be 'conditioned by the origins of the philosophical gift, by the moral character of its donor or author, by the social tradition identifying it as a source of guidance'.[44] Richard Scholar has similarly characterised Montaigne's 'turn of mind' as 'free-thinking', a phrase intended to recall the 'anti-authoritarian topos' of the *libertas philosophandi* and, more particularly, the commonplace saying 'amicus Plato, magis amica veritas' ('Plato is my friend but a greater friend is truth'). Free-thinking, in Scholar's analysis, means thinking for oneself 'in the company' of past writers, subjecting one's reading to the test of one's own experience, and striving 'to reflect upon a particular question by asking not "What does Plato [or any other figure of authority] think about it?" [. . .] but "What do I think about it? Do I accept what Plato says?"'[45]

Montaigne is concerned not merely to underline his own intellectual liberty but to encourage, in turn, a similar independence of judgment and interpretation in his readers. The *Essais* are destined not for [C]'beginners'[46] (*principians*) but for those possessed of [B]'a penetrating mind', capable of following the 'little tracks' that Montaigne has left behind and to grasp what he has merely 'pointed to with [his] finger'.[47] This statement implies not that he writes in a purposefully evasive or enigmatic manner, but rather that he allows and expects his readers to bring their own understanding and judgment to bear upon his text. As Terence Cave has put it:

> It is not that Montaigne writes indeterminately; few authors of discursive prose have been as meticulously precise as he was in momentarily arresting and recording the fugitive creatures that passed through his mind. He leaves carefully calculated spaces, gaps, suspensions of assent, shifts of direction, that allow his readers plenty of room to participate in the exercise.[48]

The self-reflexive and self-critical force of the *Essais* belies traditional interpretations of the text as a leisurely and companionable *livre de chevet*, a 'livre de sagesse' or moral handbook offering humane and aphoristic 'teachings' to an essentially docile reader.

[44] Boutcher 2005, p. 27. On the use of Montaigne in twentieth-century debates over the status of the humanities in America 'to naturalise a particular kind of philosophical-critical agency, [. . .] as an index of the receptive and self-reflexive agency, the lived mental experience, of the unsystematic critical mind', see Boutcher 2004 (quotation at p. 35).

[45] Scholar 2006, pp. 44–8; see also Scholar 2007 and 2010.

[46] III.8: P 983, V 938, F 716. [47] III.9: P 1029, V 983, F 751. [48] Cave 2007, p. 115.

[C]It is the inattentive reader who loses my subject, not I. Some word about it will always be found off in a corner, which will not fail to be sufficient, though it takes little room. [. . .] [B]I want the matter to make its own divisions. It shows well enough where it changes, where it concludes, where it begins, where it resumes: without my interlacing it with words, with links and seams introduced for the benefit of weak or heedless ears: and without writing glosses on myself. Who is there who would rather not be read, than be read sleepily or in passing?[49]

Montaigne has not produced a textbook: he is not offering lessons to his readers. He has not digested his thoughts into an easily consumable form; nor has he organised and summarised them using headings and conclusions that tell us what it is we are expected to learn. Instead of expounding a doctrine or set of teachings, Montaigne invites us to draw our own conclusions from his reflections and to appropriate and incorporate his text into our own enquiries and meditations: [C]'how many stories have I spread around which say nothing of themselves, but from which anyone who troubles to pluck them with a little more ~~ingenuity~~ <care> will produce numberless essays?'[50]

Montaigne's philosophical enterprise, as both Boutcher and Scholar make clear, is shaped not merely by a sceptical retreat from dogmatism, but by a determination to free his reason and judgment from tutelage and dependency – not merely, that is, by an epistemological concern with the conditions of human knowledge, but by an ethical interest in independent agency. My aim in what follows is to carry this analysis one step further. Montaigne's refusal to submit to the authority of his philosophical predecessors, I argue, reflects his commitment to moral, as well as intellectual, autonomy: thinking independently matters not only for its own sake, or for the sake of the truth, but for the sake of living well. For both Montaigne and his intended readers, the point of 'essaying' one's judgment is to learn how to live (not only how to think) for oneself.

The purpose of philosophy for Montaigne, as Pierre Force has recently emphasised, lies not in the pursuit of 'doctrinal coherence', but (to quote the *Essais*) in [A]'a continual exercise of the soul'. 'Exercise' here connotes

49 [C]'C'est l'indiligent lecteur, qui perd mon subject; non pas moy. Il s'en trouvera tousjours en un coing quelque mot, qui ne laisse pas d'estre bastant, quoy qu'il soit serré. [. . .] [B]J'entends que la matiere se distingue soy-mesmes. Elle montre assez où elle se change, où elle conclud, où elle commence, où elle se reprend: sans l'entrelasser de parolles, de liaison, et de cousture, introduictes pour le service des oreilles foibles ou nonchallantes: et sans me gloser moy-mesme. Qui est celuy, qui n'ayme mieux n'estre pas leu, que de l'estre en dormant ou en fuyant?' III.9: P 1041–2, V 994, F 761. See also I.25: P 178–9, V 172, F 127[A].

50 [C]'Et combien y ay-je espandu d'histoires, qui ne disent mot, lesquelles qui voudra esplucher un peu plus ~~ingenieusement~~ <curieusement>, en produira infinis Essais?' I.39: P 255, V 251, F 185.

not merely use or application but *training*: as Force explains, 'philosophers exercise their souls as athletes exercise their bodies in order to achieve spiritual health, knowing of course that perfect wisdom is out of reach and philosophers, as lovers of wisdom, can only strive for what they love'.[51] In a similar vein, Scholar presents the *Essais* as an exacting cognitive exercise, Montaigne's 'quest being to try out his mind on the questions that his experience of life and his reading raised for him and, where he could, to rescue and befriend the truth'.[52] This emphasis on the *essai* as an instrument of *intellectual* training is echoed in turn by Force: 'philosophizing is a way of exercising one's judgment'; Montaigne's concern is with 'intellectual activity as a way of exercising both mind and judgment'.[53]

Montaigne, however, conceives of philosophy in a humanist vein, as a discipline in service of life. His 'continual exercise of the soul', accordingly, is not limited to the training of the mind. The passage in *On pedantry* from which this quotation is excerpted, as Force himself notes, opposes [A]'words' (*les parolles*) and 'things' (*les choses*), and in particular the rhetorical training of the Athenians, which equipped them 'to disentangle themselves from a sophistical argument and to overthrow the imposture of words captiously interlaced', to the ascetic exercises of the Spartans, who learnt instead to confront 'the lures of sensual pleasure' and 'the threats of fortune and death'.[54] The contrast in question, then, is not merely between philosophy as the production of doctrine (*sçavoir*, *science*) and philosophy as self-reflexive, mental exercise, but between verbal and practical training, or (as Montaigne makes clear in the immediately preceding paragraph) learning and wisdom, [A]'precepts and words' and 'examples and works', 'a knowledge *in* the soul', and one that has become 'its character and habit'.[55]

This distinction between erudition and moral training is central not only to *On pedantry*, but to the chapter which immediately succeeds it, *On the education of children*. [A]'A child of noble family', Montaigne writes, is to study letters neither for (pecuniary) 'gain' nor for 'external commodities', but 'to enrich and adorn himself inwardly'. The pursuit of such outward, material advantages is not only 'unworthy of the graces and favour of the Muses', but incompatible with the self-sufficiency of the well born, because

[51] [A]'Une continuelle excercitation de l'ame'. I.24: P 148, V 143, F 105. Force 2009, pp. 530–1.

[52] Scholar 2010, p. 1. [53] Force 2005, p. 24; see Force 2009, pp. 531, 533.

[54] [A]'À Athenes on aprenoit à bien dire, et icy [en Lacedemone] à bien faire: là à se desmesler d'un argument sophistique, et à rabattre l'imposture des mots captieusement entrelassez; icy à se desmesler des appats de la volupté, et à rabatre d'un [C]grand [A]courage ~~invincible~~ les menasses de la fortune et de la mort'. I.24: P 148, V 143, F 105.

[55] [A]'Non seulement de preceptes et parolles, mais principalement d'exemples et d'oeuvres: afin que ce ne fust pas une science en leur ame, mais sa complexion et habitude'. I.24: P 148, V 142–3, F 105.

it 'looks to others and depends on them'. The purpose of education is to fashion 'able' rather than 'learned' men: the (true) [C]'gain afforded by study, as Montaigne expresses it later on in the chapter, is 'to have become better and wiser by it'. In selecting a tutor, accordingly, one should seek out a [A]'well-made rather than well-filled head', attending to 'character and understanding' rather than 'learning'.[56]

The responsibility of the instructor, on this account, is to exercise the moral as well as the intellectual faculties of his charge. The training of the 'understanding' (*entendement*) is inseparably connected to the formation of 'character' (*mœurs*), a conjunction already established in *On pedantry* through the pairing of 'judgment' with 'virtue', and of 'understanding' with 'conscience'.[57] The emancipation of thought from captivity to memory and established authority is harnessed (and subordinate) to the cultivation of *moral* freedom:

> [A]The first lessons, in which we should steep his mind, must be those that regulate his behaviour and his sense, that will teach him to know himself, and to know how to die well and live well. [C]Among the liberal arts, let us start with the art which makes us free.[58]

Only later, when [A]'his judgment is already formed', should a pupil be taught 'the meaning of logic, physics, geometry, rhetoric'.[59] Moral philosophy is here singled out, among all the liberal arts, as the most [C]'directly and professedly useful' for the 'edification and service of our life'.[60] Freedom, on this account, consists not merely in the exercise of intellectual autonomy, but in an art of existence centred around self-knowledge.

56 [A]'À un enfant de maison, qui recherche les lettres, non pour le gaing (car une ~~si vile~~ fin ~~et~~ si abjecte, est indigne de la grace et faveur des Muses, et puis elle regarde et depend d'autruy) ny tant pour les commoditez externes, que pour les siennes propres, et pour s'en enrichir et parer au dedans, ayant plustost envie d'en ~~tirer un~~ <reussir> habil' homme, qu'~~un~~ homme sçavant, je voudrois aussi qu'on fust soigneux de luy choisir un conducteur, qui eust plustost la teste bien faicte, que bien pleine: et qu'on y requist tous les deux, mais plus les mœurs et l'entendement que la science'. I.25: P 155, V 150, F 110. [C]'Le guain de nostre estude, c'est d'en estre devenu meilleur et plus sage'. I.25: P 157, V 152, F 112.

57 [A]'De vray le soing et la despence de nos peres, ne vise qu'à nous ~~garnir~~ [C]meubler [A]la teste de science: du jugement et de la vertu, peu de nouvelles. [. . .] Nous ne travaillons qu'à remplir la memoire, et laissons l'entendement [C]et la conscience [A]vuide'. I.24: P 141, V 136, F 100.

58 [A]'Les premiers discours, dequoy on luy doit abreuver l'entendement, ce doivent estre ceux, qui reglent ses mœurs et son sens, qui luy apprendront à se cognoistre, et à sçavoir bien mourir et bien vivre. [C]Entre les arts liberaux, commençons par l'art qui nous faict libres'. I 25: P 165, V 159, F 117.

59 [A]'Ayant desjà le jugement formé'. I.25: P 166, V 160, F 118.

60 [C]'Elles [les arts liberaux] servent toutes ~~aucunement~~ <voirement en quelque manière> à l'instruction de nostre vie, et à son usage: [. . .] Mais choisissons celle qui y sert directement et professoirement'. I.25: P 165, V 159, F 117.

This emphasis on living independently, as well as thinking independently, is fundamental to the rhetoric of appropriation and assimilation that pervades both *On pedantry* and *On the education of children*. Montaigne's distinction between *habile* and *docte*, between *sage* and *sçavant*, is articulated through a contrast between that which is inwardly digested and that which is merely held in keeping, or superficially lodged:

> [A]Just as birds sometimes go in quest of grain, and carry it in their beak without tasting it, to give a beakful to their little ones, so our pedants go pillaging knowledge in books, and lodge it only on the end of their lips, in order merely to disgorge it, and scatter it to the winds.[61]

A key implication of this metaphor, as we saw in the previous section, is that material may be borrowed and yet transformed in such a way that it becomes part of our own substance: [A]'it is a sign of rawness and indigestion to disgorge food just as we swallowed it: the stomach has not done its work, if it has not changed the condition and form, of what it has been given to cook.'[62] That process of incorporation, however, is figured not merely as one of appropriation, but as one of vital nourishment. It is not enough for us to simply transform what we have swallowed, to rework it in such a way that we can legitimately call it our own. It is also necessary that it should *feed* us: for [A]'what good does it do us to have our belly full of meat, if it is not digested, if it is not transformed inside us? If it does not augment and strengthen us?'[63] To transform what we read, to make it our own, is to apply it to the conduct of our own self – to subordinate it to the 'edification and service of our life' – and to thereby transform ourselves. It is in this light, I suggest, that one should understand Montaigne's own claim to [C]'promptly apply' all that he studies 'to himself, or rather within himself'.[64]

This close identification of philosophical liberty with ethical freedom helps to explain an apparent paradox within Montaigne's account of independent judgment and thought. As Scholar makes clear, 'free-thinking, for

61 [A]'Tout ainsi que les oyseaux vont quelquefois à la queste du grain, et le portent au bec sans le taster, pour en faire bechée à leurs petits: ainsi nos pedantes vont pillotans la science dans les livres, et ne la logent qu'au bout de leurs lèvres, pour la dégorger seulement, et mettre au vent'. I.24: P 141, V 136, F 100.

62 [A]'C'est tesmoignage de crudité et indigestion que de regorger la viande comme on l'a avallée: l'estomach n'a pas faict son operation, s'il n'a faict changer la façon et la forme, à ce qu'on luy avoit donné à cuire.' I.25: P 156, V 151, F 111.

63 [A]'Que nous sert-il d'avoir la panse pleine de viande, si elle ne se digere, si elle ne se transforme en nous? si elle ne nous augmente et fortifie?' I.24: P 142, V 137, F 101.

64 [C]'Et si j'estudie autre chose, c'est pour soudain le coucher sur moy, ou en moy, pour mieux dire'. II.6: P 397, V 378, F 273.

Montaigne, invariably exists in a state of tense interaction with its own limits. [. . .] Throughout the *Essais*, free-thinking is itself put to the test'.[65] This tension between liberty and self-restraint dissolves, however, when one recognises that for Montaigne the freedom to think for oneself is always dependent on the ability to govern and regulate oneself: B'there are few souls so orderly, so strong and well-born, that they can be trusted with their own guidance: and that can sail with moderation and without temerity, in the liberty of their judgments, beyond the common opinions'.[66] The freedom to dispense with conventional wisdom and established authority is to be extended only to those individuals who will exercise it with circumspection, in keeping both with their aristocratic identity and with the capacity for self-control associated with that social status.

Montaigne's own practice of 'free-thinking', accordingly, is anchored in submission rather than subversion – in discretion rather than defiance. He is A'fit only to follow',[67] abandoning his conduct to the command of custom – C'I give my prudence small share in my conduct: I readily let myself be led by the general way of the world'[68] – and his judgment to the direction of fortune – A'the uncertainty of my judgment is so evenly balanced in most occurrences, that I would willingly submit to the decision of chance and of the dice'.[69] It is his disavowal of expert knowledge and didactic authority that entitles him to write freely, in accordance with his own judgment alone:

> AI speak my mind freely on all things, even on those which perhaps exceed my capacity, and which I by no means hold to be within my jurisdiction. And so the opinion I give of them, is to declare the measure of my sight, not the measure of things.[70]

It is precisely by acknowledging and indeed advertising his worthlessness and uselessness that Montaigne is able to sidestep the jurisdiction of scholarly authorities: A'whoever shall catch me in ignorance, will do nothing

65 Scholar 2010, p. 11; see also Boutcher 2005, pp. 43, 47–9.

66 B'Certes il est peu d'ames si reglees, si fortes et bien nées, à qui on se puisse fier de leur propre conduicte: et qui puissent avec moderation et sans temerité, voguer en la liberté de leurs jugemens, au delà des opinions communes'. II.12: P 592, V 559, F 420. See also Sève 2007 on the need to discipline the erratic movements of one's *esprit*.

67 A'Propre qu'à suyvre'. II.17: P 693, V 654, F 497.

68 C'Je fay peu de part à ma prudence, de ma conduitte: je me laisse volontiers mener à l'ordre public du monde'. II.17: P 695, V 656, F 498.

69 A'L'incertitude de mon jugement, est si également balancée en la pluspart des occurrences, que je compromettrois volontiers à la decision du sort et des dets'. II.17: P 693, V 654, F 496–7.

70 A'Je dy librement mon advis de toutes choses, voire et de celles qui surpassent à l'adventure ma suffisance, et que je ne tiens aucunement estre de ma juridiction. Ce que j'en opine, c'est aussi pour declarer la mesure de ma veue, non la mesure des choses'. II.10: P 430, V 410, F 298.

against me, for I should hardly be answerable for my ideas to others, I who am not answerable for them to myself, or satisfied with them'.[71] It is by subjecting himself to the truth that he is able to free himself from bondage to received opinion: when contradicted or corrected, he [B]'cheerfully surrender[s] to [truth] and extend[s] [his] conquered arms, from as far off as [he sees] it approach'.[72] Having [B]'deprived [his] judgment of the right to make decisions',[73] his aim is simply to [C]'gratify and foster' in others 'the liberty to admonish [him], by the ease with which [he] yield[s]'.[74]

As this final quotation suggests, the intellectual freedom claimed by Montaigne is principally to be understood not as a power to express one's own opinions, but rather as a willingness to suspend such judgments in favour of continued doubt:

> [C]Scattering a word here, there another, samples separated from their context, dispersed, without a plan and without a promise: I am under no obligation to make a good job of it nor even to stick to the subject myself, without varying it, if it should it please me, and surrendering to doubt and uncertainty, and to my ruling quality, which is ignorance.[75]

To resolve in favour of any given argument or position is, in this sense, to bring one's freedom of mind to an end, to have completed one's 'de-liberations'. [A]'Irresolution', the unbecoming 'scar' which Montaigne exposes to his readers in *On presumption*, for all that it is 'very unfit to produce in public', is presented as a condition of liberty, allowing him to 'keep within [him]self doubt and the liberty to choose, until the occasion is urgent'.[76] This resolution to avoid resolution mirrors the thorough-going scepticism of the Pyrrhonians, whose abstention from choice (by neither

71 [A]'Et qui me surprendra d'ignorance, il ne fera rien contre moy: car à peine respondroy-je à autruy de mes discours, qui ne m'en responds point à moy, ny n'en suis satisfaict'. II.10: P 427–8, V 407, F 296.

72 [B]'Je festoye et caresse la verité en quelque main que je la trouve, et m'y rends alaigrement, et luy tends mes armes vaincues, de loing que je la vois approcher'. III.8: P 968–9, V 924, F 705.

73 [B]'Nous autres, qui privons nostre jugement du droict de faire des arrests'. III.8: P 967, V 923, F 704.

74 [C]'Aymant à gratifier et à nourrir la liberté de m'advertir, par la facilité de ceder'. III.8: P 969, V 924, F 705.

75 [C]'Semant icy un moy, icy un autre, eschantillons dépris de leur piece, escartez, sans dessein, sans promesse: je ne suis pas tenu d'en faire bon, ny de m'y tenir moy-mesme, sans varier, quand il me plaist, et me rendre au doubte et incertitude, et à ma maistresse forme, qui est l'ignorance'. I.50: P 321–2, V 302, F 219.

76 [A]'Ceste cicatrice, bien mal propre à produire en public. C'est l'irresolution. [. . .] J'arreste chez moy le doubte, et la liberté de choisir, jusques à ce que l'occasion me presse'. I.17: P 693, V 653–4, F 496.

affirming nor denying the truth of any given proposition) is characterised in the *Apology* as a vindication of human liberty.

> [B]Where others are carried away, either by the custom of their country, or by their parental upbringing, or by chance, as by a tempest, without judgment and without choice, indeed most often before the age of discretion, to such or such an opinion, to the Stoic or Epicurean sect, to which they find themselves pledged, enslaved, and fastened, as to a prey they have bitten into and cannot shake loose: [C]*to whatever doctrine they have been driven, as by a storm, to it they cling as to a rock.* [B]Why shall it not be granted similarly to these [C]men [B]~~here~~ [the Pyrrhonians] to maintain their liberty, and to consider things without obligation and servitude? [C]*The more free and independent because their power to judge is intact.*

Not only are they able to escape the errors and quarrels that afflict dogmatic philosophers, but the Pyrrhonians are [C]'released from the necessity that bridles others'.[77]

This freedom 'to consider things without obligation and servitude', it is important to stress, does not simply involve the power to think for oneself, independent of the influence of custom, education or allegiance to a particular school of thought. These forces are here represented as the *instruments* of subjection, not as the *masters* to whom our minds are held captive. The freedom of the Pyrrhonians is located instead in the mind's relationship to its objects – in the ability to conceive and consider ('to essay') ideas [A]'without inclination or approbation on either side', without surrendering to and becoming enslaved to them. This attitude of indifferent detachment extends even to their own profession of doubt. By [A]'taking all things in without adherence or consent', the Pyrrhonians find themselves 'exempt from the agitations we receive through the impression of the opinion and knowledge we think we have of things', and thereby 'free themselves [. . .] from jealousy on behalf of their doctrine'. Just as Montaigne refuses to pledge his judgment to the authority of another man, so the Pyrrhonians do not allow themselves to be ruled by any given proposition: they are able to 'maintain their liberty', by applying their judgment to opinions

[77] [B]'Et où les autres sont portez, ou par la coustume de leur païs, ou par l'institution des parens, ou par rencontre, comme par une tempeste, sans jugement et sans choix, voire le plus souvent avant l'aage de discretion, à telle ou telle opinion, à la secte ou Stoïque ou Épicurienne, à laquelle ils se treuvent hypothequez, asserviz et collez, comme à une prise qu'ils ne peuvent desmordre: [C]*ad quamcumque disciplinam, uelut tempestate, delati, ad eam, tanquam ad saxum, adhaerescunt* [Cicero, *Academica priora*, II.3.8]. [B]Pourquoy à ~~ceux icy~~ [C]ceux-cy, [B]ne sera-il pareillement concedé, de maintenir leur liberté, et considerer les choses sans obligation et servitude? [C]*Hoc liberiores et solutiores, quod integra illis est iudicandi potestas* [Cicero, *Academica priora*, II.3.8]. N'est-ce pas quelque advantage, de se trouver desengagé de la necessité, qui bride les autres?' II.12: P 531, V 503–4, F 373.

and arguments without committing and thereby submitting themselves to them as their masters.[78]

These two versions of liberty – freedom as the capacity to exercise one's judgment autonomously and as the ability to preserve that judgment from captivity to any one perspective or position – are found in close conjunction in *On presumption*. Montaigne concludes the catalogue of his deficiencies and imperfections with the following statement: [A]'this capacity for sifting truth, [B]whatever it may amount to in me, [A]and this free humour not to enslave my belief easily, I owe principally to myself'.[79] This assertion serves to legitimate his claim to be free of the vice of presumption, by confirming the sincerity and accuracy of his low opinion of himself. But it also focuses the reader's attention on the one quality which he is eager to attribute to himself: the ability to safeguard his *creance* from subjection. The upshot of this passage is, in the first place, to uphold Montaigne's independent jurisdiction over the formation of his judgment. He insists that [A]'the firmest and most general ideas' that he has are 'natural and all mine', that he has himself 'produced them crude and simple', and that he has merely 'established and fortified them by the authority of others and the arguments of the ancients', thereby perfecting his own original 'possession' of them. But he is also careful to emphasise his indifference towards the external objects of his mind's attention: he 'concentrates nearly all [his] affection upon [him]self and does not squander much of it elsewhere', 'turning [his] gaze inward' instead of 'looking straight ahead'.[80]

Intellectual freedom is thus best thought of not as an end in itself but as evidence of the moral status of the speaker – of the quality of his judgment and, more generally, the condition of his soul. The excellence of '*conference*' as an energetic encounter between [B]'vigorous and orderly minds' contrasts with the sycophantic performance of those who 'serve as a spectacle to the great and make a competitive parade of their wit

78 [A]'Sans inclination, ny approbation d'une part ou d'autre'. [A]'Recevant tous objects sans application et consentement'. [A]'Exempte des agitations que nous recevons par l'impression de l'opinion et science, que nous pensons avoir des choses. [. . .] Voire ils s'exemptent par là, de la jalousie de leur discipline'. II.12: P 530, V 503, F 372.

79 [A]'Ceste capacité de trier le vray, [B]quelle qu'elle soit en moy, [A]et cett' humeur libre de n'assubjectir aysément ma creance, je la dois principallement à moy'. II.17: P 697, V 658, F 499.

80 [A]'Les plus fermes imaginations que j'aye, et generalles, ~~ce sont celles mesmes~~ [B]sont celles [A]qui par maniere de dire, nasquirent avec moy: [B]elles sont naturelles, et toutes miennes. [A]Je les produisis crues et simples, [. . .] depuis je les ay establies et fortifiées par l'authorité d'autruy, et par les sains exemples des anciens, ausquels je me suis rencontré conforme en jugement: Ceux-là ~~me les ont mises en main~~ [C]m'en ont asseuré de la prinse, [A]et m'en ont donné la jouyssance et possession [C]plus [A]~~entiere~~ <claire>'. II.17: P 697, V 658, F 499. [A]'L'affection que je me porte, singuliere, comme celuy qui la ramene quasi toute à moy, et qui ne l'espands gueres hors de là. [. . .]. Le monde regarde tousjours vis à vis: moy, je replie ma veue au dedans'. II.17: P 696-7, V 657, F 499.

and chatter'.[81] Those eminent or learned persons, meanwhile, who rely on intimidating their audience into submission through their impressive demeanour and reputation are engaged in a [B]'tyrannie [. . .] parliere' that is no less hateful to Montaigne than that which is 'in acts' (*effectuelle*). [B]'The gravity, the gown, and the fortune of the speaker often give authority to vain and inept remarks', but Montaigne declares himself 'inclined to resist with all [his] mind these vain externals that delude our judgment through the senses'.[82]

Free conversation is sabotaged not only by servile flatterers driven by the pursuit of favour rather than truth or by self-appointed luminaries relying on awe rather than reason to persuade. Montaigne reserves his harshest criticism for those who are so enslaved to their own opinions that they cannot bear to hear them contested and contradicted. He admits to exasperation when dealing with interlocutors who, through [F]'ineptitude' rather than 'ignorance', lack the capacity to 'speak with order, prudently, and competently', and readily condemns his impatience in this regard: [B]'it is always a tyrannical ill humour to be unable to endure an approach different from your own'.[83] Crucially, however, what riles Montaigne is not the substance of these offending claims, but the way in which they are arrived at and defended.

Far from being irritated or unsettled when others disagree with him, he claims to [B]'enter into discussion and argument with great liberty and ease, inasmuch as opinion finds in [him] a bad soil to penetrate and take deep roots in'.[84] [B]'Contradictions of opinion [. . .] arouse and exercise' him, instead of 'offending' or 'altering' him.[85] So happy is he to see himself contradicted that he readily contradicts himself: [C]'my thinking so often contradicts and condemns itself that it is all one to me if another does the job'.[86] Indeed, even in light banter with friends, he brings [B]'more liberty

81 [B]'Esprits vigoureux et reiglez'. 'Servir de spectacle aux grands, et faire à l'envy parade de son esprit, et de son caquet'. III.8: P 967, V 923, F 704.

82 [B]'La gravité, la robbe, et la fortune de celuy qui parle, donne souvent credit à des propos vains et ineptes: [. . .] Je hay toute sorte de tyrannie, et la parliere, et l'effectuelle. Je me bande volontiers contre ces vaines circonstances, qui pipent nostre jugement par les sens'. III.8: P 975–6, V 931, F 710–11.

83 [B]'Dire ordonnement, prudemment, et suffisamment, peu d'hommes le peuvent. Par ainsi la fauceté qui vient d'ignorance, ne m'offence point: c'est l'ineptie'. 'C'est tousjours un'aigreur tyrannique, de ne pouvoir souffrir une forme diverse à la sienne'. III.8: P 973, V 928, F 708–9.

84 [B]'J'entre en conference et en dispute, avec grande liberté et facilité: d'autant que l'opinion trouve en moy le terrein mal propre à y penetrer, et y pousser de hautes racines'. III.8: P 967, V 923, F 704.

85 [B]'Les contradictions donc des jugemens, ne m'offencent, ny m'alterent: elles m'esveillent seulement et m'exercent'. III.8: P 968, V 924, F 705.

86 [C]'Mon imagination se contredit elle mesme si souvent, et condamne, que c'est tout un, qu'un autre le face'. III.8: P 969, V 924, F 705.

than wit' to the discussion, while always remaining 'perfect in forbearance [. . .], enduring retaliation, not only sharp but even indiscreet, without being disturbed'.[87] These habits of intellectual generosity and flexibility testify not only to the independence of Montaigne's judgment – to his ability to think for himself – but to a wider capacity for detachment and self-containment: to the liberty of his soul, and not only that of his mind.

IV

This concern to embrace contradiction instead of seeking to suppress or overcome it finds formal articulation in the basic structure and shape of the text itself. Montaigne refuses to conform his thoughts to linear models of argumentation and persuasion, prefering to follow the vagaries of his own judgment, as opposed to taking opinions 'on credit', and to consider things without obligation, inclination or alteration. The *essai*, as we shall see in this section, embodies a form of reflection that is peculiarly free in each of these respects: firstly, because it equips Montaigne to think in several keys at the same time, by holding competing perspectives in tension with each other; and secondly, because it maintains a critical distance between speaker and utterance, allowing him to examine ideas without engaging himself. Montaigne's commitment to liberty – in its ethical as well as intellectual aspect – thus plays a crucial role in determining the distinctive 'manner' of his thinking.

Readers of the *Essais* often think of Montaigne's approach to writing as free in some important, if ill-defined, sense. Free-ranging, free-wheeling, free-spoken and free-spirited are all adjectives that occur frequently in descriptions of the work. The text's digressive and discontinuous character evokes an apparently spontaneous and lawless mode of philosophical enquiry, confined neither in its choice of subject matter nor in its order of presentation to a predetermined, prescribed path. This emphasis on free movement and association has come to be thought of as representative not merely of Montaigne's writing but of the essay form as a whole. As a recent theorist of the essay has put it:

> The essay is an essentially ambulatory and fragmentary prose form. Its direction and pace, the tracks it chooses to follow, can be changed at will; hence its fragmentary or 'paratactic' structure. Rather than progressing in a linear and planned fashion, the essay develops around a number of topics which offer themselves along

[87] B'Plus de liberté que d'esprit'. 'Je suis parfaict en la souffrance: car j'endure la revenche, non seulement aspre, mais indiscrete aussi, sans alteration'. III.8: P 984, V 938, F 717.

the way. And this sauntering from one topic to the next together with the way in which each topic is informally 'tried out' suggests a tentativeness, a looseness, in short a randomness which seems to elude the unifying conception – syntactic, semantic, and pragmatic – of a recognizable generic identity.[88]

This representation of the essay as a walking, wandering or sauntering motion rather than a static body of prose echoes Montaigne's description of his discourse as [C]'a formless and undisciplined way of talking: A popular jargon, and a way of proceeding without definition, without division, without conclusion, confused'.[89] The rambling and stuttering structure of his writing serves to validate his assurances that he has not polished or bedecked himself for public view: [A]'I let my thoughts run on, weak and lowly as they are, as I have produced them, without plastering and sewing up the flaws' that a comparison between his opinions and those of 'good authors' reveals.[90] The *Essais* appear arbitrary in the strongest sense of the term: not only do their order and rhythm convey an impression of randomness, but these can be changed at will, in accordance with Montaigne's unbounded and spontaneous dispositions.

The *essai* represents more, however, than a mere performance of Montaigne's liberty, a fashionable and carefully fashioned pose. Its 'ambulatory and fragmentary' character is a prerequisite for the exercise of freedom both by Montaigne himself and by his readers. The author's decision to write 'without definition, without division, without conclusion' liberates the work both formally and cognitively from the straitjacket imposed by the orderly sequence of the systematic treatise, disrupting the steady, seemingly inexorable progress of arguments and explanations from first foundations and principles through to final convictions and resolutions. In revising his book between successive editions, Montaigne refuses to [A]'correct [his] first imaginings by [his] second', with the exception, [C]'perhaps', of 'a word or so, but only to vary, not to delete', in keeping with his concern [A]'to represent the course of [his] humours'.[91] This claim to represent the process of his thinking (rather than report on its results) allows him to dispense with conventional requirements of manifest pertinence and logical consistency,

[88] de Obaldia 1995, p. 2.

[89] [C]'Un parler informe et sans regle: Un jargon populaire, et un proceder sans definition, sans partition, sans conclusion, trouble'. II.17: P 675, V 637, F 483.

[90] [A]'[Je] laisse [. . .] courir mes inventions ainsi foibles et basses, comme je les ay produites, sans en replastrer et recoudre les defaux'. I.25: P 151, V 147, F 107.

[91] [A]'Je ne corrige point mes premieres imaginations par les secondes, [C]ouy à l'aventure quelque mot: mais pour diversifier, non pour oster. [A]Je veux representer le progres de mes humeurs, et qu'on voye chasque piece en sa naissance'. II 37: P 796, V 758, F 574.

in favour of more oblique and, above all, more open-ended trajectories of enquiry.

Montaigne's aim, as we have seen, is not to clarify and consolidate his opinions, but to 'essay' problems from a variety of conflicting and overlapping perspectives, without confining himself to any particular standpoint, and without setting final limits to the process of enquiry. Crucially, however, his writing cannot be classed as merely contradictory or incoherent. The tensions and uncertainties exhibited by the *essai* do not simply cancel each other out; on the contrary, the process of reflection draws fresh impetus and focus from the text's openness to digression and doubt, allowing constructive philosophical reflection to take place outside the disputed realm of dogmatic and didactic certainty.

As André Tournon has recently demonstrated, the logic of each chapter is propelled forward by semantic 'ruptures' and 'inflections' sparking unexpected, indirect and seemingly anomalous itineraries of thought ('routes par ailleurs'). These pivotal shifts in the logical development of a chapter generate a dialogical rather than dialectical process of reflection. They reconfigure the chapter's line of sight, bringing its conditions of enquiry into focus and into question, disrupting its claim to know and understand in favour of ironic self-awareness. The resulting discourse cannot be described as incoherent or indecisive, but nor is it reducible to a single point of view. Neither contradictory nor dialectical, Montaigne's writing obeys the more supple and complex logic of the *essai*, with its capacity to inhabit plural points of view; not successively, but simultaneously.[92]

A crucial implication of Montaigne's use of the *essai* to keep tensions in play instead of resolving them is that his utterances have a strictly experimental, provisional and unbinding status. The systematic deployment of certain modalising expressions (*peut être*, *à l'avanture*, *il semble que*, *il me semble que*, *je trouve que*, *je pense que*) drives a wedge between the speaking subject and the content of his utterances.[93] Montaigne draws just as much attention to the distance that separates him from his discourse as to the contact between them: he is always changing his mind, [B]'from day to day, from minute to minute'; above all, he is always forgetting his thoughts, almost as soon as he has produced them.[94]

Montaigne entertains propositions without endorsing or ratifying them; they are advanced not as statements of belief, but as candidates for appraisal.

92 Tournon 2006. 93 Sellevold 2004.

94 [B]'De jour en jour, de minute en minute'. III.2: P 845, V 805, F 611. For Montaigne's tendency to forget his own thoughts, see, for example, II.10: P 428, V 407, F 296[A].

The text speaks in a multiplicity of voices or *personae* which he 'tries out' and 'tests' in turn, while maintaining a measure of distance from the claims which they are adduced to support. As he expresses it in *On presumption*: A'I do not know which side to take in doubtful enterprises | E*Neither yes nor no my inmost heart will say.* | I can easily maintain an opinion, but not choose one'.[95]

Montaigne concludes *On the art of conversation* by commending the practice of those historians who include B'popular rumours and opinions' in their writings without seeking to suppress that which they themselves do not believe. Similarly, he does not claim to B'believe [him]self in all that [he] write[s] [. . .] often hazarding sallies of [his] mind which [he] mistrust[s], Cand certain verbal subtleties at which [he] shake[s] [his] ears; Bbut letting them run at a venture'.[96] This account of the *Essais* recalls Montaigne's description of the Pyrrhonians in the *Apology*, as not only unafraid of A'contradiction in their discussion', but 'seeking to be contradicted, so as to create doubt and suspension of judgment, which is their goal'. Far from being reduced by scepticism to silence, they 'advance their propositions' not to persuade their listeners that they are true, but 'only to combat those they think we believe in', and will 'just as gladly take the opposite one to maintain' if that will further the cause of irresolution, thereby 'separating and dividing themselves from many opinions, even from those which in many ways have upheld doubt and ignorance'.[97] This argumentative strategy, according to which a point of view is adopted not because it is credited as true but because of its capacity to loosen the hold of dogmatic convictions over us, is one that Montaigne also attributes to Socrates:

CIt is my opinion that in Plato and Xenophon Socrates argues more for the sake of the arguers than for the sake of the argument: and to instruct Euthydemus and Protagoras rather in their own impertinence, than in the impertinence of their art.

95 A'Je ne sçay pas prendre party ès entreprinses doubteuses: | B*Ne si, ne no, nel cor mi suona intero* [Petrarch, *Canzoniere*, CLXVIII]. | Je sçay bien soustenir une opinion, mais non pas la choisir'. II.17: P 693, V 653–4, F 496.

96 B'Ne m'en crois pourtant pas du tout: Je hazarde souvent des boutades de mon esprit, desquelles je me deffie: Cet certaines finesses verbales dequoy je secoue les oreilles: Bmais je les laisse courir à l'avanture'. III.8: P 989, V 943, F 720.

97 A'Ils ne craignent point la revenche à leur dispute [. . .] et cherchent qu'on les contredie, pour engendrer la dubitation et surseance de jugement, qui est leur fin. Ils ne mettent en avant leurs propositions, que pour combattre celles qu'ils pensent, que nous ayons en nostre creance. Si vous prenez la leur, ils prendront aussi volontiers la contraire à soustenir. [. . .] Et par cette extremité de doubte, qui se secoue soy-mesme, ils se separent et se divisent de plusieurs opinions, de celles mesmes, qui ont maintenu en plusieurs façons, le doubte et l'ignorance'. II.12: P 530–1, V 503, F 372.

He takes hold of the first subject that comes along, like a man who has a more useful aim than to illuminate it, to wit, to illuminate the minds, that he undertakes to manage and exercise.[98]

Montaigne's willingness to write 'experimentally', by setting utterance loose from belief, frees expression from the compulsion of assent (or dissent). Not only does the *essai* reorient philosophical discourse away from the consolidation of knowledge towards the dissemination of doubt, it releases the writer from subjection to error and obstinacy.

The *Essais* are thus imagined as a sphere of uncommon freedom and intimate self-possession in which Montaigne strives to exercise his own judgment without deferring to the authority of other thinkers and to examine arguments and propositions without attaching himself to them through either assent or dissent. Paradoxically, however, that freedom is itself construed as a source of obligation for its author, binding him to the task that he has set for himself and to the image of himself that it conveys. Montaigne's decision to write about himself deprives him of [B]'this deformed liberty to present ourselves in two aspects, the actions in one fashion and the speeches in another' practised by other writers – a monstrous and misshapen freedom, but freedom nonetheless. Whereas this grotesque liberty 'may be permissible for those who tell of things', it 'cannot' be so for 'those who tell of themselves': he is constrained to 'go the same way with my pen as with my feet'.[99] Not only is his power to shape his text in accordance with his will limited by his obligation to portray himself faithfully, the text itself exerts control over its subject. His book stands as a lasting and incorruptible witness of himself, yet he readily admits that [B]'the publication of [his] behaviour' serves him 'to some extent [. . .] as a rule', and that 'this public declaration obliges [him] to keep on his path', for fear of 'betraying ~~[his] painting~~ [C]the story of [his] life' or [B]'giving the lie to the picture of [his] qualities'.[100]

98 [C]'Il m'est advis qu'en Platon et en Xenophon Socrates dispute plus, en faveur des disputants qu'en faveur de la dispute: et pour instruire Euthydemus et Protagoras de la cognoissance de leur impertinence, plus que de l'impertinence de leur art. Il empoigne la premiere matiere, comme celuy qui a une fin plus utile que de l'aisclaircir, assavoir esclaircir les esprits, qu'il prend à manier et exercer'. III.8: P 972, V 927, F 708.

99 [B]'Ceste difforme liberté, de se presenter à deux endroicts, et les actions d'une façon, les discours de l'autre; soit loisible à ceux, qui disent les choses. Mais elle ne le peut estre à ceux, qui se disent eux mesme, comme je fais: Il faut que j'aille de la plume comme des pieds'. III.9: P 1037, V 991, F 758.

100 [B]'Je sens ce proffit inesperé de la publication de mes mœurs, qu'elle me sert aucunement de regle. Il me vient par fois quelque consideration de ne trahir ~~ma peinture~~ [C]l'histoire de ma vie. [B]Cette publique declaration, m'oblige de me tenir en ma route; et à ne desmentir l'image de mes conditions'. III.9: P 1025, V 980, F 749.

Montaigne's decision to extend his book through 'allongeails' that leave the existing text intact, instead of rewriting or replacing it, can also be understood as a form of rigorous (albeit self-imposed) discipline.

[B]When a man has mortgaged his work to the world, it seems to me that he has no further right to it. [. . .] [C]My book is always one: except that at each time, that it is to be renewed, so that the buyer may not end up completely empty-handed, I allow myself to attach to it (since it is only an ill-fitted patchwork) some supernumerary emblem. [. . .] [B]As far as I am concerned, I fear to lose by the change: My understanding does not always go forward, it goes backward too: I distrust my thoughts hardly any less for being second or third than for being first: or for being present than for being past.[101]

On the one hand, Montaigne's *allongeails* allow him to renew and perpetuate the process of deliberation and enquiry, as well as to affirm his *deffiance* of (and independence from) the arguments that he offers up for consideration. Just as importantly, however, he deprives himself of authority over those parts of the text that he has already published or 'mortgaged' (*hypothequé*) to the world. Even while allowing himself to reshape his book indefinitely by adding to his existing writings and thereby subjecting them to new inflections and juxtapositions, he refuses to disown earlier recensions of his text, however flawed or obsolete he may now take them to be. His *allongeails* are classed, in the same breath, both as a privilege which he accords to himself (or which he asks the reader to extend to him) and as the repayment of a debt owed to the 'buyer' who has purchased the book and on whom he relies for publication.[102]

The freedom of the *essai* thus consists at once in license and in self-restraint – at once in an open-ended and uninhibited proliferation of discourse and in the cultivation of distance between the author and the materials contained in his text. Montaigne relinquishes control over his book, but in so doing preserves himself at liberty.

101 [B]'Celuy qui a hypothequé au monde son ouvrage, je trouve apparence, qu'il n'y ayt plus de droict: [. . .] [C]Mon livre est tousjours un: sauf qu'à mesure, qu'on se met à le renouveller, afin que l'achetteur ne s'en aille les mains du tout vuides, je me donne loy d'y attacher (comme ce n'est qu'une marqueterie mal jointe) quelque embleme supernumeraire. [. . .] [B]Pour mon regard, je crains de perdre au change: Mon entendement ne va pas tousjours avant, il va à reculons aussi: Je ne me deffie gueres moins de mes fantasies, pour estre secondes ou tierces, que premieres: ou presentes, que passées'. III.9: P 1008–9, V 963–4, F 736.

102 The 'buyer' in question, as George Hoffmann has demonstrated, refers not to the reader who, having purchased earlier as well as later editions, would feel cheated if each successive version did not contain additional material, but rather to the publisher who, having purchased rights over the whole work, would be left 'empty-handed' once his *privilège* or monopoly over its publication had expired – a difficulty commonly circumvented by reissuing the work in question in an augmented or revised form, resulting in a new *privilège*. Hoffmann 1998, ch. 5.

V

At first sight, this emphasis on the non-identity of speaker and utterance in the *Essais* may appear at odds with Montaigne's persistent emphasis on the [A]'good faith' of his [C]'consubstantial' book.[103] The text is advanced from the outset as a *sign* of its author, making visible [A]'certain features of [his] conditions and humours' and rendering legible 'to the life' his 'defects, [. . .] <imperfections> and natural form'.[104] Its purpose, we discover in Book III, is to [A]'represent the progress of [Montaigne's] humours', to [B]'represent a continual agitation and mutation of [his] thoughts'.[105] This language of living representation recalls the terms of *On the affection of fathers for their children*, in which the offspring of the soul, that is, of [A]'our mind, our heart and ability', are said to 'represent and resemble us much more vividly' than our natural children,[106] as well as of *On the art of conversation*, where Montaigne calls upon us to offer for judgment that [B]'piece' of our 'work' (*ouvrage*) that 'represents' us 'fully', and 'by which [we] would like to be measured'.[107]

To underline the affective distance that separates Montaigne from the contents of his reflections is not, however, to deny his pervasive presence in his writing. The self-reflexive character of the *Essais* – their claim to offer knowledge of its author, rather than of the manifold topics which he treats – itself relies on the text's ability to direct its attention to an object while simultaneously detaching itself from it. His discourse folds back upon itself, applying itself to Montaigne himself rather than to the propositional content of his affirmations.[108]

As we have already established, moreover, it is by appealing to his own *agency* in producing his text that Montaigne is able to affirm it as 'exactement mien', and to thereby distinguish it from the derivative 'pastissage de lieux communs' produced by other writers. In one sense, of course,

103 [A]'Un Livre de bonne foy'. *Au lecteur*: P 27, V 3, F 2. [C]'Livre consubstantiel à son autheur'. II.18: P 703–4, V 665, F 504.

104 [A]'Aucuns traicts de mes conditions et humeurs [. . .] Mes defauts s'y liront au vif, <mes imperfections> et ma forme naïfve'. *Au lecteur*: P 27, V 3, F 2.

105 [A]'Je veux representer le progrez de mes humeurs'. II.37: P 796, V 758, F 574. [B]'Representer une continuelle agitation et mutation de mes pensées'. III.9: P 990, V 946, F 721.

106 [A]'Ce que nous engendrons par l'ame, les enfantemens de nostre esprit, de nostre courage et suffisance [. . .] nous representent et nous rapportent bien plus vivement que les autres'. II.8: P 421, V 400, F 291.

107 [B]'Laissons donc ces pieces, donnez m'en une qui vous represente bien entier, par laquelle il vous plaise qu'on vous mesure'. III.8: P 985, V 939, F 717.

108 Tournon 2006, p. 11, n. 1, and p. 29; see also the more extended discussion in Tournon 2001, pp. 257–86.

he identifies himself with the sum of all that he has ever held to be true, however tentatively and temporarily. To this extent, the *Essais* can indeed be understood as a repository of opinions and judgments, all of which he claims as part of himself, each fragment contributing to his composite self-portrait. At a deeper level, however, it is clear that he thinks of his mind as a faculty to be put to the test, rather than as a territory to be mapped, and that he seeks knowledge of himself not in the shifting lineaments of his opinions, but in the conduct of his understanding. The quality of a man's thinking, he argues in *On the art of conversation*, is to be judged on the basis of its procedure, rather than of its substantive content: [B]'when you win the advantage for your proposition, it is truth that wins; when you win the advantage for order and method, it is you who win'.[109] That which is most Montaigne, that which is most his own, is the way in which he handles the materials at his disposal. Not only are the materials themselves of secondary interest, but the preservation of a certain distance between speaker and utterance is a crucial component of this process.

The status of the *essai* as a vehicle of freedom has far-reaching implications not only for the problem of imitation in Montaigne's text, but for its status as a self-portrait, as an expression or representation of its author. In choosing to write about himself, indeed only about himself, Montaigne lays claim to a subject over which he alone may be said to exert authority. As he expresses it in *On repentance*: [B]'never did a man treat a subject which he knew or understood better than I do the subject which I have undertaken: on that subject I am the most learned man alive'.[110] He leaves the reader in no doubt as to his sovereign jurisdiction over his text, positioning himself, at the end of *On the art of conversation*, as [B]'King of the matter I treat, owing an account of it to nobody'.[111]

How are we to interpret the second part of this statement? In what sense are the *Essais* answerable to no one but their named author? In the first place, there is nobody to whom an 'account' of the text could meaningfully be made: Montaigne alone is in a position to disclose and vouch for his inner dispositions and thoughts. Yet even if there were some other person who could claim to know him better than he knows himself, he affirms himself

109 [B]'Quand vous gaignez l'avantage de vostre proposition, c'est la verité qui gaigne: quand vous gaignez l'avantage de l'ordre, et de la conduitte, c'est vous qui gaignez'. III.8: P 972, V 927, F 708.

110 [B]'Jamais homme ne traicta subject, qu'il entendist ne cogneust mieux, que je fay celuy que j'ay entrepris: et qu'en celuy là je suis le plus sçavant homme qui vive'. III.2: P 845, V 805, F 611.

111 [B]'Moy qui suis Roy de la matiere que je traicte, et qui n'en dois compte à personne'. III.8: P 989, V 943, F 720.

to be indifferent to their judgment. As he explains in *On giving the lie*, even if no one reads him, he will not have wasted his time by C'entertaining' not his audience, but himself, 'with such useful and agreeable thoughts': for 'indeed, the most delightful pleasures are digested inwardly, avoid leaving any traces, and avoid the sight not only of the public but of any other person'.[112]

This characterization of the *Essais* as a self-sufficient source of purely inward pleasure finds its consummate expression in Montaigne's assertion that his book is an inalienable and integral part of himself: C'consubstantial' in the sense that it is 'concerned with [him]self, a limb of [his] life: Not concerned with some third-hand, foreign purpose, like all other books'.[113] This passage has often been understood to convey a mimetic conception of discourse, a concern to erase the distinction between sign and signified and thus to overcome the gap that separates the self from its textual representation. As Marjorie Boyle has emphasised, however, this identification of author and book rests on a relationship of generation rather than imitation. The theological concept of consubstantiality, as it is affirmed in the Nicene Creed that Montaigne would have professed at Mass, refers not to the Trinitarian doctrine that God the Father and God the Son share one being, but rather to the Christological doctrine of the incarnation: the historical Jesus is consubstantial with the divine, according to the unity of substance binding parent and child, a man and his speech (*logos*). Montaigne's book is consubstantial with its author, just as man and God are consubstantial in Christ.[114]

This affirmation of identity through the medium of paternity or generation serves both to insist on the book's representative efficacy and to assert Montaigne's jurisdiction over the image that it contains (and its interpretation). In *On some verses of Virgil*, he describes himself as B'hungry to make myself known', or rather as having 'a mortal fear of being taken to be other than I am by those who come to know my name'.[115] Unlike La Boétie, whose posthumous memory risked being B'torn into a thousand contrary

112 C'Et quand personne ne me lira, ay-je perdu mon temps, de m'estre entretenu tant d'heures oisives, à pensements si utiles et aggreables? [. . .] Les plus delicieux plaisirs, si se digerent ils au dedans: fuyent à laisser trace de soy: et fuyent la veue, non seulement du peuple, mais d'un autre'. II.18: P 703–4, V 665, F 504.

113 C'D'une occupation propre: Membre de ma vie: Non d'une occupation et fin, tierce et estrangere, comme tous autres livres'. II.18: P 703–4, V 665, F 504.

114 Boyle 1997, esp. pp. 727, 737. See also Montaigne's description of his text as B'*Essays* of flesh and bone' ('en chair et en os'). III.5: P 885, V 844, F 640.

115 B'Je suis affamé de me faire cognoistre [. . .] je fuis mortellement, d'estre pris en eschange, par ceux à qui il arrive de cognoistre mon nom'. III.5: P 888, V 847, F 643.

faces', Montaigne advances his book as a safeguard against the distortion and speculation of others:

> [B]After all this I do not want people to go on debating, as I often see them troubling the memory of the dead: He thought thus, he lived thus; he wanted this; if he had spoken as he was dying, he would have said, he would have given; I knew him better than anyone else. [. . .] I leave nothing about me to be desired or guessed. If people are to talk about me, I want it to be truly and justly. I would willingly come back from the other world to give the lie to any man, who portrayed me other than I was, even if it were to honour me.[116]

The book is figured as a loyal child and heir, empowered to uphold Montaigne as he truly is even after his death.

On what basis then does Montaigne's text represent or express him? Consubstantiality is, to be sure, grounded in resemblance, such that acquaintance with the *Essais* yields knowledge of their author: [B]'Isn't this the way I speak everywhere? don't I represent myself to the life? Enough, then. I have done what I wanted: everyone recognises me in my book, and my book in me'.[117] The production of this likeness, however, is not so much the goal of Montaigne's enterprise, but rather evidence of the intimate role that he has played in generating and shaping his text. The book represents and expresses its author, not in the sense that it is intended as a mimetic mirror image, but because he himself has made it, and is thereby made manifest in it. What Montaigne is doing is to exercise himself, to exercise his own judgment. The result of such trials or '*essais*' is a work that bears witness to his own qualities – a 'piece' that fully 'represents' him and according to which he may justly be 'measured'. Self-expression here emerges as a symptom and guarantee of independent authorial agency, rather than as an end in itself.

Montaigne's conception of the *Essais* as a living witness of its creator echoes Erasmus' account of 'copious' (rhetorically masterful) discourse, in the *Ciceronianus* (1528), as a manifestation of the speaker's nature, as words animated by the breath of the mind ('mens illa spirans etiamnum in

116 [B]'Je ne veux pas, après tout, comme je vois souvent agiter la memoire des trespassez, qu'on aille debattant: Il jugeoit, il vivoit ainsin: il vouloit cecy: s'il eust parlé sur sa fin il eust dict, il eust donné; je le cognoissois mieux que tout autre. [. . .] Je ne laisse rien à desirer, et deviner de moy. Si on doit s'en entretenir, je veux que ce soit veritablement et justement. Je reviendrois volontiers de l'autre monde, pour démentir celuy, qui me formeroit autre que je n'estois, fust-ce pour m'honorer. [. . .] Et si à toute force, je n'eusse maintenu un amy que j'ay perdu, on me l'eust deschiré en mille contraires visages'. III.9: P 1028–9, V 983, F 751–2.

117 [B]'Est-ce pas ainsi que je parle par tout? me representé-je pas vivement? suffit. J'ai faict ce que j'ay voulu: tout le monde me recognoist en mon livre, et mon livre en moy'. III.5: P 918, V 875, F 667.

scriptus': a 'mind breathing even now in the written word').[118] His depiction of his writing as flowing directly from the inner depths of his body (*poictrine, entrailles*), in particular, parallels Erasmus' appeal to self-expression as the key to verbal plenitude ('if you do not express yourself [*si teipsum non exprimis*], your discourse [*oratio*] will be a lying mirror'), a characterization that itself builds on Quintilian's identification of a speaker's *pectus* (the chest or heart, the place where breath originates) and *vis mentis* (the power of the mind) as the sources of successful improvisation.[119]

It is in Montaigne's *maniere*, in the impression of his *forme* on the text, that the irreducibly personal character of his writing is most clearly conveyed: his is [B]'a domestic and private style, [. . .] of a form all [his] own'.[120] This emphasis on the personal *form* impressed by an author on his text is, as Kathy Eden has recently indicated, equally indebted to Erasmus. An author's style (*stilum*), Erasmus argues in his edition of the works of St. Jerome, is proper to him and marks his work as his own, as an unrepeatable, inimitable attribute of that individual and no other: 'as each individual has his own appearance, his own voice, his own character and disposition, so each has his own style of writing. And the quality of mind is manifest in speech even more than the likeness of the body is reflected in a mirror'.[121]

At first sight, this understanding of texts as vivid reflections of their authors appears to indicate a new conception of writing as a form of authentic self-expression. The anchoring of transformative imitation in the inward resources of a speaker's *pectus* or *mens*, and in the unmistakable identity of an author's personal and proper style, serves as a guarantee not of an author's sincerity, however, but of their self-reliance and self-sufficiency. Erasmus urges his readers to 'produce something that seems born of your own ability [*ingenium*], rather than begged from somewhere else, something that breathes the vigour and character of your own intellect [*mens*] and nature [*natura*]'.[122] Erasmus, like Montaigne after him, is here drawing on claims advanced by both Quintilian and Seneca. 'Arguments drawn from outside are in themselves useless,' we read in the *Institutio oratoria*, 'unless the speaker's own talent [*ingenium*] is brought into play to

118 Erasmus 1969–, vol. I, pp. 629–32; see Cave 1979, p. 42.

119 Erasmus 1969–, vol. I, p. 649; cf. Quintilian 2001, X.7.15, p. 380: 'pectus est enim quod disertos facit et vis mentis'. See Cave 1979, p. 42.

120 [B]'Un stile comique et privé: [. . .] d'une forme mienne'. I.39: P 256, V 252, F 186.

121 Erasmus 1974–, vol. LXI, p. 76, quoted in Eden 2008, pp. 29–30.

122 'In ipsum animum velut in stomachum traiicientem, ut transfusum in venas, ex ingenio tuo natum non aliunde emendicatum esse videatur, ac mentis naturaeque tuae vigorem et indolem spiret'. Erasmus 1969–, vol. I, p. 704; quoted in Moss 2000, p. 105.

apply them advantageously to the matter of his discourse'.[123] In the *Epistulae ad Lucilium*, meanwhile, we are told that it is through the application of 'our own talent and faculties' (*ingenii nostra cura et facultate*) that our borrowings are made into a new, coherent whole; an author's dependency on pre-existing sources will not be detected, Seneca argues, 'for a true copy stamps its own form upon all the features which it has drawn from what we may call the original, in such a way that they are combined into a unity'.[124] The living quality of a writer's discourse, in sum, derives from the operation of his *ingenium* – of his own ability or talent.

As Cave indicates, these Erasmian notions of personal discourse and self-expression must be sharply distinguished from a 'Romantic insistence on the intensity of emotional experience': the notion of *pectus*, in particular, 'has a range of meanings which embrace cognitive as well as affective modes of awareness, and should not be equated with "emotion" in the Romantic sense'.[125] An individual's style, as Eden emphasises, is to be understood as 'an expression of not just his language, but also his thought, his judgment, his character'.[126] The term, as Erasmus puts it in his edition of Jerome, 'comprehends all at once a multiplicity of things – manner in language and diction, texture, so to speak, and, further, thought and judgment, line of argumentation, inventive power, control of material, emotion, what the Greeks call *èthos*'.[127]

Erasmus' association of *stilum* with *èthos* is of particular significance here, as is the connection drawn by Eden between his discussion of *proprietas*, the Greek notion of *oikeion* and the Ciceronian concept of *decorum* (as adumbrated in *De officiis*) as terms at once rhetorical and forensic. As Cicero explains:

Each person should hold on to what is his, as far as it is not vicious, but is proper to him, so that the seemliness [*decorum*] that we are seeking might more easily be maintained [. . .] If anything at all is seemly, nothing, surely, is more so than an evenness both of one's whole life and of one's individual actions. You cannot preserve that if you copy someone else's nature and ignore your own. [. . .] Everyone ought to weigh the characteristics that are his own, and to regulate them, not wanting to see how someone else's might become him; for what is most seemly for a man is the thing that is most his own. Everyone, therefore, should know his

[123] 'Extra petita, nisi ad aliquam praesentis disceptationis utilitatem ingenio adplicantur, nihil per se valent'. Quintilian 2001, V.11.44, p. 454; quoted in Moss 2000, p. 11.

[124] Seneca 1989, II.84.5, p. 278. 'Puto aliquando ne intellegi quidem posse, si imago vera sit; haec enim omnibus, quae ex quo velut exemplari traxit, formam suam inpressit, ut in unitatem illa conpetant'. Seneca 1989, II.84.8, p. 280.

[125] Cave 1979, pp. 42, 37. [126] Eden 2008, p. 32.

[127] Erasmus 1974–, vol. LXI, p. 78; quoted in Eden 2008, pp. 29–30.

own natural ability [*ingenium*] and show himself a keen judge of his own good points and vices.[128]

The rhetorical notion of *decorum*, which Cicero uses to translate the Greek *to prepon*, is here applied to the problem of moral deliberation and action, combining both aesthetic and ethical considerations. An author's style is 'proper' to him, and thereby identifies his text as his own, in the sense that it becomes him, that it is consonant with the pattern of his own essential, ethical qualities. As we shall see in the next chapter, this understanding of texts as expressions of moral status, rather than psychological identity, is central to Montaigne's conception of self-study.

The extraordinary proliferation of the first-person pronoun in Montaigne's text, it has sometimes been suggested, is symptomatic of the pressures of literary borrowing: it is because the text struggles to affirm itself as the property of its author, because it cannot close the gap between imitation and appropriation, that it becomes increasingly self-reflexive, positioning itself as a study not merely of things but of Montaigne himself, bound to its author by an intimate, 'consubstantial' relation.[129] As we have seen in this chapter, however, these pressures are best understood not as a threat to the authenticity of Montaigne's discourse, but as an infringement of his liberty. The self, in this perspective, is defined first and foremost by its autonomy and independence, and only secondarily by its particularity or its sincerity.

128 'Admodum autem tenenda sunt sua cuique non vitiosa, sed tamen propria, quo facilius decorum illud, quod quaerimus, retineatur. [. . .] Omnino si quicquam est decorum, nihil est profecto magis quam aequabilitas cum universae vitae, tum singularum actionum, quam conservare non possis, si aliorum naturam imitans omittans tuam. [. . .] Quisque habeat sui, eaque moderari nec velle experiri, quam se aliena deceant; id enim maxime quemque decet, quod est cuiusque maxime suum. Suum quisque igitur noscat ingenium acremque se et bonorum et vitiorum suorum iudicem praebeat'. Cicero 1968b, I.31.110–11 and 113–14, pp. 112–14 and 116; quoted (in part) in Eden 2008, p. 37.

129 See, in particular, Cave 1979, pp. 35, 77.

CHAPTER 2

Languages of the self
Montaigne's classical inheritance

I

To the extent that the *Essais* exhibit a heightened attention to the self, it has been supposed, firstly, that this awareness of and interest in the self is a distinctively modern preoccupation, a decisive rupture with the values of the ancient world, and, secondly, that that self must take the form that it takes in our own culture – that of an authentic, deeply private self. In this chapter, I propose to read the *Essais* against the grain of this proleptic scholarship by presenting Montaigne not as the architect and exponent of a distinctively modern interiority but as a classical moralist deeply indebted to ancient patterns of thought and language. I examine the persistent and formative role of ancient discourses of self-possession and self-scrutiny in the *Essais*, uncovering the classical roots and cast of Montaigne's efforts to withdraw into and belong to himself.

The purpose of this exercise is not to call the originality of the *Essais* into question, but to allow us to see his project of self-study in a different and less anachronistic light. The question of the text's 'modernity', as I see it, is ultimately too elastic and underdetermined to be of great usefulness or interest. More importantly, there is no denying the boldness and significance of Montaigne's decision to offer himself as the subject of his own book. My point is rather that his preoccupation with the self comes into focus only when we realise how profoundly marked it is by his reading of certain classical texts. My enquiry focuses on the sources of his *language* of 'self', on the vocabulary which he uses to articulate what he 'cannot say so well'. In particular, I argue that, when he writes that we should look *into* ourselves, or that we should *own* ourselves, he is appropriating a tradition of thinking and writing found in the works of his two favourite moral philosophers: Plutarch and Seneca.

I am not suggesting that Montaigne's concerns are identical to those of these ancient writers. When we read the *Essais* from the perspective of these texts, however, it becomes clear that Montaigne constitutes the self as the object of an essentially moral endeavour of self-scrutiny and self-protection. For these writers, as for Montaigne, we should withdraw into ourselves and live for ourselves, not to realise our most individual and truthful being, but to achieve tranquillity and wisdom in a threatening and corrupt world. We must learn to own or belong to ourselves by detaching ourselves from that which is not in our power. This practice of withdrawal and reflection, turning our attention and will away from the world and towards ourselves, is presented as a vindication of our liberty, freeing us from slavery to others and allowing us to reclaim ownership over ourselves. For all its apparent familiarity and transparency, Montaigne's 'self' embodies preoccupations and assumptions quite distant from our own.

II

In order to grasp what is at stake in Montaigne's turn to 'self', we must begin by examining the exact terms in which he describes this project. As he puts it in *On practice*: [C]'it is many years now that I have had only myself as object of my thoughts, that I have been registering and studying only myself. And if I study something else, it is in order promptly to apply it to myself, or rather within myself'.[1] The reader is left in no doubt as to the purpose of the book. The *Essais* are designed to be read not merely as a collection of discourses and reflections, but as a study of Montaigne: [A]'these are my humours and opinions: I offer them as what I believe, not as that which is to be believed. My only aim here is to uncover myself'; [A]'I try to give knowledge not of things, but of myself'.[2] Montaigne's study of himself is the central focus and organising principle of the *Essais*, the thread that draws this [A]'bundle of so many disparate pieces' together as a single project.[3] He is himself the [A]'matter' of his book, his own [A]'argument' and 'subject'.[4]

Montaigne draws attention repeatedly to the radical dimensions of this enterprise. In writing about himself, he sets himself against the [A]'laws of

[1] [C]'Il y a plusieurs années que je n'ay que moy pour visée à mes pensées, que je ne contrerolle et n'estudie que moy. Et si j'estudie autre chose, c'est pour soudain le coucher sur moy, ou en moy, pour mieux dire'. II.6: P 397, V 378, F 273.

[2] [A]'Ce sont icy mes humeurs et opinions: Je les donne, pour ce qui est en ma creance, non pour ce qui est à croire. Je ne vise icy qu'à decouvrir moy-mesmes'. I.25: P 153, V 148, F 108–9. [A]'Je ne tasche point à donner à connoistre les choses, mais moy'. II.10: P 428, V 407, F 296.

[3] [A]'Fagotage de tant de diverses pieces'. II.37: P 796, V 758, F 574.

[4] [A]'Je suis moy-mesme la matiere de mon livre'. *Au lecteur*. P 27, V 3, F 2. [A]'Je me suis presenté moy-mesmes à moy pour argument et pour subject'. II.8: P 404, V 385, F 278.

ceremony', which 'allow a man neither to speak well of himself, nor to speak ill'.[5] The *Essais* are a kind of monster, [C]'the only book in the world of its kind, [A]a book with a wild and ~~monstrous~~ [C]extravagant [A]plan', devoted to 'so vain and mean' a subject that even 'the best workman in the world' could not have 'fashioned' it 'into something worthy of notice'.[6] Whenever he [A]'lead[s]' his judgment 'to a noble and well-worn subject', he finds 'the road [. . .] so beaten that it can walk only in others' footsteps'.[7] His decision to study himself, however, is [C]'a new and extraordinary amusement, which withdraws us from the ordinary occupations of the world', an undertaking which stands almost wholly without precedent: 'we have heard of only two or three ancients who opened up this road, and even of them we cannot say whether their manner in the least resembled mine, since we know only their names'.[8]

It is likely that Montaigne is here thinking of the satirical poet Gaius Lucilius, of whom Horace wrote, in a passage later quoted in *On presumption*, that he [A]'*confided, as unto trusted friends | His secrets to his books*, [. . .] *so that the old man's whole life lay revealed | As on a votive tablet*'.[9] Montaigne paraphrases this quotation by describing Lucilius as [A]'committing to his paper his actions and thoughts, and portraying himself there as he thought he was', before linking his name to two further authors through a quotation from Tacitus' *Life of Agricola*: [C]'nor did anyone doubt the honesty or disparage the motives of Rutilius or Scaurus for doing so'.[10] Montaigne may well have been justified, however, in emphasising the uniqueness of his own project. His decision to write about himself reflects a heightened mode of subjective awareness, an affirmation of his humours, conditions

5 [A]'Je me trouve icy empestré ès loix de la ceremonie: car elle ne permet, ny qu'on parle bien de soy, n'y qu'on en parle mal'. II.17: P 670, V 632, F 479. See also *Au lecteur*, P 27, V 3, F 2[A] and II.6: P 397, V 378, F 273 [C].

6 [C]'Le seul livre au monde de son espece, et d'[A]un dessein farousche et ~~monstrueux~~ [C]extravaguant [. . .] [A]à un subject si vain et si vil, le meilleur ouvrier du monde n'eust sceu donner ~~forme et~~ façon qui merite qu'on en face conte'. II.8: P 404, V 385, F 278.

7 [A]'Tantost je le promene à un subject noble et tracassé, [. . .] le chemin en estant si frayé, qu'il ne peut marcher que sur la piste d'autruy'. I.50: P 321, V 301, F 219.

8 [C]'Un amusement nouveau et extraordinaire, qui nous retire des occupations communes du monde'. 'Nous n'avons nouvelles que de deux ou trois anciens, qui ayent battu ce chemin: Et si ne pouvons dire, si c'est du tout en pareille maniere à ceste-cy, n'en connoissant que les noms'. II.6: P 396, V 377–8, F 273.

9 [A]'*Ille uelut fidis arcana sodalibus olim | Credebat libris* [. . .] *quo fit, ut omnis | Votiua pateat ueluti descripta tabella | Vita senis* [Horace, *Sermones*, II.1.30–33]'. II.17: P 670, V 632, F 479. The point is made by Villey in his edition of the *Essais* (Montaigne 2004, p. 1250).

10 [C]'Celuy là commettoit à son papier ses actions et ses pensées, et s'y peignoit tel qu'il se sentoit estre. [A]*Nec id Rutilio et Scauro citra fidem, aut obtrectationi fuit* [Tacitus, *Agricola*, I.3]'. II.17: P 670, V 632, F 479.

and fantasies in all their particularity, strangeness and vanity. This commitment to self-description and self-examination, it could well be argued, sets the *Essais* apart not only from anything to be found in classical literature, but also from the conventions of his own period.

As Ullrich Langer notes, 'what distinguishes Montaigne is his persistently personal perspective, the "study" of oneself as the goal of his enterprise'. To this extent, the *Essais*'s 'often disarming, unsystematic revealing of Montaigne's own judgments, tastes, bodily functions' may rightly be said to 'constitute the ground of what can be called the modern "self", the recentring of esthetic, epistemological and social reflection in the subject'.[11] Montaigne's rejection of universal models of wisdom,[12] his claim to study mankind through the unique lens of the self,[13] and his emphasis on the primacy of personal experience[14] all gesture towards a deeply personal, almost individualistic, moral sensibility.[15] His critique of humanist practices of imitation, his nominalist metaphysics and his 'baroque' aesthetics of grotesque singularity combine to orientate the text towards an appreciation of all that is most particular, individual and personal about the self.[16]

[11] Langer 2005, pp. 2–3.

[12] C'All the glory that I aspire to in my life is to have lived it tranquilly. Tranquilly not according to Metrodorus, or Arcesilaus, or Aristippus, but according to me' ('toute la gloire, que je pretens de ma vie, c'est de l'avoir vescue tranquille. Tranquille non selon Metrodorus, ou Arcesilas, ou Aristippus, mais selon moy'). II.16: P 660, V 622, F 471.

[13] B'You can tie up all moral philosophy with a common and private life, just as well as with a life of richer stuff: Each man bears the entire form of the human condition. CAuthors communicate with the people by some special extrinsic mark: I am the first to do so by my entire being: as Michel de Montaigne: not as a Grammarian or Poet, or Jurist' ('on attache aussi bien toute la philosophie morale, à une vie populaire et privée, qu'à une vie de plus riche estoffe: Chaque homme porte la forme entiere, de l'humaine condition. CLes autheurs se communiquent au peuple par quelque marque speciale et estrangere: moy le premier, par mon estre universel: comme, Michel de Montaigne: non comme Grammairien ou Poëte, ou Jurisconsulte'). III.2: P 845, V 805, F 611.

[14] B'Whatever may be the fruit we can reap from experience, what we derive from foreign examples will hardly be much use for our education, if we make such little profit from the experience we have of ourselves, which is more familiar to us, and certainly sufficient to inform us of what we need' ('quel que soit donq le fruict que nous pouvons avoir de l'experience, à peine servira beaucoup à nostre institution, celle que nous tirons des exemples estrangers, si nous faisons si mal nostre profit, de celle, que nous avons de nous mesme, qui nous est plus familiere: et certes suffisante à nous instruire de ce qu'il nous faut'). III.13: P 1119, V 1072, F 821.

[15] Writers who have emphasized the personal aspect of Montaigne's philosophy include Auerbach 1953, Hallie 1966, Taylor 1989, Friedrich 1991 and Nehamas 1998. Cf. Sawday 1995 on the emergence of a scientific and aesthetic culture of *autopsia* (or seeing for oneself), grounded in the direct, first-person experience of embodiment.

[16] On Montaigne and the crisis of classical exemplarity, see Hampton 1990. On Montaigne and nominalism, see Compagnon 1980 and Langer 1990. On the *Essais* as baroque text, see Sayce 1954, Buffum 1957 and Nakam 2006.

I have no quarrel with these claims. It is vital, however, to avoid projecting our own assumptions and interests onto the *Essais* and to recover some of the strangeness of this deceptively familiar text. The book is repeatedly described as a self-portrait,[17] a metaphor that has led modern readers to approach it as a 'mirror of ink'[18] purporting to disclose the deepest layer of Montaigne's being. As George Hoffmann has noted, however, 'much of the writing of Montaigne's day tends, like the *Essays* themselves, not to be a literature of expressiveness so much as one of discernment'. Whereas modern readers 'locate the aim of literature in the laying bare of emotion', Montaigne 'considered the point of his book to lie in the exercise of "judgment", in "being judged" and in "judging others"'.[19] The writing of the *Essais*, in this perspective, 'records [. . .] not so much the character of an individual person as the idiosyncratic flow of that person's thoughts'.[20] Montaigne himself tells us as much when he writes that C'what I chiefly portray is my cogitations'.[21] His C'thorny enterprise' aims to 'follow' the 'movement' of the 'mind', to 'penetrate into the opaque depths of its inner folds; to tease out and pin down so many of its subtle shades and stirrings'.[22] Montaigne's 'self', in other words, is identified not with a complex psychological identity but with a shifting pattern of cognitive dispositions; his aim is not to uncover the hidden affects of the self, but to capture the wayward movement of his thoughts.

Montaigne does, it is true, speak of the *Essais* as a B'publication of [his] manners' – revealing his A'faults', 'imperfections' and 'native form', his 'simple, natural and ordinary fashion', his B'own form', his 'mistress form',

17 A'It is myself that I portray' ('c'est moy que je peins'). *Au lecteur*: P 27, V 3, F 2. A'Whatever these ineptitudes may be, I have had no intention of hiding them, any more than I would a bald and greying portrait of myself, in which the painter had drawn not a perfect face, but mine' ('quelles que soient ces inepties, je n'ay pas deliberé de les cacher, non plus qu'un mien pourtraict chauve et grisonnant, où le peintre auroit mis non un visage parfaict, mais le mien'). I.25: P 153, V 148, F 108. A'Having here to portray myself to the life' ('ayant à m'y pourtraire au vif'). II.8: P 404, V 386, F 278. A'Why is it not permissible in the same way for each man to portray himself with the pen, as he [King René of Sicily] portrayed himself with a pencil?' ('pourquoy n'est-il loisible de mesme à un chacun, de se peindre de la plume, comme il se peignoit d'un creon?'). II.17: P 692–3, V 654, F 496. C'Painting myself for others' ('me peignant pour autruy'). II.18: P 703, V 665, F 504. A'This dead and mute portrait' ('ceste peinture morte, et muette'). II.27: P 825, V 784, F 596. B'The lines of my painting do not go astray [. . .] I do not portray being, I portray passing' ('les traits de ma peinture, ne se fourvoyent point [. . .] Je ne peinds pas l'estre, je peinds le passage'). III.2: P 844–5, V 804–5, F 610–11.

18 Beaujour 1980. 19 Hoffmann 1998, p.152. 20 Cave 2007, p. 10.

21 C'Je peins principalement mes cogitations'. II.6: P 398, V 397, F 274.

22 C'C'est une espineuse entreprinse, et plus qu'il ne semble, de suyvre une alleure si vagabonde, que celle de nostre esprit: de penetrer les profondeurs opaques de ses replis internes: de choisir et arrester tant de menus airs de ses agitations'. II.6: P 396, V 378, F 273.

his [A]'bearing', his 'air', his 'conditions and faculties'.[23] He here identifies himself not merely with the labyrinthine process of his thinking, with the 'inner folds' of the mind, but with the inclinations that make up his nature and his temperament, seen in all dimensions, [C]'standing and lying down; front and rear; to the right and to the left; in all [his] natural folds'.[24] These passages, however, invite us to think of the text not as the exploration of a unique, hermetic identity, but as the incarnation of a vivid, visible set of qualities – as an exercise in self-appraisal rather than introspection. Montaigne describes his book as an image [A]'for a nook in a library [. . .] to amuse ~~someone, who has a particular interest in knowing me:~~ a neighbour, a relative, a friend'. 'What a satisfaction,' he writes, 'it would be to me to hear someone tell me, in this way, of the habits, ~~the form, the conditions~~, [C]the face, the expression, the favourite remarks [A]and the fortunes of my ancestors'.[25] His self-portrait is here presented not as a faithful copy or simulacrum of himself, but as a votive or effigy striving 'less to resemble than to remember', offering 'a continuation of its subject as much as a representation of it, within what one might today term a metonymic rather than a mimetic relation'.[26]

The image that the text contains is offered not as the intimate trace of an elusive, authentic self, but as the bold imprint of Montaigne's moral value and character – a register of that which he can truly count as his own. As scholars have long emphasised, Montaigne is not engaged in narrating his life or his development as a person: the book is a self-portrait, not an autobiography.[27] The purpose of the *Essais* is to reveal their author as he truly is, at the moment of writing: as he famously explains, his subject is not [B]'being' but 'passage'.[28] Montaigne is not particularly interested, however, in the hopes, anxieties and obsessions that feature so prominently in our own, intensely psychological sense of self. His aim is to determine the condition of his soul, to identify the kind of man that he is, to see what can be imputed to him without injustice: [B]'those who have a false opinion

[23] [B]'La publication de mes mœurs'. III.9: P 1025, V 980, F 749. [A]'Ma façon simple, naturelle et ordinaire. [. . .] Mes defauts [. . .], <mes imperfections> et ma forme naïfve'. *Au lecteur*: P 27, V 3, F 2. [B]'Une forme sienne, une forme maistresse'. III.2: P 851, V 811, F 615. [A]'Ce mesme port, et ce mesme air [. . .] Ces mesmes conditions et facultez'. II.37: P 823, V 783, F 595.

[24] [C]'Debout, et couché; le devant et le derriere; à droitte et à gauche; et en touts mes naturels plis'. III.8: P 989, V 943, F 721.

[25] [A]'Pour le coin d'une librairie, et pour en amuser ~~quelqu'un, qui ait particulier interest à ma connoissance:~~ un voisin, un parent, un amy [. . .] Quel contentement me seroit-ce d'ouyr ainsi quelqu'un, qui me recitast les mœurs, ~~la forme, les conditions~~, [C]le visage, la contenance, les <plus communes> parolles communes, et les fortunes des mes ancestres'. II.18: P 702–3, V 664, F 503.

[26] Hoffmann 2000, pp. 150, 147. [27] Beaujour 1980, Brush 1994.

[28] [B]'Je ne peinds pas l'estre, je peinds le passage'. III.2: P 845, V 805, F 610–11.

of themselves can feed on false approbations; not I, who see myself and seek for myself down to the very entrails, I who know well what belongs to me.'[29] Montaigne's 'self' is a catalogue of attributes, albeit a contradictory one: [B]'bashful, insolent; [C]chaste, lascivious; [B]talkative, taciturn; tough, delicate; clever, stupid; surly, affable; lying, truthful; [C]learned, ignorant; liberal, miserly, and prodigal'.[30] To speak of oneself, in other words, is not to give voice to that which is hidden or repressed, to render legible that which is most ineffable and elusive about oneself, but to offer a record or account of oneself, to 'take stock' of oneself,[31] to 'essay' (weigh, try, taste) one's natural faculties and one's judgment,[32] to lay bare one's weaknesses and vices, as well as one's qualities.

Readers of the *Essais* have rightly emphasised the gulf that separates the text from the spiritual practices of confession and *examen de conscience*, with their connotations of guilt and self-abasement. Repentance, as Montaigne makes clear in the chapter of that name, is [B]'nothing but a disavowal of our will and an opposition to our fancies, which leads us about in all directions', leading a man to 'disown his past virtue and his continence'.[33]

[29] [B]'Ceux qui se mescognoissent, se peuvent paistre de fauces approbations: non pas moy, qui me voy, et qui me recherche jusques aux entrailles, qui sçay bien ce qu'il m'appartient.' III.5: P 889, V 847, F 643–4.

[30] [B]'Honteux, insolent, [C]chaste, luxurieux, [B]bavard, taciturne, laborieux, delicat, ingenieux, hebeté, chagrin, debonnaire, menteur, veritable, [C]sçavant, ignorant, et liberal et avare et prodigue'. II.1: P 355, V 335, F 242.

[31] [A]'My mind [. . .] gives birth to so many chimeras and fantastic monsters, one after another, without order or purpose, that in order to contemplate their ineptitude and strangeness at my pleasure, I have begun to keep a record of them' ('mon esprit [. . .] m'enfante tant de chimeres et monstres fantasques les uns sur les autres, sans ordre, et sans propos, que pour en contempler à mon ayse l'ineptie et l'estrangeté, j'ay commencé de les mettre en rolle'). I.8: P 55, V 33, F 21. [C]'Have I wasted my time by taking stock of myself so continually, so carefully? [. . .] I listen to my dreamings, because I have to record them' ('Ay-je perdu mon temps, de m'estre rendu compte de moy, si continuellement; si curieusement? [. . .] J'escoutte à mes resveries, par ce que j'ay à les enroller'). II.18: P 704, V 665, F 504. [B]'I cannot keep a record of my life by my actions: fortune places them too low: I keep it by my fantasies' ('je ne puis tenir registre de ma vie, par mes actions: fortune les met trop bas: je le tiens par mes fantasies'). III.9: P 989–90, V 945–6, F 721. On the metaphor of the book as *registre* or *contre-rolle*, see Benson 1989 and Mathieu-Castellani 2000, pp. 63–81.

[32] [A]'As for the natural faculties that are in me, of which this book is the essay' (quant aux facultez naturelles qui sont en moy, dequoy c'est icy l'essay'). I.25: P 151, V 146, F 107. [A]'Judgment is a tool to use on all subjects, and comes in everywhere. Therefore in the Essays that I make of it here, I use it in every sort of occasion' ('le jugement est un util à tous subjects, et se mesle par tout. A cette cause aux Essais que j'en fay icy, j'y employe toute sorte d'occasion'). I.50: P 321, V 301, F 219. [A]'This is purely the essay of my natural faculties, and not at all of the acquired ones' ('c'est icy purement l'essay de mes facultez naturelles, et nullement des acquises'). II.10: P 427, V 407, F 296.

[33] [B]'Le repentir n'est qu'une desdicte de nostre volonté, et opposition de nos fantasies, qui nous pourmene à tous sens. Il faict desadvouer à celuy-là, sa vertu passée et sa continence'. III.2: P 848, V 808, F 613. See Friedrich 1949 (pp. 267–73), Taylor 1989, and Cave 1995. On the *Essais* and Augustine's *Confessions*, see Mathieu-Castellani 2000.

Montaigne insists time and again that he accepts himself as he is, with all his follies and weaknesses: [B]'others form man, I recite him: and represent a particular one, very ill-formed, whom I should really make very different from what he is if I had to fashion him over again: but now it is done'.[34]

As Montaigne makes clear on at least two occasions, however, he is himself formed and constituted through this process of self-description:

> [C]In modelling this figure upon myself, I have had to ~~fashion~~ <groom> and compose myself so often to bring myself out, that the model has grown firm and has to some extent formed itself. Painting myself for others, I have painted myself in myself with colours clearer than my original ones. I have no more made my book than my book has made me.[35]

> [B]I feel this unexpected profit from the publication of my behavior, that to some extent it serves me as a rule. Sometimes there comes to me a feeling that I should not betray the story of my life. This public declaration obliges me to keep on my path, and not to give the lie to the picture of my qualities.[36]

This understanding of the text as a rule or pattern, modelled on oneself but also modelling oneself, unites self-scrutiny with self-transformation. Montaigne is essaying or judging himself, not in the sense that he is accusing and condemning himself, but in the sense that he is discerning that which is his. In offering an account of himself, in the strongest sense, he is both discovering and appropriating himself – surveying what is his own and claiming it as his own.

In casting doubt on our familiar understanding of the *Essais* as an exercise in psychological introspection and sincere self-expression, I am not suggesting that the 'self' which they portray is nothing more than a pose or a performance. In a powerful study of Rembrandt's self-portraits, Harry Berger rejects 'physiognomic' readings of late Renaissance portraits as windows into the sitter's soul ('the face as index of the mind'), by analysing

34 [B]'Les autres forment l'homme, je le recite: et en represente un particulier, bien mal formé: et lequel si j'avoy à façonner de nouveau, je ferois vrayement bien autre qu'il n'est: meshuy c'est fait'. III.2: P 844, V 804, F 610.

35 [C]'Moulant sur moy cette figure, il m'a fallu si souvent me ~~dresser~~ <testonner> et composer, pour m'extraire, que le patron s'en est fermy, et aucunement formé soy-mesme. Me peignant pour autruy, je me suis peint en moy, de couleurs plus nettes, que n'estoyent les miennes premieres. Je n'ay pas plus faict mon livre, que mon livre m'a faict'. II.18: P 703, V 665, F 504.

36 [B]'Je sens ce profit inesperé de la publication de mes mœurs, qu'elle me sert aucunement de regle. Il me vient par fois quelque consideration de ne trahir l'histoire de ma vie. Cette publique declaration, m'oblige de me tenir en ma route; et à ne desmentir l'image de mes conditions'. III.9: P 1025, V 980, F 749.

them as knowing parodies of mimetic representation, 'presentations of acts of self-presentation, or representations of the act of self-representation', whose true subject is not the inner self but the act of posing in itself.[37] In a related vein, David Posner has argued that Montaigne's claim to present himself without adornment or dissimulation is itself a calculated performance, designed to establish his aristocratic credentials within a theatrical court culture which demands that 'the successful nobleman [. . .] control and deploy an array of performative selves according to situational demands, while maintaining an essential separation between performer (however defined) and performance'.[38] Timothy Hampton has similarly suggested that Montaigne's 'self' is to be understood 'less as some essential interiority that must be "expressed" than as a set of postures imposed on the subject by external circumstance', 'a strategic response to particular conditions of negotiation' – a conception that seems to be indebted to Stephen Greenblatt's analysis of improvisation as 'the ability and willingness to play a role, to transform oneself, if only for a brief period and with mental reservations, into another'.[39]

My own intervention is rather different in character. In my view, Montaigne's study of himself offers not so much a subversion or performance of mimesis as an entirely different mode of self-figuration, based on a rigorous account of that which is his. My interest lies in reading the self-portrait not as a succession of postures or masks, borrowed from the outside and applied to the self, but as an index of Montaigne's moral preoccupations and sensibility. We are absolutely right, I think, to treat the *Essais* as an exercise in self-discernment and self-scrutiny, as a study of [C]'himself, his essence',[40] and of [C]'his universal being',[41] rather than as the construction of one or more rhetorically or strategically effective poses. Where we have gone wrong, however, is in identifying this enquiry with the introspection of a hidden, psychological interiority, rather than with the elucidation of one's true moral value and character. To study oneself, in this perspective, is to understand what is ours and what is not.

[37] Berger 2000, p. 12. [38] Posner 1999, p. 5.

[39] Hampton 2009, pp. 42, 71. Greenblatt 1980, p. 228. See also Timothy Reiss's influential claim that there are two subjects in Montaigne – one that is rigorously private, identified with the free process of disordered thought, enmeshed in the inconstancy characteristic of human reason and thus scarcely a subject at all, and one that is the social and political subject of the prince: Reiss 1986. On the multiple faces of Montaigne, see Rigolot 1988.

[40] [C]'C'est moy, c'est mon essence'. II.6: P 398, V 379, F 274.

[41] [C]'Mon estre universel'. III.2: P 845, V 805, F 611.

III

Having examined the terms in which Montaigne describes the project of the *Essais*, I now wish to turn to the language he uses to designate what we would call 'the self'.[42] In particular, I focus attention on his appeals for us to look or withdraw *into* ourselves, on the one hand, and to *belong* or *own* ourselves, on the other. This analysis of the *Essais*'s discourse about 'self' makes no claim to be exhaustive. My aim is simply to indicate some of the most salient features of this language, and to point to the recurrence of two striking tropes: a rhetoric of inwardness and a rhetoric of self-possession.

The first step, however, is to establish the topic under discussion. What exactly does Montaigne take himself to be writing about? Does he have a concept of 'the self'? I begin with a famous passage from *On presumption*:

> [A]Le monde regarde tousjours vis à vis: moy, je replie ma veue au dedans, je la plante, je l'amuse là. Chacun regarde devant soy, moy je regarde dedans moy: Je n'ay affaire qu'à moy, je me considere sans cesse, je me contrerolle, je me gouste. Les autres vont tousjours ailleurs, s'ils y pensent bien: ils vont tousjours avant,
>
> *nemo in sese tentat descendere:* moy, je me roulle en moy mesme.

> [A]The world always looks straight ahead: as for me, I turn my gaze inward, I plant it there and keep it busy. Everyone looks in front of himself, as for me I look inside of me: I have no business but with myself, I examine myself continually, I monitor myself, I sample myself. Others always go elsewhere, if they stop to think about it: they always go forward,
>
> *no man tries to descend into himself:* as for me, I roll myself in myself.[43]

Montaigne's contrastive and emphatic use, in this passage, of the pronouns *me*, *moy* and *moy-mesmes* (me, myself) is characteristic of his construction of 'self' in the *Essais*. When he writes that 'je me considere sans cesse' or that 'je me roulle en moy-mesmes', he is offering an elaboration of the reflexive, pronominal construction found in the quotation from Persius' *Saturae* (4.23): 'in *sese* descendere'. His subject, as announced in the preface, is not 'the self' but simply *himself*: [A]'c'est moy que je peins' ('it is myself that I am painting'); [A]'je suis moy-mesmes la matiere de mon livre' ('I am myself the matter of my book').[44]

[42] In this section, exceptionally, quotations from the *Essais* will be presented in French, followed by an English translation, in the main body of the text.

[43] II.17: P 697, V 657–8, F 499. [44] *Au lecteur*: P 27, V 3, F 2.

Montaigne does not write about *le soi* or even *le moi*, understood as an abstract or reified entity, or as a notion in philosophy requiring elucidation and justification.[45] This substantive use of 'self' as a self-standing, definite noun is to be found, in French, only from the second half of the seventeenth century onwards – for instance, in Pascal's famous retort to Montaigne: 'le moi est haïssable'.[46] (In English, the term only begins to appear towards the end of that century, notably in John Locke's pioneering definition of 'Self' as 'that conscious thinking thing [. . .] that is concerned for itself, as far as that consciousness extends').[47] Montaigne, by contrast, always uses 'moy' in its standard, pronominal form, as a reflexive rather than ontological signifier – a usage confirmed by John Florio's contemporary English translation (1603), with its recourse to the pronouns 'my selfe', 'himselfe', 'themselves', and so on.[48]

Strictly speaking, then, it is misleading to speak of 'the self' in Montaigne, because he nowhere signals his possession of such a concept through the use of the relevant term. Insofar as he can be said to be writing about 'self' at all, his efforts focus on the need to distinguish all that is properly 'moy' or 'à moy' ('myself', 'my own') from all that is not – on the need to return to ourselves, by distancing ourselves from all that is not us. Montaigne's 'moy' is defined in opposition to 'les autres' or 'le monde' its location designated by images of circular or centripetal motion. His gaze is directed '*au dedans*' instead of '*devant*', '*avant*', or '*ailleurs*'; he withdraws it or folds it (*replier*) back on himself.

This gesture of contraction and reflexion, in its most literal and etymological sense, recurs frequently in the *Essais*. In *On idleness*, Montaigne tells us that A'je me retiray chez moy' ('I retired to my home'; literally, 'to myself') to allow his mind to A's'entretenir soy-mesmes, et s'arrester et rasseoir en soy' ('to entertain itself and stay and settle itself in itself').[49] In *On solitude*, he writes of the soul that A'il la faut ramener et retirer en soy' ('we must bring it back and withdraw it into itself'), and that it is A'contournable en soy mesme' (it can be 'turned upon itself').[50] In *On vanity*, finally, he urges us to restore and seize hold of ourselves, to stem

[45] See 'Fragments d'un moi futur: de Pascal à Montaigne', in Cave 1999.
[46] Pascal 2004, fragment 509. [47] Locke 1975, II.27, §17, p. 341.
[48] Montaigne 1969. In writing 'my selfe' rather than 'myselfe', Florio is not advancing a distinctive notion of the self as something that I have, as a noun, but simply reflecting the standard orthography of the pronoun in his time (we also find 'him selfe', rather than 'his selfe').
[49] I.8: P 54-5, V 33, F 21. [50] I.38: P 244–5, V 240–1, F 176–7.

the tide of self-dispossession and self-depletion flowing from our lack of self-knowledge:

[B]Regardez dans vous, recognoissez vous, tenez vous à vous: Vostre esprit, et vostre volonté, qui se consomme ailleurs, ramenez la en soy.

[B]Look into yourself, recognise yourself, attach yourself to yourself: Bring your mind, and your will, which are consumed elsewhere, back unto yourself.[51]

This reflexive turn to oneself is figured not only as a folding *back* upon oneself, but as a reaching *into* oneself: 'je replie ma veue *au dedans*', 'je regarde *dedans moy*', 'je me roule *en* moy-mesmes'. Montaigne's 'moy' is assimilated to the visceral interior of his body.[52] In *On practice*, his self-portrait is presented as [C]'a cadaver, on which the veins, the muscles and the tendons appear at a glance, each part in its place' ('un *skeletos*, où d'une veue les veines, les muscles, les tendons paroissent, chasque piece en son siege').[53] Montaigne's 'self' is emphatically located not outside but *within*:

[A]Je ne me soucie pas tant, quel je sois chez autruy, comme je me soucie quel je sois en moy-mesme. [. . .] Les estrangers ne voyent que les evenemens et apparences externes: chacun peut faire bonne mine par le dehors, plein au dedans de fiebvre et d'effroy. Ils ne voyent pas mon cœur, ils ne voyent que mes contenances.

[A]I do not care so much what I am in others, as I care what I am in myself. [. . .] Strangers see only external events and appearances. Any man can put on a good face outside, while full of fever and fright within. They do not see my heart, they see only my countenance.[54]

The key phrase '*au dedans*' is deployed repeatedly by Montaigne. It is not enough for us to be judged [A]'by our outward actions' ('par nos actions de dehors'): 'we must probe the inside and discover what springs set the dance in motion' ('il faut sonder jusqu'au dedans, et voir par quels ressors se donne le bransle').[55] It is not [A]'for show' ('pour la montre') that our soul must play its part, but 'at home within' ('chez nous au dedans').[56] A [A]'generous heart' should not 'belie its own thoughts': it wants to be seen into its inmost depths ('jusques au dedans').[57] We need to have established [B]'a pattern within, by which to test our actions' ('un patron au dedans, auquel toucher nos actions');[58] [B]'any man can play his part in the show [*battelage*] and represent a worthy man on the stage [*en l'eschaffaut*]', but

[51] III.9: P 1047, V 1001, F 766.

[52] Hillman 2007, p. 18. On the use of corporeal metaphors of interiority in the late Renaissance, see also Sawday 1995 and Schoenfeldt 1999.

[53] II.6: P 398, V 379, F 274. [54] II.16: P 663, V 625, F 474. [55] II.1: P 358, V 338, F 244.

[56] II.16: P 661, V 623, F 472. [57] II.17: P 686, V 647, F 491. [58] III.2: P 848, V 807, F 613.

the point is to be 'ordered' (*reglé*) 'within, and inside one's breast' ('au dedans, et en sa poictrine').[59]

This inward turn, this withdrawal *into* the self, is elsewhere presented as a way of protecting, containing and appropriating oneself. We must *belong* to ourselves, Montaigne writes in *On solitude*, by separating ourselves from that which is alien to us and engaging ourselves only to ourselves:

[A]Despétrons nous de ces violentes prinses, qui nous engagent ailleurs, et esloignent de nous. Il faut desnouer ces obligations si fortes: et meshuy aymer cecy et cela, mais n'espouser rien que soy: C'est à dire, le reste soit à nous: mais non pas joint et colé en façon, qu'on ne le puisse desprendre sans nous escorcher, et arracher ensemble quelque piece du nostre. La plus grande chose du monde c'est de sçavoir estre à soy.

[A]Let us break free from these violent clutches, that engage us elsewhere, and draw us away from ourselves: We must untie these bonds that are so powerful, and henceforth love this and that, but be wedded only to ourselves: That is to say, let the other things be ours: but not joined and glued to us so strongly that they cannot be detached without tearing off our skin and some part of our flesh as well. The greatest thing in the world is to know how to belong to oneself.[60]

This emphasis on belonging to oneself, or being one's own, is anchored in a fundamental distinction between that which is ours, or proper to us, and that which is foreign. In *Our affections take us away from ourselves*, Montaigne urges us to follow Plato's [C]'great precept', 'fay ton faict, et te congnoy', insisting that each of these two 'members' of our duty enfolds or involves the other:

[C]Qui auroit à faire son faict, verroit que sa premiere leçon, c'est cognoistre ce qu'il est, et ce qui luy est propre. Et qui se cognoist, ne prend plus l'estranger faict pour le sien: s'ayme, et se cultive avant toute autre chose: refuse les occupations superflues, et les pensées, et propositions inutiles.

[C]He who would do what he has to do, would see that his first lesson is to know what he is, and what is proper to him. And he who knows himself, no longer takes foreign business for his own; he loves, and cultivates himself before anything else: he refuses superfluous occupations, and useless thoughts, and propositions.[61]

This distinction between that which is ours and that which is not provides the foundation for a striking rhetoric of self-possession. In *On vanity*, Montaigne finds [B]'nothing so dear, as that which is given to [him]', because '[his] will remains mortgaged [*hypothequée*] by the title of ingratitude'. In

[59] III.2: P 848, V 808, F 613. [60] I.38: P 246, V 242, F 178. [61] I.3: P 38–9, V 15, F 8–9.

buying offices, he only gives his money, but in receiving favours, he gives himself (B'pour ceux-cy, je ne donne que de l'argent: pour les autres, je me donne moy-mesme').[62] He has, he claims, B'nothing of [his] own, except [him]self' ('je n'ay rien mien, que moy'), although even in this case, his B'possession is partly lacking and borrowed' ('et si en est la possession en partie manque et empruntée').[63]

As Montaigne explains in *On managing the will*, B'few things touch me, or rather hold me. For it is right that they should touch, as long as they do not possess us' ('peu de choses me touchent: ou pour mieux dire, me tiennent. Car c'est raison qu'elles touchent, pourveu qu'elles ne nous possedent'). He opposes himself with all his strength to those affections B'which distract [him] from [him]self, and attach [him] elsewhere' ('qui me distrayent de moy, et attachent ailleurs'), insisting that B'we must lend ourselves to others, and give ourselves only to ourselves' ('il se faut prester à autruy, et ne se donner qu'à soy-mesme'). Other men B'give themselves for hire' ('se donnent à louage'); their faculties are 'not for themselves' ('ne sont pas pour eux') but 'for those, to whom they enslave themselves' ('pour ceux, à qui ils s'asservissent'). Yet B'we must husband the liberty of our soul, and mortgage it only on just occasions' ('il faut mesnager la liberté de nostre ame, et ne l'hypothequer qu'aux occasions justes').[64] In one important respect, at least, Montaigne claims to have succeeded in this crucial task: B'I have been able to involve myself in public office without departing one nail's breadth from myself, Cand to give myself to others without taking myself from me' (B'j'ay peu me mesler des charges publiques, sans me despartir de moy, de la largeur d'une ongle, Cet me donner à autruy sans m'oster à moy').[65]

To recapitulate: Montaigne's discourse about 'self' is structured, above all else, by two patterns of language – an appeal to 'moy' as that which is 'au dedans', the object of inward reflection; and as that which is 'à moy' or 'mien', as that which is proper to ourselves or owned by ourselves. The key question thus becomes the following: what, if any, are the sources for this way of writing about 'self'? My answer is that this discourse, far from being fundamentally new and particular to Montaigne, reflects habits of thought and language inherited from Plutarch and Seneca.

In turning to Plutarch and Seneca in search of the sources of Montaigne's 'self', I take my cue from the *Essais* themselves.[66] An entire chapter (II.32) is

[62] III.9: P 1011, V 966, F 738. [63] III.9: P 1013, V 968, F 740.
[64] III.10: P 1048-9, V 1003-4, F 766-7. [65] III.10: P 1053, V 1007, F 770.
[66] On Montaigne and Plutarch, see Aulotte 1971 and Konstantinovic 1989. On Montaigne and Seneca, see Hay 1938, Grilli 1965 and Clark 1968.

devoted to the defence of both philosophers against accusations of complicity with tyranny, in Seneca's case, and of historical credulity, in Plutarch's[67] – an intervention justified on the basis of Montaigne's [A]'familiarity with these personages and the help they give to [his] old age [C]and [his] book, built up purely from their spoils'.[68] The two authors are further singled out, in *On books*, as marking the summit of moral philosophy.[69] Montaigne emphasises their shared wisdom ([A]'these authors agree in most of the opinions that are useful and true'),[70] as well as their relative strengths, praising Plutarch above Seneca for his effortless, unforced approach to virtue, only to prefer Seneca's opinions to Plutarch's, as being, in his view, [A]'more suitable [C]for private life and [A]more sturdy'.[71] In *On physiognomy*, similarly, Montaigne judges Seneca to be [B]'~~more lively~~ <sharper>' than Plutarch: his philosophy 'pricks and startles us' and thereby 'touches our mind more'. Plutarch, conversely, is 'more ~~collected~~ <solid>' than Seneca: he 'forms us, settles us and fortifies us constantly', and in so doing 'touches our understanding more'.[72] Contrary to a widespread assumption, inherited from Pierre Villey, these comparisons are not so much to the detriment of Seneca, but rather testimony to the complementarity of these two authors in Montaigne's mind, as moral philosophers of divergent temperaments but equally exceptional calibre.[73]

Montaigne has, it is true, nothing but the highest praise for [A]'our Plutarch': 'there are in Plutarch many extensive discussions, well worth knowing, for in my judgment he is the master workman in that field'; 'in every way, Plutarch is my man'; he is 'admirable throughout, but especially where he judges human actions', 'the most judicious author in the world', 'a philosopher who teaches us virtue'.[74] Yet Seneca is also praised in the

[67] Montaigne is here responding to a comparison between Seneca and the Cardinal of Lorraine (with Charles IX as modern-day Nero) found in Protestant tracts published after the Saint Bartholomew's Day Massacre, and to Jean Bodin's criticisms of Plutarch (in Bodin 1566). See Jean Balsamo's introduction to the chapter in the Pléiade edition of the *Essais*: Montaigne 2007 pp. 1683–4.

[68] [A]'La familiarité que j'ay avec ces personnages icy, et l'assistance qu'ils font à ma vieillesse, [C]et à mon livre massonné purement de leurs despouilles'. II.32: P 757, V 721, F 545.

[69] II.10: P 433, V 413, F 300[A].

[70] [A]'Ces autheurs se rencontrent en la plus part des opinions utiles et vrayes'. II.10: P 433, V 413, F 300.

[71] [A]'Selon moy plus commodes [C]en particulier, [A]et plus fermes'. II.10: P 434, V 413, F 300.

[72] [B]'L'un, plus ~~vif~~ <aigu>, nous pique et eslance en sursaut: touche plus l'esprit. L'autre, plus ~~rassis~~ <solide>, nous informe, establit et conforte constamment: touche plus l'entendement'. III.12: P 1086, V 1040, F 795.

[73] See, for instance, Villey 1933, vol. II, p. 111.

[74] [A]'Nostre Plutarque'. I.25: P 162, V 156, F 115. [A]'Il y a dans Plutarque beaucoup de discours estandus, tres-dignes d'estre sceus: car à mon gré c'est le maistre ouvrier de telle besongne'. I.25: P 162, V 156, F 115. [A]'En toutes sortes, c'est mon homme que Plutarque'. II.10: P 437, V 416, F 303. [A]'Plutarque est admirable par tout: mais principalement, où il juge des actions humaines'. II.31: P 750, V 714, F

strongest of terms. He is cited in *On solitude*, alongside Epicurus, as an exponent of [A]'true and natural philosophy', by contrast with the 'ostentatious and wordy philosophy' of Cicero and Pliny, who remain in thrall to glory and ambition.[75] His writings, Montaigne argues, bear the unmistakable mark of a virtue [A]'so clear and entire and firm', 'so live and so vigorous' that he cannot believe any testimony to the contrary.[76] In *On three good women*, finally, he recounts at length the story of Seneca's long and painful suicide, following his condemnation by Nero. Although Montaigne's praise is ostensibly directed to Seneca's wife Paulina, who resolved to accompany her husband into death, the emotive force of the passage turns in large part on the spectacle of Seneca's [A]'peaceful and steadfast countenance' in the face of pain and death and on the 'most excellent discourses' he uttered on the occasion. Even Paulina's contempt for death is credited to Seneca's example: as she says to her husband, [A]'I do not want you to think that the virtuous examples of your life have not yet taught me to know how to die well'.[77]

Pierre Villey's painstaking inventory of the 'sources' of the *Essais* provides an initial indication of the intensity of Montaigne's engagement with these two authors. Plutarch is cited by name sixty-eight times in the *Essais*, with almost 400 direct borrowings and looser allusions to the *Ethika* and *Bioi parallèloi*. As for Seneca, the *Essais* contain almost 300 borrowings from the *Epistulae ad Lucilium*, and approximately fifty references to his moral discourses, notably *De tranquillitate animi* and *De ira*. These are, roughly speaking, evenly shared among the three books. Although the majority occur in the A-text, with only twelve borrowings from Seneca in the B-text, Montaigne draws heavily on Seneca again in his additions to the Bordeaux Copy, with eighty-nine new borrowings from the *Epistulae* alone in the C-text.[78]

Before we turn to consider Montaigne's relationship to these authors with respect to his language of 'self', we must establish the language and editions in which he is most likely to have encountered them. In the case

539. [A]'Le plus judicieux autheur du monde'. II.32: P 759, V 723, F 546. [A]'Un philosophe, qui nous apprend la vertu'. II.32: P 762, V 726, F 549.

75 [A]'La vraye et naïfve philosophie'. 'Une philosophie ostentatrice et parliere'. I.38: P 252, V 248, F 183.

76 [A]'Sa vertu si nette et entiere, [et] si ferme, [. . .] paroist si vive et si vigoureuse en ses escrits, [. . .] que je n'en croiroy aucun tesmoignage au contraire'. II.32: P 758, V 722, F 545.

77 [A]'Un visage paisible et asseuré'. [A]'Discours très-excellens'. [A]'Je ne veux pas que vous pensiez, que les vertueux exemples de vostre vie, ne m'ayent encore appris à sçavoir bien mourir'. II.32: P 785–7, V 747–9, F 566–7.

78 Villey 1933, vol. I, pp. 198–200, 214–17; see also the prefatory material to his edition of the *Essais*.

of Plutarch, Montaigne is known to have owned a Latin version of the *Bioi parallèloi*.[79] He himself indicates, however, that he read both the *Bioi* and the *Ethika* neither in the original Greek nor in Latin, but in Jacques Amyot's French translation.[80] As Villey and others have demonstrated, moreover, Montaigne quotes from the text of Amyot's *Vies des hommes illustres* (in either the 1565 edition or a later edition),[81] and from the first 1572 edition of the *Œuvres morales*.[82] In the case of Seneca, meanwhile, it is safe to assume that Montaigne read the *Epistulae ad Lucilium* in the original Latin, most likely in the 1557 Basel (Froben) edition of his complete works.[83] In addition, however, Montaigne almost certainly would have had some familiarity with a French translation of a selection of the *Epistulae* first published by his brother-in-law Geoffroy de la Chassaigne, souldan de Pressac, in 1582.[84]

IV

The guiding aspiration of the *Essais*, it has been widely argued, is 'to convey personality through the use of words, [. . .] to capture the internal self'.[85] The text dramatises a 'constant tension between inside and outside, between private self and public persona [. . .] between the parts played and the real, essential dimension of being' – between 'the borrowed form of the actor (*forme empruntée*)' and 'that personal ruling pattern (*forme sienne, forme maistresse*) which is the very heart of individuality'.[86] Montaigne's 'opaque depths' and 'inner folds' gesture towards subconscious impulses and repressed desires: 'what is being pointed to here is the place of the *id* [. . .] the location of the inexpressible'.[87] To this extent, the *Essais*

79 Plutarch 1560. Montaigne's copy is now housed in the Bibliothèque Nationale: Rés. Z. Payen 499. Villey 1933, vol. I, pp. 219–20.

80 II.4: P 382, V 363–4, F 262. See also I.46: P 298, V 277, F 202. On Amyot's translation, see Aulotte 1965.

81 Plutarch 1565. Villey 1933, vol. I, p. 221. All references to the *Vies* in what follows are to the Pléiade edition by Gérard Walter (Plutarch 1951), which is based on the 1567 edition.

82 Plutarch 1572. Villey 1933, vol. I, p. 320. Further arguments are supplied in Konstantinovic 1989, pp. 17–18. All references to the *Œuvres morales* are to this edition, which is also available in facsimile (Plutarch 1971).

83 Seneca 1557. This is a revised version of Erasmus' annotated edition of 1529, with prefatory material by Curione. Another possibility, rejected by Villey, is Seneca 1585, an edition published in Rome by Marc-Antoine Muret which was later reprinted in Paris in 1587. Villey 1933, vol I, pp. 237–42.

84 Seneca 1582. On Montaigne and Pressac, see Balsamo 2001.

85 Brush 1994, p. 9.

86 Regosin 1977, pp. 233–4.

87 'Ce qui est indiqué, est le lieu du *ça* [. . .] le lieu de l'indicible'. Garavini 1995, p. 238; see also Garavini 1994. The quotation is from II.6: P 396, V 378, F 273.

embody 'the dilemma of modern man', torn between 'on the one hand, a social being, prey to the demands of society, and on the other, an existential being whose responsibility is to the Self'.[88] For Montaigne, 'the outside world is the realm of delusive appearance; there we fragment, and ultimately lose, ourselves by being reflected in the eyes of innumerable spectators, each with his own – limited, biased, misleading – point of view'.[89] Montaigne's dialogue with himself 'must inevitably lead to an exploration of the self as opposed to others, who are always entangled and imprisoned by socially governed actions ('nos actions accoustumées'), tending to mask rather than reveal. [. . .] By looking inward, Montaigne will be freed from the prejudicial and distorting vision of others'.[90]

For the majority of these scholars, the possibility of an unmediated, authentic selfhood, freed from artifice and distortion, is ultimately a fiction. Montaigne's 'self' is not ontologically prior to the act of description, but brought into being through the process of self-portraiture, which serves to impose a consistent and prescriptive shape upon the complex of 'things, attitudes, and actions' that make up his being.[91] The histrionic and alienating dimensions of social life can never be fully transcended: 'life is theater and the self a role at the point where illusion and reality converge and intermingle. [. . .] Man even plays at being himself'.[92] The 'self' of the *Essais* is a literary artefact, displacing its referent even as it seeks to describe it: 'can the discourse of self ever be more than a gloss? a mask upon the face of the subject? [. . .] Can writing [. . .] ever be more than a "writing over" or a blemish on the natural, legible self?'[93] The conviction that interiority is about authenticity, however, continues to structure these accounts, even where belief in an essential self as the source of our identity and as the origin of our discourse is itself jettisoned as an illusion.

Jean Starobinski is perhaps the most influential and sophisticated exponent of this approach. Montaigne's central insight, in Starobinski's reading, is the role of the other in shaping, but thereby also enabling, individual subjectivity and self-definition. The 'movement' of the *Essais* is a dialectical one, taking Montaigne from an initial condition of 'dépendence irraisonnée' or irrational dependency upon the judgment of others, to its antithesis, 'le refus autarcique', an ultimately self-defeating effort to cut the self off from the world and from others. The dialectic is finally resolved, however,

[88] Norton 1975, p. 23. [89] Bencivenga 1990, pp. 116–17. [90] Polachek 1992, pp. 264, 267.
[91] Bencivenga 1990, pp. 10–12, 15. [92] Regosin 1977, p. 235.
[93] Glidden 1993, pp. 71, 82. See also Brush 1994, pp. 8–9 and Delègue 1998, p. 9.

through Montaigne's acknowledgement that a pure, autonomous authenticity is unattainable, his acceptance of a 'relation maîtrisée' with others and his search for a measured reconciliation with the world of appearances. An initial thirst for independence gives way to an understanding of the self as embedded in shared narratives, as a sense of connectedness as well as distinctiveness, constituted through our negotiation of our relations with others. 'Autarchy' is thereby rejected as a mirage, an act of desertion abandoning others to the world of illusion and leaving the self stranded in an objectified, atomised space. The quest for veracity, however, is not abandoned but reaffirmed through a new understanding of identity – not as an autonomous essence, but as a relation. The task of self-portrayal itself allows Montaigne to maintain himself in a truthful, relational identity, requiring him 'not to keep to himself in silent self-sufficiency, but rather to be honest in representing himself to others and to seek from them guarantees of his presence to himself'.[94]

This emphasis on truthful self-presence and self-expression has decisively shaped our understanding of the historical significance of Montaigne's project. The *Essais*, it has recently been argued, 'gave poignant expression to a widely-felt need, in the age of the court, to find certain spaces – in one's own room, or library, or friendships, or writings – to provide a comparatively honest or sincere account of oneself and one's feelings'. Montaigne is here identified with a gradual reconfiguration of ethical discourse, in the final decades of the sixteenth century, linked both to a disillusionment with the artifices of court culture and to the influence of Protestant and evangelical ideas privileging inward conscience over outward performance. The *Essais*, in this reading, dramatise the conflict between the demands of prudent artifice and dissimulation and a new ethical ideal of 'sincerity', understood as being 'true to one's nature and temperament', not only in private but also in public. This emphasis on personal integrity, it is claimed, marked a profound shift away from medieval ideas of *concordia* and towards the affirmation of *individual* identity as the measure of authentic self-expression.[95]

In all these accounts, it is through the negotiation of a fundamental and unprecedented divide between a visible exterior and a hidden interior

[94] 'Qui n'enferme pas l'individu dans le devoir de la silencieuse autarcie, mais qui l'assigne à l'exigence de la véracité dans la représentation qu'il donne de soi à un destinataire extérieur, et qui l'oblige à chercher en autrui la garantie de sa présence à soi-même'. Starobinski 1993, quotation at p. 44. English translation from Starobinski 1985, p. 29.

[95] Martin 2004, quotation at p. 119. See also his earlier article: Martin 1997.

that Montaigne constructs his 'self'. How legitimate is this way of picturing interiority in relation to the *Essais*? In his study of the rhetoric of inwardness and human depth in seventeenth-century French literature, Nicholas Paige has suggested that 'the whole enterprise of retreat for Montaigne has little to do with introspection as such, if one understands that term [. . .] as the search for a truth located metaphorically inside each one of us'. Withdrawing into oneself, in a chapter such as *On solitude*, is instead about 'engaging in a practice of self-government ("[se] gouverner") by which one prepares oneself for misfortune through the contemplation of hypothetical events or exemplary figures'. Paige's account of the reception of the *Essais* and their role in the development of modern conceptions of authorship reveals that it is only in the two centuries following Montaigne's death that his text came to be thought of as, above all else, an intimate autobiography, disclosing the deepest secrets of its author's life and character.[96]

Paige locates the explanation for this shift not only in the emergence of a 'cult' of interiority in the seventeenth century, but in an ambiguity inherent in Montaigne's text. As he puts it, 'the modern tendency to privilege autobiographical readings can and should be understood not as something totally foreign to the texts themselves, but rather as part of a diachronic process in which these important works have *become*, bit by bit, autobiographies'.[97] The crux of his analysis is that the *Essais* 'mark the intersection or overlapping of two different models of identity', of 'two discordant technologies of self' – a Foucauldian 'care of the self' positing the 'self as practice' and a 'hermeneutic of the self' 'as the locus of a pre-existent truth (i.e., an interiorised subject)'.[98] Our confusion about Montaigne can thus be traced to his having 'begun the deployment of interiorizing tropes in a first-person text still massively dedicated to the care of the self'.[99]

Foucault's distinction between practices of ethical self-fashioning and self-cultivation, on the one hand, and more familiar forms of self-discovery and self-interpretation, on the other, provides one possible starting point for thinking about interiority in Montaigne. This paradigm has its limits, however, not least because it imposes a predetermined frame onto the *Essais*, rather than working up and out of the text itself. Nor does it get us to the heart of the problem to be addressed in this section: what kind of work is the language of inwardness doing in Montaigne's text? Paige appears at times to rely on a number of questionable assumptions – that Montaigne is deploying these tropes for the first time, that he is feeling his way towards modern interiority, that interiority just *is* psychological

96 Paige 2001, p. 30. 97 Paige 2001, p. 60. 98 Paige 2001, p. 29. 99 Paige 2001, p. 35.

introspection. My aim in this section is to take Paige's central claim – that interiority as we now understand it is a historical artefact rather than a principle of universal human experience – one stage further, by drawing attention to a further complexity in that artefact's history. Montaigne's 'au dedans', I suggest, is part of a pattern of discourse inherited from classical texts. Being interior has not always meant living in accordance with our most private and authentic selves: it can also be about living for the sake of that which is inside me, in the sense that it is *in my power*, as opposed to that which takes me outside of myself, in the sense that it subjects me to someone or something other than myself.

We might begin by observing that the ability to reveal what is *within* is offered by Montaigne not only as a defining characteristic of his own work, but as the mark of Plutarch's excellence as a historian and as a judge of human actions.[100] As he explains in *On books*:

> [C]Man in general, the knowledge of whom I seek, appears in them [the historians] more alive and entire than in any other place – the diversity and truth of his internal conditions in the mass and in detail, the variety of the ways he is put together, and the accidents that threaten him. [A]Now those who write lives, since they spend more time on plans than on happenings, more on what comes from within than on what happens without, are most proper to me. That is why in every way Plutarch is my man.[101]

Montaigne here opposes 'ce qui part du dedans' to 'ce qui arrive au dehors', our 'conditions internes' to those that are external. What is at stake in this distinction? Our actions are here thought of as lying 'without', not only in the sense that they are easily visible, on public display, but also in that they are merely adventitious, the product of chance. By focusing our attention on 'plans' or 'counsels' ('conseils') rather than on 'happenings' or 'events' ('evenemens'), biographers such as Plutarch teach us to see beyond the superficial contingency of worldly success and reputation, in order to judge men according to their nature rather than their glory – to take stock not only of their famous deeds, but of their intentions, and their most ordinary and hidden actions. Montaigne elaborates on this theme by stating that he is [A]'very sorry' that Diogenes Laertius did not

[100] On Plutarch's *Lives* as a model for the *Essais*, see Mathieu-Castellani 1988, ch. 2.

[101] [C]'L'homme en general, de qui je cherche la cognoissance, y paroist plus vif et plus entier qu'en nul autre lieu: la ~~diversité~~ <varieté> et verité de ses conditions internes, en gros et en detail, la ~~varieté~~ <diversité> des moyens de son assemblage, et des accidents qui le menacent. [A]Or ceux qui escrivent les vies, d'autant qu'ils s'amusent plus aux conseils qu'aux evenemens: plus à ce qui part du dedans, qu'à ce qui arrive au dehors: ceux là me sont plus propres. Voylà pourquoy en toutes sortes, c'est mon homme que Plutarque'. II.10: P 437, V416, F 303.

spread himself [A]'more widely [C]or more wisely' in his own biographical writings, and that he himself is as curious about [A]'the fortunes and the life of those great teachers of the world' as he is about their 'teachings and fantasies'.[102] Only the most gifted historians, in his judgment, are able to attribute [A]'counsels' and 'suitable words' to princes by deducing them from their known 'condition' and 'humours'; the most common sort twist their narrative to suit their teachings, [A]'often conceal[ing] from us a given word, a given private action, that would instruct us better'.[103]

This distinction between inner condition and outward accident turns not on the difference between an authentic self and an artificial role, but on a contrast between that which is proper to us, or which can justly be attributed to our agency, and that which we are merely reputed to be, or which can more accurately be assigned to fortune. Montaigne makes the same point in his defence of the *Vies des hommes illustres* against Jean Bodin, who had criticised Plutarch for unfairly matching Cicero with Demosthenes and Cato the Elder with Aristides, arguing that the two Greeks were unworthy of their Roman counterparts. Bodin, Montaigne writes, is simply seduced by [A]'the great and dazzling lustre that the Roman names take on in our mind' and by their 'more swollen, glorious, and pompous' exploits, forgetting that 'the finest and most virtuous actions, either in war or elsewhere, are not always the most famous'. Plutarch, by contrast, aimed [A]'to consider the truth of the thing, and men in themselves' and to compare men rather on the basis of 'their manners, their natures, their abilities' than of their 'fortune'.[104] This ability to disclose that which we are *in ourselves* is also true of Plutarch's own self-revelation in his writings, which, [A]'if we savour them aright, discover him to us well enough', such that Montaigne feels able to 'know him even into his soul'.[105]

102 [A]'Je suis bien marry que nous n'ayons une douzaine de Laërtius, ou qu'il ne soit plus estendu, [C]ou plus entendu: [A]Car je suis pareillement curieux de cognoistre les fortunes et la vie de ces grands precepteurs du monde, comme de cognoistre la diversité de leurs dogmes et fantasies'. II.10: P 437, V 416, F 303.

103 [A]'De la condition des Princes et de leurs humeurs, ils en concluent les conseils, et leur attribuent les paroles convenables'. [A]'Ils [. . .] nous cachent souvent telle parole, telle action privée, qui nous instruiroit mieux'. II.10: P 438, V 417, F 304.

104 [A]'Ce grand et esclatant lustre des noms Romains, que nous avons en la teste'. 'Leurs exploits de guerre [. . .] enflez, glorieux, et pompeux'. 'Les actions les plus belles et vertueuses, non plus en la guerre qu'ailleurs, ne sont pas tousjours les plus fameuses'. 'Qui considerera la verité de la chose, et les hommes en eux mesmes, [. . .] et à balancer leurs mœurs, leurs naturels, leur suffisance, que leur fortune'. II.32: P 763, V 726, F 549.

105 [A]'Les escrits de Plutarque, à les bien savourer, nous le descouvrent assez; et je pense le cognoistre jusques dans l'ame'. II.31: P 752, V 716, F 541.

This way of understanding 'au dedans' – in terms of moral judgment rather than psychological introspection – echoes Plutarch's own account of his subject matter – for example, in this famous passage from the life of Alexander:

The most elevated and glorious exploits are not always the ones that best display the vice or virtue of a man; but very often a slight thing, a word or a game, make the natural character of persons more apparent, than do defeats where ten thousand men are left dead, or great battles, or the seizure of cities by siege or by assault. So just as painters who portray from life look for likenesses only or principally in the appearance and traits of the face, in which we see as if an impressed image of the conduct and character of men, without being much concerned with the other parts of the body, so should one concede to us that we shall principally attend to the signs of the soul, forming through these a natural portrait of the life and manners of each man, leaving to historians to write about wars, battles and other such great things.[106]

Plutarch's subject – the term that Amyot translates as 'le naturel des personnes' or 'des meurs, et du naturel' – is *èthos*, or character. For Plutarch as for other ancient thinkers, character was 'less about what somebody was like, more about recognizing right and wrong deeds; its consequence was a desire to judge and evaluate'.[107] In common with ancient convention, Plutarch linked *èthos* (character) to its homonym *ethos* (habituation), as that set of dispositions and inclinations, towards both virtue and vice, acquired through education and habit. Character is, quite literally, an *ethical* category: moral virtue is character-virtue (*èthike-aretè*).[108] When Plutarch describes himself as depicting *èthos*, he simply means that he is a moralist, 'a philosopher who teaches us virtue', in Montaigne's formulation.

[106] 'Les plus hauts et les plus glorieux exploits ne sont pas toujours ceux qui montrent mieux le vice ou la vertu de l'homme; mais bien souvent une légère chose, une parole ou un jeu, mettent plus clairement en évidence le naturel des personnes, que ne font pas des défaites où il sera demeuré dix mille hommes morts, ni les grosses batailles, ni les prises des villes par siège ni par assault. Tout ainsi donc comme les peintres qui portraient au vif, recherchent les ressemblances seulement ou principalement en la face, et aux traits du visage, sur lesquels se voit comme une image empreinte des mœurs, et du naturel des hommes, sans guères se soucier des autres parties du corps, aussi nous doit-on concéder que nous allions principalement recherchant les signes de l'âme, et par iceux formant un portrait au naturel de la vie et des mœurs d'un chascun, en laissant aux historiens à écrire les guerres, les batailles et autres telles grandeurs'. *Vie d'Alexandre-le-Grand*, Plutarch 1951, vol. II, p. 323.

[107] Duff 1999, p. 14. Duff is here drawing on Christopher Gill's distinction between character (which pertains to the evaluation of individuals) and personality (which places more emphasis on understanding what is unique about a person); see Gill 1983. This division is articulated in Gill's more recent work as a contrast between 'objective-participant' and 'subjective-individualist' conceptions of personality. See Gill 1996, esp. pp. 10–13, and Gill 2006, esp. sec. 6.2.

[108] Duff 1999, p. 74.

Plutarch's claim to be forming 'un portrait au naturel de la vie d'un chascun', modelled on those painters who 'portraient au vif' (as Amyot translates it), is echoed in Montaigne's description of the *Essais*: A'ayant à m'y pourtraire au vif'.[109] The latter's claim, in *On practice*, that his book is a C'cadaver', an anatomical dissection in which his whole body (and not just his face) is put on display, is at once an inversion and an extension of the passage from *Alexandre* quoted in the previous paragraph, with its insistence that the rest of the body can safely be ignored, just as spectacular exploits are to be set aside in the writing of a life. For Montaigne, like Plutarch, it is 'vice' and 'vertu', our 'meurs', our 'naturel' and the 'signes de l'ame' that matter: our actions and deeds are, as Montaigne puts it, C'*effects*', which 'say more about fortune, than they would about me. They bear witness to their part, not to mine, unless it be by conjecture and without certainty: they are samples that reveal only particulars'. Montaigne inverts Plutarch, by insisting that he C'expose[s] [him]self whole', so that all parts, muscles, tendons and veins are seen together 'at a glance', instead of being disclosed 'dubiously', through an occasional 'cough' or 'palpitation of the heart'.[110] Whereas Plutarch must content himself with this kind of fragmentary conjecture, Montaigne, as author of his own life, testifies to his whole self – to his whole body and not just to his face: as he puts it in *On glory*, A'all those judgments that are founded on external appearances are marvelously uncertain and doubtful: and there is no witness so sure as each man to himself'.[111]

Montaigne's inversion of Plutarch's image in *On practice*, however, simply extends and confirms the distinction between outward fortune and inward nature that is fundamental to both writers: C'it is not my deeds that I write down; it is myself, it is my essence'.[112] The implied antonym of 'essence', in this much-quoted passage, is not only 'appearance', I suggest, but 'accident'. Our 'gestes' belong to the realm of conjecture, doubt, uncertainty and fortune. Montaigne's 'moy' is situated 'au dedans'

[109] II.8: P 404, V 386, F 278.

[110] C'Les effects diroyent plus de la fortune, que de moy. Ils tesmoignent leur roolle, non pas le mien, si ce n'est conjecturalement et incertainement: Eschantillons d'une montre particuliere. Je m'estalle entier: C'est un *skeletos*, où d'une veue les veines, les muscles, les tendons paroissent, chasque piece en son siege. L'effect de la toux en produisoit une partie: l'effect de la palleur ou battement de cœur un'autre, et doubteusement'. II.6: P 398, V 379, F 274.

[111] A'Tous ces jugemens qui se font des apparences externes, sont merveilleusement incertains et douteux: et n'est aucun si asseuré tesmoing, comme chacun à soy-mesme.' II.16: P 664, V 626, F 474.

[112] C'Ce ne sont mes gestes que j'escris; c'est moy, c'est mon essence'. II.6: P 398, V 379, F 274.

and not 'au dehors', not in the sense that his identity originates in himself, that he is able to constitute himself as a subject, instead of being interpellated by power, ideology, or the alienating gaze of others – but in the sense that his public reputation and outward countenance are a doubtful guide to the inner disposition of his heart or soul.

Montaigne's appeal to medical anatomy serves not only to emphasise the [B]'marvelously corporeal'[113] nature of humanity, but to identify health and disease as the objects of self-study, moving from uncertain symptoms to a complete diagnosis of his 'condition'. As he puts it in *On glory*:

> [A]I do not care so much what I am to others as I care what I am in myself. [. . .] Strangers see only external events and appearances. Any man can put on a good face outside, while full of fever and fright within. They do not see my heart, they see only my countenance. [. . .] We can perfectly well hide our game for the moment with a good face and a confident word, though our soul trembles within us.[114]

In painting himself, Montaigne paints not what he is to others, but what he is in himself. When we 'hide our game', we are not acting a part, impersonating ourselves instead of being ourselves; we are struggling to maintain an appearance of constancy and equanimity in the face of inner turmoil. The cleavage that separates 'coeur' and 'contenance', the inside and the outside, relies not so much on a distinction between self and mask, reality and role, as on the rift that separates our true moral state from its external manifestations – a contrast familiar to Montaigne from his reading of Plutarch.

Tropes of interiority and exteriority feature prominently in Plutarch's writing, as well as Montaigne's. 'Au dedans' names that which springs from the inside, from our own qualities, rather than from fortune or reputation, and those true goods which are pursued for their own sake, in secret, rather than for ostentation. The gentle and happy life consists not 'in beautiful, large houses', or 'a great number of slaves', or 'a hefty sum of gold and silver': joy 'does not proceed from without man' (*du dehors de l'homme*;

113 [B]'Merveilleusement corporelle'. III.8: P 975, V 930, F 710.

114 [A]'Je ne me soucie pas tant, quel je sois chez autruy, comme je me soucie que je sois en moy-mesme. [. . .] Les estrangers ne voyent que les evenemens et apparences externes: chacun peut faire bonne mine par le dehors, plein au dedans de fiebvre et d'effroy. Ils ne voyent pas mon cœur, ils ne voyent que mes contenances. [. . .] Nous sçaurons bien pour ce coup, couvrir nostre jeu d'un bon visage, et d'une parolle asseurée, quoy que l'ame nous tremble au dedans'. II.16: P 663, V 625, F 474.

exothen) but is rather imparted by man to 'all those things that are around him' (*autour de luy*; *peri auton*), when his 'inward character' (*son naturel et ses mœurs au dedans*) is 'well composed', as the 'living fountain and source' from which all contentment proceeds (*ek pègès tou èthous prostithesin*).[115] Our curiosity and spitefulness about the doings of other men can be traced to our unwillingness 'to look on [our] life' and to 'fold back [*replier*] and turn [our] reason as a light onto ourselves'. Our soul, 'being full of all kinds of evils and fearful of what she feels inside herself [*au dedans d'elle mesme*; *endon*] [. . .] leaps outside [*dehors*; *thurasde*], scurrying to and fro to search into the business of others, feeding and fattening up her own sickness'.[116] Instead of being duped by the spectacle of all 'that is dazzling and renowned in those men whom [we] admire, and whom [we] take to be happy', we should 'open a little, so to speak, the curtain, and the veil of appearance and opinion, that covers them, and enter inside [*au dedans*; *entos*],' where 'great travails, and annoyances, and frustrations' lie.[117] The best way to distinguish flatterers from friends is to remember that 'the service or office that proceeds from the friend shall, like a living animal, have its principal faculties hidden deep within [*au fond du dedans*; *en bathei tas kuriotatas echei dunameis*], and nothing on display or parade up front' (*epideiktikon de kai panègurikon ouden epestin*),[118] because the 'good will and affection' of the true friend is 'impressed within his heart' (*dedans son coeur*; *endothen*).[119]

This appeal to a living quality hidden within the depths of the body, within our very entrails (*entos*, *entera*), is to be found not only in Plutarch, but in Seneca's *Epistulae* as well.[120] The disorders of the mind are here assimilated to an invisible, inward sickness, concealed from the world by a deceptive layer of false appearances. Citing the example of his wife's clown, Harpaste, who has suddenly become blind but blames the darkness of her living quarters for her inability to see, Seneca urges Lucilius to recognise that the diseases of the soul stem not from outward circumstances

115 *Du vice et de la vertu*, Plutarch 1971, vol. I, p. 38, B-C. Cf. Plutarch 1962, vol. II, p. 94.

116 *De la curiosité*, Plutarch 1971, vol. I, p. 64, B-C. Cf. Plutarch 1962, vol. VI, p. 478.

117 *De la tranquillité de l'ame et repos de l'esprit*, Plutarch 1971, vol. I, p. 72, B-C. Cf. Plutarch 1962, vol. VI, p. 202.

118 *Comment on pourra discerner le flatteur d'avec l'amy*, Plutarch 1971, vol. I, p. 48v, G. Cf. Plutarch 1962, vol. I, p. 336.

119 *Comment on pourra distinguer le flatteur d'avec l'amy*, Plutarch 1971, vol. I, p. 48, B. Cf. Plutarch 1962, vol. I, p. 332.

120 On interiority in Seneca, see Traina 1987 and Lotito 2001. A recent study of Seneca's *Lebenskunst* includes a short discussion of 'innere Freiheit' in Montaigne along similar lines to that pursued in this chapter: Albrecht 2004, pp. 173–92.

but from ourselves: 'the evil that afflicts us is not external [*extrinsecus*], it is within us [*intra nos est*], situated in our very vitals [*in visceribus ipsis*]'.[121] Seneca is himself affected not by 'a swollen foot', or 'an inflamed hand', or 'some shrivelled sinews in a withered leg', but by an evil 'greater than any of these, which he cannot show to [us]': 'the abscess or ulcer is within [his] breast [*in pectore*]'.[122] Conversely, 'an absolutely strong and happy mind [*ingenium*] can lie under any kind of skin [*sub qualibet cute*]'.[123] Just as we judge horses without their cover, so should we judge men without their finery and other adornments, and so also should we value ourselves: 'if you wish to set a value [*perpendere*] on yourself, put away your money, your estates, your honours, and look into yourself [*intus te ipse*]'; 'at present, you are entrusting that which you are to others' (*qualis sis, aliis credis*).[124]

The *Essais* are profoundly marked by this appeal to the interior as the location of our true moral state – so much so that *On the inequality that is between us* is structured largely around (usually unattributed) quotations on this theme lifted directly from the *Epistulae*.[125] Where Seneca had asked, in *Epistula* 41, 'what is more foolish than to praise in a man those things which are alien to him?', Montaigne wonders [A]'why do we not [. . .] judge a man by what is his own?' A man is valued for his [A]'great retinue', his 'beautiful palace', his 'influence' and his 'income', yet these things are all 'around [*autour*], not in him' – a phrase which, together with Montaigne's punning insistence that a man should be judged 'by himself, not by his attire [*atours*]', derives *verbatim* from Seneca ('nihil in ipso, sed circa ipsum').[126] In judging a man, Montaigne writes, we should ask: [A]'what sort of soul does he have? Is it beautiful, capable, and happily furnished with all its pieces? Is it rich of its own, or of others?' Here again, he is quoting from *Epistula* 41: 'consider his soul, its quality and stature,

121 Seneca 1989, I.50.4, p. 332. Cf. Pressac's translation: 'nostre mal ne vient pas du dehors, il est au dedans de nous: Il a sa source dans nos entrailles'. Seneca 1582, p. 104.

122 'Maius malum est hoc, quod non possum tibi ostendere; in pectore ipso collectio et vomica est'. Seneca 1989, II.68.8, p. 48.

123 Seneca 1989, II.66.1, p. 2. 124 Seneca 1989, II.80.10, p. 218.

125 These quotations are identified by Villey in his edition of the *Essais*.

126 [A]'Pourquoy [. . .] n'estimons nous un homme par ce qui est sien? Il a un grand train, un beau palais, tant de credit, tant de rente: tout cela est autour de luy, non en luy [. . .] Il le faut judger par luy mesme, non par ses atours'. I 42: P 281, V 259, F 189. Cf. 'Nullo bono nisi suo nitet; quid enim est stultius quam in homine aliena laudare? [. . .] Nemo gloriari nisi suo debet. [. . .] In homine [. . .] id laudandum est, quod ipsius est. Familiam formasam habet et domum pulchram, multum serit, multum fenerat; nihil horum in ipso est, sed circa ipsum'. Seneca 1989, I.41.6–8, pp. 274 and 276.

whether its greatness is borrowed, or its own'.[127] In arguing that an emperor should be judged A'behind the curtain' (*derriere le rideau*), and not A'on the boards' (*sur l'eschaffaut*), Montaigne appropriates Seneca's comparison between powerful and successful men and actors who seem so mighty on the stage but return to their true stature when the play is over.[128] Finally, he combines two quotations from Seneca into a single summary phrase, C'*this man is inwardly happy: that man's happiness is a veneer*' – compare *Epistulae* 118 ('the felicity of all men looks to the public; but the man whom we have snatched from the people and from Fortune is happy inwardly') and 115 ('all the famous men whom you see strutting about with head in air, have nothing but a gold-leaf prosperity').[129]

It is certainly tempting to dismiss passages such as this as unremarkable, 'impersonal' exercises in plagiarism – as evidence of unreflective and indifferent commonplacing, and of an impressionable, 'immature' author who has not yet found his own voice. This was Pierre Villey's view,[130] and something of that prejudice remains with us to this day. There are good reasons, however, for resisting it. Even in those chapters that are almost exclusively built out of extracts from Seneca's writings, Montaigne is not simply engaging in slavish and uncritical imitation. As Alberto Grilli has put it, Montaigne's practice of quotation, drawing widely and freely from these texts, suggests 'a fine tapestry of reminiscences absorbed into the mind', rather than a collection of 'bookish citations'.[131] Instead of treating these borrowed fragments as distractions from or obstacles to our understanding of Montaigne's thought, we might ask instead what they can tell us about his preoccupations: why is he so interested in these passages and not in others? What is it that these quotations are helping him to articulate?

In the context of the *Epistulae*, the distinction between inner and outer happiness is an aspect of the Stoic principle that everything except virtue

127 A'Quelle ame a il? Est elle belle, capable, et heureusement pourveue de toutes ses pieces? Est elle rich du sien, ou de l'autruy?' I.42: P 282, V 260, F 190. Cf. 'Animum intuere, qualis quantusque sit, alieno an suo magnus'. Seneca 1989, II.76.32, p. 166.

128 I.42: P 283, V 261, F 191A. Cf. Seneca 1989, II.76.31, p. 164.

129 C'*Ille beatus introrsum est: istius bracteata felicitas est*'. I.42: P 283, V 261, F 191. Cf. 'Omnium istorum felicitas in publicum spectat; ille, quem nos et populo et fortunae subduximus, beatus introsum est'. Seneca 1989, III.119.11, p. 376. 'Omnium istorum, quos incedere altos vides, bratteata felicitas est'. Seneca 1989, III.115.9, p. 324.

130 See Villey 1933, vol. II, pp. 56–9.

131 'Un fine intreccio di reminiscenze penetrate nell' animo, non de libresche citazioni'. Grilli 1965, p. 307.

is indifferent and that worldly goods such as glory, wealth, power and the health of the body are only good in name:

> The true goods are those which reason bestows, solid and eternal, they cannot fall away, neither can they grow less or be diminished. Other things are goods according to opinion, and though they are called by the same name as the true goods, the property of goodness is not in them.[132]

These goods are external, both in the sense that they lie outside us and beyond our power and in the sense that their goodness is itself external to them, existing merely in public opinion rather than being an intrinsic property of them. Wisdom, moreover, consists in the rule of reason over the soul, for 'that which is proper to man' is 'soul, and reason brought to perfection in the soul'.[133] For Seneca, then, that which is inside or intrinsic to us is reason, by virtue of our universal nature as men: 'in each thing that quality should be best for which the thing is brought into being and by which it is judged. And what quality is best in man? It is reason'.[134] Not only this, but the self is *identified* with reason: 'rejoice only in that which is your own. But what is "your own"? You yourself and that which is the best part of you'.[135]

This ethics of rational self-control places a strong emphasis both on the inviolability of that which is internal to us and on the almost divine power of the wise man: 'it is reason alone that is unchangeable, that holds fast to its decisions. For reason is not a slave to the senses, but a ruler over them'.[136] We must come to recognise that 'great and hallowed soul', the '*deus intus*' or god within us, that is 'resplendent with no other good but its own'.[137] The inner self is an inviolable fortress, entirely sufficient unto itself. The wise man's joy 'depends on nothing external and looks for no favour from man or fortune': his happiness is 'domestic'; it does not 'enter' the soul but

[132] 'Bona illa sunt vera, quae ratio dat, solida ac sempiterna, quae cadere non possunt, ne decrescere quidem aut minui. Cetera opinione bona sunt et nomen quidem habent commune cum veris, proprietas in illis boni non est'. Seneca 1989, II.74.16-17, p. 122.

[133] 'Quod proprium hominis est [. . .] animus et ratio in animo perfecta'. Seneca 1989, I.41.8, p. 276.

[134] 'Id in quoque optimum esse debet, cui nascitur, quo censetur. In homine optimum quid est? Ratio'. Seneca 1989, II.76.8–9, p. 150.

[135] 'Unum potest praestare felicem: dissice et conculca ista, quae extrinsecus splendent, quae tibi promittuntur ab alio vel ex alio, ad verum bonum specta et de tuo gaude. Quid est autem hoc "de tuo"? Te ipso et tui optima parte'. Seneca 1989, I.23.6, p. 162. On the tendency of ancient Stoicism to 'regard the essence of a human being, the real self, as identical to the *hègemonikon*' or rational soul, see Long 1996, p. 248.

[136] 'Sola ratio immutabilis et iudicii tenax est. Non enim servit, sed imperat sensibus'. Seneca 1989, II.66.32, p. 22.

[137] 'Animus magnus ac sacer [. . .] Qui nullo bono nisi suo nitet'. Seneca 1989, I.41.5–6, pp. 274–6.

is 'born' there; that which is 'external' merely 'grazes his skin'.[138] The soul 'stands on unassailable ground, if it has abandoned external things', 'it has freed itself in its own fortress'.[139]

As we shall see in Chapter 4, this emphasis on rational self-mastery and invulnerability is strikingly absent from the *Essais*, even in their earliest incarnation. What Montaigne takes from Seneca is not a triumphant ethics of self-overcoming, but a way of separating that which is fully our own from that which is merely accidental – a way of distinguishing sword and sheath, horse and harness, that defines the limits of our powers: A'why in judging a man do you judge him all wrapped up and packaged? He displays to us only parts that are not at all his own, and hides from us those by which alone can truly judge of his value'.[140] This distinction provides the starting point both for meaningful self-appraisal and for the redirection of our attention and care towards ourselves. Instead of living for the sake of outward favour and glory, we should regulate ourselves from within.

Seneca urges Lucilius to distinguish the dazzling lustre of worldly success from the true radiance of wisdom and virtue, which spring from inside ourselves.

There is the same difference between these two lives as there is between mere brightness and real light; the source of the latter is definite and its own, the other borrows its radiance; the one is called forth by an illumination coming from the outside, [. . .] but the other is lit up by its own light.[141]

This is certainly an ethics of concordance, encouraging us to reconcile that which is within with our outward words and deeds. But the harmony in question is moral rather than ontological, a matter of constancy rather than sincerity.

Philosophy teaches us to act, not to speak; it exacts of every man that he should live according to his own law, that his life should not dissent from his words, and that the life within him should be of one hue and not out of harmony with all

138 'Non enim ex alieno pendet nec favorem fortunae aut hominis expectat. Domestica illi felicitas est; exiret ex animo, si intraret; ibi nascitur. Aliquando extrinsecus, quo admoneatur mortalitatis, intervenit, sed id leve et quod summam cutem stringat'. Seneca 1989, II.72.4–5, p. 98.

139 'In insuperabili loco stat animus, qui externa deseruit, et arce se sua vindicat'. Seneca 1989, II.82.5, p. 242.

140 A'Pourquoy estimant un homme l'estimez vous tout enveloppé et empacqueté? Il ne nous faict montre que des parties, qui ne sont aucunement siennes: et nous cache celles, par lesquelles seules on peut vrayement juger de son estimation'. I.42: P 281, V 259, F 190.

141 'Quod interest inter splendorem et lucem, cum haec certam originem habeat ac suam ille niteat alieno, hoc inter hanc vitam et illam; haec fulgore extrinsecus veniente percussa est, crassam illi statim umbram faciet quisquis obstiterit; illa suo lumine inlustris est'. Seneca 1989, I.21.2, pp. 140, 142.

his activities. This is the highest duty and proof of wisdom – that deed and work should be in accord, that a man should be always equal to himself and always the same.[142]

In Seneca, the rational self acts as prosecutor and inquisitor: 'prove yourself guilty, hunt up charges against yourself', acting as one's own accuser, judge and intercessor.[143] Montaigne's repudiation of repentance, in the chapter of that name, rejects this hierarchy of reason and passion within the soul. Like Seneca, however, Montaigne argues that our true satisfaction and approval come from within, that there is [B]'a certain gratification in doing good which makes us rejoice in ourselves' and in being able to 'say in oneself' that 'whoever should see me right into my soul, would not even then find me guilty, either of anyone's affliction or ruin, or of vengeance or envy, of public offence against the laws, or of innovation and disturbance, or of failing in my word'.[144] Montaigne insists that he alone can be the judge of himself – that he alone can bear witness to what lies within. He has established [B]'a pattern within', as a touchstone for his actions, according to which to 'sometimes caress' and 'sometimes punish' himself: 'I have my own laws and court to judge me [. . .] Others do not see you, they guess at you by uncertain conjectures: they see, not so much your nature, as your art. Therefore do not hold to their verdict, but to your own'.[145]

In turning his attention to what lies within, Montaigne connects himself with a classical tradition of self-examination and self-regulation.[146] When he explains that he retired from all occupations and affairs to allow his mind to [A]'entertain itself and stay and settle itself in itself',[147] or when he appeals for us to [A]'bring back unto ourselves, and unto our ease, our thoughts and our intentions',[148] he echoes Seneca's claim that the wise man, faced with

[142] 'Facere docet philosophia, non dicere, et hoc exigit, ut ad legem suam quisque vivat, ne orationi vita dissentiat, ut ipsa intra se vita unius sit omnium actionum sine dissensione coloris. Maximum hoc est et officium sapientiae et indicium, ut verbis opera concordent, ut ipse ubique par sibi idemque sit'. Seneca 1989, I.20.2, pp. 132, 134.

[143] 'Te ipse coargue, inquire in te; accusatoris primum partibus fungere, deinde iudicis, novissime deprecatoris'. Seneca 1989, I.28.10, p. 202.

[144] [B]'Il y a certes je ne sçay quelle congratulation, de bien faire, qui nous resjouit en nous mesmes, [. . .] de dire en soy: Qui me verroit jusques dans l'ame, encore ne me trouveroit-il coupable, ny de l'affliction et ruyne de personne: ny de vengeance ou d'envie, ny d'offence publique des loix: ny de nouvelleté et de trouble: ny de faute à ma parole'. III.2: P 847, V 807, F 612.

[145] [B]'Un patron au dedans, auquel toucher nos actions: et selon iceluy nous caresser tantost, tantost nous chastier. J'ay mes loix et ma cour, pour juger de moy [. . .] Les autres ne vous voyent point, ils vous devinent par conjectures incertaines: ils voyent, non tant vostre naturel, que vostre art. Par ainsi, ne vous tenez vous pas à leur sentence, tenez vous à la vostre' III.2: P 848, V 807–8, F 613.

[146] Foucault 1984b, Hadot 1987. For self-scrutiny in Seneca, see Edwards 1997.

[147] [A]'S'entretenir soy-mesmes, et s'arrester et rasseoir en soy'. I.8: P 55, V 33, F 21

[148] [A]'Ramenons à nous, et à nostre aise nos pensées et nos intentions'. I.38: P 246, V 242, F 178.

adversity, will 'return into himself and be with himself'.[149] When he urges us to A'sequester ourselves and repossess ourselves',[150] or when he writes of the soul that A'we must bring it back and withdraw it into itself',[151] his language mimics Seneca's injunction to Lucilius: 'retreat into yourself, as far as you can', rather than face moral corruption in the midst of the vices of the mob.[152]

Montaigne is here appropriating a gesture of renunciation and retreat – to turn back upon oneself, to return into oneself – that recurs frequently in the *Epistulae*. To withdraw into oneself, to settle one's soul in itself, is to redirect our affections and thoughts towards oneself, away from the contamination of the crowd and the vanity of external goods. The mark of a 'composed mind' is that it is able to 'consist in and remain with itself', instead of seeking the company of vicious and foolish men.[153] We should not entreat the gods to bring us happiness, for 'there is only one good, the cause and the support of a happy life: to entrust ourselves to ourselves'.[154] The wise man is '*se contentus*', content or contained within himself, both in the sense that he is 'sufficient unto himself' and that 'he is allowed to order his affairs according to his own will'.[155] Happiness is to be sought within the boundaries of one's own self: 'let your thoughts, your cares, your desires, help to make you content with yourself and the goods that spring from yourself'.[156]

Seneca's text, like the *Essais*, is haunted by images of erosion, depletion and dissipation. Montaigne's preoccupation with the need to *mesnage* (economise, manage, govern) his will and his liberty[157] echoes Seneca's

149 'In se reconditur, secum est'. Seneca 1989, I.9.16, p. 52. Cf. Pressac's translation: 'il est revolu en soy: il est seulement avec soy'. Seneca 1582, p. 27v.

150 A'Se [. . .] sequestrer et r'avoir de soy'. I.38: P 243, V 239, F 176.

151 A'Il la faut ramener et retirer en soy'. I.38: P 244, V 240, F 176.

152 'Recede in te ipsum, quantum potes'. Seneca 1989, I.7.8, p. 34. Cf. Pressac's translation: 'retire toy donc en toy-mesme autant que tu pourras'. Seneca 1582, p. 81.

153 'Primum argumentum conpositae mentis existimo posse consistere et secum morari'. Seneca 1989, I.2.1, p. 6. Cf. Pressac's translation: 'le premier tesmoignage d'une ame bien composée soit de se contenir, et demeurer avec soy-mesme'. Seneca 1582, pp. 3–3v.

154 'Unum bonum est, quod beatae vitae causa et firmamentum est, sibi fidere'. Seneca 1989, I.31.3, p. 222. Cf. Pressac's translation: 'il y a un bien, qui est la cause, et le firmament de la vie heureuse, se fier à soy-mesme'. Seneca 1582, p. 94.

155 'Sibi ipse sufficiat [. . .] illi licet suo arbitrio res suas ordinare'. Seneca 1989, I.9.3, 17, pp. 44, 52. Cf. Pressac's translation: 'le sage est [. . .] content de soy-mesme [. . .] il luy est loisible d'ordonner ses affaires à son plaisir, et à sa volunté'. Seneca 1582, pp. 23v, 27v.

156 'Huc ergo cogitationes tuae tendant, hoc cura, hoc opta, [. . .] ut contentus sis temet ipso et ex te nascentibus bonis'. Seneca 1989, I.20.8, p. 136.

157 'De mesnager sa volonté' (title of III.10). B'We must husband the liberty of our soul, and mortgage it only on just occasions' ('il faut mesnager la liberté de nostre ame, et ne l'hypothequer qu'aux occasions justes'). III.10: P 1049, V 1004, F 767. See Ch. 5.

emphasis on the need to fortify ourselves, to assume control over ourselves, to hold ourselves in our own grasp or in reserve, safe (*securus*) from these ubiquitous forces of destruction and disempowerment. The dangers involved in wasting time and the need to make oneself master of one's time are recurrent themes in the *Epistulae*: 'gather and save your time, which till lately has been forced from you, or filched away, or has merely slipped from your hands'.[158] We must act today instead of depending upon tomorrow, by 'holding every hour in our grasp', for 'nothing [. . .] is ours, except time'.[159] This emphasis on urgency and the elusiveness of time are translated by Montaigne into a discourse of *self*-emptying: B'you are running out, you are dispersing yourself; concentrate yourself, sustain yourself; you are being betrayed, dissipated, and stolen from yourself'.[160]

This condition of self-containment is figured in both Seneca and Montaigne as a way of living for oneself, being a friend to oneself or keeping company with oneself. The summit of human happiness and wisdom, Montaigne writes, lies in true 'friendship' with ourselves, not a C'false friendship, that makes us embrace glory, learning, riches, and such things with principal and immoderate affection, as members of our being', nor B'an indulgent and indiscriminate friendship; in which it happens as we see with the ivy, that it corrupts and ruins the wall it clings to', but 'a salutary and regulated friendship, useful and pleasant alike', in which 'knowing exactly what he owes to himself', a man 'finds in his role, that he must apply to himself, his experience of other men and of the world; and in order to do so, to contribute to public society those duties and offices that pertain to him'. As he concludes, quoting Seneca, a man who is C'*a friend to himself*', is by the same token '*a friend to all men*'.[161]

158 'Tempus, quod adhuc aut auferebatur aut subripiebatur aut excidebat, collige et serva'. Seneca 1989, I.1.1, p. 2.

159 'Omnes horas complectere. [. . .] Omnia [. . .] aliena sunt, tempus tantum nostrum est'. Seneca 1989, I.1.2–3, pp. 2, 4. Cf. Pressac's translation: 'Embrasse, et estrain toutes les heures. [. . .] Toutes autres choses sont à autruy, le temps seulement est nostre'. Seneca 1582, p. 1. According to Lewis and Short (1987), the meanings of the verb 'complectere' include the following: to clasp or embrace; to grasp, seize, encircle, surround, compass, enclose; to take into possession, to lay hold of, to make oneself master of.

160 B'Vous vous escoulez, vous vous respandez: appilez vous, soustenez vous: on vous trahit, on vous dissipe, on vous desrobe à vous'. III.9: P 1047, V 1001, F 766.

161 B'Non une Camitié faulce, qui nous faict embrasser la gloire, la science, la richesse, et telles choses, d'une affection principalle et immoderée, comme membres de nostre estre; ny Bune amitié molle et indiscrette; en laquelle il advient ce qui se voit au lierre, qu'il corrompt et ruyne la paroy qu'il accole: Mais une amitié salutaire et reiglée; esgalement utile et plaisante'. B'Cettuy-cy, [. . .] sçachant exactement ce qu'il se doit trouve dans son rolle, qu'il doit appliquer à soy, l'usage des autres hommes, et du monde; et pour ce faire, contribuer à la societé publique les devoirs et offices qui le touchent [. . .] C*Qui sibi amicus est, scito hunc amicum omnibus esse*'. III.10: P 1051–2, V 1006–7, F 769. Cf. Seneca 1989, I.6.7, p. 28.

V

If Montaigne's rhetoric of interiority can be traced back to Plutarch and Seneca, does the same also hold true for his appeal for us to 'estre à soy' (to belong to ourselves, to be one's own)?

The high incidence of an allegedly 'commercial' vocabulary in the *Essais* has been described by Philippe Desan as constituting a novel and distinctive 'economic discourse', mirroring the ascendancy of a modern capitalist society driven by trade and contractual exchange between equals, as opposed to an older 'feudalism' based on principles of natural obligation. According to Desan,

> the wide diffusion of this economic discourse and its overflow into literature soon lead to a reorganisation of the imagination on the basis of an exchangist and mercantile model. [. . .] In the case of Montaigne, [. . .] economic discourse proliferates to such an extent that it becomes an integral component of his way of thinking, insinuating itself so well into the literary text that it comes to structure it.[162]

Elsewhere, Desan has analysed what he calls the 'rhétorique comptable' of the *Essais*, arguing that Montaigne rejects classical rhetorical models as obsolete, writing instead according to 'a model of an exchangist type very close to that adopted by contemporary merchants in their account books'. This discursive style privileges the present moment of exchange with the other, allowing Montaigne to record his 'commerces' with others in their spontaneity and fortuity, through a pragmatic, open and sincere way of writing.[163] Desan stops short of labelling Montaigne 'bourgeois', and is careful to counterbalance the appeal of this new merchant discourse and ideology with the continued sway of traditional, 'chevaleresque' ideals of nobility and honour over the *Essais*. Ultimately, however, the *Essais* bear witness to 'the great epistemic transformation of the second half of the sixteenth century', a rupture directly linked to 'the impossibility of conceiving the world and mankind in anything other than economic terms'.[164]

162 'La généralisation du discours économique et son débordement dans la littérature réorganisent bientôt l'imaginaire à partir d'un modèle échangiste et marchand. [. . .] Chez Montaigne, [. . .] le discours économique se généralise à un tel point qu'il devient partie intégrante d'un mode de pensée et s'insinue si bien dans le texte littéraire qu'il finit par le structurer'. Desan 1992, pp. 12–13.

163 'Un modèle de type échangiste très proche de celui adopté par les marchands de l'époque dans leurs livres de comptes'. Desan 1995, pp. 178, 186.

164 'La grande transformation épistémique de la seconde moitié du XVIè siècle [. . .]. L'impossibilité de penser le monde et l'homme en termes qui ne seraient pas économiques'. Desan 1992, p. 19.

These claims lose much of their force, however, when we realise that Seneca uses the same language of ownership and repossession deployed by Montaigne. The author of the *Epistulae* rejoices at the thought of Lucilius judging himself worthy 'to become [his] own'.[165] The man who has come to terms with the inevitability of death and who is therefore able to face tomorrow 'without care' is described as 'a secure owner of himself'.[166] We must ensure 'that all time belongs to us', but that cannot be 'unless we ourselves begin to belong to ourselves'.[167] We must take care that 'adventitious things [. . .] depend on us, and not we on them', for 'all things that fortune looks upon become productive and pleasant, only if he who possesses them is also in possession of himself, and not in the power of his things'.[168]

This language of self-ownership is also found in Plutarch, although somewhat less prominently. Cato's suicide, for instance, is presented as an act of self-appropriation. Taking hold of the sword with which he had resolved to take his life, the hero is reported to have declared 'je suis [. . .] maintenant à moy' (I am now my own; I belong to myself).[169] The great consolation of exile, we are told in *Du bannissement*, is that it restores us to ourselves. Released from public duties, we are able to enjoy 'a stable, tranquil life, full of rest, being distracted by no superfluous occupation, but living properly and truly for oneself'. This self-sufficient, self-contained state is contrasted with the mendicancy of public life: 'we are no longer involved in intrigues, we are no longer dependent, we are no longer subject to paying court at the doors of governors'. Visited only by close friends and relatives, the exile shall find that 'there is no one to come and bother us, no one to ask for us, no one to borrow from us, no one who begs us to come and answer for him, or to help him to conduct his plot'. Banishment, in short, brings 'rest, leisure, and liberty': the exile can take comfort in the thought that 'all the rest of his time and life remains free and unindebted'.[170]

165 'Si vales et te dignum putas, qui aliquando fias tuus, gaudeo'. Seneca 1989, I.20.1, p. 132.

166 'Ille beatissimus est et securus sui possessor, qui crastinum sine sollicitudine expectat'. Seneca 1989, I.12.9, p. 70. Cf. Pressac's translation: 'Celuy est tres-heureux, et asseuré possesseur de soy-mesme, qui atteint le jour du lendemain sans sollicitude'. Seneca 1582, p. 39.

167 'Id agamus, ut nostrum omne tempus sit. Non erit autem, nisi prius nos nostri esse coeperimus'. Seneca 1989, II.71.36–7, p. 94.

168 'Fragilibus innititur, qui adventicio laetus est [. . .] si illa ex nobis pendent, non ex illis nos [. . .] Omnia, quae fortuna intuetur, ita fructifera ac iucunda fiunt, si qui habet illa se quoque habet nec in rerum suarum potestate est'. Seneca 1989, III.98.1–2, p. 118.

169 *Vie de Caton d'Utique*, Plutarch 1951, vol. II, p. 598.

170 'Une vie stable, tranquille, pleine de repos, n'estant distrait d'aucune superflue occupation, ains vivant proprement et veritablement à soy. [. . .] Il n'y a personne qui luy aille rompre la teste,

Living for oneself and owning oneself (as opposed to living in a state of debt) are here closely identified. It is in Seneca, however, that this language of self-possession is developed most fully. The wise man's ownership of himself is contrasted with the emptiness of material possessions: 'the happy man is not he whom the crowd deems happy, namely, he to whom great sums of money have flowed, but he whose goods are all in his soul' and 'whom no violence can deprive of his possessions'.[171] Wisdom consists in distinguishing between those goods which are truly our own, and those which are merely borrowed from others and not goods at all. It is a matter of judicious economy, of balancing one's accounts, of not being in others' debt, of recognizing what is truly of value and in our possession, and what are mere baubles, or worse, chains. Instead of 'allow[ing] the cheapest and most useless things, which can easily be replaced, to be charged in the reckoning', we should take care to 'save what is really [ours]', for 'it is too late to spare when you reach the dregs of the cask'.[172]

The force of this rhetoric of self-possession is to emphasise that we do not own what we think we own, and that in seeking to increase our possessions we are in fact alienating our most treasured belongings: 'we hold that "buying" refers only to the objects for which we pay money, and we regard as free gifts the things for which we spend our very selves. [. . .] Each man regards nothing as cheaper than himself'.[173] In judging a man, we must take stock of what he owns, as opposed to what is borrowed, on loan or on pledge to others:

> You estimate no man according to his own. When property is concerned, you reckon up in this way with most scrupulous calculation those to whom you shall either lend money or benefits [. . .]. 'His estates are wide, but his debts are large'. 'He has a fine house, but he has built it on borrowed capital'. [. . .] I suppose you call a man rich just because his gold plate goes with him even on his travels,

personne qui luy aille demander, personne qui luy emprunte, nul ne le prie de venir respondre pour luy, nul de luy aider à conduire sa brigue. [. . .] Tout le reste du temps et de la vie luy demeure franc et quitte, sans qu'on luy puisse violer ny troubler. [. . .] Aussi ne sommes nous plus en brigues, aussi ne despendons nous plus, aussi ne sommes nous plus subjects à aller faire la court aux portes des gouverneurs. [. . .] Le repos, le loisir et la liberté'. *Du bannissement, ou de l'exil*, Plutarch 1971, vol. I, pp. 127–7v, B-F.

171 'Beatum non eum esse, quem vulgus appellat, ad quem pecunia magna confluxit, sed illum, cui bonum omne in animo est [. . .] cui bona sua nulla vis excutit'. Seneca 1989, I.45.9, pp. 294, 296.

172 'Quae minima et vilissima sunt, certe reparabilia, imputari sibi. [. . .] Serves tua [. . .] sera parsimonia in fundo est'. Seneca 1989, I.1.3, 5, p. 4.

173 'Ex eo licet stupor noster appareat, quod ea sola putamus emi, pro quibus pecuniam solvimus, ea gratuita vocamus, pro quibus nos ipso inpendimus. [. . .] Adeo nihil est cuique se vilius'. Seneca 1989, I.42.7, p. 282. Cf. Pressac's translation: 'Et en cela pouvons nous cognoistre nostre bestise, que nous pensons achepter seulement les choses, pour lesquelles nous donnons de l'argent, et celles nous semblent gratuites, pour lesquelles nous nous donnons nous mesmes'. Seneca 1582, p. 101v.

because he farms land in all the provinces [. . .]. But after you have mentioned all these facts, he is poor. And why? He is in debt. 'To what extent?' you ask. For all that he has. Or perchance you think it matters whether one has borrowed from another man or from Fortune.[174]

Fortune's 'gifts' (*munera*) are better thought of as 'snares' (*insidiae*): we think that we have hold of them when it is they that have hold of us (*habere nos putamus, haeremus*).[175] That which fortune has granted us is not truly ours.[176] 'Individuals have riches just as we say that we "have a fever", when really the fever has us': we should really say that 'riches hold them'.[177]

This vocabulary of debt and credit, of true and false goods, is pervasive in Seneca, and it is here that Montaigne finds the words with which to express the vicissitudes of obligation. His insistence that [B]'one should lend oneself to others, but give oneself only to oneself'[178] is closely modelled on Seneca's claims that 'wherever I am, I am my own' and that the great soul 'counts none of the things which are around him as his own, but uses them as if they were a loan'.[179] As Seneca expresses it, 'I do not surrender myself to my affairs, but only lend myself to them. [. . .] When I give myself to my friends, I do not remove myself from myself'.[180]

This state of self-ownership, moreover, is identified by Seneca as one of freedom, notably in the opening command of the *Epistulae*: 'ita fac, mi Lucili, *vindica te tibi*'.[181] This cryptic expression, which Pressac renders as 'entre en possession de toy-mesme',[182] has been variously translated as 'claim yourself for yourself',[183] 'reclaim yourself' or 'assert your ownership over

[174] 'Neminem aestimatis suo. Cum ad patrimonium ventum est, diligentissimi computatores sic rationem ponitis singulorum, quibus aut pecuniam credituri estis aut beneficia, [. . .]: late possidet, sed multum debet; habet domum formosam, sed alienis nummis paratam: [. . .] Divitem illum putas, quia aurea supellex etiam in via sequitur, quia in omnibus provinciis arat [. . .] Cum omnia dixeris, pauper est. Quare? Quia debet. "Quantum?" inquis. Omnia. Nisi forte iudicas interesse, utrum aliquis ab homine an a fortuna mutuum sumpserit'. Seneca 1989, II.87.5–7, p. 326.

[175] Seneca 1989, I.8.3, p. 38. Cf. Pressac's translation: 'Vous pensez, que ce soient des presans de la fortune, et ce sont des embuches. [. . .] Nous les pensons tenir, et elles nous tiennent'. Seneca 1582, p. 20v.

[176] 'Non est tuum, fortuna quod fecit tuum'. Seneca 1989, I.8.10, p. 42. Cf. Pressac's translation: 'Ce que le sort a faict tien, n'est pas tien'. Seneca 1582, p. 22v.

[177] 'Divitias habent, quomodo habere dicimur febrem, cum illa nos habeat [. . .] divitiae illum tenent'. Seneca 1989, III.119.12, p. 376.

[178] [B]'Il se faut prester à autruy, et ne se donner qu'a soy-mesmes'. III.10: P 1049, V 1004, F 767.

[179] 'Ubicumque sum, ibi meus sum'. Seneca 1989, I.62.1, p. 426. 'Magnus animus [. . .] ceterum nihil horum, quae circa sunt, suum iudicat, sed ut commodatis utitur'. Seneca 1989, III.120.18, p. 392.

[180] 'Rebus enim me non trado, sed commodo. [. . .] Cum me amicis dedi non tamen mihi abduco'. Seneca 1989, I.62.1–2, pp. 426, 428.

[181] On freedom in Seneca, see Inwood 2005 and, above all, Edwards 2009.

[182] Seneca 1582, p. 1.

[183] Edwards 1997, p. 28.

yourself',[184] and 'set yourself free for your own sake'.[185] The verb *vindicare* combines the meaning of 'laying claim to something as one's property', or 'asserting ownership over something', in particular something disputed or lost, with that of 'setting free' or 'placing into a condition of freedom'.[186] Hence by becoming one's owner one is also freeing oneself from a state of slavery. Freedom here consists in the absence of dependency – in placing ourselves within our own power, rather than being subject to that which is alien to us. The true spirit (*animus*) is one 'that will never come under the will of another' (*in alienum ... arbitrium*).[187] He 'who has not placed his happiness in the power of others' (*in aliena potestate*) has attained the 'summit' of wisdom.[188] Happiness can consist only in the life of virtue, in what is honourable, 'for anyone who deems other things to be good, comes under the power of fortune [*in fortunae venit potestatem*], and goes under the will of another [*alieni arbitrii fit*]'.[189]

Some men who are free in name, in the eyes of the law, can more truthfully be described as slaves, and conversely those whom we conventionally refer to as slaves may in fact be freer than their masters:

> 'He is a slave.' His soul, however, may be that of a free man. 'He is a slave.' But shall that stand in his way? Show me a man who is not a slave; one is a slave to lust, another to greed, another to ambition, and all men are slaves to fear.[190]

To be free, in the truest sense, is to have withdrawn the will from those things which we take to be evil but which are in fact indifferent, in particular from fear of death and of poverty.[191] Evil simply is 'the yielding to those things which are called evils, the surrendering of one's liberty to them', and 'liberty is lost, unless we despise those things which put the yoke upon our necks'.[192] The life of virtue brings 'peace of mind' and 'absolute

184 Bartsch and Wray 2009, pp. 12–13.

185 This is Richard Gunmere's translation in the Loeb parallel text edition. Seneca 1989, I.1.1, p. 2.

186 Lewis and Short (1987) define *vindicare* as 'to lay legal claim to a thing, whether as one's own property or for its restoration to a free condition', hence 'to lay claim to as one's own, to make a claim upon, to demand, claim, arrogate, assume, appropriate' or 'to place a thing in a free condition', 'to deliver, liberate, protect, defend'.

187 Seneca 1989, I.13.1, p. 72. Cf. Pressac's translation: 'Les choses contraires, et difficiles sont la vraye touche d'une ame, qui est toute à soy, et qui n'est pour se soumettre à la puissance de personne'. Seneca 1582, p. 40.

188 Seneca 1989, I.23.2, p. 158.

189 Seneca 1989, II.74.1, p. 114.

190 '"Servus est." Sed fortasse liber animo. "Servus est." Hoc illi nocebit? Ostende, quis non sit; alius libidini servit, alius avaritiae, alius ambitioni, omnes timori'. Seneca 1989, I.47.17, p. 310.

191 See, for example, Seneca 1989, II.80.5–6, pp. 214, 216.

192 'Quaeris quid sit malum? Cedere iis, quae mala vocantur, et illis libertatem suam dedere, pro qua cuncta patienda sunt. Perit libertas, nisi illa contemnimus, quae nobis iugum imponunt'. Seneca 1989, II.85.28, pp. 300, 302.

liberty', which consists in 'not fearing either men or gods' and 'not craving wickedness or excess', and therefore 'having the greatest power over oneself', or 'becoming one's own' (*suum fieri*).[193]

Seneca's vision of human freedom is, in certain important respects, radically unlike Montaigne's. In the *Epistulae*, it should be stressed, the vindication of our liberty is presented in heroic and martial terms. 'To live is to do battle': the man who complains of hardship and toil, and longs to be free of them, is 'effeminate'.[194] To shake off the yoke, we must 'reject pleasures' and 'spurn wealth', for 'liberty cannot be gained for nothing'.[195] For a man to 'live for himself', it is not enough for him to live at his own leisure, for that would mean 'living for his belly, his sleep, and his lust'.[196] To own oneself is to 'have conquered', to have 'subdued all the passions and brought them under our own will' – to have overcome 'greed, ambition, and the fear of death', far greater enemies than those faced by the conquerors of the world.[197] We are only in our power, on this view, where we are able to exert dominion over our affections:

> The evils that afflict the mind do not admit of moderation. You can more easily remove than control them. [. . .] If you grant jurisdiction to sadness, fear, desire, and all the other wrong impulses, they will cease to lie within our power. And why? Simply because the means of arousing them lie outside us.[198]

The body, it follows, is to regarded as 'nothing but a chain which manacles my freedom'; indeed, 'to despise our bodies is sure freedom'.[199] The soul should treat the body as 'a burden which must be borne, not as a thing to

[193] 'Expectant nos, si ex hac aliquando faece in illud evadimus sublime et excelsum, tranquillitas animi et expulsis erroribus absoluta libertas. Quaeris quae sit ista? Non homines timere, non deos; nec turpia velle nec nimia; in se ipsum habere maximam potestatem. Inaestimabile bonum est suum fieri'. Seneca 1989, II.75.18, p. 146.

[194] 'Atqui vivere, Lucili, militare est'. 'Tam effeminata vox virum dedecet'. Seneca 1989, III.96.4–5, p. 106.

[195] 'In primis autem respuendae voluptates; enervant et effeminant et multum petunt, multum autem a fortuna petendum est. Deinde spernendae opes: auctoramenta sunt servitutum. [. . .] Non potest gratis constare libertas'. Seneca 1989, III.114.34, p. 210.

[196] 'Ille sibi non vivit, sed, [. . .] ventri, somno, libidini'. Seneca 1989, I.55.5, p. 368.

[197] 'Quando continget omnibus oppressis adfectibus et sub arbitrium suum adductis hanc vocem emittere "vici"? Quem vicerim quaeris? Non Persas nec extrema Medorum nec si quid ultra Dahas bellicosum iacet, sed avaritiam, sed ambitionem, sed metum mortis, qui victores gentium vicit'. Seneca 1989, II.71.37, p. 94.

[198] 'Non recipiunt animi mala temperamentum. Facilius sustuleris illa quam rexeris. [. . .] Deinde si das aliquid iuris tristitiae, timori, cupiditati, ceteris motibus pravis, non erunt in nostra potestate. Quare? Qui extra nos sunt, quibus inritantur'. Seneca 1989, II.85.10–11, p. 290.

[199] 'Maior sum et ad maiora genitus, quam ut mancipium sim mei corporis, quod equidem non aliter aspicio quam vinculum aliquod libertati meae circumdatum. [. . .] Contemptus corporis sui certa libertas est'. Seneca 1989, I.65.21–2, p. 456.

love, but as a thing to oversee', for 'no man is free, who is a slave to the body'.[200]

As we shall see in Chapters 4 and 5, Montaigne rejects this robust model of virtuous self-overcoming in favour of a weak-willed, effortless and natural innocence, based on an acceptance of the fragility, vanity and folly of the human condition – and of the limits of our voluntary power over ourselves. What Montaigne does take from Seneca, however, is the idea that wisdom consists in independence – in disengaging ourselves from that which subjects us to the power of other agents and forces. The free man refuses to be a supplicant, living by favour or through borrowed goods: he contains himself within the limits of his power and distances himself from all superfluous commodities.

In order to banish hunger and thirst, it is not necessary for you to pay court at the doors of the proud, or to submit to the stern frown, or to the kindness that humiliates; nor is it necessary for you to scour the seas, or go campaigning; nature's needs are easily provided and ready to hand. It is the superfluous things for which men sweat – the superfluous things that wear our togas threadbare, that force us to grow old in camp, that dash us upon foreign shores. That which is enough is ready to our hands.[201]

The measured self-containment of the free man, for Seneca as for Montaigne, is to be contrasted with the ambitious venality of the slave. The health of the mind consists in its being 'content with itself' and 'trusting in itself', indifferent to 'all those things for which men pray, all the benefits which are bestowed and sought for'.[202] The man who owns himself does so by 'leaning upon none but himself,' in the knowledge that 'one who sustains himself by any prop may fall'.[203]

In Plutarch, similarly, the flatterer is depicted as a servile chameleon, passively imitating those whose favour he seeks, regulating himself by another, rather than taking charge of his own conduct. He is a 'mask, dressed and adorned with another's colours and clothing, as Plato says, for lack of

[200] 'Cum se in hanc sublimitatem tulit [anima], corporis quoque ut oneris necessarii non amator, sed procurator est nec se illi, cui inpositus est, subicit. Nemo liber est, qui corpori servit'. II.92.33, p. 468.

[201] 'Ut famem sitimque depellas, non est necesse superbis adsidere liminibus nec supercilium grave et contumeliosam etiam humanitatem pati, non est necesse maria temptare nec sequi castra; parabile est, quod natura desiderat, et adpositum. Ad supervacua sudatur. Illa sunt, quae togam conterunt, quae nos senescere sub tentorio cogunt, quae in aliena litora impingunt. Ad manum est, quod sat est'. Seneca 1989, I.4.10–11, p. 18.

[202] 'Dicam, quomodo intellegam sanum: si se ipso contentus est, si confidit sibi'. 'Omnia vota mortalium, omnia beneficia quae dantur petunturque'. Seneca 1989, II.72.7, p. 100.

[203] 'Ne ulli quidem nisi sibi innixus. Nam qui aliquo auxilio sustinetur, potest cadere'. Seneca 1989, II.92.2, p. 448.

any of his own',[204] 'like a man who does not have a single home within his manners, and who does not live a life that he has shaped according to his will, but who forms himself and composes himself according to the pattern of others'.[205] He is a figure of contrivance and affectation, full of effort, care and premeditation:

> . . . a transpiring face, running here and there, a mournful and pensive appearance, all signs which give an appearance and opinion of laborious work, executed with great pains and great care: no more and no less than an affected painting, which with exaggerated colours, broken folds, wrinkles and angles seeks to make itself appear more lifelike.[206]

Deception, effort and vice are closely identified, and contrasted with the carelessness and plainness of the virtuous friend, who is identified by his willingness to 'speak freely' (*parler librement*), that is, to offer frank remonstrance and counsel, and to gently but plainly criticise the vices, failings and errors of judgment of his friend. Freedom is here identified with frankness, an identity captured in Amyot's French by the single word *franchise*.

This contrast between boldness and dissimulation, faithfulness and affectation, is strongly emphasised in the lives of Cato, Phocion and Aristides – those exemplars whom Montaigne cites in *On solitude* as inner governors guiding us on the right path of self-containment:

> [A]Until you have made yourself such, that you do not dare to trip up in your own presence, and until you feel shame and respect for your self, [C]*keep honourable images before your mind*: [A]keep ever in your imagination Cato, Phocion, and Aristides, in whose presence even fools would hide their faults, and establish them as controllers of all your intentions: If they go off track, your reverence for these men will set you back on course: they will contain you in this path, to content yourself with yourself, to borrow nothing except from yourself, to arrest and settle your soul in certain and limited cogitations, where it may please itself: and having understood the true goods, which we may enjoy insofar as we understand them,

[204] 'Ce masque qui se vest et se pare des couleurs et habits d'autruy, ainsi que dit Platon, à faulte d'en avoir de propres à luy'. *Comment on pourra discerner le flatteur d'avec l'amy*, Plutarch 1971, vol. I, p. 41v, F.

[205] 'Comme celuy qui n'a pas un seul domicile en ses meurs, et qui ne vit pas d'une vie qu'il ait elevée à son gré, mais qui se forme et compose au moule d'autruy'. *Comment on pourra discerner le flatteur d'avec l'amy*, Plutarch 1971, vol. I, p. 42, A.

[206] 'Une sueur au visage, un courir ça & là, une face chagrine et pensive, tous signes qui donnent apparence et opinion d'oeuvre laborieuse, et faitte avec une grand peine et grand' soing: ne plus ne moins qu'une peinture affettee, qui avec couleurs renforcees, avec plis rompus, et avec rides et angles chercheroit de se monstrer bien vivement apparente'. *Comment on pourra discerner le flatteur d'avec l'amy*, Plutarch 1971, vol. I, p. 49, A.

to be content with these, without any desire to prolong either one's life or one's name.[207]

Plutarch describes Aristides, the commander of the Athenians during the Persian wars, as 'cool, collected, constant and arrested', claiming that he 'would not err from the right path of justice for anything' and that he 'would not have made use of lies, affectation, or deceit, even in jest'.[208] This antipathy towards deception and treachery is picked up by Montaigne and applied to himself in *On custom*, where he professes to [A]'have trained himself in [his] childhood, to always walk in [his] own great and open road, and to have had an aversion for mixing trickery or ruse in [his] childish games', and where he states that 'there is no pastime so trivial' that he does not 'bring to it from within, from a natural propension, and without study, an extreme repugnance to deceit'.[209] Plutarch praises Aristides above all else for his civic virtue, his ability to undertake public affairs and serve the common good without regard for private interest, ambition or faction, and for his refusal to be bought: 'never for any honour done to him, did he raise himself up, nor did he lower himself for any rebuttal or refusal that he suffered', serving 'the republic, without hoping or expectating any mercenary wages, either of money, or honour and glory'. Aristides' defence of Greek liberty against the threat of Persian subjugation mirrors his own inward freedom. He was neither a slave to other men nor a slave to destructive passion: 'he was not only so firm and so straight as to resist favour and grace alone, but also anger and hatred'.[210]

207 [A]'Jusques à ce que vous vous soyez rendu tel, devant qui vous n'osiez clocher, et jusques à ce que vous ayez honte et respect de vous mesmes, [C]*obuersentur species honestae animo* [Cicero, *Tusculanae disputationes*, II.22.52]: [A]presentez vous tousjours en l'imagination Caton, Phocion, et Aristides, en la presence desquels les fols mesme cacheroient leurs fautes, et establissez les contrerolleurs de toutes vos intentions: Si elles se detraquent, leur reverence vous remettra en train: ils vous contiendront en cette voye, de vous contenter de vous mesmes, de n'emprunter rien que de vous, d'arrester et fermir vostre ame en certaines et limitées cogitations, où elle se puisse plaire: et ayant entendu les vrays biens, desquels on jouyt à mesure qu'on les entend, s'en contenter, sans desir de prolongement de vie ny de nom'. I.38: P 252, V 247–8, F 183.

208 'Froid, reposé, constant et arrêté, qui pour rien n'eût devoyé du droit sentier de la justice, et n'eût usé de mensonge, d'afféterie, ni de tromperie, non pas en jeu seulement'. Plutarch 1951, *Vie d'Aristide*, vol. I, p. 711.

209 [A]'Pour m'estre duict en ma puerilité, de marcher tousjours mon grand et plein chemin, et avoir eu à contrecœur de mesler ny tricotterie ny finesse à mes jeux enfantins, [. . .] il n'est passetemps si leger, où je n'apporte du dedans, et d'une propension naturelle, et sans estude, une extreme contradiction à tromper'. I.22: P 113, V 110, F 79.

210 'Jamais pour honneur qu'on lui fit il ne s'éleva, ni pour rebut ou refus qu'il souffrît aussi ne s'abaissa [. . .] Servir la chose publique, sans en espérer ou attendre aucun loyer mercenaire ni d'argent, ni d'honneur et de gloire. [. . .] Il n'estait pas seulement ainsi ferme et roide pour résister à faveur et à grace seulement, mais aussi à ire et à haine semblablement'. *Vie d'Aristide*, Plutarch 1951, vol. I, p. 713.

The same parallel is found in Cato, who devoted himself to 'the defence of liberty against tyrants', and who was hailed by the people as 'the only free and invincible man'.[211] Montaigne's account of Cato's virtue, in particular its heroic inflexibility, is an ambivalent one – although it is worth noting here that Plutarch writes of a 'natural goodness and charity towards his family, mingled with firm rigidity and inflexible hardness in the face of pleasures, fears, and unlawful and dishonourable prayers'.[212] What is especially interesting here, however, is the emphasis that Plutarch places on *la franchise de son parler*, a 'speech full of meaning and sane judgment, with which he [. . .] frankly berated others', without 'powder or paint, or youthful affectation, but being straight, full of meaning and vehemence'. 'Mingled with the brevity of this speech', he continues, 'was a grace which gave pleasure to those who heard him, his natural character showing through, grave and venerable, bringing them I know not what pleasant affection, which invited them to smile'.[213] This ideal of speech – unbridled and yet gracious – is expressed strongly in the *Ethika* as well. The language of the 'wise governor' must in no way be 'affected', 'pompous' or 'made-up', free from any 'ruse' or 'orator's artifice', or 'any affectation of praise for having spoken in a learned, subtle, or ingenious manner', but rather 'full of a natural affection, of a true greatness of soul, of a paternal frankness in remonstrance [. . .] having attractive grace conjoined with honest dignity'.[214]

As these examples suggest, Montaigne derives from both Plutarch and Seneca a powerful language opposing free men and slaves as rival models of *moral* selfhood. 'Estre à soy', in this perspective, is indeed a condition of my integrity, but not in the quasi-ontological sense of an 'equal and stable

[211] 'La défense de la liberté à l'encontre des tyrans'. 'Seul homme libre et invincible'. *Vie de Caton d'Utique*, Plutarch 1951, vol. II, pp. 568, 599.

[212] 'La naïve bonté et charité envers les siens, qui était en luy mêlée parmy sa roideur ferme et dureté inflexible à l'encontre des voluptés, des craintes, et des prières illicites et déshonnêtes'. *Vie de Caton d'Utique*, Plutarch 1951, vol. II, p. 537.

[213] 'Une parole pleine de sens et de sain jugement, par laquelle il [. . .] tançait franchement'. 'Son langage n'avait rien de fard, ny d'afféterie de jeunesse, mais était roide, plein de sens et de véhémence, et néanmoins parmy la brièveté de ses sentences, y avait une grâce qui donnait plaisir aux écoutants, et son naturel se montrant à travers grave et vénérable leur apportait ne sais quoi d'affection agréable, qui les conviait à rire'. *Vie de Caton d'Utique*, Plutarch 1951, vol. II, pp. 563, 532.

[214] 'Puisqu'il est donc ainsi, que le principal instrument d'un sage gouverneur est la parole, il fault tout premierement qu'elle ne soit point affettee, ny pompeuse et fardee [. . .] qu'il apparoisse non une ruze, ny un artifice d'orateur, non une affectation de louange d'avoir parlé doctement, subtilement, et ingenieusement, mais [. . .] plein d'une affection naïfve, d'une vraye magnanimité, d'une franchise de remonstrance paternelle, [. . .] aiant la grace attraiante conjoincte avec l'honeste dignité'. *Instruction pour ceulx qui manient affaires d'estat*, Plutarch 1971, vol. I, p. 164, B-C.

relation of self to self'.[215] The question to which 'myself' is the answer is not 'Who am I? or 'How can I be true to myself?', but 'What is mine?', 'What is in my power?' Who is in control: myself or another? Am I rich with borrowed goods, or with my own? Do I belong to myself, or am I mortgaged to another? Freedom for Montaigne is not about being able to shape one's true identity, a power to preserve one's inward being from the oppressive conditioning of external structures.[216] The enemy of liberty is servitude, in the sense of a subjection of the will, rather than an alienation of authentic or self-constituting identity. In the next chapter, we shall see how this set of preoccupations is put to work in Montaigne's meditations on public life, engagement and retreat.

[215] 'Rapport égal et stable de soi à soi'. Starobinski 1993, p. 40.

[216] Cf. Schwartz 2000: '[for Montaigne] we must free ourselves from the authority of others, from custom, from ideology, even from language, and from all that conspires to rob us of our authenticity' (p. 155).

CHAPTER 3

Self-possession, public engagement and slavery

I

In April 1570, Montaigne resigned his office as a counsellor to the *parlement* of Bordeaux, a position he had held for the past decade. The following year, he commemorated this decision by having a Latin inscription painted on the wall of a little room adjacent to his library:

> In the year of Christ 1571, at the age of thirty-eight, on the last day of February, anniversary of his birth, Michel de Montaigne – long wearied of the servitude of the court and of public charges, and yearning to hide himself, while still whole, in the bosom of the learned Virgins, where in calm and freedom from all cares (if the fates permit it) he will complete what little remains of his life now more than half run out – has consecrated this seat, this sweet ancestral refuge, to his liberty, tranquillity and leisure.[1]

Montaigne's departure from the *parlement* has been linked to a number of pivotal events in his life, including the death of Estienne de La Boétie in 1563; his accession to the family estate following the death of his father in 1568; and his own involvement in a violent collision on horseback sometime towards the end of 1569. Montaigne himself, however, attributed a specific meaning to his decision. In this inscription, he cast his resignation from public office as a vindication of his liberty, freeing him, on the approach of old age and death, from a lifelong condition of *servitium* or slavery. By dedicating his ancestral home to 'libertati suae, tranquillitatique et otio', Montaigne sought not only to celebrate the beginning of a new life, timed to coincide with the anniversary of his birth, but also to set forth for himself a model for a certain way of living and dying, by dedicating himself to the

[1] 'An[no] Chr[isti] M.D. LXXXI. aet[ate] 38. pridie cal[endas] Mart[ias] die suo natali Mich[aelis] Montanus servitii aulici et munerum publicorum iamdudum pertaesus dum se integer in doctarum Virginum abdere gestit sinus ubi quietus et omnium securus quantillum id tandem superabit decursi multa iam plus parte spatii si modo fata duint exigat istas sedes et dulces latebras avitasq[ue] libertati suae tranquillitatiq[ue] et otio consecravit'. P 1315. English translation from Frame 1965, p. 115.

performance of a particular philosophical persona: that of a man in full possession of his liberty.

Montaigne's retirement from the *parlement* did not commit him to a life of seclusion and contemplation. The sale of his office seems to have been triggered by a failure to secure promotion from the *Chambre des Enquêtes* to either the *Grand' Chambre* or the *Tournelle*, the problem being that many of his relatives already held posts in these two more important chambers. This obstacle would usually have been circumvented by applying for a dispensation from the king, but Montaigne either neglected or declined to set this procedure in motion.[2] His retreat to the estate did not, however, mark the end of his public career. As well as a double term of office as Mayor of Bordeaux from 1582 to 1585, he held appointments as *gentilhomme de la chambre* to both Henri III and Henri de Navarre, serving as an intermediary and negotiator between opposing parties in the wars of religion ravaging late sixteenth-century France.[3]

Public service aside, Montaigne was a busy man, responsible for the management of his family's property, income and servants. His study window looked out, not (as tradition would have it) upon open fields and beyond, but upon the courtyard at the centre of household activity. For all his protestations to the contrary, the task of writing, revising and proofreading the *Essais* – to say nothing of arranging and financing its publication – would have cost him considerable time and effort. Nor will it do to imagine him as a recluse, working in isolation from all company. A substantial part of the *Essais* was dictated to a secretary, and (as the dedications of certain chapters attest) Montaigne seems to have shared his work in progress with friends and visitors to the estate.[4] In an age in which the humanities were thought to lay the foundations for public service, the *Essais* may have served not as a distraction but as a complement to his career, as a public testimony to his sound judgment, effortless learning and rhetorical skill: he did, after all, present a copy of the 1580 edition to the king.[5]

From the vantage point of the text itself (which he probably began writing about a year after his retirement), it is clear that Montaigne thought of his retreat not as a wholesale withdrawal from public life, but as an exile

[2] Frame 1965, p. 114.

[3] This point is well made by Fontana 2008, p. 6. On Montaigne's continuing public career, see Frame 1965, pp. 223–45 and 266–88, Maskell 1979 and Cocula 2003.

[4] *On the education of children* (I.25) is dedicated to 'Madame de Foix, contesse de Gurson', the *Twenty-nine sonnets of Estienne de la Boetie* (I.28) to 'Madame de Grammont, contesse de Guissen' and *On the resemblance of children to their fathers* (II.37) to 'Madame de Duras'.

[5] For an excellent account of these matters, see Hoffmann 1998; cf. Sayre 1978, pp. 20–5. On Montaigne's political ambitions and the gift of his book to the king, see Balsamo 2006.

of the will – a transformation of the conditions of his engagement with the world.

> [A]We must reserve for ourselves a room at the back of the shop, entirely ours, entirely free, in which to establish our true liberty and our principal retreat and solitude. Here our ordinary conversation must be between us and ourselves, and so private, that no outside association or communication can find a place.[6]

In this early and much-quoted passage from *On solitude*, liberty is closely associated with seclusion and privacy. Even here, however, the 'arriereboutique' designates a refuge within the soul as well as a physical retreat. In *On three kinds of association*, meanwhile, Montaigne is at pains to insist that his quarrel is not with society as such, but only with its capacity to enslave us. His [B]'essential form', he writes, is 'suited to communication and revelation'; he is 'born for company and friendship'. His retreat is spiritual rather than physical, driven by a quest for freedom rather than seclusion:

> [B]The solitude that I love, and that I preach, is primarily nothing but leading my feelings and thoughts back to myself, restraining and shortening not my steps, but my desires and my care: abandoning foreign solicitude, and mortally fleeing from servitude and obligation: [C]and not so much the press of people as the press of business.[7]

This deep-seated hatred of slavery and obligation lies at the heart of Montaigne's critique of public society and service. The solitude that he seeks provides space neither for the sincere expression of his feelings, nor for the discovery of his authentic self, but for the preservation of his liberty.

II

Montaigne's alignment of *libertas* with *tranquillitas* and *otium* links the 1571 inscription to a long-standing tradition of humanist reflection on the ethics of civic engagement and service. Like Thomas More, like Justus Lipsius, the author of the *Essais* is anxious not merely to set retreat against engagement,

6 [A]'Il se faut reserver une arriereboutique, toute nostre, toute franche, en laquelle nous establissions nostre vraye liberté et principale retraicte et solitude. En cette-cy faut-il prendre nostre ordinaire entretien, de nous à nous mesmes, et si privé, que nulle accointance ou communication de chose estrangere y trouve place'. I.38: P 245, V 241, F 177.

7 [B]'Ma forme essentielle, est propre à la communication, et à la production: je suis [. . .] nay à la societé et à l'amitié: La solitude que j'ayme, et que je presche, ce n'est principallement, que ramener à moy mes affections, et mes pensées: restreindre et resserrer, non mes pas, ains mes desirs et mon soucy, resignant la solicitude estrangere, et fuyant mortellement la servitude, et l'obligation: [C]et non tant la foule des hommes, que la foule des affaires'. III.3: P 864, V 823, F 625.

but to explore the possibility of their reconciliation.[8] What place, if any, is there for liberty in public life? Can service be fully distinguished from servitude?[9] Is freedom a precondition for good counsel[10] or, on the contrary, incompatible with political life?

In a manner characteristic of the *Essais*, Montaigne's reflections on public engagement do not coalesce into a single doctrine or prescribed course of action.[11] His approach is exploratory rather than expository, an essaying of dissonant possibilities in a context of uncertainty and doubt. Montaigne's account of his own involvement in public life, in particular, is somewhat ambiguous, as we can see if we analyse a series of passages from the third book positioned no more than twenty pages apart.

I should like to begin with a quotation situated towards the end of *On vanity*, in which Montaigne claims to have long disentangled himself from [B]'affairs of state' and 'the service of public dealings'.[12] In an echo of Hythloday's protestations, in More's *Utopia*, that the life of counsel is not only incompatible with his happiness but with his liberty,[13] Montaigne claims to be fundamentally unsuited to such pursuits:

[B]I feel that if I had to train myself thoroughly for such occupations, I should need a great deal of change and reclothing for it. Even if I had enough power over myself to do it (and why could I not, with time and pains?) I would not want to. By what little I have essayed myself in that occupation, I am just that much disgusted with it: I sometimes feel rising in my soul the fumes of certain temptations toward ambition: but I stiffen and hold firm against them:

But thou, Catullus, persevere, persist.

[8] On More's distinctive contribution to humanist debates about *otium* and *negotium*, see Skinner 2002b and Parrish 1997; on the emergence in England of a 'Lipsian paradigm' in service of political engagement rather than resignation, see McCrea 1997.

[9] For the proximity of *inservire* and *servire*, see More's *Utopia* (1516): 'Bona verba, inquit Petrus, mihi visum est non ut servias regibus, sed ut inservias. Hoc est, inquit ille [Hythlodaeus], una syllaba plus quam servias' ('"Well said", Peter replied, "but I do not mean that you should be in servitude to any king, only in his service". "The difference is only a matter of one syllable", said Hythlodaeus'). More 1995, p. 50.

[10] See Lipsius' *Politicorum libri sex* (1589), where 'libertas' is listed alongside 'pietas', 'constantia', 'modestia' and 'silentium' as one of five fundamental warnings or commands (*monita*) for true and good counsellors. 'Libertatem secundo. ut fortiter, non obnoxie, sententias dicant' ('that they may give their opinion boldly, not submissively'). Lipsius 2004, III.5, p. 358.

[11] On the question of public engagement in the *Essais*, see Abecassis 1995, Baldwin 2001 and Brahami 2006.

[12] [B]'Affaires d'estat [. . .] service des maniemens publiques'. III.9: P 1037, V 991, F 758.

[13] 'Feliciorem me, inquit Raphael, ea via facerem, a qua abhorret animus? Atque nunc sic vivo ut volo, quod ego certe suspicor paucissimis purpuratorum contingere' ('"Would a way of life", said Raphael, "so absolutely repellent to my spirit make me happier? As it is now, I live as I wish, something which I suspect can be said of very few splendid courtiers"'). More 1995, p. 50.

I am seldom summoned to them, and I offer myself to them just as little. [C]Liberty and idleness, which are my ruling qualities, are qualities diametrically opposite to that trade.[14]

As we shall see in the next chapter, idleness (*oysiveté*) refers to a kind of ponderous inertia, a lack of effort and care stemming from a deep aversion towards business and restless agitation. Let us focus for now, however, on the connection drawn in this passage between the disciplining of ambition, the renunciation of public charges, and a natural inclination towards liberty.

The upshot of this self-description is not, it should be emphasised, that Montaigne has wholly removed himself from public occupations, but only that he tries to avoid them as far as he can: the enemy of liberty is not involvement as such, but the active pursuit of public office, and the concern for glory and social advancement which it implies. 'Private life', as Montaigne presents it a few pages earlier, consists not in the abnegation of all public activity and service to princes, but rather in indifference towards public renown:

[B]I love a private life, because it is by my own choice that I love it, not because of unfitness for public life: which is perhaps just as well suited to my nature. I serve my Prince the more gaily, because I do so by the free election of my judgment, and of my reason, [C]without personal obligation. [B]And because I am not thrown back on his service, and constrained to it, by being unacceptable and unwelcome to every other party.[15]

Montaigne serves the prince voluntarily, because he has freely chosen to do so, and not simply for lack of an alternative or (as the phrase inserted in the Bordeaux Copy suggests) out of a personal debt of gratitude. His independence remains intact.

These readings from *On vanity* identify liberty with privacy, that is, with a life hidden from public view and thus purged of the corruptions

[14] [B]'Je sens que si j'avois à me dresser tout à fait à telles occupations, il m'y faudroit beaucoup de changement et de rabillage. Quand je pourrois cela sur moy, (et pourquoy ne le pourrois je, avec le temps et le soing?) je ne le voudrois pas. De ce peu que je me suis essayé en ceste vacation, je m'en suis d'autant desgousté: Je me sens fumer en l'ame par fois, aucunes tentations vers l'ambition: mais je me bande et obstine au contraire: *At tu Catulled* [sic] *obstinatus obdura* [Catullus, VII.19].

On ne m'y appelle gueres, et je m'y convie aussi peu. [C]La liberté et l'oysiveté, qui sont mes maistresses qualitez, sont qualitez, diametralement contraires à ce mestier là.' III.9: P 1038, V 992, F 759.

[15] [B]'J'ayme la vie privée, par ce que c'est par mon choix que je l'ayme, non par disconvenance à la vie publique: qui est à l'avanture, autant selon ma complexion. J'en sers plus gayement mon Prince, par ce que c'est par libre eslection de mon jugement, et de ma raison, [C]sans obligation particuliere. [B]Et que je n'y suis pas rejecté, ny contrainct, pour estre irrecevable à tout autre party, et mal voulu'. III.9: P 1034, V 988, F 756.

of ambition. In the next chapter, however, Montaigne strikes a slightly different note, boasting that he has [B]'been able to involve [him]self in public charges, without departing even a nail's breadth from [him]self'.[16] He begins (as he had in *On vanity*) by claiming (in a phrase borrowed from Ovid) to [B]'*flee from affairs*' and to be '*born for untroubled leisure*'.[17] Here too, he insists on the importance of safeguarding our freedom: [B]'we must husband the liberty of our soul and mortgage it only on the right occasions. Which are in very small number, if we judge sanely'.[18] As this passage and the chapter's title suggest, however, *On managing the will* is not about recoiling from public life, but about bringing an inner sense of equanimity and detachment to the performance of our public duties:

> [B]I do not want a man to refuse, to the charges he takes on, attention, steps, words, and sweat and blood if need be:
>
> *To die for dear friends,*
> *Or for my country, I do not fear.*
>
> But this is by way of loan and accidentally: The mind holding itself ever in repose and health, not without action, but without vexation, without passion.[19]

Liberty, in this perspective, is an inner disposition of the will, allowing us not only to protect ourselves from the vicissitudes of fortune, but to execute our functions both prudently and justly.

> [B]We never conduct well the thing that possesses and conducts us.
>
> [C]*Impulse handles all things ill.*
>
> [B]He who employs in it only his judgment, and his skill, proceeds more gaily: he feints, he bends, he plays for time entirely at his ease, according to the need of the occasions: he misses the target, without torment, and without affliction, ready and intact for a new undertaking: he always walks bridle in hand. In the man who is intoxicated with that violent and tyrannical intention, we see of necessity much imprudence and injustice. The impetuosity of his desire carries him away.

16 [B]'J'ay peu me mesler des charges publiques, sans me despartir de moy, de la largeur d'une ongle'. III.10: P 1053, V 1007, F 770.

17 [B]'*Fugax rerum, securáque in otia natus* [Ovid, *Tristia*, III.2.9]'. III.10: P 1048, V 1003, F 767.

18 [B]'Il faut mesnager la liberté de nostre ame, et ne l'hypothequer qu'aux occasions justes. Lesquelles sont en bien petit nombre, si nous jugeons sainement'. III.10: P 1049, V 1004, F 767.

19 [B]'Je ne veux pas, qu'on refuse aux charges qu'on prend, l'attention, les pas, les parolles, et la sueur, et le sang au besoing: | *non ipse pro charis amicis* | *Aut patria timidus perire* [Horace, *Carmina*, IV.9.51]. | Mais c'est par emprunt et accidentalement; L'esprit se tenant tousjours en repos et en santé; non pas sans action, mais sans vexation, sans passion'. III.10: P 1052, V 1007, F 770.

These are rash movements, and, unless fortune lends them a great hand, of little fruit.[20]

It is worth drawing attention here to the quotation from Statius inserted into the Bordeaux Copy version of this passage. This excerpt is also cited by Lipsius, in his *Politicorum libri sex* (1589), as part of a discussion of the 'obstacles' (*impedimenta*) and 'shoals' (*vada*) upon which good counsel may founder, and more especially of the dangers posed by *affectus* (emotion, passion, affect), of which the prime example for Lipsius is anger (*ira*).[21] The ability to handle public affairs – to steer the ship of state – is here dependent on self-control and self-restraint, and in particular on the overcoming of private interest, including obstinacy (*contumacia*), personal enmity (*privati odii pertinacia*) and the pursuit of private wealth (*avaritia*). If we are to dispense sound, prudent advice, we must first prevent ourselves from becoming a mere 'plaything of the winds'.[22]

For Montaigne, similarly, the passionate and impulsive man does not belong to himself. He is 'conduct[ed]' and 'possess[ed]' by a 'violent and tyrannical intention', tossed about and carried away by powerful and unruly forces. The man who governs his will, by contrast, displays the measured control of a skilled fencer or horseman: his ability to regulate himself is mirrored in his mastery of the tasks entrusted to him. Liberty and active participation in public life here seem rather to complement than to contradict one another: far from precluding a public career, freedom is here a precondition for it.

One way of explaining the tension between the two passages is to treat Montaigne's self-presentation as thinly disguised self-promotion.[23] His purported lack of ambition and his capacity for dispassionate involvement, it could be argued, are two sides of the same disingenuous coin: for all his protestations of disinterest, both serve to recommend him for public office. There is probably an element of truth in this claim: as we noted in the introduction to this chapter, Montaigne's 'retirement' ought not to

20 B'Nous ne conduisons jamais bien la chose de laquelle nous sommes possedez et conduicts. | C*Malè cuncta ministrat* | *Impetus* [Statius, *Thebaid*, 10.704–5]. | BCeluy qui n'y employe que son jugement, et son addresse, il y procede plus gayement: il feint, il ploye, il differe tout à son aise, selon le besoing des occasions: il faut d'atteinte, sans tourment, et sans affliction, prest et entier pour une nouvelle entreprinse: il marche tousjours la bride à la main. En celuy qui est enyvré de cette intention violente et tyrannique, on voit par necessité beaucoup d'imprudence et d'injustice. L'impetuosité de son desir l'emporte. Ce sont mouvemens temeraires, et, si fortune n'y preste beaucoup, de peu de fruict'. III.10: P 1053, V 1007–8, F 770.

21 Lipsius 2004, III.6, p. 362.

22 'Quia ludibrium profecto ventis debet, quisquis non cavet'. Lipsius 2004, III.5, p. 360.

23 For a persuasive reading of *On presumption* along these lines, see Farquhar 1995.

be interpreted too literally. Yet it would be both simplistic and unfair to reduce his meditations on retreat to mere rhetorical posturing.

The asymmetry between the two passages is partly a matter of emphasis and a reflection of their different textual contexts. The pretext of *On vanity* is to defend Montaigne's journey to Italy from September 1580 to November 1581, whereas *On managing the will* centres on his period of office as Mayor of Bordeaux from 1582 to 1585. Nor should the tension between these two chapters be overstated: Montaigne's reflections on exile and engagement are consistent in their suspicion towards public life and in their insistence that public office is a dangerous, although sometimes unavoidable, undertaking.

At the deepest level, however, the *Essais* offer two contrasting accounts of the proper relationship between liberty and the active life. On the one hand, the *arriereboutique*, the tower library, the estate and the text itself are imagined as a shelter and escape, both literal and symbolic, from a threatening and enslaving world: these are the spaces into which one withdraws, the only corners of the world in which we can be said to be free. On the other, these spaces are imagined as an inner equilibrium or anchor, equipping us for public service by allowing us to act in the world without placing our liberty under threat.[24]

Montaigne's reflections on the problem of public engagement draw on two distinct but related notions of independence. In the first instance, to be free is to be governed and ruled by none other than oneself: it is the mark of the man who refuses to live by another man's favour, and whose judgment, speech and conduct are his own, instead of being mortgaged or sold to another. This understanding of liberty as a condition of personhood and independent agency is essentially juridical in origin and in character. Self-possession is not only, however, about releasing oneself from subjection to and domination by other men. It is also about withdrawing our attention and care from a dangerous and turbulent world, curbing those desires that take us away from ourselves, and learning to live for ourselves. In this perspective, freedom consists in disengaging our will from all that is not in our power, and allowing it to rest within ourselves. Liberty, in this second and more immediately ethical sense, is a matter of psychological rather than forensic independence, grounded in self-knowledge and self-care, rather than self-jurisdiction.

[24] See Timothy Hampton's recent description of Montaigne's project of self-representation as a 'struggle to define a position for the subject that is both politically engaged and psychologically and emotionally disengaged'. Hampton 2006, p. 34.

These two conceptions of freedom – as a juridical or forensic quality, and as an ethical or psychological state – are inseparably connected for Montaigne: it is only by withdrawing into ourselves and understanding what is properly ours that we are able to free ourselves from subjection to others. At the most fundamental level, they are united by a common preoccupation with the status of the will. Liberty, in this perspective, is about owning oneself, as opposed to living at the mercy of someone or something other than oneself. It is about being one's own man, in one's own power, instead of being mastered.

This understanding of self-possession as a property of the will is all but absent from existing studies of the *Essais*. Hugo Friedrich seems to have had something along these lines in mind when he wrote, in connection to *On solitude*, of Montaigne's 'inner chamber of self-possession and self-regulation' and of his commitment to 'the soul being with itself, gathering itself upon itself, assuring itself of its own inclinations and strengths'.[25] Similarly, in a recent study of Montaigne's political engagement, Frédéric Brahami glosses 'être à soi' as 'to possess oneself, to belong to nobody, to not enslave one's contentment "to the power of others"'.[26] The vast majority of scholars, however, have taken 'I own myself' to mean not 'I am my own master', but 'I am my own property'. 'Estre à soy', in this perspective, points towards a 'bourgeois' or 'liberal' understanding of the self as a form of private property.

This approach reflects a wider concern to connect the emergence of modern modes of self-awareness to the rise of capitalist ideology. For Stephen Greenblatt, for example, the 'crucial consideration' in Renaissance understandings of identity is not biological and psychic continuity but 'ownership', in the sense that selfhood is understood as a form of private property and as a title to wider material possessions. The trial of Arnaud du Tilh, the famous impostor who impersonated Martin Guerre, involves 'the community's determination that this particular body possesses by right a particular identity and hence a particular set of possessions'. In Shakespeare as in English parish records, 'purse and person are [. . .] inseparably linked'. Renaissance identities are 'communally secured proprietary rights to a name and a place in an increasingly mobile social world', witnesses to an understanding of 'identity *as* property'.[27]

[25] 'Innenraum des Selbstbesitzes und der Selbstgesetzlichkeit'. 'Besichselbersein der Seele, eine Sammlung auf sich selbst, ein Sich-Vergewissern der eigenen Neigungen und Kräfte'. Friedrich 1949, p. 233. English translation adapted from Friedrich 1991, p. 247.

[26] 'Se posséder soi-même, n'appartenir à personne, ne pas asservir son contentement "à la puissance d'autrui"'. Brahami 2006, p. 41. Brahami is here quoting from I.38: P 247, V 243, F 179.

[27] Greenblatt 2007, pp. 192, 184, 189, 190.

One of Montaigne's few appearances in *Renaissance self-fashioning* is telling in its insistence that inward-looking selfhood is inextricably intertwined with the trappings of bourgeois individualism. For Greenblatt, the *arriereboutique*

> conjures up a world of *negotium*, in effect a world of private property. If Montaigne counsels a retreat from the world, he is, at the same time, assuming its existence; that is, his sense of self is inseparable from his sense of the *boutique* and all it represents. We are returned forcefully to More's insight in *Utopia* that there is an essential relationship between private property and private selves.[28]

To have a self is, in this light, dependent on a distinctly proprietary stance towards the world, and towards one's own humanity. Montaigne's sense of self is a product of what C. B. Macpherson termed 'possessive individualism': *negotium*, the classical opposite of *otium* or learned leisure, here takes on an inescapably capitalist meaning.[29]

This analysis of self-possession as a proto-capitalist 'property in one's person' has been advanced in a number of recent studies of the *Essais*. Louis van Delft has characterised Montaigne as 'the founder and steadfast supporter of what could be termed "interior capitalism"'.[30] 'Estre à soy', in this reading, translates the principles of capital accumulation to the sphere of ethics, as an 'economy of the self' grounded in 'economic deliberation'.[31] Montaigne pleads for 'a judicious management of the self, of that precarious and fragile plot of being that has momentarily fallen to our share. The self is considered as *capital*. [. . .] Therein lies the meaning of the famous formula: "I *have* nothing that is *mine* but myself"'.[32] Van Delft underlines the roots of such claims in ancient ethical *loci communes*, but does not shy away from a more Weberian interpretation: 'Montaigne weighs, he evaluates each action before engaging himself. [. . .] If this measure of the scope of each "pledge" hearkens back to that very old opposition between *vita activa* and *vita contemplativa*, it is not without reminding us of the bourgeois mentality that, precisely at the time of the *Essais*, is acquiring some of its characteristic traits'.[33]

28 Greenblatt 1980, pp. 46–7. 29 Macpherson 1962.

30 'Le fondateur et le tenant indéfectible de ce qu'on pourrait appeler le "capitalisme intérieur"'. Van Delft 1990, p. 48.

31 'Économie du moi'. 'Delibération économique'. Van Delft 1990, pp. 41, 47.

32 'Une judicieuse gestion du moi, de cette précaire et fragile parcelle d'être qui nous est momentanément échue en partage. Le moi est considéré comme *capital*. [. . .] C'est là le sens de la célèbre formule: "Je n'*ai* rien *mien* que moi" [Van Delft's italics]'. Van Delft 1990, p. 46. Van Delft is here quoting III.9: P 1013, V 968, F 740.

33 'Montaigne soupèse, il évalue toute action avant de s'engager. [. . .] Si cette mesure de la portée de toute "engageure" renvoie à la très ancienne opposition entre *vita activa* et *vita contemplativa*, elle

In a similar vein, Constance Jordan presents Montaigne as the spokesman of a new, recently ennobled merchant class and as the exponent of 'a liberal politics of the individual, based on recognizing a man as having a property in himself and therefore self-owned'.[34] According to Jordan, Montaigne takes himself to be free of all natural obligations to other individuals and to the state. He claims to 'own' himself, in the sense that he has a right to dispose of himself at will – to serve others only where he has voluntarily agreed to do so, in exactly the same way as it is his exclusive and inalienable right to dispose of his material property. In other words, Montaigne adheres to a political ideology of 'self-ownership' commonly (but, as Janet Coleman has shown, disputably) associated with Locke, and of continuing appeal in modern-day, right-wing libertarian discourse.[35] Montaigne thereby distinguishes his own career of public service, in which the exclusive property he has in himself is contractually leased to the use of the prince, from a life of political servitude (or feudal serfdom), in which one's powers of judgment and will are permanently forfeited.[36]

In the Introduction, I suggested that freedom, as Montaigne presents it, is best understood as an aspect of aristocratic rather than bourgeois ideology. Montaigne's 'self', according to scholars such as Jordan and Van Delft, is a private commodity, to be preserved at all costs from outside interference and usurpation by other men or by the state. Yet liberty is clearly identified in the *Essais* with a refusal to be *mastered*, a refusal to surrender one's will to the power of others. Coercion and constraint are presented as deeply antipathetic to Montaigne's character, but it is dependency – the fact of having a master, of living in subjection to someone or something other than ourselves – that constitutes the deepest and most basic affront to his liberty.

There is no doubt that Montaigne takes the fact of being fettered or forced to be an infringement of his freedom. Images of confinement and chains abound in the *Essais*. His polemic against the jurisprudence of his times, in *On experience*, leads him to reflect that the mere sight of a prison, even from the outside, is intolerable to him: [B]'I am so sick for liberty that if anyone should forbid me access to some corner of the Indies, I should live distinctly less comfortably. [. . .] All my little prudence in these civil wars, in which we are now involved, is employed to keep them from interrupting

n'est pas non plus sans rappeler la mentalité marchande, bourgeoise, qui, précisément du temps des *Essais*, acquiert quelques-uns de ses traits les plus caractéristiques'. Van Delft 1990, p. 46.

34 Jordan 2003, p. 432.

35 Coleman 2005. For a critique of contemporary arguments about self-ownership, see Cohen 1995.

36 See also Schaefer 1990, pp. 315–21.

my liberty of coming and going'.[37] In *On vanity*, meanwhile, the image of a man who is physically jostled and constrained by a crowd provides a vivid analogy for the restrictions and pressures imposed by public life:

> [B]He who walks in the crowd, must step aside, keep his elbows in, step back or advance, even leave the straight way, according to what he encounters: He must live not so much according to himself, as according to others, not according to what he proposes to himself, but according to what others propose to him, according to the time, according to the men, according to the business.[38]

This emphasis on unconstrained movement, on having space in which to manoeuvre, echoes Montaigne's claim, earlier in the chapter, that the [C]'bond of an obligation' is a 'cruel stranglehold for a man who likes to free up elbow room for his liberty in all directions'.[39] The idea of freedom of movement is indeed fundamental to the chapter as a whole, which offers an extended apology for Montaigne's restless appetite for travel and for the wandering motion of his own text: [C]'my style and my mind alike go a-roaming'.[40]

This antipathy towards confinement is paralleled by an equally visceral hatred of compulsion. In *On the education of children*, he writes that his own upbringing was conducted in such a way as to make him [A]'taste knowledge and duty' of his 'own unforced will and desire', his 'soul' being educated 'in all gentleness and liberty, without rigour and constraint'.[41] This [A]'mild and free fashion, exempt from rigorous subjection',[42] he complains in *On presumption*, has taught him to chafe against all manner of prescription and command, such that his actions are successful only when moved by 'some pleasure' and by his 'own pure and free will'.[43] His soul is [A]'<free and> all its own, accustomed to conducting itself in its own way'. Having had 'neither forced governor nor master to this day', he has become 'soft

37 [B]'Je suis si affady après la liberté, que qui me deffendroit l'accez de quelque coin des Indes, j'en vivrois aucunement plus mal à mon aise. [. . .] Toute ma petite prudence, en ces guerres civiles où nous sommes, s'employe à ce, qu'elles n'interrompent ma liberté d'aller et venir'. III.13: P 1119, V 1072, F 820–1.

38 [B]'Celuy qui va en la presse, il faut qu'il gauchisse, qu'il serre ses couddes, qu'il recule, ou qu'il avance, voire qu'il quitte le droict chemin, selon ce qu'il rencontre: Qu'il vive non tant selon soy, que selon autruy: non selon ce qu'il se propose, mais selon ce qu'on luy propose: selon le temps, selon les hommes, selon les affaires.' III.9: P 1037, V 991, F 758.

39 [C]'L'engageure d'une obligation [. . .] Cruel garrotage, à qui ayme d'affranchir les coudées de sa liberté, en tout sens'. III.9: P 1014, V 1097, F 740.

40 [C]'Mon stile et mon esprit vont vagabondant de mesmes'. III.9: P 1041, V 994, F 761.

41 [A]'De me faire gouster la science et le devoir, par une volonté non forcée, et de mon propre desir; et d'eslever mon ame en toute douceur et liberté, sans rigueur et contrainte'. I.25: P 181, V 174, F 129.

42 [A]'Une façon molle et libre, [. . .] exempte de subjection rigoureuse'. II.17: P 682, V 643, F 488.

43 [A]'Par quelque plaisir, [. . .] ma pure et libre volonté'. II.17: P 680, V 642, F 487.

and useless for serving others, and no good to anyone' but himself.[44] Like a [C]'restive and wind-broken horse', he has taken charge of other people's affairs only 'on condition of managing them at [his] own times and in [his] own way, commissioned by people who trusted [him] and did not press [him], and knew [him]'.[45] Further on in this chapter, we learn that this aversion to command is so deeply ingrained that Montaigne is himself unable to press himself into action against his will: [A]'I flee command, obligation, and constraint. What I do easily and naturally, I can no longer do if I order myself to do it by strict and express command.'[46] His memory and his sexual organs fail under the pressure of advance urging, weakened and repulsed by the suggestion of [A]'necessary service' and 'constrained and tyrannical preordinance'.[47]

The dominant emphasis of the *Essais*, however, falls not on coercion and interference as impediments to free action, but on *dependency* as a source of slavery. This order of priorities becomes clear if we return to *On vanity*. The 'cruel stranglehold' suffered by 'the man who likes to free up elbow room for his liberty in all directions', when read in the context of the passage as a whole, turns out to refer not to a limit imposed on his power to act, but to a state of subjection, an alienation suffered by the will. The quotation forms part of an extended complaint about the uncertainty and dependency experienced by Montaigne as a result of the civil wars. His house, we are told, [B]'has always been free, ~~open~~ [C]very accessible [B]and at any one's service'. It has therefore won 'considerable popular affection', and remained miraculously 'virgin of blood and pillage' amid so much local disturbance and unrest. Yet Montaigne is deeply troubled by the fact that he owes this lucky escape not to 'the protection of the laws' but to the good will of other men: 'as things stand, I live more than half, by others' favour: which is a harsh obligation. I do not want to owe my safety, either to the kindness, and goodness of the great, who approve of my obedience to the laws and my liberty: or to the easy ways of my predecessors and myself'.[48]

44 [A]'Une ame libre et toute sienne, accoustumée à se conduire à sa ~~poste~~ <mode> N'ayant eu jusques à cett' heure ny commandant ny maistre forcé [. . .]. Cela m'a amolli et rendu inutile au service d'autruy, et ne m'a faict bon qu'à moy'. II.17: P 681, V 643, F 487.

45 [C]'En condition de les manier à mon heure et à ma façon: commis par gents, qui s'en fioyent à moy, et qui ne me pressoyent pas, et me cognoissoyent'. 'Un cheval restif et poussif'. II.17: P 681–2, V 643, F 488.

46 [A]'Je fuis le commandement, l'obligation, et la contrainte. Ce que je fais aysement et naturellement, si je m'ordonne de la faire, par une expresse et prescrite ordonnance, je ne sçay plus le faire.' II.17: P 688, V 650, F 493.

47 [A]'Service necessaire [. . .] preordonnnance contraincte et tyrannique'. II.17: P 688, V 649–50, F 493.

48 [B]'De tout temps libre, ~~ouverte,~~ [C]de grand abbord, [B]et officieuse à chacun'. 'Assez d'affection populaire'. 'Vierge de sang, et de sac'. 'Me desplait d'estre hors la protection des loix, et soubs autre

To depend on others in this way is to be condemned to a state of subjection. When we are under obligation to others, our will ceases to be our own, and to alienate one's will is to alienate oneself. That is, of course, the definition of a slave: a man who belongs to another rather than to himself.

[B]I hold that we should live by right, and by authority, not [C]by reward or [B]favour. How many gallant men have preferred to lose their lives, than to owe them? I shun to submit myself to any manner of obligation. But especially to any that attaches me by a debt of honour. I find nothing so dear, as that which is given to me: and for which, my will remains mortgaged by the title of ingratitude: And I more willingly receive offices, that are for sale. Rightly so I think: For the latter I give only money: for the others, I give myself.[49]

The word 'mortgaged' here takes on its full connotations, as a form of subjugation as well as expropriation – placing us quite literally *en gage*, on pledge, as if we had pawned ourselves to others. Those men who 'engage' themselves so easily to others by accepting favours from them, Montaigne continues, would not do so [C]'<if they relished>', as he does, '<the sweetness of a pure liberty, and> if they weighed the bond [*engageure*] of an obligation as much as a wise man ought' – if, like him, they had 'conceived a mortal hatred of being bound [*tenu*] either to another or by another than myself'.[50] To live by favour is to be under the power of another: [C]'as giving is an ambitious quality and a prerogative, so is accepting a quality of submission'.[51] It is the mere fact of living under obligation, of being in debt to others, that reduces us to a condition of slavery.

The point is not to obtain greater latitude for the unimpeded fulfilment of our desires, but to achieve self-sufficiency through continence, by teaching our soul [C]'to be contented with itself and manfully to do without the

sauvegarde que la leur. Comme les choses sont, je vis plus qu'à demy, de la faveur d'autruy: qui est une rude obligation. Je ne veux debvoir ma seureté, ny à la bonté, et benignité des grands, qui s'aggréent de ma legalité et liberté: ny à la facilité des mœurs de mes predecesseurs, et miennes.' III.9: P 1010–11, V 965–6, F 738.

49 [B]'Je tiens, qu'il faut vivre par droict, et par auctorité, non par [C]recompense ny par [B]grace. Combien de galans hommes ont mieux aymé perdre la vie, que la devoir? Je fuis à me submettre à toute sorte d'obligation. Mais sur tout, à celle qui m'attache, par devoir d'honneur. Je ne trouve rien si cher, que ce qui m'est donné: et ce pourquoy, ma volonté demeure hypothequée par tiltre d'ingratitude: Et reçois plus volontiers les offices, qui sont à vendre. Je croy bien: Pour ceux-cy je ne donne que de l'argent: pour les autres, je me donne moy-mesme'. III.9: P 1011, V 966, F 738.

50 [C]'Ceux que je voy si familierement employer tout chacun et s'y engager: ne le feroient pas, <s'ils sçavouroient comme moy la douceur d'une pure liberté: et> s'ils poisoient autant que doit poiser à un sage homme, l'engageure d'une obligation. [. . .] Par tout cela, j'ay prins à haine mortelle, d'estre tenu ny à autre, ny par autre que moy'. III.9: P 1014, V 969, F 740.

51 [C]'Comme le donner est qualité ambitieuse, et de prerogative, aussi est l'accepter qualité de summission'. III.9: P 1014, V 969, F 740.

comforts that come to it from outside, when fate so ordains'.[52] In seeking to shore up his liberty, by freeing himself of all debts and obligations, Montaigne's aim is not to preserve his 'interior capital' from depredation and invasion, but to curb and restrain the centripetal forces of ambition and desire. As far as he understands [B]'the science of benefaction and gratitude', he continues a few pages later, 'I see no one freer and less indebted, than I am up to this point'. All that he owes, he owes simply [B]'to the ordinary and natural obligations'. His point is not that he is free of all obligations to the state or to society, but that he has not allowed himself to be bought, to become a bondsman: [B]'*the gifts of the powerful are to me unknown*. Princes [C]give me plenty if they take nothing from me, and [B]do me enough good when they do me no harm'.[53]

Freedom, for Montaigne, does not simply designate a sphere of action and existence that is free from interference or trespass. It names the condition of the man who acts, thinks and speaks independently, by virtue of the fact that he is his own master; indeed, it is a condition of being an agent or person in the first place, as opposed to another man's creature or instrument. Liberty consists in having a 'pure and free will', that is, an independent will, a will of one's own: it is about belonging to oneself, instead of owing one's tranquillity and security to others. The free man has cast off the yoke of tutelage and subordination, by refusing to live by favour or by grace. He lives under his own will, rather than under the will of another.

III

This characterisation of freedom as a condition of self-jurisdiction is, in certain crucial respects, powerfully illuminated by the work of Philip Pettit and Quentin Skinner.[54] These scholars contrast an entrenched, liberal understanding of freedom as the mere absence of impediments, a view which finds its classical expression in the work of Thomas Hobbes, with a 'neo-Roman' or 'republican' concept of liberty, 'in which the antonym is not interference as such but rather [. . .] domination', defined as

[52] [C]'De se contenter d'elle, et se passer virilement des commoditez qui luy viennent du dehors, quand le sort l'ordonne'. III.9: P 1013, V 969, F 740.

[53] [B]'Selon que je m'entends en la science du bien-faict et de recognoissance, [. . .] je ne vois personne, plus libre et moins endebté, que je suis jusques à cette heure. Ce que je doibs, je le doibs simplement aux obligations communes et naturelles. [. . .] | *nec sunt mihi nota potentum* | *Munera* [adapted from Virgil, *Aeneid*, XII, 519–20]. | Les Princes [C]me donnent prou, s'ils ne m'ostent rien: et [B]me font assez de bien, quand ils ne me font point de mal'. III.9: P 1013, V 968, F 739.

[54] Pettit 1997 and 2002; Skinner 1998, 2002a, 2006, 2008a and 2008b.

'subjection to an arbitrary power of interference on the part of another – a *dominus* or master – even another who chooses not actually to exercise that power'.[55]

This understanding of liberty, which dominated sixteenth and early seventeenth-century discussions of public service, power and moral agency, was built not on the difference between self and others, or between individual and society, but on a foundational Roman law distinction between freemen and slaves. To be a slave, according to the rubric 'De statu hominum', is to be subject to another's will, to be within the power of a master (*in potestate dominorum*, *in dominio alieno* or *in alieno iure*). The freeman, by contrast, has his own will: he is able to act *sui iuris* ('in his own right'), being responsible for his conduct and speech to no one but himself.[56] He may be said to own his actions or to be his own man. As Skinner puts it, 'the condition of self-ownership is equated with the ability to act according to one's will, and hence with the ability to 'own' (i.e., take responsibility for) the consequences of one's actions. [. . .] What it means to have full property in yourself [. . .] is simply to act independently of the arbitrary will of anyone else'.[57]

This understanding of freedom is central to the *Discours de la servitude volontaire*, or *Contr'un*, a polemical tract [A]'in honour of liberty against tyrants' of special significance to Montaigne, who attributed it to his late friend Estienne de La Boétie, describing it in the *Essais* as the 'means of our first acquaintance', and comparing his own writings to a collection of mere 'grotesques and monstrous bodies' designed to surround La Boétie's masterpiece.[58] The voluntary servitude in question is the unthinking subjection of an entire nation to the tyranny of a single man, a servitude which is voluntary in the sense that it depends only on our will to free ourselves from it. To be a slave is to be dependent on the good will and kindness of one's master; to live, act and speak on condition of his favour: 'to speak in earnest, it is a great misfortune to be subject to a master of whose goodness one can never be assured, since it is always in his power to be bad when he wants to'.[59]

55 Pettit 2002, p. 340.

56 Mommsen and Krueger 1985, vol. I, I.5. (*De statu hominum*) and I.6 (*De his qui sui vel alieni iuris sunt*).

57 Skinner 2006, pp. 164–5.

58 [A]'À l'honneur de la liberté contre les tyrans'. 'Moyen à nostre premiere accointance'. 'Crotesques et corps monstrueux'. I.27: P 189–90, V 183–4, F 135–6. On Montaigne and the *Discours*, see Tournon 1990 and Gray 2004.

59 'À parler à bon escient, c'est un extreme malheur d'estre subject à un maistre duquel on ne se peut jamais asseurer qu'il soit bon puis qu'il est tousjours en sa puissance d'estre mauvais quand il voudra'. La Boétie 1987, p. 33.

In this subjection, we have nothing left which we can call our own, because everything we possess is dependent upon the arbitrary will of another:

> What a vice, or rather what an unfortunate vice, to see an infinite number of persons not only obeying, but serving, not only being governed but tyrannised, having neither goods, nor relatives, nor wives nor children nor even their life belonging to themselves.[60]

This condition of servitude is at its most wretched, however, not for the simple labourer or artisan, but for those closest to the tyrant, 'soliciting and begging for his favour'.[61] These ambitious and avaricious men hope to 'have a share in the bounty and to become, under the great tyrant, tyrantlets themselves'.[62] Yet it is they, more than anyone else who live as slaves, living by and for the favour of their master rather than themselves:

> It is not enough for them to obey him, they must also please him, they must break themselves, they must torment themselves, they must kill themselves in labouring in his business, and then they must find pleasure in his pleasure, they must abandon their own taste for his, they must force their complexion, and undo their natural character.[63]

To live in this condition of subjection is to give all that is ours and all that is us up to another, to substitute his will for ours: 'what condition is more wretched than to live thus, having nothing that is one's own, holding one's ease, liberty, body and life from another?'[64]

What Montaigne and the neo-Roman tradition have in common is an aspiration to a certain vision of moral selfhood: a vision of the free man as the man who has no master, the man who lives under his own will, the man who owns himself. In what we have come to think of as the liberal tradition, freedom is a predicate of actions: to be free is nothing more than to be able to act freely. Montaigne, by contrast, describes freedom (alongside idleness) as his 'ruling quality', defining the kind of man he

[60] 'Quel vice, ou plustost quel malheureux vice, voir un nombre infini de personnes non pas obéir, mais servir, non pas estre gouvernés mais tirannisés, n'aians ni biens, ni parens, femmes ny enfans ni leur vie mesme qui soit à eux'. La Boétie 1987, p. 35.

[61] 'Coquinans et mendians sa faveur'. La Boétie 1987, p. 70.

[62] 'Avoir part au butin et estre sous le grand tiran tiranneaus eusmesmes'. La Boétie 1987, p. 68.

[63] 'Ce n'est pas tout à eus de lui obeir, il faut ancore lui complaire, il faut qu'ils se rompent, qu'ils se tourmentent, qu'ils se tuent à travailler en ses affaires, et puis qu'ils se plaisent de son plaisir, qu'ils laissent leur goust pour le sien, qu'ils forcent leur complexion, qu'ils despouillent leur naturel'. La Boétie 1987, p. 69.

[64] 'Quelle condition est plus miserable que de vivre ainsi, qu'on n'ait rien à soy, tenant d'autrui son aise, sa liberté, son corps et sa vie?' La Boétie 1987, p. 70.

wants and takes himself to be. His freedom is forfeited by the mere fact of being obligated (i.e., in debt) to another – by the mere fact of his will being mortgaged (by gratitude as much as by fear) to that of another. This characterisation of liberty as a property of Montaigne's person shifts attention away from the conditions that shape his ability to perform, or refrain from, specific actions (whether these are framed under the category of interference or under that of domination), towards a consideration of his own status as an agent, and in particular of his relationship to princes and powerful men.

Montaigne does not, however, subscribe to the political theory of self-rule with which the 'neo-Roman' concept of liberty has come to be associated. Skinner has always emphasised, it is true, that there is nothing exclusively *republican* about the claim that liberty consists in nondomination: although no early modern writer 'who professed to be a republican (in the strict sense of an opponent of monarchy)' contested that definition, 'it was also espoused by thinkers (for example, John Locke) who would have been shocked to hear themselves described as republican in their political allegiances'.[65] The crux of the neo-Roman account lies instead, he argues, in its attack on the presence of arbitrary or discretionary power within the commonwealth. It follows directly from this view, however, that the liberty of the individual can be secured only through participation in a self-determining polity: the legal state of self-ownership, as Skinner defines it, is the distinctive property of the citizen.[66]

The *Essais* evidently do not belong to that tradition of political thought linking the civic ideology of the ancient Roman republic, the city-republics of Renaissance Italy, the political debates of the English civil war, and the foundation of the American republic. In the first place, and this is an obvious point, the text is not a political work. But even if one were to read it as such, in violation of Montaigne's insistence that he studies no subject but himself, one would find that he has relatively little to say about government, except to condemn the vanity of political philosophy, to present himself as a loyal subject of the French monarchy, and to distance himself from all efforts to challenge or reform the existing constitution of the state.

65 Skinner 2008b, p. ix.

66 In other words, political participation is a *precondition* for the preservation of individual liberty. As Philip Petitt has emphasized, however, for these early modern writers, freedom was not 'definitionally tied' to 'participation in a self-determining polity': liberty is not in itself *identified* with political participation. Pettit 2002, pp. 339–40.

Montaigne, as we have seen, is deeply troubled by the mechanisms of ambition, favour and dependency. But the way to liberty, according to the *Essais*, lies not in a constitution which protects citizens from domination, but in a practice of retreat and self-regulation allowing us to disentangle ourselves, both physically and mentally, from our public servitude. He stops short of advocating a life of pure *otium*, dispensing with all public duties and offices. Yet it is only by withdrawing his will, as much as he can, from a world ruled by opinion, fortune and public necessity – by stepping back, if only symbolically, from 'the servitude of the court and of public charges' – that he is able to preserve his liberty.

In Montaigne's hands, accordingly, the juridical terminology of neo-Roman liberty unites with the moral language of Stoic freedom. In *On physiognomy*, for example, he writes that [B]'true freedom consists in having power over oneself for everything', a declaration to which he later adds a sentence from Seneca's *Epistulae* (110.34): [C]'he is most powerful who is in his own power' (*qui se habet in potestate*).[67] Slavery (and Montaigne is here quoting from Cicero's *Paradoxa stoicorum*) is [C]'the obedience of a broken and abject soul, lacking its own will' (*arbitrio carentis suo*).[68]

Montaigne's relationship to La Boétie's text, moreover, is steeped in ambiguity. He begins by telling us that he has decided to include the *Discours* as the centrepiece both of *On friendship* and of the *Essais* as a whole. At the end of the chapter, however, he performs an abrupt and anticlimactic *volte-face*, unexpectedly announcing that he has decided not to print the tract after all because it has already been published [A]'with evil intent, by those who seek to trouble and change the state of our polity, without worrying whether they will improve it'.[69] This reference to the inclusion of the text, either in part or in its entirety, in a number of radical Huguenot publications put together in the mid-1570s[70] leads to a lengthy

67 [B]'La vraye liberté c'est pouvoir toute chose sur soy'. III.12: P 1092, V 1046, F 800.

68 Cicero, *Paradoxa stoicorum*, 35. On the Bordeaux Copy, Montaigne began by inserting this quotation into *On physiognomy*, immediately after the passage from Seneca. He then deleted it, however, moving it to *On vanity*, III.9: P 998, V 958, F 728.

69 [A]'À mauvaise fin, par ceux qui cherchent à troubler et changer l'estat de nostre police, sans se soucier s'ils l'amenderont'. I.27: P 201, V 194, F 144.

70 Two fragments from *De la servitude volontaire* were used in the Protestant pamphlet *Dialogi ab Eusebio Philadelphio cosmopolita* ([Anonymous] 1574a), which was immediately translated into French under the title of *Reveille-matin des François* ([Anonymous] 1574b). The tract was first published in its entirety in the third volume of Simon Goulart's collection, *Mémoires de l'estat de France, sous Charles Neufiesme* ([Goulart] 1577). Soon after, it reappeared by itself under the title of *Vive description de la tyrannie, et des tyrans, avec les moyens de se garantir de leur joug* ([Anonymous] 1577). See Trinquet 1964.

and enigmatic defence of La Boétie's memory against any such association with sedition.

[A]And so that the memory of the author may not be damaged in the eyes of those who could not know his opinions and actions at close hand: I advise them that this subject was treated by him in his childhood, only by way of exercise, as a common theme hashed over in a thousand places in books. I have no doubt that he believed what he wrote: for he was so conscientious, as not to lie even in jest: and I know further that if he had had the choice, he would rather have been born in Venice than Sarlat; and with reason. But he had another maxim sovereignly imprinted in his soul, to obey and submit himself most religiously to the laws, under which he was born. There never was a better citizen, or one more devoted to the tranquillity of his country, or more hostile to the commotions and innovations of his time: he would much rather have used his ability to suppress them, than to give them material that would excite them further. His mind was moulded in the pattern of other ages than this.[71]

How are we to make sense of this ambiguous passage, and of Montaigne's strange insistence on drawing attention to a text that he then denies to the reader?

Montaigne's characterisation of his late friend as an enemy of political unrest is not, it should be said, inconsistent with the tone of the *Discours*, which reads as a plea for lucidity and bitter counsel of despair, rather than as a call to arms.[72] The central theme of the text is that the power of the tyrant is a product of the people's collusion in their own slavery. A single man cannot compel a whole nation to submit to him by force: the people have instead allowed themselves to be dazzled and duped. In order to recover our liberty, it follows, we need not overthrow or challenge the tyrant, but only refuse him our consent:

There is no need to fight him, there is no need to undo him: he is undone by himself, as soon as the nation stops consenting to its slavery. There is no need to

71 [A]'Et affin que la memoire de l'autheur n'en soit interessée en l'endroit de ceux qui n'ont peu cognoistre de près ses opinions et ses actions: je les advise que ce subject fut traicté par luy en son enfance, par maniere d'exercitation seulement, comme subject vulgaire et tracassé en mil endroits des livres. Je ne fay nul doubte qu'il ne creust ce qu'il escrivoit: car il estoit assez conscientieux, pour ne mentir pas mesmes en se jouant: et sçay d'avantage que s'il eust eu à choisir, il eust mieux aymé estre nay à Venise qu'à Sarlac; et avec raison: Mais il avoit un' autre maxime souverainement empreinte en son ame, d'obeyr et de se soubmettre très-religieusement aux loix, sous lesquelles il estoit nay. Il ne fut jamais un meilleur citoyen, ny plus affectionné au repos de son païs, ny plus ennemy des remuements et nouvelletez de son temps: il eust bien plustost employé sa suffisance à les esteindre, qu'à leur fournir dequoy les emouvoir d'avantage: il avoit son esprit moulé au patron d'autres siecles que ceux-cy'. I. 27: P 201, V 194, F 144.

72 This point is also made by Fumaroli 1984, pp. 27–8.

take anything from him, but only to give him nothing. [. . .] In order to have freedom we need only desire it.[73]

And yet what hope can there be of rousing slaves from their slumbers, when they have fallen so low as to cherish their own chains? 'Liberty alone, men do not desire, and for no other reason, it seems, than that if they did desire it, they would already have it'.[74] There are always a few, 'better born that the others', who 'never tame themselves to subjection'.[75] As a general rule, however, 'as soon as it is subjected, the people suddenly falls into such a profound oblivion of freedom, that it is not possible that it should wake itself to regain it'.[76]

'Montaigne's defense of his friend's loyalty to his country', it has been suggested, 'resembles the rhetoric by which [. . .] the essayist seeks to obscure the revolutionary import of his own teaching'.[77] This approach relies on dismissing much of what Montaigne says as window dressing designed to deflect the suspicion of conservative readers.[78] His recurrent appeals for obedience and conformity to the established legal order, on this Straussian account, are concessions to the threat of censorship and prosecution, to be discounted in favour of a hidden, subversive message: a radical commitment to kingless government. But this is to obliterate the complexity of the position that Montaigne is trying to elaborate. La Boétie, he writes, would have preferred Venice, that symbol of republican liberty, to Sarlat, his actual birthplace in the Périgord – 'and with reason'. Yet the demon lies in the qualifying phrase: 'if he had had the choice'. La Boétie may have yearned for Venice – or indeed, as the final sentence in the excerpt suggests, for 'other ages than this' – but, exiled in the present and under a monarchy, he serves the cause of peace and tranquillity. His longing for liberty marks him out as a great soul, but so does his willingness to submit to the accident of his birth, by obeying and lending his support to the laws of his country.

73 'Il n'est pas besoin de le combattre, il n'est pas besoin de le defaire: il est de soymesme defait, mais que le païs ne consente à sa servitude. Il ne faut pas luy oster rien, mais ne luy donner rien. [. . .] Pour avoir liberté il ne faut que la desirer'. La Boétie 1987, pp. 37–8.

74 'La seule liberté, les hommes ne la desirent point, non pour autre raison, ce semble, sinon que s'ils la desiroient ils l'auroient'. La Boétie 1987, p. 39.

75 'Mieulx nés que les autres [. . .] qui ne s'apprivoisent jamais de la sujetion'. La Boétie 1987, p. 50.

76 'Le peuple, deslors qu'il est assujetti, tombe si soudain en un tel et si profond oubly de la franchise, qu'il n'est pas possible qu'il se resveille pour la ravoir'. La Boétie 1987, p. 46.

77 Schaefer 1998, p. 14.

78 'I try to show how remarks that seem on the surface to belie my interpretation do not really do so, either because a careful reading shows their true meaning to be different from the surface one or because Montaigne directly or indirectly indicates that these remarks are not to be taken seriously'. Schaefer 1990, p. xi. Schaefer 1998 argues that Montaigne is the true author of the *Discours*.

This emphasis on the gap that separates freedom from its practical realisation recalls the pessimistic, ambivalent line of thought pursued by More in *Utopia*, with its reprisal of Seneca's claim, in *De otio*, that the commonwealth in which the philosopher may preserve and exercise his liberty is, quite literally, 'nowhere' to be found. There is truly 'no place' for the wise man within public life, on this account, at least not in any existing commonwealth.[79] The *Essais* register the full force of this Stoic critique of civic engagement. For Montaigne, however, the life of *otium*, of contemplative leisure and retreat, is no more viable an alternative that the imaginary republic described by Hythloday.

Montaigne's friendship with La Boétie, we are told, reflects the unity [A]'of one soul in two bodies, according to Aristotle's very apt definition'.[80] His apology for La Boétie can thus be read as a description of his own position as much as that of his friend: a love of liberty reconciled with disenchanted submission to the constitution of our birth. This approach finds fuller expression in *On vanity*:

> [B]We may regret better times: but not escape the present ones: we may wish for other magistrates, but we must nevertheless, obey those that are here: And perhaps there is more merit, in obeying the bad, than the good. As long as the image of the received and ancient laws of this monarchy shines in some corner, there will I be planted.[81]

This emphasis on patient obedience to the ancient and established laws – or at least to the 'image' of those laws – forms part of a wider appeal for us to detach ourselves, as far as we can, from the storm of public events and in particular from the violence and uncertainty of the civil wars. Montaigne's departure from his country, on the occasion of his travels across Europe in the early 1580s, is justified with the claim that human action has no purchase on political outcomes, which are governed by forces beyond our understanding and control. This emphasis on our powerlessness in the face of fortune leads to a repudiation of political philosophy as

79 Parrish 1997. Cf. *De otio*, VIII.3 in Seneca 1932, vol. II, p. 200: 'Quodsi non invenitur illa res publica, quam nobis fingimus, incipit omnibus esse otium necessarium, quia quod unum praeferri poterat otio, nusquam est' ('But if that state which we dream of can nowhere be found, leisure begins to be a necessity for all of us, because the one thing that might have been preferred to leisure nowhere exists').

80 [A]'Une ame en deux corps, selon la très-propre definition d'Aristote'. I.27: P 197, V 190, F 141. Cf. *Nicomachean ethics*, IX.8.2, 1168b (Aristotle 1968, p. 548).

81 [B]'On peut regretter les meilleurs temps: mais non pas fuyr aux presens: on peut desirer d'autres magistrats, mais il faut ce nonobstant, obeyr à ceux icy: Et à l'advanture y a il plus de recommendation, d'obeyr aux mauvais, qu'aux bons. Autant que l'image des loix receues, et anciennes de ceste monarchie, reluyra en quelque coin, m'y voilà planté'. III.9: P 1040, V 994, F 760.

an exercise in vain theorizing: all [B]'descriptions of government, feigned by art' are 'ridiculous and unfit to put into practice', all those 'great and long altercations about the best form of society and the rules most suitable to bind us' being fit 'only for the exercise of our minds'.[82]

Our thirst for change and reform, for Montaigne, is an expression of our inconstancy, a contagious impulse of instability hurtling states and peoples towards unknown and unpredictable disasters:

> [B]Not in theory, but in truth, the best and most excellent polity for each nation, is the one under which it has preserved itself. Its form and essential fitness depend on habit. We are prone to be discontented with the present state of things: but I maintain nevertheless, that to wish for the government of a few, in a popular state, or another type of government, in a monarchy, is vicious and foolish.
>
> *Love the state such as you find it.*
> *If it is royal, love royalty;*
> *If it is of few, or of many,*
> *Love it also, since God had you born into it.*[83]

Montaigne's stance is here one of equivocal reversibility, privileging neither monarchy nor popular government, nor indeed aristocracy, but rather a multivalent conventionalism in which custom and fortune, rather than reason, underpin political norms.

Political controversies of this kind are to be treated both with suspicion and derision, as weapons coloured by private interest and contests of power. As he puts it in *On the incommodity of greatness*:

> [B]There are few things, on which we can give a sincere judgment, because there are few, in which we have not in some fashion a private interest. Superiority and inferiority, mastery and subjection, are forced into a natural envy and contention: they must pillage one another perpetually. I do not believe either one, about the rights of its companion: let us give the floor to reason, which is inflexible and impassible, when we can prevail on her. Less than a month ago, I was leafing through two Scottish books, fighting each other on this subject. The popular one

[82] [B]'Toutes ces descriptions de police, feintes par art, se trouvent ridicules et ineptes à mettre en practique. Ces grandes et longues altercations, de la meilleure forme de la société: et des reigles plus commodes à nous attacher, sont altercations propres seulement à l'exercice de nostre esprit'. III.9: P 1001, V 957, F 730.

[83] [B]'Non par opinion, mais en verité, l'excellente et meilleure police, est à chacune nation, celle soubs laquelle elle s'est maintenue. Sa forme et commodité essentielle despend de l'usage. Nous nous desplaisons volontiers de la condition presente: Mais je tiens pourtant, que d'aller desirant le commandement de peu, en un estat populaire: ou en la monarchie, une autre espece de gouvernement, c'est vice et folie. | *Ayme l'estat tel que tu le vois estre,* | *S'il est royal, ayme la royauté,* | *S'il est de peu, ou bien communauté,* | *Ayme l'aussi, car Dieu t'y a faict naistre* [Guy de Pibrac, *Quatrains*, no. 106].' III.9: P 1001–2, V 957, F 731.

makes the King's station worse than a carter's, the monarchist lodges him several fathoms above God, in power and sovereignty.[84]

Montaigne is here referring to George Buchanan's defence of popular sovereignty in *De iure regni apud Scotos* (1579) and to Adam Blackwood's monarchist counterblast, the *Apologia pro regibus* (1581).[85] If constant, dispassionate reason were used to draw the line between the relative 'rights' of kings and subjects, as Montaigne urges, our judgment might come to rest in a middle ground between these two extreme, absurd positions. Reason, however, remains silently inaccessible, confined to the realm of hypothetical discussion ('when we can prevail on her'). Rather than attempt to resolve the conflict between carters and gods, it is better to acknowledge our impotence in such matters, and to merely 'leaf through' such texts, with an attitude of collected detachment and disinterest.

It is equally misleading, however, to see Montaigne as the advocate of a sceptical, Tacitean 'reason of state', positing a prudential, outward subject, conforming or conformed to power and deception, and a sceptical, dissident, but rigorously private self.[86] Although active resistance is decisively condemned, outward submission is not without its limits. In contrast to Lipsius, for whom the virtue of prudence must be 'mixed, a little' with 'a bit of the sediment of deceit', Montaigne casts himself as the exemplar of an ingenuous, innocent 'good faith'.[87] Far from sanctioning dissimulation (and simulation) as strategic necessities within a world of appearances and amorality, Montaigne refuses to be used as an instrument of deceit – and in doing so, as we shall see later in this chapter, he appeals above all else to his liberty.

Nor is the value of conformity left wholly unquestioned in the *Essais*. *On custom, or not easily changing an accepted law* is often read as a forceful endorsement of external subjection. But the piece also opens up an ambiguous space between the need to reject custom's tyranny over our judgment and the need to submit our conduct to her laws. In a well-known passage,

84 [B]'Il est peu de choses, ausquelles nous puissions donner le jugement syncere, parce qu'il en est peu, ausquelles en quelque façon nous n'ayons particulier interest. La superiorité et inferiorité, la maistrise et la subjection, sont obligées à une naturelle envie et contestation: il faut qu'elles s'entrepillent perpetuellement. Je ne crois ny l'une ny l'autre, des droicts de sa compagne: laissons en dire à la raison, qui est inflexible et impassible, quand nous en pourrons finer. Je feuilletois, il n'y a pas un mois, deux livres Escossois, se combattans sur se subject. Le populaire rend le Roy de pire condition qu'un charretier, le monarchique le loge quelques brasses au dessus de Dieu, en puissance et souveraineté'. III.7: P 962–3, V 918, F 701.

85 Buchanan 1579 and Blackwood 1581.

86 For versions of this view see Battista 1966, Reiss 1986, Burke 1991, Tuck 1993 and Abecassis 1995.

87 'Fasne est ut leviter misceam, et iungam aliquid e fraudiam faece? Ego puto'. Lipsius 2004, IV.13, p. 506. See *Au lecteur*: P 27, V 3, F 2 ([A]'un Livre de bonne foy').

Montaigne establishes a strict distinction between outward obedience to custom and the inner liberty of the mind: [A]'the wise man should, within, withdraw his soul from the crowd, and keep it in liberty and power to judge of things freely: but as for the outside, [. . .] he should wholly follow the accepted ways and forms'.[88] This concession to the 'empire' of custom is cast in a more problematic light, however, in an addition to the Bordeaux Copy:

> [C]Nations brought up to liberty and to ruling themselves, consider any other form of government monstrous and against nature: Those who are accustomed to monarchy do the same. And whatever easy chance fortune offers them to change, even when with great difficulties they have rid themselves of the importunity of one master, they run to supplant him with another, with similar difficulties, because they cannot make up their minds to hate mastery.[89]

The implications of this passage are strikingly double-edged. On the one hand, this appeal to custom drains constitutional allegiances of all normative value. The citizen's commitment to self-government is no less contingent and no more objectively 'natural' than the subject's unthinking loyalty to his king. Despite this apparent symmetry, however, the passage also echoes the problem posed by La Boétie: why cannot men brought up under kingship bring themselves to hate mastery? Which is more laughable: to rebel against our rightful masters on a whim, or to sink back into subjection as soon as we have rid ourselves of their yoke?

Montaigne, it should now be clear, is no republican: the only principle of political morality that he espouses without ambiguity is that our duty is to uphold the established laws of our country which, in his case, meant serving as a loyal subject of the French monarchy. Yet that longing for liberty which he ascribed to La Boétie – that yearning to be born in Venice rather than in France – is not, for all that, invalidated. In a striking passage towards the close of *On vanity*, Montaigne reflects on his sense of kinship with the ancient world – and, in particular, with republican Rome. He claims to have [B]'started a hundred quarrels in defence of Pompey, and for the cause of Brutus' and declares himself to be 'bewitched' by 'the state of that

88 [A]'Le sage doit au dedans retirer son ame de la presse, et la tenir en liberté et puissance de juger librement des choses: mais quant au dehors, [. . .] il doit suivre entierement les façons et formes receues'. I.22: P 122, V 118, F 86.

89 [C]'Revenons à l'Empire de la coustume. Les peuples nourris à la liberté et à se commander eux mesmes, estiment toute autre forme de police monstrueuse et contre nature: Ceux qui sont duits à la monarchie en font de mesme. Et quelque facilité que leur preste fortune au changement, lors mesme qu'ils se sont avec grandes difficultez deffaitz de l'importunité d'un maistre, ils courent à en replanter un nouveau avec pareilles difficultez, pour ne se pouvoir resoudre de prendre en haine la maistrise'. I.22: P 119–20, V 116, F 83–4.

ancient Rome, free, just, and flourishing', adding that he 'love[s] neither her birth nor her old age'.[90] This vision of Roman liberty is presented as an object of nostalgia and regret – an image of a vanished world. Yet this cherished 'fantasie' remains valid, or at least valuable, for all its vanity.

As Montaigne explains earlier in the chapter, [B]'I apply myself to make use of vanity itself, and asininity, if it brings me any pleasure'.[91] Montaigne here reprints in full the [B]'authentic bull of Roman citizenship' granted to him on his recent visit to the city, 'pompous in seals and gilt letters'.[92] Being [B]'a citizen of no city', he confesses that he is 'very pleased to be one of the noblest city that ever was or ever will be'. The pleasure that this document brings him, he concedes, is 'full of inanity and nonsense' – yet, he insists, he cannot 'get rid of' such vanity 'without getting rid of [him]self'.[93] Montaigne is here drawing attention to his acceptance of his own weakness: what little wisdom he can hope for, he suggests, lies not in overcoming his flights of folly, but in acknowledging them as his own. But it might not, perhaps, be too fanciful to also see in this passage a veiled echo of La Boétie's spiritual kinship with Venice and of his juvenile 'essay' in the name of liberty.

IV

In what ways does this aspiration to freedom shape Montaigne's account of his relationship with princes and powerful men? In *On the education of children*, he carefully distinguishes service or subjection (which consist in reasoned submission to lawful authority) from servitude (which stems from dependency on the personal favour of a prince). Among 'the most profitable lessons of philosophy' which a young man is to be taught, he lists [A]'the difference between [. . .] servitude and subjection, licence and liberty'.[94] The significance of this elliptical remark is made clear a few pages earlier by an addition to the Bordeaux Copy inserted into an existing

90 [B]'J'ay attaqué cent querelles pour la deffence de Pompeius, et pour la cause de Brutus'. 'Si embabouyné'. 'L'estat de ceste vieille Rome, libre, juste, et florissante (car je n'en ayme, ny la naissance, ny la vieillesse)'. III.9: P 1043, V 996–7, F 763.

91 [B]'Je m'employe à faire valoir la vanité mesme, et l'asnerie, si elle m'apporte du plaisir'. III.9: P 1042, V 996, F 762.

92 [B]'Une bulle authentique de bourgeoisie Romaine: qui me fut octroyée dernierement que j'y estois, pompeuse en seaux, et lettres dorées'. III.9: P 1045, V 999, F 764–5.

93 [B]'N'estant bourgeois d'aucune ville, je suis bien aise de l'estre de la plus noble qui fut et qui sera onques'. 'Pleins d'inanité et de fadaise: De m'en deffaire, je ne puis, sans me deffaire moy-mesmes'. III.9: P 1047, V 1000, F 766.

94 [A]'Les plus profitables discours de la philosophie'. 'Ce qu'il y à dire entre [. . .] la servitude et la subjection, la licence et la liberté'. I.25: P 164-5, V 158, F 117.

discussion of the conduct to be adopted [A]'in discourse and contestation'. A young man, Montaigne argues in the 1580 edition, should be taught to obey the commands of truth rather than those of any man, for that is what it means to judge freely. He must learn 'above all to surrender and throw down his arms before truth as soon as he perceives it, whether it be found in the hands of his opponents, or in himself through reconsideration'. He shall be neither 'set in a chair to say a prescribed role', nor 'pledged to any cause, except by the fact that he approves it'; unlike courtiers (and perhaps lawyers), he shall not be 'of that trade, where one sells for ready cash the liberty to repent and reconsider'.[95]

It is at this point, in the Bordeaux Copy, that Montaigne inserts a quotation from Cicero's *Academica priora*, followed by an explanation of the difference between being a servant of one's prince and being a courtier:

> [C]*Nor is he forced by any necessity to defend everything that has been prescribed and commanded.* If his tutor is of my humour, he will form his will to be a very loyal servant of his Prince, and a very affectionate, and very courageous one: but he will cool in him any desire to attach himself to that prince otherwise than by public duty. Besides several disadvantages, which harm our ~~freedom~~ <liberty>, by these private obligations, the judgment of a man who is hired and bought, is either less whole and less free, or tainted with imprudence and ingratitude. A <pure> Courtier can have neither the right nor the will, to speak and think otherwise than favourably of a master, who among so many thousands of other subjects, has chosen him to nourish and raise up with his own hand. This favour and utility corrupt his freedom, not without some reason, and dazzle him. Therefore we habitually find the language of those people different from any other language, in a state, and little to be trusted in such matters.[96]

Instead of being bound by 'public duty' alone, the courtier is 'attached' to his prince through 'private obligations': he is personally in his debt,

95 [A]'Qu'on l'instruise sur tout à se rendre, et à quitter les armes à la verite, tout aussi tost qu'il l'appercevra: soit qu'elle naisse ès mains de son adversaire, soit qu'elle naisse en luy-mesmes par quelque ravisement. Car il ne sera pas mis en chaise pour dire un rolle prescript, il n'est engagé à aucune cause, que par ce qu'il l'appreuve. Ny ne sera du mestier, où se vend à purs deniers contans, la liberté de se pouvoir repentir et recognoistre.' I.25: P 160, V 155, F 114.

96 [C]'*Neque, ut omnia, quae praescripta et imperata sint, defendat, necessitate ulla cogitur* [Cicero, *Academica priora*, II.3.8]. Si mon gouverneur tient de mon humeur, il luy formera la volonté à estre très-loyal serviteur de son Prince, et très-affectionné, et très-courageux: mais il luy refroidira l'envie de s'y attacher autrement que par un devoir publique. Outre plusieurs inconvenients, qui blessent nostre ~~franchise~~ <liberté>, par ces obligations particulieres, le jugement d'un homme gagé et achetté, ou il est moins entier et moins libre, ou il est taché et d'imprudence et d'ingratitude. Un <pur> Courtisan ne peut avoir ny loy ny volonté, de dire et penser que favorablement d'un maistre, qui parmi tant de milliers d'autres subjects, l'a choisi pour le nourrir et elever de sa main. Cette faveur et utilité corrompent non sans quelque raison, sa franchise, et l'esblouissent. Pourtant void on coustumierement, le langage de ces gens là, divers à tout autre langage, en un estat, et de peu de foy en telle matiere'. I.25: P 160–1, V 115, F 114.

because he owes him his position, his power and his possessions. His liberty is compromised and corrupted: he has been 'hired and bought'; he no longer belongs to himself. The consequence of such dependency is that the courtier cannot judge or speak freely: his language cannot be trusted. He has alienated his liberty to repent and reconsider; he surrenders not to the truth, but to the demands of his uncertain and subservient condition.

Why is the courtier 'forced', as Montaigne has it, 'to defend everything that has been prescribed and commanded'? In the first place, he is 'dazzled' and flattered by the favour shown to him, his judgment clouded by gratitude and wonder at the prince's power: he does not, Montaigne suspects, have the 'will' to do anything other than please. Even more importantly, it is not within his power to speak or think openly, even if he wanted to: he does not have the 'right' (*loy*). It is not merely that the courtier owes it to the prince to show gratitude for his favour. In addition, it would be imprudent for him to say anything that might displease the man who is, as Montaigne makes clear, not only his prince but his 'master'.

This representation of the courtier as a flatterer whose speech cannot be reckoned upon is a recurring motif in the *Essais*. In an early passage from *On the inequality that is between us*, Montaigne paraphrases with approval a complaint made by the Syracusan tyrant Hieron, as recounted by Xenophon:

> [A]What testimony of affection and good will, can I extract from a man, who owes me, whether he will or not, everything he can do? Can I take any stock in his humble speech and courteous reverence, seeing that it is not in his power to refuse me them? [. . .] All they [my subjects] say to me, and do for me, is only powder and paint, their liberty being bridled on all sides by the great power I have over them: I see nothing around me except what is covered and masked.[97]

The emphasis of this passage, and of the chapter as a whole, is on the unenviable and unhappy state of kings, and thus on the foolhardiness of aspiring to their power. Hieron is a lonely and melancholy figure, [A]'deprived of all mutual friendship and society', his 'height' placing him 'outside of human association'.[98] This miserable condition also serves to reveal the

97 [A]'Quel tesmoignage d'affection et de bonne volonté, puis-je tirer de celuy, qui me doit, veuille il ou non, tout ce qu'il peut? Puis-je faire estat de son humble parler et courtoise reverence, veu qu'il n'est pas en luy de ma la refuser? [. . .] Tout ce qu'ils me dient, et font, ce n'est que fard, leur liberté estant bridée de toutes parts par la grande puissance que j'ay sur eux: je ne voy rien autour de moy que couvert et masqué.' I.42: P 288, V 266, F 195. Cf. Xenophon, *Hieron*, esp. I, III.1–9, IV.1–2, and VI.1–16.

98 [A]'Privé de toute amitié et societé mutuelle [. . .] Ma hauteur m'a mis hors du commerce des hommes'. I.42: P 288, V 266, F 195.

mechanism of subjugation: the liberty of Hieron's subjects is curtailed by the mere fact of his power over them. He himself wants nothing more than to be dealt with honestly: yet they 'owe' him all that they can do and, precisely for that reason, it is not in their power to speak freely. All of their words and actions have the status of permissions, conditioned by their need to please the king and obtain his favour.

Montaigne would return to this theme in later years. The 'incommodity of greatness', he argues in the 1588 version of the chapter of that name (III.7), is that in B'the trials of strength we have with one another, in rivalry of honour and worth, whether in exercises of the body or of the mind [. . .] sovereign greatness has no true share', and that the status of rulers 'stifles and consumes their other true and essential qualities'. Everyone lets the prince win in any contest or challenge. When the Senate awarded a prize for eloquence to Tiberius, he turned it down, B'thinking that from a judgment so far from being free, even if it had been true, he could have no satisfaction'. Not only do subjects approve the defects of their kings, but they go so far as to copy them: B'every one of the followers of Alexander carried his head on one side, as he did. And the flatterers of Dionysius bumped into one another in his presence, stumbled upon and knocked over what was at their feet, to signify that they were as shortsighted as he'.[99]

In a late addition to *Our affections reach out beyond ourselves*, finally, the connection between subjection to a prince, self-censorship and the curtailment of our liberty is made clear. In the 1588 version of the chapter, Montaigne had inserted a passage expressing his approval for the idea that the actions of princes should be examined after their death. In the Bordeaux Copy, he extends this thought through a discussion of the obedience owed to princes and the limit imposed upon it by their death:

CWe owe subjection and obedience equally to all Kings: for that concerns their office: but we do not owe esteem, any more than affection, except to their virtue. Let us make this concession to the political order: to suffer them patiently if they are unworthy: to conceal their vices, to assist their indifferent actions with our recommendation, as long as their authority requires our support. But, our dealings over, it is not reasonable to deny to justice, and to our liberty, the expression of our true feelings. And especially to deny to good subjects, the glory of having reverently

99 B'Les essays que nous faisons les uns contre les autres, par jalousie d'honneur et de valeur, soit aux exercices du corps ou de l'esprit: ausquels la grandeur souveraine n'a aucune vraye part'. B'Estouffe et consomme les autres qualitez vrayes et essentielles'. B'N'estimant pas que d'un jugement si peu libre, quand bien il eust esté veritable, il s'en peust ressentir'. B'Chacun des suivans d'Alexandre portoit comme luy, la teste à costé. Et les flateurs de Dionisius, s'entrehurtoient en sa presence, poussoyent et versoient ce qui se rencontroit à leurs pieds, pour dire qu'ils avoient la veue aussi courte que luy'. III.7: P 963–4, V 918–19, F 701–2.

and faithfully served a master whose imperfections were so well known to them: depriving posterity of so useful an example. And those who, out of respect for some private obligation, unjustly espouse the memory of a blameworthy Prince, do private justice at the expense of public justice. Livy says truly, that the language of men brought up under a Monarchy, is always full of ~~mad~~ <vain> ostentations and ~~vain~~ <false> testimonies: each man indiscriminately raising his King, to the highest level of worth and sovereign greatness.[100]

In *On the education of children*, Montaigne had suggested that one may be a 'servant' and a 'subject' and yet preserve one's liberty, as long as one's attachment to the prince is conditioned by law and not by favour, by the demands of 'public duty' and not by the heat of passion: any 'desire' for 'private obligations' is to be 'cooled', and our service is to be 'très-affectionné' but also 'très-loyal' ('very loyal' or 'very lawful'). In this passage from *Our affections*, which belongs to the same state of the text, the prospects for liberty under a monarchy seem rather more bleak. As the quotation from Livy implies, we can expect nothing more from men who live under a monarchy than false speech, flattery and adulation. Again, the relevant distinction is between those 'good subjects' who are able to look upon the prince without unmerited affection, their judgment untarnished by any 'private obligation', and those creatures of the prince whose approval has been bought with favour. Although we may refuse to flatter, however, it is clear that our liberty is condemned to silence, as long as the prince is still alive. Unworthy kings are not merely to be suffered and obeyed: the good subject must play his part in hiding their imperfections, supporting them in their indifferent actions, and placing all criticism in abeyance until their death. It is in this obedience without illusions, but also without resistance, that the excellence and glory of the subject lies.

Crucially, however, the silence of the good subject springs not from private affection or interest, but from the obedience that is due to the *office* of kings. This contrast between a dispassionate and lawful submission

100 [C]'Nous devons la subjection et obeïssance egalement à tous Rois: car elle regarde leur office: mais l'estimation, non plus que l'affection, nous ne la devons qu'à leur vertu. Donnons à l'ordre politique de les souffrir patiemment, indignes: de celer leurs vices: d'aider de nostre recommandation leurs actions indifferentes, pendant que leur auctorité a besoin de nostre appuy. Mais nostre commerce finy, ce n'est pas raison de refuser à la justice, et à nostre liberté, l'expression de noz vrays ressentiments. Et nommément de refuser aux bons subjects, la gloire d'avoir reveremment et fidelement servi un maistre, les imperfections duquel leur estoient si bien cognues: frustrant la posterité d'un si utile exemple. Et ceux, qui, par respect de quelque obligation privée, espousent iniquement la memoire d'un Prince meslouable, font justice particuliere aux despends de la justice publique. Titus Livius dict vray, que le langage des homme nourris sous la Royauté, est tousjours plein de ~~folles~~ <vaines> ostentations et ~~vains~~ <faux> tesmoignages: chascun eslevant indifferemment son Roy, à l'extreme ligne de valeur et grandeur souveraine'. I.3: P 39, V 16, F 9. See Livy, XXXV.48.2–3.

that leaves our liberty intact and a slavish attachment moved by private passion had already been explored by Montaigne in the first chapter of the third book, *On the useful and the honourable*, in connection not with the problem of flattery and self-censorship, but with the seditious impact of private interest in politics. One of the aims of this latter chapter is to defend the *politique* cause of moderation, peace and subjection in the midst of the civil wars, by arguing that those who resist royal authority act not for the sake of the common good but on the impulse of passion and vice:

> [B]We must not call duty, as we do every day, an inner bitterness and asperity that is born of private interest and passion; nor courage, a treacherous and malicious conduct. Their propensity to malignity and violence they call zeal. It is not the cause that inflames them, it is their interest: They kindle war not because it is just, but because it is war.[101]

Montaigne's own allegiance and subjection, by contrast, is to the laws. He aligns himself with [B]'the cause of the laws and the defence of the old order',[102] and declares that 'the laws have freed [him] from great anxiety', in that 'they have chosen [him] a party and given [him] a master', such that 'any other superiority and obligation must be relative to that one, and restricted'.[103] His freedom is here advanced as a mark both of his sound and moderate judgment and of the honesty and fearlessness of his counsel:

> [B]I am not pressed by any passion, either of hate, or of love, toward the great: nor is my will bound by personal injury, or obligation. [C]I look upon our kings with an affection that is simply loyal and civil, neither moved nor removed by private interest. For this I congratulate myself. [B]I am attached to the general and just cause only with moderation and without fever. I am not subject to these penetrating, intimate mortgages and engagements. [. . .] That is what makes me walk everywhere head high, face, and heart, open.[104]

Montaigne has no master but the laws: his will is not 'bound' to any powerful man; he has not pledged himself; he acts and speaks in his own

101 [B]'Mais il ne faut pas appeller devoir, comme nous faisons tous les jours, une aigreur et une intestine aspreté, qui naist de l'interest et passion privée, ny courage, une conduite traistresse et malitieuse. Ils nomment zele, leur propension vers la malignité, et violence: Ce n'est pas la cause qui les eschauffe, c'est leur interest: Ils attisent la guerre, non par ce qu'elle est juste, mais par ce que c'est guerre'. III.1: P 833, V 793, F 602.

102 [B]'La cause des loix, et defence de l'ancien estat'. III.1: P 833, V 793, F 602.

103 [B]'Les loix m'ont osté de grand peine, elles m'ont choisi party, et donné un maistre: toute autre superiorité et obligation doibt estre relative à celle-là, et retranchée.' III.1 P 834, V 794–5, F 603.

104 [B]'Je ne suis pressé de passion, ou hayneuse, ou amoureuse, envers les grands: ny n'ay ma volonté garrotée d'offence, ou d'obligation particuliere. [C]Je regarde nos Roys d'une affection simplement legitime et civile, ny emeue ny demeue par interest privé, dequoy je me sçay bon gré. [B]La cause generale et juste ne m'attache non plus, que moderément et sans fièvre. [. . .] C'est ce qui me faict marcher par tout, la teste haute, le visage, et le cœur ouvert'. III.1: P 831–2, V 792, F 601.

right. Why? Because he is ruled not by passion but by law – not by hatred or love, but by 'an affection that is simply loyal and civil'. In subjecting himself to the law, rather than to the will of another man, he is able to preserve his liberty.

Montaigne is far from blind to the fact that it is not always easy to reconcile lawful obedience and freedom, and that, in practice, princes tend to treat their subjects as if they were slaves. In one of the shortest chapters of the first book, *A trait of certain ambassadors*, he turns his attention to the problem of authority and judgment in the performance of public office: is it lawful for an ambassador to speak and act on the basis of his own judgment, or is he simply the instrument of his master?[105] The chapter centres on an anecdote from the *Mémoires* of Guillaume du Bellay, in which two French ambassadors take it upon themselves to omit from their reports some insulting and inflammatory remarks made against France by the Emperor Charles V. In both the 1580 and 1588 versions of the text, Montaigne appears to condemn such behaviour. He declares it [A]'very strange that it should be in the power of an Ambassador' to 'exercise dispensation' over the information given to 'his master'. 'The office of a servant', he argues, extends only so far as 'to represent things faithfully in their entirety, just as they happened'. 'The liberty to order, judge, and choose' ought to remain 'with the master', as it 'belongs' to 'he, who gives the law, not to he who receives it', as to 'a curator or school master'. In their public capacity as ambassadors, these men act not in their own right, but as vehicles and instruments of another man's judgment and affairs.[106]

In the additions made to the Bordeaux Copy, Montaigne begins by making the challenge to lawful authority represented by the French ambassadors even clearer than in previous editions. To follow their example, Montaigne now writes, is not to obey but rather to [C]'usurp mastery', for 'we corrupt the office of command, when we obey through discretion, not subjection'.[107] A tension immediately insinuates itself, however. The same natural love of independence and 'mastery' ('everyone aspires so naturally to liberty and authority') seems to underlie both the superior's rightful claim to 'simple and natural obedience' from his inferiors, and those inferiors' unacceptable

[105] For an important discussion of this chapter, see Hampton 2009.

[106] [A]'Bien estrange, qu'il fust en la puissance d'un Ambassadeur de dispenser sur les advertissemens qu'il doit faire à son maistre [...] Et m'eust semblé l'office du serviteur estre, de fidelement representer les choses en leur entier, comme elles sont advenues: afin que la liberté d'ordonner, juger, et choisir demeurast au maistre'. 'À celuy, qui donne la loy, non à celuy qui la reçoit, au curateur et maistre d'eschole'. I.16: P 75–6, V 75–6, F 51.

[107] [C]'Nous [...] usurpons sur la maistrise. [...] On corrompt l'office du commander, quand on y obeit par discretion, non par subjection'. I.16: P 76, V 74, F 51.

abuses of power in their public functions.[108] A further doubt is raised when Montaigne cites the example of Crassus, who had an engineer whipped for returning from Athens, not (as he was ordered to do) with the larger of two shipmasts, but with the smaller of the two, having 'on the strength of his knowledge, granted himself permission' to fetch 'the more suitable one according to the rules of his craft'.[109] Although this reference is ostensibly deployed in defence of an abnegation of individual judgment, it actually triggers an opposite train of thought, leading Montaigne to openly question the virtue of 'natural' (as opposed to discretionary or voluntary) obedience that he has thus far praised.

'On the other hand', Montaigne suggests, ambassadors are subject not to 'precise and stated commands' but to 'a freer charge, which, in several parts, depends absolutely on their disposition'.[110] Not only do they form and direct their master's will by their counsel, but their effectiveness as representatives depends precisely on their adjusting their commands to the circumstances in which they find themselves, instead of following their instructions to the letter. The final sentence of the chapter casts doubt not only on the expediency of 'constrained obedience', but also on its justice: did not Crassus, in instructing an engineer in his expert capacity, 'enter in conference with his deliberation and invite him to interpose his decree?'[111]

This discussion raises some uncomfortable questions without offering any definite answers: as so often in Montaigne, we are left to draw our own moral from the story. Perhaps the engineer should have known better than to challenge his master's authority: he ought to have adopted the path of least resistance, erring on the side of 'simple and natural obedience', like the 'good subjects' of *Our affections reach out beyond ourselves*. Perhaps princes should know better than to exact such 'constrained obedience' from their subjects, recognizing, as Hieron did to his regret in *On the inequality that is amongst us*, that the only service of any value to them is that which is free. Perhaps, finally, the message simply *is* that, as subjects we are caught on the horns of an insoluble dilemma: how can our duties of obedience and service be reconciled with the exercise of our liberty? It may well have

108 C'Chascun aspire si naturellement à la liberté et authorité'. 'Leur simple et naïfve obeissance'. I.16: P 76, V 74, F 51.

109 C'Sous titre de sa science, se donna loy de choisir autrement, et mena le plus petit, et selon la raison de l'art, le plus commode'. I.16: P 76, V 74, F 51.

110 C'D'autre part pourtant on pourroit aussi considerer, que cette obeïssance si contreinte, n'appartient qu'aux commandements precis et prefix. Les Ambassadeurs ont une charge plus libre, qui en plusieurs parties depend souverainement de leur disposition'. I.16: P 76, V 74, 51.

111 C'Et Crassus, escrivant à un homme du mestier, et luy donnant advis de l'usage auquel il destinoit ce mas, sembloit-il pas entrer en conference de sa deliberation, et le convier à interposer son decret?' I.16: P 77, V 74, F 51.

been inconsistent of Crassus to employ an expert and then punish him for exercising that expertise, but that in itself does nothing to change the engineer's unhappy fate. For what is to stop us from being reduced not merely to subjection but to slavery?

Faced with this danger, it sometimes appears in the *Essais* that the only path to liberty lies in shunning all public occupations and offices, at least in our old age. In *On solitude*, Montaigne exhorts the wise man to remove himself from A'the titles, the offices, and the hustle and bustle of the world' – 'not that [he] cannot live anywhere content, even alone in a palace crowd', but 'if he has the choice, he will flee even the sight of a throng'.[112] Cicero's claim A'that we are not born for ourselves, but for the public' is nothing but a 'fine saying under which ambition and avarice take cover'.[113] Quite on the contrary, nothing should be more precious to us than ourselves: A'*what! Shall a man establish in his soul, or prize, anything dearer than himself in his own eyes?*' To this quotation from Terence, Montaigne adds, in the Bordeaux Copy, what sounds like a correction: C'solitude seems to me more appropriate and reasonable for those who have given to the world their most active and flourishing years, following the example of Thales'.[114] But this insertion serves only to add a note of humility and weakness to his appeal for absolute retreat: C'our powers are failing us; let us withdraw them and concentrate them on ourselves'.[115]

Writing sometime between 1572 and 1580, Montaigne had argued in *On age* that we enter public service too late and leave it too early: A'to send men back into retirement before the age of fifty-five or sixty seems not very reasonable to me. I should be of the opinion that our employment and occupation should be extended as far as possible, for the public welfare; but I find the fault in the other direction, that of not putting us to work soon enough'.[116] When he came to revise *On solitude*, sometime between 1588

112 A'Les estats, les charges, et cette tracasserie du monde'. I.38: P 241, V 237, F 174. A'Ce n'est pas que le sage ne puisse par tout vivre content, voire et seul, en la foule d'un palais: mais s'il est à choisir, il en fuira, dit-il, mesmes la veue'. I.38: P 242, V 238, F 175.

113 A'Ce beau mot, dequoy se couvre l'ambition et l'avarice, Que nous ne sommes pas naiz pour nostre particulier, ains pour le public'. I.38: P 241, V 237, F 174. Cf. Cicero 1968b, p. 22; Cicero 1991, pp. 9–10.

114 A'*Vah quemquámne hominem in animum instituere, aut | Parare, quod sit charius, quàm ipse est sibi?* [Terence, *Adelphi*, I.1.38] CLa solitude me semble avoir plus d'apparence, et de raison, à ceux qui ont donné au monde leur aage plus actif et fleurissant, à l'exemple de Thales'. I.38: P 246, V 242, F 178.

115 C'Noz forces nous faillent: retirons les, et resserrons en nous'. I.38: P 246, V 242, F 178.

116 A'De renvoyer les hommes au sejour avant cinquante cinq ou soixante ans, il me semble n'y avoir pas grande apparence. Je serois d'advis qu'on estendit nostre vacation et occupation autant qu'on pourroit, pour la commodité publique: mais je trouve la faute en l'autre costé, de ne nous y embesogner pas assez tost'. I.57: P 346, V 327, F 237.

and his death in 1592, he drew instead on the authority of Socrates, who taught [C]'that the young should get instruction; that grown men should practise doing good; and that old men should withdraw from all civil and military occupations and live at their own discretion, without being tied down to any fixed office'.[117]

By appealing to his advanced years as grounds for retirement, Montaigne suggests that he is too weak and too useless for public life, a strategy that finds its fullest expression in the third book, in *On vanity* (as we have seen) and *On the useful and the honourable*. In the second of these chapters, Montaigne claims to avoid political functions and charges whenever they require him to compromise his conscience and his virtue in the name of public necessity. Whereas in *On solitude* he had deplored the moral bankruptcy of political life, Montaigne here adopts the language of reason of state, only to subvert it.[118] Like beneficial poisons, vice, cruelty and deception are both integral to human nature and unavoidable in politics, detestable as they may be: [B]'the public welfare requires that a man betray, and lie, [C]and massacre'. Montaigne himself, however, refuses to surrender himself in this way: [B]'let us resign this commission to other more obedient and flexible men', 'to more vigorous and less fearful citizens who sacrifice their honour and conscience just as the ancients sacrificed their lives in order to save their country'.[119]

Montaigne does not want, he insists, [B]'to deprive treachery of its rank'. He readily concedes that there are 'lawful vices, just as there are many either good or excusable actions that are unlawful'. In a particularly double-edged statement, offered both as a maxim of political realism and as a criticism of its limits, he writes that [B]'justice in itself, natural and universal, is regulated otherwise and more nobly than that other, [C]special, national [B]justice, constrained to the need of our governments'.[120] Pomponius Flaccus may have been found fit by the Romans to exact justice for them, by subjecting a traitor to a new act of betrayal and deceit – and indeed 'let he who will

117 [C]'Les jeunes se doivent faire instruire; les hommes s'exercer à bien faire: les vieux se retirer de toute occupation civile et militaire, vivants à leur discretion, sans obligation à certain office'. I.38: P 246–7, V 242, F 178.

118 On Montaigne's critique of reason of state in this chapter, see Collins 1992.

119 [B]'Le bien public requiert qu'on trahisse, et qu'on mente, [C]et qu'on massacre: [B]resignons cette commission à gens plus obeissans et plus souples'. [C]'Il faut laisser jouer cette partie, aux citoyens plus vigoureux, et moins craintifs, qui sacrifient leur honneur et leur conscience, comme ces autres anciens sacrifierent leur vie, pour le salut de leur pays'. III.1: P 830, V 791, F 600.

120 [B]'Priver la tromperie de son rang [. . .] Il y a des vices legitimes, comme plusieurs actions, ou bonnes, ou excusables, illegitimes. La justice en soy, naturelle et universelle, est autrement reglée, et plus noblement, que n'est cette autre justice [C]speciale, nationale, [B]contrainte au besoing de nos polices'. III.1: P 836, V 795–6, F 604.

be a Pomponius Flaccus, and there are enough who will' – but Montaigne himself is unsuitable for such service. He readily admits that he owes his service to the common good: 'as for me', he writes, 'both my word and my faith, are, like the rest, part of this common body: their best effect, is public service: I take that for granted'. Yet he insists on refusing all orders 'to lie, to betray, and to perjure myself', preferring rather to be punished than to corrupt himself: 'if I have robbed anyone or stolen anything, send me rather to the galleys'.[121] His assertion, in *On presumption*, that his liberty has made him [A]'soft and *useless* for serving others', takes on a fresh significance in this context.[122] Unlike Crassus' unlucky engineer, Montaigne makes no claims to expertise. He cannot be put to *use*, both in the sense that he has nothing to contribute to public utility, and in the sense that he cannot bear to be used as an instrument: he cannot be made fit for a political universe ruled by expediency rather than honesty.

To [B]'prostitute one's conscience' for the sake of public necessity, Montaigne suggests, is to consent to slavery.[123] He quotes the judgment of a wise man named Dandamys, who (according to Plutarch) thought that Socrates, Pythagoras, and Diogenes, for all their greatness, were [B]'too enslaved to reverence for the laws, to authorise and support which true virtue has to give up much of its original vigour'.[124] Of the hangman who was ordered to deflower Sejanus' daughter, because virgins could not be executed under Roman law, Montaigne writes that [B]'not only his hand, but even his soul, is a slave to public convenience'.[125] In all his dealings with princes, accordingly, Montaigne makes clear that his own freedom must come first:

> [B]I do not want to be considered either so affectionate or so loyal a servant, as to be found fit to betray anyone. He who is unfaithful to himself, is excusably so to his master. But these are Princes, who do not accept men by halves and scorn limited and conditional services. There is no remedy: I freely tell them my limits: for a slave, I must be to reason alone, and I can barely even do that properly.

121 [B]'Sera Pomponius Flaccus qui voudra, et en est assez qui le voudront; Quant à moy, et ma parolle et ma foy, sont, comme le demeurant, pieces de ce commun corps: leur meilleur effect, c'est le service public: je tiens cela pour presupposé'. 'À mentir, à trahir, et à me parjurer'. 'Si j'ay volé ou desrobé quelqu'un, envoyez moy plutost en gallere.' III.1: P 836–7, V 796–7, F 605.

122 [A]'Cela m'a amolli et rendu inutile au service d'autruy'. II.17: P 681, V 643, F 487.

123 [B]'La prostitution de conscience'. III.1: P 839, V 799, F 606.

124 [B]'Trop asservis à la reverence des loix: Pour lesquelles auctoriser, et seconder, la vraye vertu a beaucoup à se desmettre de sa vigueur originelle'. III.1: P 836, V 796, F 604. Cf. *Vie d'Alexandre-le-Grand*, Plutarch 1951, vol. I, p. 401.

125 [B]'Non sa main seulement, mais son ame, est esclave à la commodité publique'. III.1: P 839, V 799, F 606.

[C]And they too are wrong, to expect from a free man, such subjection to their service, and such obligation, as they do from a man, that they have made and bought: or whose fortune depends particularly and expressly on their own.[126]

Montaigne here draws once more on the now familiar contrast between the free man and the man who has been bought. It is hard not to see this passage as a response and correction to the 'very-affectionate' and 'very-loyal' subject from *On the education of children*. Princes may be 'wrong' to treat him as if he were a slave, and yet, Montaigne here suggests, it is in their nature to disdain the 'limited and conditional services' provided by free men.[127] There is 'no remedy' to this state of affairs: all that Montaigne can do is to stand his ground and allow his 'services' to be scorned.

Freedom and subjection here appear to be locked in a dead heat. Montaigne's commitment to his liberty, it would seem, leaves him with little choice but to withdraw from public life, by retreating to the one part of the world where he may be said to belong to himself: the *domus* of which he is *dominus*. In *On the inequality that is amongst us*, similarly, the unhappy condition of the king, who is always on display, is contrasted with the king-like jurisdiction of [B]'a retired and stay-at-home Lord', who 'hears speak of his master once a year, as if of the King of Persia'. Instead of envying the state of kings and seeking their favour through public service, Montaigne urges us to take comfort in our considerable jurisdiction over our own estates:

[B]In truth our laws are free enough; and the weight of sovereignty scarcely touches a French gentleman twice in his life: The real and essential subjection, is only for those among us, who go seeking it, and who like to gain honours and riches by

[126] [B]'Je ne veux estre tenu serviteur, ny si affectionné, ny si loyal, qu'on me treuve bon à trahir personne. Qui est infidelle à soy-mesme, l'est excusablement à son maistre. Mais ce sont Princes, qui n'acceptent pas les hommes à moytié, et mesprisent les services limitez et conditionnez. Il n'y a remede: je leur dis franchement mes bornes: car esclave, je ne le doibs estre que de la raison, encore n'en puis-je bien venir à bout. [C]Et eux aussi ont tort, d'exiger d'un homme libre, telle subjection à leur service, et telle obligation, que de celuy qu'ils ont faict et achetté: ou duquel la fortune tient particulierement et expressement à la leur'. III.1: P 834, V 794, F 603.

[127] In the Villey-Saulnier edition, this sentence is transcribed without a comma after 'Princes': 'Mais ce sont Princes qui n'acceptent pas les hommes à moytié'. Villey glosses this ambiguous passage as 'Les princes auxquels je pense sont des princes qui . . . ' ('the princes of whom I am thinking are princes who do not accept men by halves'). If we look at the Bordeaux Copy itself (fol. 354v), however, it is clear that the 1588 edition read, 'ce sont Princes, qui n'acceptent' and that instead of deleting this comma, Montaigne replaced it with a semi-colon ('ce sont Princes; qui n'acceptent'). The 1595 text, which I have used here, reinstates the comma. Yet it seems clear to me, both from the Bordeaux Copy and the posthumous edition, that Montaigne's intention was to reinforce the caesura between the clauses, thus making his meaning clear: 'but these are princes; and princes do not accept men by halves'.

such service: for anyone who wants to ensconce himself by his hearth, and who knows how to conduct his house without quarrels, and lawsuits, is as free as the Duke of Venice. [C]*Slavery holds but few; many hold fast to slavery.*[128]

The one place in the world where we may rightly claim to be free from subjection, Montaigne suggests in *Ceremony of the interviews of kings*, is in our own home. In the first edition of 1580, this brief chapter was devoted to discussing a minor point of etiquette. With each successive addition, however, the piece develops into a meditation on the home as a refuge from ceremony, and thus from servitude.

In the A-text, Montaigne begins by observing that it is held to be a great discourtesy for a man to be absent from his house when an equal or superior person comes to meet him there by prior appointment. He then concludes simply by noting that, nonetheless, among princes it is considered respectful for the least distinguished party to arrive last at the place of meeting. In the 1588 edition, Montaigne adopts a more personal approach, by confessing that he himself often forgets these [B]'vain offices' when he is at home: 'I cut back ~~all~~ ceremony in my house <as much as I can>'. To follow deferential rituals such as these, in the privacy of one's own home, is irksome and absurd, because it introduces subjection into the one realm where we stand a chance of resisting it: [B]'someone takes offence: what of it? It is better for me to offend him once, than to offend myself every day: it would be a continual subjection. What is the use of fleeing the servitude of the courts, if we drag it back to our lair?'[129]

The Bordeaux Copy draws a general inference about the relativity of manners: [C]'not only each country, but each city <and each occupation> has its own particular civility'. Despite its relativity, this civility should nonetheless be respected: the chapter now concludes by affirming these rules of politeness as 'encouraging the first beginnings of society and familiarity; and consequently opening the door for us to instruct ourselves using the example of others'. At the same time, however, Montaigne is careful

128 [B]'Un Seigneur retiré et casanier [. . .] oyt parler de son maistre une fois l'an, comme du Roy de Perse. [. . .] À la verité nos loix sont libres assez; et le pois de la souveraineté ne touche un gentilhomme François, à peine deux fois en sa vie: La subjection essentielle et effectuelle, ne regarde d'entre nous, que ceux qui s'y convient, et qui ayment à s'honnorer et enrichir par tel service: car qui se veut tapir en son foyer, et sçait conduire sa maison sans querelle, et sans procès, il est aussi libre que le Duc de Venise. [C]*Paucos seruitus, plures seruitutem tenent* [Seneca, *Epistulae ad Lucilium*, 22.11]'. I.42: P 287–8, V 265–6, F 194–5.

129 [B]'Je retranche en ma maison ~~toute~~ <autant que je puis de la> cerimonie. Quelqu'un s'en offence: qu'y ferois-je? Il vaut mieux que je l'offence pour une fois, que moy tous les jours: ce seroit une subjection continuelle. À quoy faire fuit-on la servitude des cours, si on l'entraine jusques en sa taniere?' I.13: P 70, V 48, F 32.

to restate his deep distrust of the servile trappings of ceremony and their capacity to constrain us: 'I like to follow these laws, but not in so cowardly a manner that my life would remain constrained'.[130]

Montaigne's objection to ceremony is not that its practices are artificial or merely conventional, but that they are slavish, unbecoming of the free man he aspires to be. If these were empty, brittle rituals, their mere formality exposed by their arbitrariness and variability, he would perhaps not have had any qualms about rejecting them outright. But ceremonies *are* meaningful: they underpin sociability, and to be ignorant of them is always a disgrace. Yet they include [C]'some troublesome forms, which a man may forget, provided he does so by discretion, rather than by error, without losing any grace'.[131]

Montaigne urges us to limit the binding power of ceremony to the court and to society, preserving for ourselves a sphere of inviolable independence when we are at home. In his own house, as he explains in *On three kinds of association*:

> [B]I reserve, both for myself, and for others, [A]an unusual liberty: there we have a truce on ceremony, on waiting on people, on escorting them here and away, and other such troublesome prescriptions of our courtesy (oh what a servile and importunate practice!), each man governs himself as he pleases, any one who wants to communing with his thoughts: I hold myself mute, dreamy, and closed, without offending my guests.[132]

The figurative space of the library provides a closeted, private refuge in which one can hide oneself, dispensing with all company and ceremony. Crucially, however, this state of seclusion is represented by Montaigne not as a locus of introspective self-discovery, but as a condition of dominion and self-mastery:

> [B]There is my seat. I try to make my dominion over it pure: and to withdraw this one corner from all community, conjugal, filial, and civil. Everywhere else, my authority is only verbal: in essence, impure. Wretched to my mind is the man who

[130] [C]'Non seulement chasque païs, mais chasque cité <et chasque vacation> a sa civilité particulière'. 'Conciliatrice des premiers abords de la société et familiarité: et par consequent nous ouvre la porte à nous instruire par les exemples d'autruy'. 'J'aime à les ensuivre, mais non pas si couardement, que ma vie en demeure contraincte'. I.13: P 70–1, V 48–9, F 32–3.

[131] [C]'Elles ont quelques formes penibles, lesquelles pourveu qu'on oublie par discretion, non par erreur, on n'en a pas moins de grace'. I.13: P 70, V 48, F 32.

[132] [B]'Je reserve là, et pour moy, et pour les autres, [A]une liberté inusitée: Il s'y faict trefve de ceremonie, d'assistance, et convoiemens, et telles autres ordonnances penibles de nostre courtoisie (ô la servile et importune usance) chacun s'y gouverne à sa mode, y entretient qui veut ses pensées: je m'y tiens muet, resveur, et enfermé, sans offence de mes hostes'. III.3: P 865, V 823–4, F 625.

has nowhere in his home where he can be his own: where he can pay court to himself privately: where he can hide.[133]

To withdraw from the world, from the 'servitude of the court and of public charges', is to remove ourselves from the temptations of dependency and servility, by seeking refuge in that one corner in the world in which we are our own master – in that one room that is 'toute nostre, toute franche', entirely ours and entirely free.

V

It is not enough, however, simply to flee all public obligations. Montaigne's point is not that we should shun or sunder our relationships with the external world, retreating within the forbidding fortress of an autarchic and solipsistic solitude: we must live within and with the world, but not enslave ourselves to it. His economy of freedom invites us to place our will into abeyance, to protect it from enslavement by detaching it from that which lies beyond its control, so as to ensure – if necessity requires it – that tranquillity and contentment may be found within the narrow confines of our power. As he argues in *On solitude*, [A]'we have lived enough for others; let us live at least this remaining bit of life for ourselves', so that we may 'live more at leisure and at [our] ease'.[134] Yet freedom cannot be achieved merely by removing ourselves from the scene of our slavery: [A]'often [people] think they have left business, and they have only changed it [. . .] we take our chains along with us, our freedom is not complete; we still turn our eyes to what we have left behind, our fancy is full of it'.[135] We must withdraw our will from all that is not truly ours, by learning to live for and by ourselves, and by honouring the obligations that we have to ourselves. We cannot truly set ourselves apart without first learning how to order ourselves: [A]'retire into yourself, but first prepare to receive yourself there; it would be madness to trust in yourself if you do not know how to govern yourself'.[136]

133 [B]'C'est là mon siege. J'essaye à m'en rendre la domination pure: et à soustraire ce seul coing, à la communauté et conjugale, et filiale, et civile. Par tout ailleurs je n'ay qu'une auctorité verbale: en essence, confuse. Miserable à mon gré, qui n'a chez soy, où estre à soy: où se faire particulierement la cour, où se cacher'. III.3: P 870, V 828, F 629.

134 [A]'C'est assez vescu pour autruy, vivons pour nous au moins ce bout de vie'. I.38: P 246, V 242, F 178. 'Vivre plus à loisir et à son aise'. I.38: P 242, V 238, F 175.

135 [A]'Souvent on pense avoir quitté les affaires, on ne les a que changez. [. . .] Nous emportons nos fers quand et nous: Ce n'est pas une entiere liberté, nous tournons encore la veue vers ce que nous avons laissé; nous en avons la fantasie pleine'. I.38: P 242, 244; V 238, 240; F 175, 176.

136 [A]'Retirez vous en vous, mais preparez vous premierement de vous y recevoir: ce seroit folie de vous fier à vous mesmes, si vous ne vous sçavez gouverner'. I.38: P 252, V 247, F 182.

In *On solitude*, this practice of self-regulation includes three distinct but inter-related commands. We must begin by overcoming those affections which (as Montaigne puts it in the title of the third chapter of the first book) 'reach out beyond ourselves', and which he here names as [A]'ambition, avarice, irresolution, fear and lusts'.[137] Above all, as we saw in Chapter 2, we must silence in ourselves all temptations towards glory, by recognising that our reputation and renown lie outside of ourselves, because they are not within our power. Unlike Pliny and Cicero who [A]'have only stepped back [from the world] to make a better jump', we must learn to 'abandon with the other pleasures that which comes from the approbation of others'.[138]

Next it is crucial that we [A]'make our contentment depend on ourselves' and that we 'cut ourselves loose from all the ties that bind us to others, [. . .] winning over ourselves the power to live really alone and to live that way at our ease'.[139] We should accustom ourselves to the possibility of losing our goods, our property, our servants, even our children and our wives, by coming to realise that these commodities lie beyond our power, and that we may lose them and yet have lost nothing that is truly our own. We need not reject these gifts of fortune: [A]'to sleep on the hard ground; to put out our eyes; to throw our riches into the river; to seek pain [. . .] these are the acts of an excessive virtue'. But we should prepare ourselves at all times for their loss, by picturing to ourselves 'while still at ease, the evil that is to come, as far as our imagination can reach'.[140]

We should not treasure these external things, because we can do nothing to ensure that they are not taken from us. By becoming dependent upon that which we cannot claim to possess, we allow ourselves in turn to become dependent upon other men and their favour: [A]'why should we [. . .] enslave our contentment to the power of others?'[141] We ought instead to cherish those [A]'treasures that can be secured from harm, and to hide them in a place

[137] 'Nos affections s'emportent au delà de nous' (title of I.3). [A]'L'ambition, l'avarice, l'irresolution, la peur et les concupiscences'. I.38: P 243, V 239, F 176.

[138] [A]'Ils se sont seulement reculez pour mieux sauter. [. . .] Quittez avecq les autres voluptez, celle qui vient de l'approbation d'autruy'. I.38: P 251–2, V 247, F 182.

[139] [A]'Faisons que nostre contentement despende de nous: Desprenons nous de toutes les liaisons qui nous attachent à autruy: Gaignons sur nous, de pouvoir à bon escient vivre seuls et y vivre à nostr' aise'. I.38: P 244, V 240, F 177.

[140] [A]'Coucher sur la dure, se crever les yeux, jetter ses richesses emmy la riviere, rechercher la douleur [. . .] c'est l'action d'une vertu excessive. [. . .] Il me suffit souz la faveur de la fortune, me preparer à sa défaveur; et me representer estant à mon aise, le mal advenir, autant que l'imagination y peut attaindre'. I.38: P 247, V 243, F 179.

[141] [A]'Pourquoy [. . .] asservirons nous nostre contentement à la puissance d'autruy?' I.38: P 247, V 243, F 179.

where no one may go and which can be betrayed only by ourselves'.[142] We shall then be able to follow the examples of Stilpo who, despite having lost all his family and goods in the destruction of his city, could still say that 'thanks to God he had lost nothing of his own', and of Paulinus, Bishop of Nola, who, after his city was sacked by barbarians, prayed God to keep him from feeling his loss, 'since they have yet touched nothing of what is mine'.[143]

Finally, we must focus our attention, time and care on the only task that truly concerns us: the art of living and dying. The main emphasis of this chapter, however, falls not on the pleasures of self-possession, but on the depiction of its absence:

> [A]Among our customary actions there is not one in a thousand that concerns ourselves. The man you see climbing atop the ruins of that wall, frenzied and beside himself, a mark for so many harquebus shots; and that other, all scarred, pale and faint with hunger, determined to die rather than open the gates to him: do you think they are there for their own sake? They are there for the sake of a man whom perhaps they never saw, who is not in the least concerned about their doings, and who at that very moment is plunged in idleness and pleasures. This fellow, all dirty, with running nose and eyes, whom you see coming out of his study after midnight, do you think he is seeking among his books how to make himself a better, happier, and wiser man? No such news. He is going to teach posterity the metre of Plautus' verses and the true spelling of a Latin word, or die in the attempt.[144]

The two crazed soldiers risk their lives in another's cause, their furious agitation signalling not only their abandonment to passion, but their mercenary status and their failure to live for themselves. The grubby, dusty scholar is, in his own way, a slave – sacrificing his time and ease for the sake of glory and immortality, and a particularly small-minded and pedantic glory at that.

142 [A]'Voylà que c'est de bien choisir les thresors qui se puissent affranchir de l'injure: et de les cacher en lieu, où personne n'aille, et lequel ne puisse estre trahi que par nous mesmes'. I.38: P 244–5, V 241, F 177.

143 [A]'Il n'y avoit Dieu mercy rien perdu de sien'. 'Ils n'ont encore rien touché de ce qui est à moi'. I.38: P 244, V 240–1, F 177.

144 [A]'En noz actions accoustumées, de mille il n'en est pas une qui nous regarde. Celuy que tu vois grimpant contremont les ruines de ce mur, furieux et hors de soy, en bute de tant de harquebuzades: et cet autre tout cicatricé, transi et pasle de faim, deliberé de crever plustost que de luy ouvrir la porte: penses-tu qu'ils y soyent pour eux? pour tel à l'adventure, qu'ils ne virent onques, et qui ne se donne aucune peine de leur faict, plongé cependant en l'oysiveté et aux delices. Cettuy-cy tout pituiteux, chassieux et crasseux, que tu vois sortir apres minuict d'un estude, penses-tu qu'il cherche parmy les livres, comme il se rendra plus homme de bien, plus content et plus sage? nulles nouvelles. Il y mourra, ou il apprendra à la posterité la mesure des vers de Plaute, et la vraye orthographe d'un mot Latin'. I.38: P 245, V 241, F 177–8.

To belong to ourselves, then, is to live neither for the sake of a master, nor for reputation, nor for those things which are not in our power, but for the sake of wisdom, by learning to live well and (above all, in this chapter) to die well. By withdrawing our will and retreating into ourselves, we are in a sense undertaking the first step of our journey towards death: A'since God gives us leisure to make arrangements for moving out, let us make them; let us pack our bags; let us take an early leave of the company'.[145] To live well, in this perspective, is to prepare to die, by shunning A'any desire to prolong our life or our name'.[146]

The self is here a pure remainder, an essence defined only in negative terms, through the subtraction of all accidental and external objects of desire. In the C-text, however, Montaigne explores the possibility of a richer conception of self, constructed through inward conversation and a respectful, loving self-discipline:

> CHe who can turn the offices of friendship and fellowship around and fuse them into himself, let him do so. [. . .] Let him indulge and care for himself, and especially govern himself, respecting and fearing his reason and conscience, so that he cannot make a false step in their presence without shame. *For it is rare for anyone to respect himself enough.*[147]

It is in *On managing the will*, arguably Montaigne's most sustained reflection on the problem of public engagement, however, that this rich friendship with ourselves finds its fullest expression.

Montaigne here presents the world as a theatre, in which the essential and the accidental, 'le propre' and 'l'estranger', are characteristically confused – in which our public roles are mistaken for ourselves.

> BMost of our occupations are farcical. *The whole world is acting a part.* We must play our role duly, but as the role of a borrowed personage. Masks and appearances must not be made into a real essence, nor that which is alien into that which is proper. We cannot distinguish the skin from the shirt. CIt is enough to make up our face, without making up our heart.[148]

145 A'Puis que Dieu nous donne loisir de disposer de nostre deslogement; preparons nous y; plions bagage; prenons de bon'heure congé de la compagnie'. I.38: P 246, V 242, F 178.

146 A'Sans desir de prolongement de vie ny de nom'. I.38: P 252, V 248, F 183.

147 C'Qui peut renverser et confondre en soy les offices de tant d'amitiez, et de la compagnie, qu'il le face. [. . .] Qu'il se flatte et caresse, et sur tout se regente, respectant et craignant sa raison et sa conscience: si qu'il ne puisse sans honte, broncher en leur presence. *Rarum est enim, ut satis se quisque uereatur* [Quintilian, *Institutio oratoria*, X.7.24]'. I.38: P 246, V 242, F 178.

148 B'La plus part de noz vacations sont farcesques. *Mundus uniuersus exercet histrioniam* [Petronius]. Il faut jouer deuement nostre rolle, mais comme rolle d'un personnage emprunté. Du masque et de l'apparence, il n'en faut pas faire une essence réelle, ny de l'estranger le propre. Nous ne sçavons pas distinguer la peau de la chemise. C'C'est assés de s'enfariner le visage, sans s'enfariner la poictrine'. III.10: P 1057, V 1011, F 773.

This passage has typically been interpreted as evidence of Montaigne's alleged appeal to an inner 'essence' of the self, incommensurable with its artificial roles. To describe our public charges as masks (or as *personae*), however, is not so much to indict social life for its dishonesty and inauthenticity as it is to offer a subversive rewriting of a widespread, humanist ethics of public office, as articulated most influentially by Cicero in *De officiis*.[149] Montaigne continues:

> BI see some who transform and transubstantiate themselves into as many new figures, and new beings, as they undertake charges: and who make themselves prelates down to their liver and guts: and drag their office with them right into their privy. I cannot teach them to distinguish between hats doffed to them and those doffed to their commission, or their retinue, or their mule. *They give themselves so much over to fortune that they forget their own nature.* [. . .] The Mayor and Montaigne have always been two, by a very clear separation.[150]

From the perspective of *De officiis*, virtue is an essentially public quality, realised in visible, outward expression and inseparably connected to the performance of duties (*officia*) identified with our social roles. A man's identity lies in the performance of his *personae* – as father, son, friend, patron, citizen, magistrate, and so on. But Montaigne is *not* exhausted by his offices: there is an all-important difference between the world of our public charges and that of 'real essences', a clear and evident distinction between the Mayor of Bordeaux and Michel de Montaigne.

A public charge is like a cumbersome costume or like the insubstantial, powdery make-up used by comedians. There is an unmistakable gap between shirt and skin, between face and heart, between the world of public office and the extreme inward privacy of the closet. To 'prelate' oneself – the subsuming of one's identity into one's public offices that was taken for granted in *De officiis* – is now to 'transsubstantiate' ourselves, to lose the 'form' that gives us life: to confuse that which is essential with that which is accidental, that which is ours with that which is another's.

Montaigne's point is not that we should simply abandon our public duties: we 'must play our role duly'. But we must not give *ourselves* up to these parts: they are borrowed ('emprunté'), alien ('estranger'). They

149 See Baldwin 2001.

150 B'J'en vois qui se transforment et se transsubstantient en autant de nouvelles figures, et de nouveaux estres, qu'ils entreprennent de charges: et qui se prelatent jusques au foye et aux intestins: et entrainent leur office jusques en leur garderobe. Je ne puis leur apprendre à distinguer les bonnetades, qui les regardent, de celles qui regardent leur commission, ou leur suitte, ou leur mule. *Tantum se fortunae permittunt, etiam ut naturam dediscant* [Quintus Curtius, III.2.18]. [. . .] Le Maire et Montaigne, ont tousjours esté deux, d'une separation bien claire'. III.10: P 1057, V 1011–2, F 773–4.

belong to someone or something other than ourselves; they are under the sway of fortune, not nature. We must learn to act for ourselves, to *own our actions* by performing our own part, by distinguishing our true offices from those that properly belong to others. Even in the performance of our borrowed roles, we must remember that we are acting on behalf of another – and that our true contentment and our true role lie elsewhere.

[B]I have enough business ordering and arranging the domestic pressures that oppress my entrails and veins, without giving myself the trouble of adding extraneous pressures to them: And I am enough involved in my essential, proper, and natural affairs, without inviting in foreign ones. Those who know how much they owe to themselves, and for how many offices they are obligated to themselves, find that nature has given them in this a commission full enough and not at all idle.[151]

We must 'husband our will' and 'husband our liberty', by disengaging ourselves from that which is not truly ours – in the sense that it is not subject to our will.

To be free in this context is to assume responsibility for ourselves as independent moral agents. The point is not to reject the theatrical dimensions of conduct, but to accept no one but oneself as the arbiter of one's performance:

[B]Any man can play his part in the play, and represent an honourable person on the stage: but within, in one's breast, where everything is permissible where everything is hidden, that's the point. The next step to that is to be so in our own house, in our ordinary actions, for which we need render account to no one, where nothing is studied or artificial.[152]

What truly matters to Montaigne, in other words, is his ability to realise within himself the part of the free man – not the introspection of a hermetic, interior identity. Here as elsewhere, the self-portrait functions as an instrument of self-regulation, serving him (as he puts it in *On vanity*) as a [B]'rule' (*regle*), a 'public declaration' that 'obliges [him] to keep on

[151] [B]'J'ay assez affaire à disposer et ranger la presse domestique que j'ay dans mes entrailles, et dans mes veines, sans y loger, et me fouler d'une presse estrangere: Et suis assez interessé de mes affaires essentiels, propres, et naturels, sans en convier d'autres forains. Ceux qui sçavent combien ils se doivent, et de combien d'offices ils sont obligez à eux, trouvent que nature leur a donné cette commission plaine assez, et nullement oysive.' III.10: P 1049, V 1049, F 767.

[152] [B]'Chacun peut avoir part au battelage, et representer un honneste personnage en l'eschaffaut: mais au dedans, et en sa poictrine, où tout nous est loisible, où tout est caché, d'y estre reglé, c'est le poinct. Le voisin degré, c'est de l'estre en sa maison, en ses actions ordinaires, desquelles nous n'avons à rendre raison à personne; où il n'y a point d'estude, point d'artifice'. III.2: P 848–9, V 808, F 613.

[his] path, and not to give the lie to the picture of [his] qualities'.[153] [B]'I do not', he tells us in this later chapter, 'engage myself easily': he enjoys by both nature and study a 'privilege of insensibility'.[154] Unlike those men who [B]'give themselves to hire', having been taught 'to let themselves be seized and carried away' and to 'push in indiscriminately wherever there is business [C]and involvement', his will is marked by slackness and inertia: [B]'I commonly desire mildly what I desire, and desire little: I occupy and busy myself likewise, rarely and with tranquillity'.[155] Things [B]'touch' him but do not 'hold' or 'possess' him; he takes charges 'in hand, not in lungs and liver'; [C]'I give myself to others without taking myself from myself'.[156] This practice of detachment has allowed him to maintain himself [B]'in equanimity and pure indifference', his understanding uncontaminated by any 'violent obligation'.[157]

In *On solitude*, Montaigne had urged the man who [A]'retires from common life, weary and disgusted, to model this [life] on the rules of reason'.[158] In *On managing the will*, by contrast, he writes that he is, on the approach of death, [B]'in the act of finishing up this man, not of making another out of him'.[159] Instead of seeking to reform our acquired dispositions, [B]'let us also call the habits and condition of each of us nature; let us rate and treat ourselves according to this measure, let us stretch our appurtenances and our accounts that far'.[160] But we should still contain our desires within these limits, and always ensure that they are 'reflective', bringing us back to ourselves rather than casting us into the arms of fortune:

[B]The more we amplify our need and our possession, the more we involve ourselves in the blows of fortune and adversity. The range of our desires should be

153 [B]'Cette publique declaration, m'oblige de me tenir en ma route; et à ne desmentir l'image de mes conditions'. III.9: P 1025, V 980, F 749.

154 [B]'J'ay grand soin d'augmenter par estude, et par discours, ce privilege d'insensibilité [. . .] Je m'engage difficilement'. III.10: P 1048, V 1003, F 766.

155 [B]'Voyez les gens appris à se laisser emporter et saisir [. . .] ils s'ingerent indifferemment où il y a de la besongne'. 'Et communément desire mollement ce que je desire, et desire peu: M'occupe et embesongne de mesme, rarement et tranquillement'. III.10: 1049–50, V 1004–5, F 767–8.

156 [B]'Peu de choses me touchent: ou pour mieux dire, me tiennent. Car c'est raison qu'elles touchent, pourveu qu'elles ne nous possedent'. [B]'J'ay promis de les prendre en main, non pas au poulmon et au foye'. [C]'Me donner à autruy sans m'oster à moy'. III.10: P 1048, 1049, 1053; V 1003, 1004, 1007; F 766, 767, 770.

157 [B]'Violente obligation'. 'En equanimité, et pure indifference'. III.10: P 1057–8, V 1012, F 774.

158 [A]'Celuy qui se retire ennuié et desgousté de la vie commune, doit former cette-cy, aux regles de la raison'. I.38: P 250, V 245, F 181.

159 [B]'Me voicy après d'achever cet homme, non d'en refaire un autre'. III.10: P 1056, V 1011, F 773.

160 [B]'Dispensons nous de quelque chose plus outre; appellons encore nature, l'usage et condition de chacun de nous; taxons nous, traitons nous à cette mesure; estendons noz apparetenances et noz comtes jusques là'. III.10: P 1055, V 1009, F 772.

circumscribed and restrained to a narrow limit of the nearest and most contiguous commodities. And moreover their course should be directed not in a straight line that ends up elsewhere, but in a circle whose two extremities by [C]a short sweep [B]meet and terminate in ourselves.[161]

This practice of circular reflection aims at humble self-protection rather than heroic self-fortification. In withdrawing our will from the world, we are evading its dangers rather than overcoming them: [B]'we little men must flee the storm from further away; we must try to avoid feeling it, not try to endure it, and dodge the blows we cannot parry'.[162] Montaigne's self-possession is as fragile and imperfect as it is necessary:

> [B]We ourselves, who are the most proper and certain place for us to turn to, have not made ourselves secure enough. I have nothing that is my own but myself, and even there my possession is partly defective and borrowed.[163]

Montaigne makes no claim to rule himself, if ruling means exercising full control and mastery over his will, and living wholly within his own right, free of all manner of debt and obligation. But although he may not control himself, it is still (as we shall see in Chapter 5) within his power to 'regulate' and 'order' himself, however weakly and falteringly.

VI

Montaigne's call for us to return to and live for ourselves, it should now be clear, is not only or even mainly about inwardness and sincerity – about calling an end to play-acting and exiting the stage of public life, in order to discover (and live in accordance with) one's most authentic and irreducibly particular self. 'Belonging to oneself', 'estre à soy', entails both knowing how to live for ourselves, by understanding what it is that we owe to ourselves, and knowing how to own ourselves, by shunning all that renders us dependent upon, or subject to, the power of others.

161 [B]'Plus nous amplifions nostre besoing et possession, d'autant plus nous engageons nous aux coups de la fortune, et des adversitez. La carriere de nos desirs doit estre circonscripte, et restraincte, à un court limite, des commoditez les plus proches et contiguës. Et doit en outre, leur course, se manier, non en ligne droite, qui face bout ailleurs, mais en rond, duquel les deux pointes se tiennent et terminent en nous, par [C]un brief contour'. III.10: P 1056, V 1011, F 773.

162 [B]'À nous autres petits, il faut fuyr l'orage de plus loing: il faut pourvoir au sentiment, non à la patience; et eschever aux coups que nous ne sçaurions parer'. III.10: P 1061, V 1015, F 777.

163 [B]'Nous mesmes qui est la plus juste adresse, et la plus seure, ne nous sommes pas assez asseurez. Je n'ay rien mien, que moy; et si en est la possession en partie manque et empruntée'. III.9: P 1013, V 968, F 739–40.

Before drawing this chapter to a close, I should like to raise and respond to a possible objection to the argument that I have so far laid out. If, as I have claimed, independence and not sincerity lies at the heart of Montaigne's preoccupation with 'self', what are we to make of his insistence, in the preface, that he intends to be seen A'in his own simple, natural, ordinary fashion, without study or artifice?'[164] Montaigne's 'self' is clearly identified, in this passage, with natural plainness and effortless simplicity, against all that is borrowed or contrived. Does this commitment to undisguised self-revelation not imply that being true to oneself *is*, after all, at the core of his project?

Deceit and hypocrisy are, it is true, forcefully denounced by Montaigne as symptoms of an epidemic of false self-presentation and self-delusion. It is crucial, however, that we see just what is at stake in this critique. Despite his deep concern with the immorality of lies, his desire to promote a sincere civility based on friendship and equity, and his heightened awareness of the disparity between appearance and reality, Montaigne indicts art, not as evidence of inauthenticity, but as an expression of servility. His rhetoric of openness and naturalness, purged of all false glosses and accretions, is inseparable from, and subordinate to, his identification of himself as a free man.

In Jean Starobinski's reading of the *Essais*, Montaigne's concern with the concordance of inner and outer states of feeling and being is not only an ethical imperative in its own right but a condition of meaningful self-identity:

> Lying is not merely a matter of culpable disloyalty to my neighbor; it is an ontological catastrophe for myself: I lose my true self, because it is impossible for me to preserve its form intact within my own mind, and because, deprived of all outside relations, my mind is nothing but uncertainty.[165]

Deception is loathsome to Montaigne because it signals the unavoidable corruption of his being by artifice and appearance:

> For wasn't the natural law that propels and governs us perverted once we became aware of the possibility of artifice? And when I turn my affection upon myself,

[164] A'En ma façon simple, naturelle et ordinaire, sans estude et artifice'. *Au lecteur*: P 27, V 3, F 2.

[165] 'Le mensonge n'est pas seulement une déloyauté coupable envers mon prochain; il est, pour nous-mêmes, une catastrophe ontologique: je perds ma vraie forme, puisqu'il n'est pas possible de la préserver intacte en mon for intérieur, et puisque mon for intérieur, privé de toute relation externe, n'est qu'incertitude'. Starobinski 1993, pp. 193–4; English translation from Starobinski 1985, p. 98.

eager as I may be to possess the truth about myself, isn't artifice incorporated into each of my acts and each of my perceptions? Hasn't appearance – that cause of all great change – insinuated its evil effects between me and myself? Even worse, hasn't it cast its spell over me as both subject and object?[166]

A world of histrionic appearances strips individuals not only of their honesty but also of their power over their own identities. Montaigne realises that

> he is hypocritical because he is alienated (as a later vocabulary would have it): he has made his being dependent on opinion, on esteem, on the *words* by which others (the 'world', 'society') confer 'reputation' and 'glory'. (Rousseau's formulation of the first count in his indictment of society scarcely differs from this in its language).[167]

Montaigne's revolt against 'the theft of our being by the gaze of others' is 'a judgment that Sartre would repeat in his phenomenological description of the *pour autrui*, or "for others"'.[168]

The *Essais* are adamant in their condemnation of lying as a fundamental betrayal of human sociability and as a perversion of language and communication. As Montaigne argues in *On liars*: [C]'we are men, and hold together, only by our word. If we recognised the horror and the gravity of lying, we would persecute it with fire more justly than other crimes'.[169] To lie is to corrupt speech, to render meaningful communication impossible. As he explains in *On giving the lie*, [A]'mutual understanding is brought about solely by way of words', as 'the only instrument by means of which our wills and thoughts communicate'. He who 'falsifies' his word 'betrays human society', for 'if it fails us, we have no more hold on each other, no

[166] 'La loi naturelle qui nous porte et nous traverse, n'a-t-elle pas été pervertie une fois pour toutes lorsque nous nous sommes éveillés à la possibilité de l'artifice? Et lorsque je tourne sur moi mon affection, si désireux que je sois de me posséder dans ma vérité, l'artifice n'est-il pas incorporé dans chacun de mes gestes, dans chacun des mes regards? Le paraître – cet exécuteur des hautes oeuvres de la mutation – n'insinue-t-il pas ses maléfices entre moi et moi, et pis encore, ne tient-il pas sous son charme à la fois le moi-sujet et le moi-objet?' Starobinski 1993, pp. 186–7; translation from Starobinski 1985, p. 94.

[167] 'Il est hypocrite parce que aliéné (comme le dira un langage plus tardif): il a mis son être sous la dépendance de l'opinion, du regard, des mots par lesquels les autres (le 'monde', la 'société') confèrent la 'réputation' et la 'gloire'. Rousseau ne formulera pas en termes différents son premier acte d'accusation'. Starobinski 1993, pp. 34–5; translation from Starobinski 1985, p. 10.

[168] 'Le rapt de notre être par le regard d'autrui'. 'Un constat qui sera repris par Sartre dans sa description phénoménologique du "pour autrui"'. Starobinski 1993, p. 180; translation from Starobinski 1985, p. 90.

[169] [C]'Nous ne sommes hommes, et ne nous tenons les uns aux autres que par la parole. Si nous en connoissions l'horreur et le poids, nous le poursuivrions à feu, plus justement que d'autres crimes'. I.9: P 58, V 36, F 23.

more knowledge of each other', and 'if it deceives us, it breaks up all our relations and dissolves all the bonds of our polity'.[170]

The problem with dissimulation, however, lies not in its inherent artifice or bad faith, but in its fraudulence, as a debasement of the currency which we use to judge the morals of men: [A]'our truth of nowadays is not what is, but what others can be convinced of; just as we call 'money' not only that which is legal, but also any counterfeit that will pass'.[171] False speech, in this sense, [B]'enfolds cowardice and faintness of heart',[172] there being no more obvious cowardice than 'to deny our own word' and, worse yet, 'to deny what we know'. The man who dissimulates and hides himself is guilty not of insincerity, but of moral turpitude and weakness.

The courtier, as we have seen, is condemned to flattering and ingratiating himself with his master, contorting himself into whatever posture shall best please the man who holds him in his power. But nor is he able, as a consequence, to judge or speak freely about himself. As Montaigne writes in *On presumption*:

> [A]It is a craven and servile humour to disguise ourselves and hide under a mask, and not to dare to show ourselves as we are. [. . .] [B]A generous heart should not belie its thoughts; it wants to reveal itself even to its inmost depths.[173]

This connection between freedom and frankness is then reaffirmed through an appeal to Aristotle, who [C]'considered it the function of magnanimity to hate and love openly, to judge, to speak with complete frankness, and to have no regard for the approbation or reprobation of others in comparison with truth', and Apollonius, who [A]'said that it was for slaves to lie, and for free men to speak truth'.[174]

Montaigne, we are told in the same chapter, does not know [A]'how to please, or delight, or tickle', knowing only how to talk 'in good earnest',

170 [A]'Nostre intelligence se conduisant par la seule voye de la parolle, celuy qui la fauce, trahit la societé publique. C'est le seul util, par le moyen duquel se communiquent nos volontez et nos pensées: c'est le truchement de nostre ame: s'il nous faut, nous ne nous tenons plus, nous ne nous entrecognoissons plus. S'il nous trompe, il rompt tout nostre commerce, et dissoult toutes les liaisons de nostre police'. II.18: P 705–6, V 666–7, F 505.

171 [A]'Nostre verité de maintenant, ce n'est pas ce qui est, mais ce qui se persuade à autruy: comme nous appelons monnoye, non celle qui est loyalle seulement, mais la fauce aussi, qui a mise'. II.18: P 705, V 666, F 505.

172 [B]'Envelopper la couardise et lascheté de cœur'. 'Se desdire de sa parolle [. . .] se desdire de sa propre science' II.18: P 705, V 666, F 505.

173 [A]'C'est un' humeur couarde et servile de s'aller desguiser et cacher sous un masque, et de n'oser se faire veoir tel qu'on est. [. . .] [B]Un cœur genereux ne doit desmentir ses pensées: il se veut faire voir jusques au dedans'. II.17: P 685, V 647, F 491.

174 [C]'Aristote estime office de magnanimité, hayr et aimer à descouvert: juger, parler avec toute franchise: et, au prix de la verité, ne faire cas de l'approbation ou reprobation d'autruy. [A]Apollonius disoit que c'estoit aux serfs de mentir, et aux libres de dire verité'. II.17: P 686, V 647, F 491.

a defect that makes him ill-suited to 'tirelessly amusing the ear of a prince with all kinds of talk': [B]'princes are not very fond of serious talk, nor I of telling stories'. His language has [A]'no ease or polish', being 'harsh, with free and unruly dispositions'.[175] His soul [A]'shuns lying by its own complexion, and hates even to think a lie', so much so that he feels 'an inward shame and a stinging remorse if one escapes me, as sometimes it does on unexpected occasions.[176]

Montaigne's study of himself, as I argued in Chapter 2, is an account of himself in the strongest sense – a *registre* or *contre-rolle* of that which is truly his own, an act of stocktaking and public testimony, offered not as the introspection of an elusive, authentic self, but as a bold imprint of his moral value and character. This commitment to bold self-scrutiny and self-disclosure, I now wish to suggest, is advanced by Montaigne as a public witness to his independence. As he maintains in *On the art of conversation*:

[B]Not to dare to speak roundly of oneself shows some lack of heart: A stout and lofty judgment which judges sanely and surely, uses its own examples on all occasions as well as others, and testifies as frankly about itself as about a third party: We must pass over these common rules of civility in favour of truth, and liberty. [C]I dare not only to speak of myself, but to speak only of myself.[177]

To those men, finally, who claim that what Montaigne calls [B]'frankness, simplicity and naturalness' in his conduct is mere 'art and subtlety, and rather prudence than goodness, artifice than nature, good sense than good luck',[178] he boldly responds:

[B]But surely they make my subtlety too subtle. And if anyone follows and watches me closely, I will concede him the victory if he does not confess, that there is no rule in their school that could reproduce this natural movement, and maintain a

175 [A]'Je ne sçay ny plaire, ny resjouyr, ny chatouiller. [. . .] Je ne sçay parler qu'en bon escient'. [A]'Amuser sans se lasser, l'oreille d'un prince, de toute sorte de propos'. [B]'Les princes n'ayment guere les discours fermes, ny moy à faire des comptes'. '[A]Mon langage n'a rien de facile et fluide: il est aspre, ayant des dispositions libres et desreglées'. II:17: P 675–6, V 637–8, F 483.

176 [A]'Mon ame de sa complexion refuit la menterie, et hait mesme à la penser'. 'Un'interne vergongne et un remors piquant, si par fois elle m'eschappe, comme par fois elle m'eschappe'. II.17: P 686, V 648, F 491.

177 [B]'Le n'oser parler rondement de soy, accuse quelque faute de cœur: Un jugement roide et hautain, qui juge sainement, et seurement: il use à toutes mains, des propres exemples, ainsi que de chose estrangere: et tesmoigne franchement de luy, comme de chose tierce: Il faut passer par dessus ces regles populaires de la civilité, en faveur de la verité, et de la liberté. [C]J'ose non seulement parler de moy: mais parler seulement de moy'. III.9: P 988, V 942, F 720.

178 [B]'Que ce que j'appelle franchise, simplesse, et naïfveté, en mes mœurs, c'est art et finesse: et plustost prudence, que bonté: industrie, que nature: bon sens, que bon heur'. III.1: P 835, V 795, F 603.

picture of liberty, and licence, so constant and inflexible, on such tortuous and varied paths: and that all their attention and ingenuity could not bring them to it.[179]

Montaigne's unabashed examination and exposition of himself in the *Essais*, is, from this perspective, a final testament to his liberty.

179 B'Mais certes ils font ma finesse trop fine. Et qui m'aura suyvi et espié de près, je lui donray gaigné, s'il ne confesse, qu'il n'y a poinct de regle en leur escole, qui sceust rapporter ce naturel mouvement, et maintenir une apparence de liberté, et de licence, si pareille, et inflexible, parmy des routes si tortues et diverses: et que toute leur attention et engin, ne les y sçauroit conduire'. III.1: P 835, V 795, F 603.

CHAPTER 4

Oysiveté *and* nonchalance

Liberty as carelessness

I

Public life, as we established in Chapter 3, is for Montaigne a source of slavery. Men 'give themselves to hire', by placing themselves at the mercy of other men, for the sake of reputation, wealth, influence and other external commodities that are not truly their own. They are slaves in the sense that they have mortgaged or expropriated themselves, by rendering themselves dependent on the will of another. The free man, by contrast, belongs to himself.

Self-possession, however, is only one part of the story. The man who engages himself to others, who lives *in potestate dominorum* rather than *sui iuris*, is not only subject to a master, he is also a slave to care. His mind and his will are not his own: not merely because he lives under the power of another, but because he labours under the burden of endless vexations and troubles. To a life of restless agitation and anxiety, full of 'empeschemens', 'tracasserie', 'presse' and 'pois', Montaigne opposes his own laziness, negligence and irresponsibility. Liberty, in this perspective, is associated not with independence but rather with carelessness.

In *On vanity*, let us recall, Montaigne writes that C'idleness and freedom', his 'favourite qualities', have bred in him 'a mortal hatred, of being held to another, or by another' than himself.[1] Later on in the same chapter, he claims to have turned his back on public occupations because C'liberty and idleness', his 'ruling qualities', are 'diametrically opposed to that trade'.[2] In Chapter 3, these appeals to freedom were shown to form part of a bold discourse of self-jurisdiction, grounded in a refusal to live by grace or under obligation to others. I should now like to extend and complete this

[1] C'Et mes qualitez plus favories, l'oysiveté, la franchise. Par tout cela, j'ay prins à haine mortelle, d'estre tenu ny à autre, ny par autre que moy'. III.9: P 1014, V 969, F 741.

[2] C'La liberté et l'oysiveté, qui sont mes maistresses qualitez, sont qualitez, diametralement contraires à ce mestier là'. III.9: P 1038, V 992, F 759.

analysis by turning to the second of these all-important qualities. What does Montaigne mean by 'idleness' (*oysiveté*), and what does this concept contribute to his understanding of freedom?

Idleness, in the first instance, consists in laziness and inertia. Liberty here comes to be identified not merely with an absence of dependency, but with a lack of effort, difficulty and strain. In the first extract just cited, Montaigne's unwillingness to accept favours from others reflects his reluctance to repay them with services of his own. Freedom is associated with both leisure and pleasure: he '<relish[es] the tenderness of a pure liberty>' discharged of all duties.[3] In the second passage, similarly, idleness is adduced alongside liberty to explain his lack of enthusiasm for the thorough 'reclothing' needed to make him fit for public occupations: [B]'even if I had enough power over myself to do that (and why couldn't I, with time and care?), I wouldn't want to'.[4] Not only is he too protective of his independence to submit to the temptations of ambition, but he is also too indolent to train himself for such a career.

Montaigne's point is not to commend pure inactivity and lethargy, but rather to free himself from mental disquiet.[5] His aversion towards effort and strain reflects an antipathy towards care (*soing*, *soucy*, *solicitude*), a concern to protect himself and his indolent, fragile will from discomfort and distress. He is [C]'easy <and ready> for any man's need', but only as long as they ask of him 'nothing involving business or care', for he has 'declared war to the death against all care'.[6] He avoids binding himself to others [B]'to relieve [him]self a little of the inner tension and solicitude of [his] will, ~~and of the internal obligation of [his] affection~~. [. . .] Which is a little ~~violent~~ [C]too urgent [B]and pressing where [he] give[s] [him]self to it, at least for a man who has no wish to be under pressure'.[7]

It is worth drawing attention here to Montaigne's use, in the first passage just quoted, of the motif of weight. When he claims to [C]'weigh the bond of an obligation' as heavily as it 'weighs upon' him,[8] he is playing with

3 '<S'ils sçavouroient comme moy la douceur d'une pure liberté>'. III.9: P 1014, V 969, F 740.

4 [B]'Rabillage'. 'Quand je pourrois cela sur moy, (et pourquoy ne le pourrois je, avec le temps et le soing?) je ne le voudrois pas'. III.9: P 1038, V 992, F 759.

5 On leisure and tranquillity in Montaigne, see O'Loughlin 1978, Tournon 1996, Petit 1997 and Krause 2000.

6 [C]'Commodement facile <et prest> au besoing de chacun'. 'Chose negotieuse et soucieuse'. 'Car j'ay denoncé à tout soing guerre capitale'. III.9: P 1015, V 970, F 741.

7 [B]'Me soulager un peu, de l'attention et sollicitude, de ma volonté au dedans, ~~et de l'obligation interne de mon affection~~. [. . .] Laquelle j'ay ~~peu bien violente~~, [C]trop urgente [B]et pressante, où je m'adonne: aumoins pour un homme, qui ne veut estre aucunement en presse'. III.9: P 1012, V 967, F 739.

8 [C]'S'ils poisoient autant que doit poiser à un sage homme, l'engageure d'une obligation'. III.9: P 1014, V 969, F 740.

the meanings of the transitive verb *poiser* (to weigh, to evaluate) and the reflexive *me poiser* (to weigh upon me). The weight or value that he attaches to such bonds is the same as their weight – their burden, their impression – on his soul. As he puts it elsewhere in *On vanity*, he is C'no philosopher': evils 'trample' him insofar as they 'weigh upon' him.[9] Similarly, in a passage that appears towards the start of the chapter, Montaigne gives two reasons for excepting himself from public duties and occupations: he departs from them B'partly out of conscience', for just as he sees 'the weight attached to such employments', he sees 'the little means' that he has to bring to them, and 'partly out of cowardice', because he is 'content to enjoy the world without being all empressed in it, to live a life, that is merely excusable: and which will merely not weigh on [him]self or others'.[10]

Montaigne here juxtaposes the importance and gravity of public occupations, a weight which he is unworthy to bear, with the intolerable burdens that such charges impose on his mind. His aspiration to a weightless life 'qui seulement ne poise, ny à moy, ny à autruy' is, by this token, a plea at once for tranquillity and for obscurity. As he puts it a few pages earlier, B'I seek only to pass by', without notice, his C'principal profession in this life' being 'to live it comfortably, and rather relaxedly than busily'.[11]

This association of public occupations with a crippling burden of care is also to be found in the following chapter, *On managing the will*. Montaigne states that he is B'too tender, both by nature and by practice' to cope with the strain and stress of public life: 'if I were to bite off as much as others do, my soul would never have the strength to bear the alarms and emotions that afflict those who embrace so much'.[12] Those men who 'enslave themselves' to others have been defrauded of their 'faculties': 'their tenants' (the men who have 'hire[d]' their services) 'are at home inside, not they'.[13] Slavery, in this context, signifies not only dispossession, but ceaseless and forced labour.

9 C'Je ne suis pas philosophe. Les maux me foullent selon qu'ils poisent'. III.9 P 994, V 950, F 725.

10 B'Partie par conscience: (car par où je vois le poix qui touche telles vacations, je vois aussi le peu de moyen que j'ay d'y fournir [. . .]) partie par poltronerie. Je me contente de jouir le monde, sans m'en empresser: de vivre une vie, seulement excusable: et qui seulement ne poise, ny à moy, ny à autruy'. III.9: P 997, V 952–3, F 727.

11 B'Je ne cherche qu'à passer [. . .]. C Ma principale profession en cette vie, estoit de la vivre mollement, et plustost laschement qu'affaireusement'. III.9: P 993, V 949, F 724.

12 B'Je suis trop tendre, et par nature et par usage [. . .]. Si je mordois à mesme, comme font les autres; mon ame n'auroit jamais la force de porter les alarmes, et emotions, qui suyvent ceux qui embrassent tant'. III.10: P 1048–9, V 1003–4, F 767.

13 B'Les hommes se donnent à louage. Leurs facultez ne sont pas pour eux; elles sont pour ceux, à qui ils s'asservissent; leurs locataires sont chez euz, ce ne sont pas eux'. III.10: P 1049, V 1004, F 767.

[B]See the people who have been taught to let themselves be seized and carried away, they do so everywhere. In little things as in big; in what does not touch them, as in what does. They push in indiscriminately whenever there is business and involvement, and are without life, when they are without tumultuous agitation.[14]

This satire on the restlessness of ambitious men takes on a more tragic appearance through a description of his father's selfless devotion to public service during his time as Mayor of Bordeaux.

[B]I remember having seen him old, in my boyhood, his soul cruelly agitated by this public turmoil; forgetting the sweet air of his home, to which the weakness of years had attached him long since, and his household, and his health; and, truly heedless of his life, which he thought to lose in this, engaged for them in long and painful journeys.[15]

Montaigne [B]'commend[s]' this course of action, which in his father 'sprang from a great goodness of nature', but he himself does not 'like to follow it'.[16] In accepting the post of Mayor in his turn, he writes, he made it clear to the magistrates of Bordeaux that he should be [B]'very sorry if anything whatsoever were to make such an impression on my will, as their affairs and their city had formerly done' on his father's.[17] His point is not that his independence requires him to shun all manner of debt and private obligation (although, as we have seen, that pattern of thought is evident elsewhere in this chapter of the text), but that he cannot bear to forfeit his tranquillity and ease, even in the name of public duty. Like his ageing and weakened father, he cannot be brought to 'forget the sweet air of his home' without 'cruel' agitation and distress. His rejection of too intimate or passionate an engagement with public life stems not only from his aversion towards ambition, partisan judgments and violent affections, but from an awareness of the fragility and delicacy of his will.

Liberty, as these examples suggest, appears in the *Essais* in two contrasting guises, overlapping and intersecting so closely as to be present in the

14 [B]'Voyez les gens appris à se laisser emporter et saisir, ils le font par tout. Aux petites choses comme aux grandes; à ce qui ne les touche point, comme à ce qui les touche. Ils s'ingerent indifferemment où il y a de la besongne; et sont sans vie, quand ils sont sans agitation tumultuaire'. III.10: P 1049, V 1004, F 767.

15 [B]'Il me souvenoit, de l'avoir veu vieil, en mon enfance, l'ame cruellement agitée de cette tracasserie publique; oubliant le doux air de sa maison, où la foiblesse des ans l'avoit attaché long temps avant, et son mesnage, et sa santé; et mesprisant certes sa vie, qu'il y cuida perdre, engagé pour eux, à des longs et penibles voyages'. III.10: P 1051, V 1005–6, F 769.

16 [B]'Luy partoit cette humeur d'une grande bonté de nature. [. . .] Ce train, que je loue en autruy, je n'ayme point à le suivre'. III.10: P 1051, V 1006, F 769.

17 [B]'Très-marry que chose quelconque fist autant d'impression en ma volonté, comme avoyent faict autrefois en la sienne, leurs affaires, et leur ville'. III.10: P 1050–1, V 1005, F 768–9.

same passage. From the perspective of Chapter 3, freedom is about governing oneself in accordance with one's own will. It is about holding one's head high and accepting no one but oneself as the arbiter of one's judgment, speech and conduct. Dependency and moral corruption are inextricably linked: flattery, dissimulation, and pusillanimity are inescapable consequences of living under the power of others. As I have now begun to suggest, however, this muscular language intersects with a seemingly antithetical understanding of liberty as a state of idleness, ease, passivity, and even weakness. Freedom is here associated with a negligent and irresponsible absence of concern and application, a ponderous indifference and inertia, a lack of premeditation and effort, and an untamed resistance to discipline and control. To be free, in this light, is to live at one's leisure, unburdened and untroubled by any duties or business, in a manner suited to Montaigne's natural tenderness and laziness. It is about being careless – a conception that unites idleness with negligence (*nonchalance*).

How are we to make sense of this apparent disjunction? Is Montaigne's use of the term 'liberty' simply confused or incoherent? The *Essays* certainly make no claim to offer a consistent or systematic treatment of this or any other topic. On the contrary, as Montaigne explains in a crucial passage from *On Democritus and Heraclitus*,

> CI do not see the whole of anything: Nor do those who promise to show it to us. Of a hundred members and faces that each thing has I take one [. . .]. Scattering a word here, there another, samples separated from their context, dispersed, without a plan, without a promise: I am not bound to make something of them, or to adhere to them myself, without varying, when I please, and giving myself up to doubt and uncertainty, and to my ruling quality, which is ignorance.[18]

It would not be surprising then if, in 'essaying' liberty, Montaigne were to deploy the term in dissonant ways. B'I may well contradict myself now and then', whether because 'I am different myself' or because 'I take hold of my subjects in different circumstances and aspects' – although 'truth', he insists, 'I do not contradict'.[19]

It would be wrong, however, to conclude from such statements that he writes about 'liberty' in a muddled or unthinking way. Montaigne's

18 C'Car je ne voy le tout de rien: Ne font pas, ceux qui nous prometttent de nous le faire veoir. De cent membres et visages, qu'à chasque chose j'en prens un [. . .] Semant icy un mot, icy un autre, eschantillons dépris de leur piece, escartez, sans dessein, sans promesse: je ne suis pas tenu d'en faire bon, ny de m'y tenir moy-mesme, sans varier, quand il me plaist, et me rendre au doubte et incertitude, et à ma maistresse forme, qui est l'ignorance'. I.50: P 321–2, V 302, F 219.

19 B'Soit que je sois autre moy-mesme, soit que je saisisse les subjects, par autres circonstances, et considerations. [. . .] Je me contredis bien à l'advanture, mais la verité [. . .] je ne la contredy point'. III.2: P 845, V 805, F 611.

construction of freedom is composite but not incoherent. Self-possession and carelessness are to be understood neither as chronologically successive positions, nor as stages in an overarching, dialectical argument, but as structures of thought and language held in persistent and reciprocal dialogue with each other. Their juxtaposition results not in mere confusion or inconsistency, but in a process of constructive self-questioning drawing strength from the text's capacity to inhabit multiple points of view.

Montaigne's characterisation of himself as weak, indolent and neglectful has featured prominently in both older and more recent studies of the *Essais*.[20] These studies rightly draw attention to the paradoxical or ironic dimensions of this self-presentation: his uselessness and lack of application function as forms of indirect self-praise, his powerlessness being recovered as the mark of an unlearned, effortless, natural goodness.[21] What is lacking in these accounts, however, is a sense of the wider context governing this rhetoric of laziness and artlessness – a sense of the contribution made by carelessness to Montaigne's efforts to construct himself as a free man.

This point can be illustrated most clearly with reference to David Quint's landmark study, *Montaigne and the quality of mercy* (1998), arguably the most influential and accomplished contribution to the recent 'ethical turn' in Montaigne studies (which it did so much to inaugurate).[22] One of Montaigne's principal aims in the *Essais*, Quint argues, is to intervene in the unfolding crisis of the French civil wars 'by propounding a new ethics to counter the model of heroic virtue that prevailed in his culture and his noble class'.[23] Faced with a political morality that equates resistance and revenge with aristocratic honour and Stoic autonomy, the *Essais* redefine nobility, according to Quint, as a willingness to yield for the sake of peace, in particular through the exercise of clemency toward one's enemies and submission to royal authority. Montaigne's depiction of himself as a nonchalant, trusting, innocent weakling is 'rhetorically designed to show that morality in action and to persuade us to follow it'.[24] Independence, constancy and firmness are repudiated as elements of an obstinate, violent and unforgiving Stoicism: the exercise of power over the self, for Montaigne, results both in cruelty to others and to oneself.

In this reading, the *Essais* stage a dramatic confrontation between two irreconcilable visions of morality: an ethics of self-government and self-discipline derived from the classics, and a more humane and distinctively

[20] Among recent contributions, see Langer 1999, pp. 105–21, 163–79; Giocanti 2001, pp. 485–542; Naya 2005; Hartle 2003 and 2006; and Noirot-Maguire 2007.

[21] On Montaigne's appeal to nature, see Micha 1956, Atkinson 1973, Beaudry 1976 and Schneider 1996.

[22] Quint 1998. See also his study of *On anger*: Quint 2000.

[23] Quint 1998, p. ix. [24] Quint 1998, p. xiv.

modern ethics of innocent weakness, compassion and self-acceptance.[25] This dichotomy becomes unsustainable, however, when we realise that carelessness is itself part of a wider discourse about liberty. Idleness and nonchalance are, in their deepest sense, about not being a slave to care, by freeing ourselves from the oppressive burdens of 'affaires' and mental disquiet. Carelessness is about being unaffected, both in the sense that one's conduct and speech are unrehearsed and uncontrived, and in the sense that one's will is preserved in a state of indifference and equanimity. Far from being defined in *opposition* to independence and self-regulation, Montaigne's slackness and softness (*mollesse, lascheté, facilité*), his idleness and lethargy (*oysiveté, langueur, paresse*), and above all his artlessness (*naïfveté, nonchalance*) take their place, *alongside* self-possession, within a single, powerful vision of what it means to be free.

II

Montaigne's emphasis on his ordinary, lowly, human weakness is one of the most striking and appealing features of his self-presentation. As he declares in *On presumption*, he feels himself, [A]'floating and bending with weakness', so much so that [A]'it would be very difficult [. . .] for anyone to esteem himself less, or indeed for anyone to esteem [him] less' than he does.[26] The ensuing pages illustrate this point by listing all of the ways in which he has found himself to be wanting: his poetry and style are untouched by grace; his physical appearance is unremarkable; he lacks physical skill and athletic distinction. This catalogue of imperfections includes the same conjunction of terms encountered in *On vanity*: he is [C]'extremely idle, extremely free, both by nature and by art'.[27]

Montaigne's liberty – he has had [A]'neither governor nor master forced on [him] to this day'; his soul is [A]'free and all its own' – is here identified not merely with a hatred of subjection, but with an inability to tolerate care.[28] He has [A]'no liveliness' either in his body or his soul, only a 'full, firm vigour', which allows him to 'stand up well under hard work', but only 'so far as [his] desire leads [him] to it'.[29] He has [A]'come to the point where,

[25] On this point, see also Hallie 1977.

[26] [A]'Il est bien difficile [. . .] qu'aucun s'estime moins, voire qu'aucun autre m'estime moins, que ce que je m'estime. [. . .] Je me [C]~~desadvoue sans cesse; et me~~ [A]sens [C]~~par tout~~ [A]flotter et fleschir de foiblesse'. II.17: P 672–3, V 635, F 481.

[27] [C]'Extremement oisif, extremement libre, et par nature et par art'. II.17: P 681, V 642, F 487.

[28] [A]'N'ayant eu jusques à cett' heure ny commandant ny maistre forcé'. 'Une ame libre et toute sienne'. II.17: P 681, V 643, F 487.

[29] [A]'Rien d'allegre: [. . .] seulement une vigueur pleine et ferme. Je dure bien à la peine, [. . .] autant que mon desir m'y conduit'. II.17: P 680, V 642, F 487.

except for health and life, there is nothing [C]for which [he is] willing to bite [his] nails, and [A]that [he is] willing to buy at the cost of mental torment and constraint'.[30] He [C]'would as willingly lend [his] blood, as [his] care',[31] and has always gone in life [A]'just so far as [he] pleased, and at [his] own pace'.[32] His is a [A]'ponderous, lazy and do-nothing nature'[33] and [A]'a delicate complexion, incapable of solicitude'.[34]

This rhetoric of inertia, uselessness and passivity is pervasive in the *Essais*. Montaigne's self-portrait, he states with regret, does not [A]'represent' him in his 'best state', but 'fallen far' from his 'earlier vigour and cheerfulness, and beginning to grow withered and rancid': he is now 'at the bottom of the barrel, which smells at turns of rot and of the lees'.[35] Even as a child, his [A]'heavy complexion', 'slow mind', 'tardy understanding' and 'weak invention' meant that 'nothing worthwhile' could be got out of him.[36] His father's enthusiasm for education was thus wasted on him: [A]'although my health was sound and complete, and my nature gentle and tractable, I was withal so ponderous, slack and drowsy, that one could not tear me from my idleness, not even to make me play'.[37]

Being a man of no true knowledge, distinction, or merit, Montaigne cannot claim, like other authors, to have anything of value to offer to those who buy his book. In his prefatory address, he warns that he has written the *Essais* for [A]'the private convenience of my relatives and friends', without thought for the 'service' of others, his 'powers' being inadequate for such a task. The reader is abruptly dismissed with the unwelcoming assertion that it would be 'unreasonable to spend your leisure on so frivolous and vain a subject' as Montaigne himself.[38] The *Essais*, we are told in *On vain subtleties*, will please neither [A]'common and vulgar minds' nor 'singular and excellent'

[30] [A]'Car j'en suis là, que sauf la santé et la vie, il n'est chose [C]pourquoy je vueille ronger mes ongles, et [A]que je vueill' acheter au prix du tourment d'esprit, et de la contrainte'. II.17: P 681, V 642, F 487.

[31] [C]'Je presteroy aussi volontiers mon sang, que mon soing'. II.17: P 681, V 642, F 487.

[32] [A]'J'ay marché aussi avant, et le pas qu'il m'a pleu'. II.17: P 681, F 487.

[33] [A]'Ce naturel poisant, paresseux et fayneant'. II.17: P 681, V 643, F 487.

[34] [A]'Une complexion delicate et incapable de sollicitude'. II.17: P 682, V 643, F 488.

[35] [A]'Cette peinture [. . .] ne se raporte pas à mon meilleur estat, mais beaucoup descheu de ma premiere vigueur et allegresse, tirant sur le flestry et le rance. Je suis sur le fond du vaisseau, qui sent tantost le bas et la lye'. II.37: P 825, V 784, F 596.

[36] [A]'Cette complexion lourde [. . .] l'esprit, je l'avois lent [. . .] l'apprehension tardive, l'invention lasche'. 'Rien [. . .] qui vaille'. I.25: P 181, V 174–5, F 129.

[37] [A]'Quoy que j'eusse la santé ferme et entiere, et quant et quant un naturel doux et traitable, j'estois parmy cela si poisant, mol et endormy, qu'on ne me pouvoit arracher de l'oisiveté, non pas pour me faire jouer'. I.25: P 181, V 174, F 129.

[38] [A]'Je n'y ay eu nulle consideration de ton service, [. . .] mes forces ne sont pas capables d'un tel dessein. Je l'ay voué à la commodité particuliere de mes parens et amis'. 'Ce n'est pas raison que tu employes ton loisir en un subject si frivole et si vain'. *Au lecteur*: P 27, V 3, F 2.

ones, although they may 'get by in the middle region'.[39] Montaigne here classes himself among those [C]'half-breeds who have disdained the first seat, ignorance of letters, and have not been able to reach the other', caught between simple peasants and philosophers, 'the rear end between two saddles'. Because he has no hope of attaining or even approaching wisdom, his only aim is to 'draw back as much as [he] can into the first and natural stage, which for naught [he] attempted to leave'.[40] He certainly has nothing to teach us, except perhaps by counter-example. As he puts it in the final chapter of the book: [B]'in the end, this whole fricassee that I am scribbling here, is nothing but a record of the essays of my life, which, for inward health is exemplary enough, if one takes its instruction in reverse'.[41]

The uselessness of the *Essais* reflects the carelessness with which Montaigne claims to have written them.[42] His soul [C]'ordinarily produces its most profound and maddest fancies, and those [he] like[s] the best, unexpectedly and when [he is] least looking for them', disappearing before he has a chance to write them down.[43] He claims to only write [A]'when pressed by too slack an idleness, and nowhere but at home', and 'with diverse interruptions and intervals'.[44] His book, in sum, is a collection of [B]'trifles' (*fadaises*) which, instead of being spoken 'with care' (*curieusement*) or 'great pains' (*magno conatu*), 'escape [him] as nonchalantly [*nonchalamment*] as they are worth'.[45]

This appeal to *nonchalance*, which John Florio typically translates as 'carelessenesse', is particular striking given the predominantly negative connotations of the word in sixteenth-century French usage. According to Edmond Huguet's *Dictionnaire de la langue française du seizième siècle*, the verb 'nonchalloir' meant to neglect or abandon ('être insoucieux de, négliger'; 'abandonner, laisser'), or to be indifferent or oblivious to something ('ne pas songer à, oublier, ne pas s'occuper de').[46] Huguet defines

39 [A]'Ils ne plairoient guere aux esprits communs et vulgaires, ny guere aux singuliers et excellens: [. . .] ils pourroient vivoter en la moyenne region'. I.54: P 333, V 313, F 227.

40 [C]'Les mestis, qui ont dedaigné le premier siège de l'ignorance des lettres, et n'ont peu joindre l'autre (le cul entre-deux selles: desquels je suis, et tant d'autres) [. . .] Je me recule tant que je puis, dans le premier et naturel siege, d'où je me suis pour neant essayé de partir'. I.54: P 332, V 313, F 227.

41 [B]'En fin, toute ceste fricassée que je barbouille ici, n'est qu'un registre des essais de ma vie: qui est pour l'interne santé exemplaire assez, à prendre l'instruction à contrepoil'. III.13: P 1126, V 1079, F 826. See also III.8: P 965, V 921, F 703[B].

42 Lapp 1971 and Noirot-Maguire 2007.

43 [C]'Mon ame [. . .] produit ordinairement ses plus profondes resveries, plus folles, et qui me plaisent le mieux, à l'improuveu, et lors que je les cherche moins'. III.5: P 919, V 876, F 668.

44 [A]'Lors qu'une trop lasche oysiveté me presse, et non ailleurs que chez moy. Ainsin il s'est basty à diverses poses et intervalles'. II.37: P 796, V 758, F 574.

45 III.1: P 829, V 790, F 599. 46 Huguet 1925–67.

nonchalance as 'insouciance', a lack of diligence, concern or care, citing a passage from Jean Calvin's *Institution de la religion chrestienne* (first French edition, 1541): 'le Seigneur par ses preceptes poinct et resveille les consciences des iniques, à fin qu'ilz ne se flattent point en leurs peschez par nonchallance de son jugement' ('the Lord by his precepts pricks and awakens the consciences of the wicked, in order that they should not flatter themselves in their sins through nonchalance of his judgment').[47] This emphasis on sinful indifference or complacency is found again, in the following century, in Pascal's well-known condemnation of Montaigne for inspiring 'une nonchalance du salut, sans crainte et sans repentir. [...] Il ne pense qu'à mourir lâchement et mollement par tout son livre' ('a *nonchalance* about salvation, without fear and without repentance. [...] He thinks only of dying loosely and limply throughout all his book').[48] These connotations of improvidence and neglect are confirmed by Randall Cotgrave's *Dictionarie of the French and English Tongues* (1611), which offers 'heedlessenesse, carelessnesse, retchlessenesse' and 'idlenesse', along with 'negligence', as English equivalents of *nonchalance*.[49]

The *Essais* offer several examples of this understanding of nonchalance as negligence or the literal negation of diligence. In a discussion of the art of 'mesnagerie' (the government of the household) in *On solitude*, Montaigne contrasts [A]'that base and vile care, tense and full of anxiety, which is seen in those men who plunge themselves deeply into it' with 'that profound and extreme neglect [*nonchalance*] letting everything go to ruin, which we see in others'.[50] This contrast between *nonchalance* and *soing* or *solicitude* is echoed in *Let business wait until tomorrow*, where he writes that [A]'the vice contrary to curiosity, is nonchalance: [B]'towards which I clearly lean by my complexion'.[51] Montaigne's nonchalance can thus quite literally be understood as carelessness, a lack of *cura* – a failure of application or effort, a detrimental idleness. This interpretation is confirmed by a comparison with Florio's translation, which substitutes 'that profound and extreame retchlesnesse to let all things goe' and 'rechlesness' for *nonchalance* in each of these two passages.[52]

47 Calvin 1911, vol. II, p. 101.

48 Pascal 2004, fragment 574. For Pascal's disagreement with Montaigne, see Meijer 1984.

49 Cotgrave 1611.

50 [A]'Ce bas et vil soing, tendu et plein de solicitude, qu'on voit aux hommes qui s'y plongent du tout. [...] Cette profonde et extreme nonchalance laissant tout aller à l'abandon, qu'on voit en d'autres'. I.38: P 248–9, V 244, F 180.

51 [A]'Le vice contraire à la curiosité, c'est la nonchalance: [B]vers laquelle je panche evidemment de ma complexion'. II.4: P 383, V 364, F 263.

52 Montaigne 1969, pp. 122; 211.

Nonchalance, finally, is a word that Montaigne would have encountered in French editions of Baldassare Castiglione's immensely popular *Libro del Cortegiano* (first published in 1528), as a translation of the key concept of *sprezzatura*.[53] There is no doubt that he had enough knowledge of Italian to read Castiglione in the original – a significant portion of his own *Journal de voyage* is in fact written in that language. It seems likely, however, from one of two explicit allusions to the work in the *Essais*, that he is referring instead to an unidentified French version of the text.[54] Of the three different translations to which Montaigne might have had access, the most successful (by 'J. Colin') rendered *sprezzatura* simply as 'nonchalance'. A second, anonymous translator, who contributed a version of Book I (alongside Colin's translation of Books II to IV) to the first (1537) French edition of the text, substituted 'nonchalance et mesprizon' or simply 'mesprizon'. The third version, by Gabriel Chappuys (1580), which came to displace the Colin translation towards the end of the century, offers 'mespris et nonchalance'.[55]

There is a strong case for interpreting *nonchalance* as a version of *sprezzatura*. The meaning of *sprezzatura* itself is, of course, notoriously elusive.[56] The term is, as Castiglione himself emphasises, 'a new word', making its first appearance in the following, oft-quoted definition offered by Count Ludovico da Canossa in Book I of the dialogue:

> But, having thought many times already about how this grace is acquired (leaving aside those who have it from the stars), I have found quite a universal rule [. . .] and that is to avoid affectation in every way possible as though it were some very rough and dangerous reef; and (to pronounce a new word perhaps) to practise in all things a certain *sprezzatura*, so as to conceal all art and make whatever is done or said appear to be without effort and almost without any thought about it.[57]

Sprezzatura allows the courtier to steer clear of *affettazione* and to achieve the perfection of *grazia*. Paradoxically, it seems to consist both in the concealment of art, and in its absence, 'demonstrating' a lack of effort

[53] On Montaigne and Castiglione, see Friedrich 1949, pp. 166, 370; Tetel 1979; and Noirot-Maguire 2007.

[54] Tetel 1979, p. 71, n. 3.

[55] Klesczewski 1966, pp. 168–9; Burke 1995, p. 69. For Colin's translation, see Castliglione 1538. The anonymous version of Book I is found in Castiglione 1537. For Chappuys' version, see Castiglione 1580.

[56] Saccone 1983.

[57] 'Ma avendo io già più volte pensato meco onde nasca questa grazia, lasciando quelli che dalle stelle l'hanno, trovo una regula universalissima [. . .] e cio è fuggir quanto più si po, e come un asperissimo e pericoloso scoglio, la affettazione; e, per dir forse una nova parola, usar in ogni cosa una certa sprezzatura, che nasconda l'arte e dimostri ciò che si fa e dice venir fatto senza fatica e quasi senza pensarvi'. Castiglione 1981, I.xxvi, pp. 59–60. English translation from Castiglione 2002, p. 32.

(‘fatica’) and premeditation (‘quasi senza pensarvi’). It is clear that Montaigne has a similarly unlaboured, improvised quality (and a similar paradox) in mind, in *On vanity*, when he writes that his [B]‘design is, to represent in speaking, a profound carelessness [*nonchalance*] <of accent and of face>, and fortuitous and unpremeditated gestures, as arising from the immediate occasions’.[58] Carelessness, in the sense of a lack of diligence, is here valorised as artlessness: *nonchalance* becomes a negligent pose or effortless manner attesting to one’s lack of affectation or premeditation.

Montaigne’s protestations of uselessness and weakness are designed to reinforce his *èthos* or authority as a speaker, by attesting not only to his lack of presumption and self-love, but to his naturalness (*naïfveté*), untainted by affectation, art or learning. As he puts it in *On repentance*, his is [B]‘a lowly life without lustre’, offering ‘crude and simple effects of nature, and of a very feeble nature at that’.[59] His aversion towards strain and effort is here recovered as the sign of an unforced, unlearned grace. In the sphere of ethics, meanwhile, his idleness and negligence come to be closely identified with ideas of innocence or natural goodness. In *On vanity*, he consoles himself in the knowledge that whereas other [B]‘more powerful’ men are guilty of ‘treason’, ‘injustice’, ‘irreligion’, ‘tyranny’, ‘avarice’ and ‘cruelty’, he himself has proved capable of no more than ‘stupidity, vanity and idleness’, and that ‘in an age, where it is so common to do evil, to do what is merely useless is as if praiseworthy’.[60] From childhood onwards, he claims in *On the education of children*, he has [A]‘had no other vice than ~~heaviness~~ [C]inertia and ~~softness~~ [B]laziness’, the danger being not that he should ‘do ill’, but that he should ‘do nothing’; not that he should become ‘wicked, but only useless’; not that he should be guilty of ‘malice’, but only of ‘~~stupidity~~ [C]idleness’.[61] As he explains in *On cruelty*, [A]‘what good I have in me I have [. . .] by the chance of my birth’; [B]‘the innocence that is in me, is a childish innocence; little vigour, and no art’.[62]

58 [B]‘Mon dessein est, de representer en parlant, une profonde nonchalance <d’accent et de visage>, et des mouvemens fortuites et impremeditez, comme naissans des occasions presentes’. III.9: P 1007, V 963, F 735.

59 [B]‘Une vie basse, et sans lustre. [. . .] Des effects de nature et crus et simples, et d’une nature encore bien foiblette’. III.2: P 845, V 805, F 611.

60 [B]‘La trahison, [. . .] l’injustice, l’irreligion, la tyrannie, l’avarice, la cruauté’. ‘La sottise, la vanité, l’oisiveté’. ‘En un temps, où le meschamment faire est si commun, de ne faire qu’inutilement, il est comme louable’. III.9: P 990, V 946, F 722.

61 [A]‘Aussi n’avoit la mienne [complexion] autre vice, que ~~la pesanteur~~ [C]langueur et ~~mollesse~~ [B]paresse. Le danger n’estoit pas que je fisse mal, mais que je ne fisse rien. Nul ne prognostiquoit que je deusse devenir mauvais, mais inutile: on y prevoyoit de la ~~stupidité~~ [C]faineantise, [A]non pas de la malice.’ I.25: P 183, V 175–6, F 130.

62 [A]‘Ce que j’ay de bien, je l’ay [. . .] par le sort de ma naissance [. . .]. [B]L’innocence qui est en moy, est une innocence niaise; peu de vigueur, et point d’art’. II.11: P 450–1, V 429, F 313.

As David Quint has demonstrated, this weak, artless, childish innocence is set in opposition to an ethics of arduous, even heroic, self-control. True virtue, Montaigne argues in *On cruelty*, signifies [A]'something greater and more active, than to let oneself, by a happy disposition, be led gently and peacefully in the footsteps of reason'.[63] It [A]'refuses facility for her companion', demanding 'a rough and thorny road', not 'the easy, gentle, and sloping path that guides the measured footsteps of a good natural disposition'.[64] His own [A]'virtue, or rather innocence', however, is 'accidental and fortuitous', an instinctive shunning of vice due to his natural complexion, rather than to reason and self-discipline.[65]

Socrates and Cato, he notes, exhibit [A]'so perfect a habituation to virtue that it has passed into their complexion'.[66] In these exceptional cases, a lifelong habit of virtuous self-control has brought the soul to such a point of moral perfection that its [A]'strength and rigidity [. . .] stifle and extinguish ~~bodily passions~~ [C]lusts, [A]as soon as they begin to stir', allowing them to act virtuously without effort, struggle or pain.[67] Montaigne's innocence, by contrast, is a [A]'condition so close to imperfection and weakness' that he does not 'very well know how to separate their confines and distinguish them'.[68] [A]'I have not', he writes, 'put myself to great effort to curb the desires by which I have found myself pressed'; indeed, [A]'I have not essayed much firmness in my soul to withstand passions, if they are even the least bit vehement'. In sum, [A]'I cannot give myself any great thanks because I find myself free from many vices', since 'I owe it more to my fortune than to my reason'.[69]

Montaigne's hatred of vice is an [A]'instinct and impression' formed in the nursery, a tender immaturity which he has never been able to shrug off and which remains obdurately deaf even to his own reasonings' (*discours*).[70]

63 [A]'La vertu sonne je ne sçay quoy de plus grand et de plus actif, que se laisser par une heureuse complexion, doucement et paisiblement conduire à la suite de la raison'. II.11: P 442, V 422, F 306.

64 [A]'La vertu refuse la facilité pour compagne; [. . .] cette aisée, douce et panchante voie, par où se conduisent les pas reglez d'une bonne inclination de nature, n'est pas celle de la vraye vertu. Elle demande un chemin aspre et espineux'. II.11: P 443–4, V 423, F 308.

65 [A]'Une vertu, ou innocence, pour mieux dire, accidentale et fortuite'. II.11: P 448, V 427, F 311.

66 [A]'Une si parfaicte habitude à la vertu, qu'elle leur est passée en complexion'. II.11: P 446, V 425, F 310.

67 [A]'La force et roideur de leur ame, estouffe et esteint les ~~passions corporelles~~ [C]concupiscences, [A]aussi tost qu'elles commencent à s'esbranler'. II.11: P 446–7, V 426, F 310.

68 [A]'Cette condition est si voisine à l'imperfection et à la foiblesse, que je ne sçay pas bien comment en demesler les confins et les distinguer'. II.11: P 447, V 426, F 310.

69 [A]'Je ne me suis mis en grand effort, pour brider les desires dequoy je me suis trouvé pressé. [. . .] Je n'ay essayé guere de fermeté en mon ame, pour soustenir des passions, si elles eussent esté tant soit peu vehementes. [. . .] Ainsi, je ne me puis dire nul granc-mercy, dequoy je me trouve exempt de plusieurs vices: [. . .] Je le doy plus à ma fortune qu'à ma raison'. II.11: P 448, V 427, F 311.

70 II.11: P 449, V 428, F 213.

This infantile goodness manifests itself in squeamishness (he hates cruelty to [A]'such a point of softness' that he can neither see 'a chicken's neck wrung without displeasure', nor 'suffer to hear the scream of a hare in the teeth of [his] dogs')[71] and in a childish affection towards other creatures (his [C]'nature is so tender, so childish' that he 'cannot well refuse [his] dog the play he offers [him] or asks of [him] outside the proper time').[72] This easy, weak-willed playfulness offers an elaboration and inversion of [A]'that brave and generous Epicurean pleasure' described at the start of the chapter, 'which undertakes to bring up virtue softly in her bosom and make it frolic, giving it as its playthings shame, fevers, poverty, death, and tortures'.[73] Whereas Epicurean virtue delights in its own courageous indifference, playing with hardship and evils like a child with its toys, Montaigne's childish innocence consists rather in a naïve and tender sensitivity towards suffering and affliction.

For all its weakness and indiscipline, however, this effortless, careless goodness closely resembles the perfected virtue of Cato and, above all, Socrates – a virtue which is no longer [C]'laborious' or 'maintained by a stiffening of the soul', but which corresponds to 'the very essence of the soul, its natural and ordinary gait'.[74] Moral excellence, in this perspective, consists not in a violent straining or exertion of the will, but rather in the experience of pleasure and ease in the performance of noble and honourable acts. Cato's suicide, Montaigne writes, is [A]'more tragic, and more tense' than that of Socrates. But Socrates' 'blithe cheerfulness in his last words and actions' is 'still, I know not how, more beautiful' than Cato's heroic and spectacular death.[75] This contrast between Cato and Socrates is repeated and further elaborated in *On physiognomy*. [B]'In Cato', Montaigne writes, 'we see very clearly that his is a pace ~~forced and~~ strained far above the ordinary'.[76] Socrates, however, [B]'raised himself, not by sallies, but by

71 [A]'Jusques à telle mollesse, que je ne voy pas esgorger un poulet sans desplaisir, et ois impatiemment gemir un lievre sous les dents de mes chiens'. II.17: P 451, V 429, F 313.

72 [C]'Je ne crain point à dire la tendresse de ma nature si puerile, que je ne puis pas bien refuser à mon chien la feste, qu'il m'offre hors de saison, ou qu'il me demande'. II.11: P 457, V 435, F 318.

73 [A]'Cette brave et genereuse volupté Epicurienne, qui fait estat de nourrir mollement en son giron, et y faire follatrer la vertu; luy donnant pour ses jouets, la honte, les fievres, la pauvreté, la mort, et les gehennes'. II.11: P 444, V 424, F 308.

74 [C]'Ce n'est plus vertu penible, ny des ordonnances de la raison, pour lesquelles maintenir il faille que leur ame se roidisse: c'est l'essence mesme de leur ame, c'est son train naturel et ordinaire'. II.11: P 446, V 425–6, F 310.

75 [A]'Plus tragique, et plus tendue'. 'Une allegresse enjouée en ses propos et façons dernieres'. 'Encore, je ne sçay comment, plus belle'. II.11: P 446, V 425, F 310.

76 [B]'En Caton, on void bien à clair, que c'est une alleure ~~forcée, et~~ tendue bien loing au dessus des communes'. III.12: P 1083, V 1037–8, F 793.

disposition, to the utmost point of vigour', or, rather, 'he raised nothing, but brought vigour, hardships, and difficulties down and back to his own natural and original level, and subjected them to it'.[77] Montaigne himself, finally, takes this artlessness one step further. Unlike Socrates, he writes, he has not [B]'corrected [his] natural disposition by ~~training and by~~ force of reason'. He has not 'troubled [his] inclination at all by art': 'I let myself go as I have come'.[78]

This vision of easy, unstrained goodness draws strength not from the exercise of power over the self, but from the absence of such power. Instead of labouring to achieve control over himself, Montaigne claims simply to abandon himself to his own benevolent, innocent nature. This valorisation of weakness as artlessness, as Quint shows, allows Montaigne to undercut contemporary identifications of noble virtue with a kind of unyielding, imperious constancy, by associating it instead with a capacity for mercy and reconciliation. However, to characterise this unlearned weakness as a repudiation of autonomy and independence, as Quint does, is profoundly misleading. Carelessness, I argue, is inseparably connected to liberty, and thus to self-possession.

III

At the heart of Montaigne's rhetoric of *oysiveté*, *mollesse* and *lascheté* is a vision of liberty as a state of tranquillity and ease, in which the mind comes to rest at its own leisure, and the will is released from all external pressures and burdens. His weakness reinforces his independence rather than undermining it, by allowing him to present himself as a man who, by his very nature, cannot bear to be ruled by, or to engage himself, to others.

Montaigne's flight from care is presented as an escape not merely from public occupations (as we saw in the case of *On managing the will*), but also from the responsibilities that pertain to him as the governor of his household. His appetite for travel, as he explains in *On vanity*, stems in the first instance from its allowing him to free himself, albeit temporarily,

77 [B]'Et se monta, non par boutades, mais par complexion, au dernier poinct de vigueur. Ou pour mieux dire: il ne monta rien, mais ravala plustost et ramena à son poinct, originel et naturel, et luy soubmit la vigueur, les aspretez et les difficultez'. III.12: P 1083, V 1037, F 793.

78 [B]'Je n'ay pas corrigé come Socrates, par ~~institution, et~~ [C]la [B]force de la raison, mes complexions naturelles: et n'ay aucunement troublé par art, mon inclination. Je me laisse aller, comme je suis venu'. III.12: P 1106, V 1059, F 811.

from the continual vexations involved in the running of his estate – an occupation to which he has never been able to apply himself in good earnest.

> [B]In the eighteen years that I have been managing an estate, I have not succeeded in prevailing upon myself to look at a title deed or my principal affairs, which necessarily have to pass within my knowledge and care. This is not a philosophical scorn for transitory and mundane things: my taste is not so refined, and I value them at least at their worth: but it certainly is inexcusable and childish ~~indolence and slackness~~ [C] laziness and negligence. What would I not do rather than read a contract? Rather than go and disturb those dusty masses of papers, a serf to my affairs? or still worse, to those of others, as so many people are for the sake of money. Nothing costs me dear except care and pains, and I seek only to make myself nonchalant and slack.[79]

Montaigne's negligent attitude towards the management of property and goods is here presented as a refusal to *enslave* himself, either to his own affairs or to those of other men. Liberty is here found alongside weakness. It is his laziness, his aversion to 'trouble and pains', that makes him so sensitive to slavery. It is his feeble, childish disposition that leaves him vulnerable to such frustrations, the difficulty lying not in the gravity of these stumbling blocks, but in their ubiquity: [B]'there is always something that goes wrong'. These are but [B]'trivial pinpricks', and yet [B]'as small letters ~~hurt and~~ tire the eyes most, so do small matters sting us most'.[80]

Montaigne's idleness is here linked to his tenderness and sensitivity. He flees from troublesome occupations out of a concern to shelter himself from affliction and distress. Elsewhere, however, this same laziness is presented as a mark of temperance and continence, Montaigne's sluggishness making him incapable of vehement agitation and commotion. In *On sadness*, he cites several examples of the petrifying and sometimes fatal effects of excessive grief and other extreme forms of emotion, before adding by way of conclusion that he himself is [B]'little subject to these violent passions', his 'apprehension' being 'naturally tough' and deliberately 'hardened and

79 [B]'Depuis dix-huict ans, que je gouverne des biens, je n'ay sceu gaigner sur moy, de voir, ny tiltres, ny mes principaux affaires, qui ont necessairement à passer par ma science, et par mon soing. Ce n'est pas un mespris philosophique, des choses transitoires et mondaines: je n'ay pas le goust si espuré, et les prise pour le moins ce qu'elles valent: mais certes c'est ~~faitardise et mollesse~~ [C]paresse et negligence inexcusable et puerile. Que ne feroy je plustost que de lire un contract? Et plustost, que d'aller secouant ces paperasses poudreuses, serf de mes negoces? ou encore pis, de ceux d'autruy, comme font tant de gents à prix d'argent. Je n'ay rien cher que le soucy et la peine: et ne cherche qu'à m'anonchalir et avachir'. III.9: P 998, V 953–4, F 727–8.

80 [B]'Il y a tousjours quelque piece qui va de travers'. 'Vaines pointures'. 'Comme les petites lettres ~~offensent et~~ lassent plus les yeux, aussi nous piquent plus les petits affaires'. III.9: P 994, V 950, F 725.

thickened' each day.[81] In *On the resemblance of children to their fathers*, he claims that, although he is touched deeply by bodily pains, [A]'those sufferings that affect us simply through the soul, afflict [him] much less than they do most men'. This insensitivity he attributes partly to his judgment' – 'for the world considers many things horrible, or to be avoided at the cost of life, which are almost indifferent' to him – and partly to 'a stupid and insensible complexion' that he has 'towards accidents that do not come to [him] head-on', which he considers 'one of the best parts of [his] natural condition'.[82] This ponderous slackness lies at the heart of his aversion to engagement. As he declares in *On solitude*, exile and retreat are easiest for those men [A]'whose susceptibility is weak and lax, and whose affection and will are fastidious and slow to enter service or employment', a category in which he falls 'both by natural disposition and application'.[83]

Self-possession and carelessness are to be thought of as complementary rather than antagonistic patterns of ideas: Montaigne's antipathy towards obligation and his hatred of care are two sides of the same coin. The convergence between these two strands of thought is made clear in his treatment of the topic of ingratitude, a charge to which his freedom makes him particularly vulnerable. As he explains in *On the education of children*:

> [C]The complaints that ring in my ears are ~~of this sort~~ <as follows>: Idle, cool in the duties of friendship and kinship: and in public duties, too particular, too disdainful. <Even> the most insulting do not say, Why did he take what he did, why didn't he pay for it? but, Why doesn't he cancel what is owed him? <why> doesn't he give more?[84]

Montaigne's neglect of the offices of friendship and public service is here linked both to his refusal to be under pledge or indebted to other men, and to his sheer laziness: he is able to dispose of his [C]'fortune' and of '[him]self'

[81] [B]'Je suis peu en prise de ces violentes passions: j'ay l'apprehension naturellement dure; et l'encrouste et espessis tous les jours par discours'. I.2. P 38, V 14, F 8.

[82] [A]'Les souffrances qui nous touchent simplement par l'ame, m'affligent beaucoup moins qu'elles ne font la pluspart des autres hommes· Partie par jugement: car le monde estime plusieurs choses horribles, ou evitables au prix de la vie, qui me sont à peu près indifferentes· Partie, par une complexion stupide et insensible, que j'ay aux accidents qui ne donnent à moy de droit fil: laquelle complexion j'estime l'une des meilleures pieces de ma naturelle condition'. II.37: P 797, V 759–60, F 575.

[83] [A]'L'apprehension molle et lasche, et une affection et volonté ~~difficile et qui ne se prend pas aysément~~ [C]delicate, et qui ne s'asservit <ny> ~~et ne~~ s'employe pas aysément, [A]desquels je suis, et par naturelle condition, et par discours'. I.38: P 247, V 242, F 178–9.

[84] [C]'Les plaintes qui me cornent aux oreilles, sont ~~comme cela~~ <telles>: Il est oisif, froid aux offices d'amitié, et de parenté: et aux offices publiques, trop particulier, trop desdaigneux. Les plus injurieux <mesmes> ne disent pas, Pourquoy a il prins, pourquoy n'a-il payé? mais, Pourquoy ne quitte-il, <pourquoy> ne donne-il?' I.25: P 183, V 176, F 130.

all 'the more freely', the more they are '[his] own'.[85] The same conjunction is found in *On repentance*, where he describes himself as C'quite as jealous of the rights of [his] repose as of the rights of [his] authority', and thus quite happy when other men ignore or do not seek his advice. Idleness and independence here go hand in hand. Montaigne links his C'professed principle, which is to be wholly contained and established within [him]self' to the 'pleasure' that he finds in not being 'concerned in other people's affairs' and being 'discharged of responsibility for them'.[86] He himself, he insists, has C'never up to this moment followed any [judgment] but [his] own', the opinions of other men being to him 'nothing but flies and atoms that distract [his] will'.[87]

Belonging to oneself, instead of living under obligation to others, and being free from care, instead of a slave to business and occupations, come together in their focus on the enslavement of the will. In the first case, servitude arises when the will finds itself bound to others, mortgaged by a debt of gratitude or by the demands of subjection. In the second instance, slavery consists rather in the pressures and weight imposed on the will by the burdens of responsibility and care. Although analytically distinct, these two conceptions are closely interwoven by Montaigne – for instance, in this discussion in *On vanity*:

> BI am lax in following duties to which I should be dragged, if I did not go to them. C*Even a just action is just only in so far as it is voluntary.* BIf the action does not have something of the splendour of liberty, it has neither grace nor honour.
>
> *When I am forced by law, my will gives scant assent.*
>
> When necessity tugs me, I like to relax my will. *Because whatever is exacted by power is ascribed rather to him who commands than to him who executes.*[88]

Montaigne's laxness and laziness are inseparably connected with his resistance to mastery and command. Liberty is associated both with that

85 C'Je puis d'autant plus librement disposer de ma fortune, qu'elle est plus mienne: et de moy, que je suis plus mien'. I.25: P 183, V 176, F 130.

86 C'Bien autant jaloux des droits de mon repos, que des droits de mon auctorité'. 'Ma profession, qui est, de m'establir et contenir tout en moy'. 'Ce m'est un plaisir, d'estre désinteressé des affaires d'autruy, et desgagé de leur gariement'. III.2: P 856, V 814–5, F 812.

87 C'Je n'en ay creu jusqu'à cette heure que les miennes [raisons]. [. . .] Ce ne sont que mousches et atomes, qui promeinent ma volonté'. III.2: P 855, V 814, F 618.

88 B'Je suy laschement les debvoirs ausquels on me traineroit, si je n'y allois. C*Hoc ipsum ita iustum est quod rectè fit, si est uoluntarium* [Cicero, *De officiis*, I.9.28]. BSi l'action n'a quelque splendeur de liberté, elle n'a point de grace, ny d'honneur. | *Quod me ius cogit, uix uoluntate impetrent* [Terence, *Adelphi*, III.4.490]. | Où la necessité me tire, j'ayme à lacher la volonté. *Quia quicquid imperio cogitur, exigenti magis, quàm praestanti acceptum refertur* [Valerius Maximus, II.2.6]'. III.9: P 1012, V 967, F 739.

condition of independent self-jurisdiction in which we are ruled by our own will, rather than being subject to that of another, and with a state of relaxation and grace in which the will is relieved of all pressure and tension.

This conjunction is not, however, wholly without difficulty. If we return to the passage from *On vanity* with which this section began, we find that Montaigne's commitment to self-sufficiency and his longing for irresponsibility are sometimes brought into tension with each other. To exercise authority, it seems, is to be subject to care: although [B]'there is a certain satisfaction in being in command, were it only of a barn, and in being obeyed of one's people', it is 'too monotonous and languid a pleasure', and one which is 'necessarily mingled with many bothersome thoughts', 'the poverty and oppression of your people', a 'quarrel amongst your neighbours' and their 'encroachments upon you' all taking it in turns to 'afflict you'.[89] So overwhelmed is he by the ceaseless throng of such everyday difficulties that he dreams of yielding to the guardianship of another man and falling back into a heedless and cossetted senility: [B]'never did a man abandon himself more fully and more loosely to the care and government of another than I would, if I had someone', for example a son-in-law, 'who could cajole my old age comfortably and put it to sleep' and into whose hands 'I could deposit in full sovereignty the management and use of my possessions'.[90] We can only escape from care, Montaigne here suggests, by surrendering ourselves to the care of another.

> [B]I was, I think, better fitted to live on another man's fortune, if that could be done without obligation and servitude. And at that I do not know, when I look it at closely, whether, given my disposition and my lot, there is not more abjection, irksomeness, and bitterness in what I have to endure from business, and servants, and household, than there would be in serving a man, born greater than myself, who would lead me according to my ease. [C]*Servitude is the obedience of a broken and abject mind lacking free will.*[91]

89 [B]'Il y a quelque commodité à commander, fust ce dans une grange, et à estre obey des siens. Mais c'est un plaisir trop uniforme et languissant. Et puis il est par necessité meslé de plusieurs pensements fascheux. Tantost l'indigence et l'oppression de vostre peuple: tantost la querelle d'entre vos voysins: tantost l'usurpation qu'ils font sur vous, vous afflige'. III.9: P 992, V 948, F 723.

90 [B]'Jamais homme ne se laisser aller plus plainement et plus laschement, au soing et gouvernment d'un tiers, que je ferois, si j'avois à qui'. 'Un gendre, qui sceust appaster commodément mes vieux ans, et les endormir: entre les mains de qui je deposasse en toute souveraineté, la conduite et usage de mes biens'. III.9: P 997, V 953, F 727.

91 [B]'J'estoy, ce croi-je, plus propre, à vivre de la fortune d'autruy, s'il se pouvoit, sans obligation et sans servitude. Et si ne sçay, à l'examiner de près, si selon mon humeur et mon sort, ce que j'ay à souffrir des affaires, et des serviteurs, et des domestiques, n'a point plus d'abjection, d'importunité, et d'aigreur, que n'auroit la suitte d'un homme, nay plus grand que moy, qui me guidast un peu à mon aise. [C]*Servitus obedientia est fracti animi et abiecti, arbitrio carentis suo* [Cicero, *Paradoxa stoicorum*, 35]'. III.9: P 998, V 954, F 727–8.

In this passage, Montaigne draws attention to a difficulty inherent in the condition of the master. Because slavery consists in dependency, it follows that we are free only where we live under our own power, rather than under the jurisdiction of another man: we cannot be subject to another 'without obligation and servitude'. At the same time, however, that independence brings with it a heavy burden of responsibility and toil. Like the melancholy princes of *On the inequality that is between us* and *On the incommodity of greatness*, the man who is his own master may find himself to be more wretched than those individuals who are subject to his authority, suffering more 'abjection', 'importunité' and 'aigreur' at the hands of his 'affaires', 'serviteurs' and 'domestiques' than he would if were himself a servant. Is he not then a greater slave than any of his men? This passage explores the friction between self-possession and carelessness as rival understandings of liberty. Which is worse, to be subject to a master or to be condemned to a life of toil, trouble and pains?

The insertion of a quotation from Cicero's *Paradoxa stoicorum* contributes further to this sense of tension by juxtaposing domination ('arbitrio carentis suo') and disquiet ('fracti animi et abiecti') as characteristics of the slave. If we turn to the source of this definition, we find that it is offered by Cicero in explication and defence of the Stoic view 'that only the wise man is free, and that every foolish man is a slave'.[92] This doctrine, as Cicero explains in the preface to the work, is a *paradoxa* not because it is an apparent contradiction (as we now usually understand the term), but in the sense that it is 'surprising' and 'counter to universal opinion' (in Greek, *doxa*).[93] The paradox lies in the fact that the man whom all regard as 'commander' is, in truth, 'altogether unworthy to be deemed not merely a commander but even a free man'. Why? Because he 'cannot command his own desires'.[94]

> For what is freedom? the power to live as you will. Who then lives as he wills except one who follows that which is right? [...] All wicked men are slaves therefore, slaves! Nor is this really so startling a paradox as it sounds. For [the Stoics] do not mean that [the wicked] are slaves in the sense of chattels that have become the property of their lords by assignment for debt or some law of the state; but, if slavery means, as it does mean, the obedience of a broken and abject spirit that

92 'Solum sapientem esse liberum, et omnem stultum servum'. Cicero 1968a, p. 284.

93 'Admirabilia contraque opinionem omnium'. Cicero 1968a, §4, p. 256. Cf. Montaigne's description of the Delphic injunction 'know thyself' as a B'commandement paradoxe' (III.9: P 1047, V 1001, F 766). On this point, see Steczowicz 2007.

94 'Imperator quo modo? [...] qui non potest cupiditatibus suis imperare?' Cicero 1968a, §33, p. 284.

has no will of its own, who would deny that all light-minded and covetous people and indeed all the vicious are really slaves?[95]

It is a great mistake, Cicero argues, to imagine that liberty consists simply in doing as one pleases. Only the wise man who has subordinated his appetites to the authority of reason, may truly be said to have 'a will of his own', and thus to act freely. Freedom consists not in the power to live as we wish, but in the ability to subject one's will to the demands of reason.

Like Cicero's, Montaigne's argument in this passage takes the form of a paradox: those men who think themselves free are in truth slaves. By adducing this definition in defence of idleness and irresponsibility, however, he is [B]'deforming it to a new purpose'[96] and subverting Cicero's appeal to rational self-mastery and self-overcoming. His antipathy towards 'soing' and 'soucy' takes the form not of philosophical indifference but of childish irresponsibility: not only is he unable to overcome his 'faitardise et mollesse' (as he put it in the 1588 edition), his 'paresse et negligence' (as he expressed it in later versions of the text), but he seems to succeed only in entrenching himself further in his lethargic, bloated negligence ('je ne cherche qu'à m'anonchalir et m'avachir'). For Cicero, the slave's 'broken and abject spirit' denotes the disorder and unrest of a mind enthralled to the passions. In Montaigne's hands, it comes to represent the vulnerable and unhappy condition of a man oppressed by paperwork.

The tone of this passage, and of much of *On vanity* as a whole, is somewhat bathetic and not entirely serious. There should be [B]'some legal restraint', Montaigne claims, against 'inept and useless writers such as him, just 'as there is against vagabonds and idlers'.[97] His own domestic plight – 'a thousand things give me reason to desire and fear' – is humorously juxtaposed with the troubles faced by Aeneas in his flight from Troy, through a quotation adapted from Virgil ('*then is our soul distraught with countless cares*').[98] For all his playful self-deprecation, however, Montaigne

[95] 'Quid est enim libertas? Potestas vivendi ut velis. Quis igitur vivit ut vult nisi qui recta sequitur? [. . .] Servi igitur omnes improbi, servi! Nec hoc tam re est quam dictu inopinatum atque mirabile. Non enim ita dicunt eos esse servos ut mancipia quae sunt dominorum facta nexu aut aliquo iure civile; sed si servitus sit, sicut est, obedientia fracti animi et abiecti et arbitrio carentis suo, quis neget omnes leves omnes cupidos omnes denique improbos esse servos?' Cicero 1968a, §34–5, pp. 284, 286.

[96] [B]'Et parmy tant d'emprunts, suis bien aise d'en pouvoir desrober quelqu'un le desguisant et difformant à nouveau service'. III.12: P 1103, V 1055, F 808.

[97] [B]'Il y devroit avoir quelque coerction des loix, contre les escrivains ineptes et inutiles, comme il y a contre les vagabons et faineants'. III.9: P 990, V 946, F 721.

[98] [B]'*Tum uerò in curas animum diducimus omnes*: mille choses m'y donnent à desirer et craindre'. III.9: P 995, V 951, F 725. Cf. Virgil, *Aeneid*, V.720.

is also making a more serious point. Freedom consists in an inner state of repose and leisure, released from unwanted and troublesome care: that, he suggests, is what it means to have 'a will of one's own'. Montaigne is certainly not proposing that we should abandon all attempts to lead a reasoned and ordered life, by giving free rein to the passions. In seeking to exercise mastery over ourselves, however, we may find that we are simply replacing one form of slavery with another.

The need to distinguish liberty from mere licence was a commonplace of Renaissance ethics.[99] As Jean Jacques Boissard put it in his *Emblematum liber* (1593), 'true liberty consists in not being a slave to the passions'.[100] Montaigne himself endorses this distinction in *On the education of children*, by including it among the key points of moral philosophy that all young gentlemen ought to study.[101] Elsewhere, however, he appears to elide this opposition, by urging us to relax our grip, releasing our will from pressing constraints and burdens, including those of excessive self-discipline and self-containment.

It is worth noting, in this connection, the recurrent appearance in the *Essais* of the image of an unbridled and unruly horse. This motif offers an implicit echo and subversion of the Platonic comparison of the rational soul to a charioteer who must keep a tight rein over the passions lest he be driven and controlled by them. In Montaigne's hands, however, the bolting horse becomes a metaphor not for the licentious disorder of the appetites, but for the troubled state of a mind haunted by care. In *On idleness*, his *esprit* is figured as a [A]'runaway horse', which, instead of becoming 'more heavy, and more mature, with time' in its new-found idleness and retreat from worldly occupations, 'gives itself a hundred times more ~~trouble~~ <free rein> than it ~~takes~~ [B]took [A]for others', 'giving birth' to countless 'chimeras and fantastic monsters'.[102] In *On solitude*, he cites a line from Horace's *Carmines* – [A]'*behind the horseman sits black care*' – to illustrate the claim that in 'getting rid of the Court and the market place, we do not get rid of the principal worries of our life', because 'they often follow us even into

[99] Skinner 2008b, pp. 26–32.

[100] 'Libertas vera est affectibus non servire'. Boissard 1593, p. 11; quoted in Skinner 2008b, pp. 31–2.

[101] Montaigne here argues that a young man should be told [A]'what the difference is between [. . .] licence and liberty' ('ce qu'il y a à dire entre [. . .] la licence et la liberté'). I.25: P 165, V 158, F 117.

[102] [A]'J'esperois qu'il peust meshuy faire plus aysément, devenu avec le temps, plus poisant, et plus meur: Mais je trouve, [. . .] qu'au rebours faisant le cheval eschappé, il se donne cent fois plus ~~d'affaire~~ <de carriere> à soy-mesmes, qu'il ~~n'en prent~~ [B]ne prenoit [A]pour autruy: et m'enfante tant de chimeres et monstres fantasques'. I.8: P 55, V 33, F 21.

the cloisters and the schools of Philosophy'.[103] In *On the affection of fathers for their children*, the abdication of Emperor Charles V is compared to the turning loose of a tired and broken horse, again through the insertion of a quotation from Horace: '*set free the aging horse before it is too late, | Lest he go stumbling broken-winded at the end*'.[104] In *On presumption*, finally, Montaigne compares himself to a [C]'restive and disobedient horse', whom only experts can cajole into service.[105] What these examples suggest, however, is not that inactivity and rest provide a simple answer to our distress, but that, on the contrary, excessive idleness, as well as excessive occupation, can lead us to fall prey to the spectre of care.[106] The aim, then, is not simply to abandon oneself to the undisciplined movement of the horse, but to know when to slacken the reins, and when to harness them, so as to keep ourselves in our *assiette* or saddle.

Montaigne's goodness, as we saw in Section II, is linked to weakness and a *lack* of power over oneself. That powerlessness, however, is itself tied to liberty, as the mark of an unacquired, unmastered goodness, owed to no one but himself. Socrates, he argues in *On physiognomy*, [B]'did a great ~~service~~ [C]favour to human nature by showing it how much it can do by itself'. By seeking to derive our wisdom from books, we train ourselves 'to borrow and beg, [. . .] to use the resources of others more than our own'.[107] Yet Socrates [B]'teaches us that it is in us, and the way to find it and help ourselves with it', which is to 'collect yourself' and 'find in yourself Nature's arguments against death, true ones, and the fittest to serve you in case of necessity'.[108] [A]'That which is good in me', Montaigne writes in *On cruelty*, 'I hold neither from law, nor precept, nor other apprenticeship'.[109] Like that of Socrates and Cato, his goodness is [A]'the very essence of [his]

103 [A]'Pour nous estre deffaits de la Cour et du marché, nous ne sommes pas deffaits des principaux tourmens de nostre vie: [. . .] *Et post equitem sedet atra cura* [Horace, *Carmina*, III.1.4]. Elles nous suivent souvent jusques dans les cloistres, et dans les escholes de Philosophie'. I.38: P 243, V 239, F 175–6.

104 [A]'*Solue senescentem maturè sanus equum, ne | Peccet ad extremùm ridendus, et ilia ducat* [Horace, *Epistulae*, I.1.8–9]'. II.8: P 410, V 391, F 283.

105 [C]'Un cheval restif et poussif'. II.17: P 682, V 643, F 488.

106 On the ambivalence of leisure or *otium* in Renaissance culture, see Vickers 1990.

107 [B]'Il a faict grand ~~service~~ [C]faveur [B]à l'humaine nature, de monstrer combien elle peut d'elle mesme. [. . .] On nous dresse à l'emprunt, et à la queste: on nous duict à nous servir plus de l'autruy, que du nostre'. III.12: P 1084, V 1038, F 794.

108 [B]'Socrates nous apprend qu'elle est en nous, et la maniere de l'y trouver, et de s'en ayder. [. . .] Recueillez vous, vous trouverez en vous, les argumens de la nature, contre la mort, vrais, et les plus propres à vous servir à la necessité'. III.12: P 1085, V 1039, F 794.

109 [A]'Ce que j'ay de bien, [. . .] je ne le tiens ny de loy ny de precepte ou autre apprentissage'. II.11: P 450, V 429, F 313.

soul, its natural and ordinary gait',[110] [A]'an attitude so natural and so much [his] own' that he himself cannot do anything to change it.[111]

In this chapter, as we also observed in Section II, Montaigne identifies his natural goodness with a form of childish simplicity. In addition, however, he aligns himself implicitly with a wild and untamed goodness, free from the jurisdiction of the laws. He is less offended by those [A]'savages' who roast and eat dead bodies than by the European practice of tearing apart and torturing the living.[112] Although cruelty has become commonplace in the midst of France's civil catastrophe, this has not [A]'tamed' him to its horrors.[113] Goodness, he writes, is 'without law', a claim that appears twice in *On cruelty*, first in the extract cited in the previous paragraph ('that which is good in me, [. . .] I hold neither from law . . . '), and, second, in a passage linking [C]'being wholly good' to an 'occult, natural, and universal property, without law, without reason, without example'.[114]

This phrase ('sans loy') also occurs twice in the chapter immediately following *On cruelty*, the *Apology for Raymond Sebond*, on both occasions with reference to the peoples of the New World, whose existence 'without law' is endowed with a simple, uncoerced, purely natural goodness that is all but absent from European society. In the first instance, Montaigne praises the native peoples of Brazil for the [C]'tranquillity and serenity of their souls, discharged of any tense or unpleasant passion, thought and occupation, as people who spent their life in admirable simplicity and ignorance, without letters, without law, without King, without religion of any kind'.[115] A few pages later, he speaks of [A]'those nations, without magistrates and without law', discovered by the Spanish, who 'live more lawfully and more regulatedly than ours, where there are more officers and laws than there are other men and actions'.[116]

Liberty is here connected not only to the ease of the mind, but to a form of natural self-regulation and self-legislation, independent of the authority of external law or precept.

[110] [A]'L'essence mesme de leur ame [. . .] son train naturel et ordinaire'. II.11: P 446, V 426, F 310.

[111] [A]'Une opinion si naturelle et si mienne'. II.11: P 449, V 428, F 312.

[112] II.11: P 452, V 430, F 314. [113] II.11: P 454, V 432, F 315.

[114] [C]'Seroit-il vray, que pour estre bon <tout> à faict, il nous le faille estre par occulte, naturelle et universelle proprieté, sans loy, sans raison, sans exemple?' II.11: P 449–50, V 428, F 312.

[115] [C]'La tranquillité et serenité de leur ame, deschargée de toute passion, pensée et occupation tendue et desplaisante, comme gents qui passoyent leur vie en une admirable simplicité et ignorance, sans lettres, sans loy, sans Roy, sans relligion quelconque'. II.12: P 517, V 491, F 362.

[116] [A]'Ces nations, sans magistrat, et sans loy, vivent plus legitimement et plus reglément que les nostres, où il y a plus d'officiers et de loix, qu'il n'y a d'autres hommes, et qu'il n'y a d'actions'. II.12: P 524, V 497, F 367.

[C]Shall I say this in passing: that I see held in greater price than it is worth a certain idea of scholastic prudence, almost the only one practised among us, a slave to precepts, held down beneath fear and hope? What I like is the virtue that laws and religions do not make but perfect and authorise, that feels in itself enough to sustain itself without help: born in us from our own roots, from the seed of universal reason that is implanted in each man who is not denatured.[117]

Far from diminishing his commitment to self-possession, Montaigne's carelessness is an integral component of his moral independence.

This contrast between a lawless, unmastered goodness and a servile, fearful obedience to 'precepts' leads Montaigne to repudiate the tension of rigorous self-discipline as a source of both subjection and care. [B]'Wisdom has its excesses, and has no less need of moderation than does folly',[118] as he argues in the opening paragraphs of *On some verses of Virgil*.

[B]To the extent that useful thoughts are fuller, ~~more grave~~ and more solid, they are also more obstructive and more burdensome. Vice, death, poverty, disease, are grave subjects, and which grieve us. We should have a soul instructed in the means to sustain and combat evils, and instructed in the rules for living and believing well: and should often arouse it and exercise it in this fine study. But for a soul of the common sort, this must be done with respite and moderation: it goes mad, if it is too continually tense.[119]

His advancing years, he continues, have imparted to him a morbid prudence and ponderous constancy, which he contrasts unfavourably with the wanton liveliness of his youth. Whereas once he had to [B]'warn and sollicit' himself to 'keep [him]self in his duty', he now finds that he is 'too sedate, too heavy, and too mature'. For that reason, he writes, 'I deliberately let myself go a bit to wantonness and sometimes occupy my soul with playful and youthful thoughts, to give it a rest' – a principle put in practice in

117 [C]'Diray-je cecy en passant: que je voy tenir en plus de prix qu'elle ne vaut, qui est seule quasi en usage entre nous, certaine image de preud'hommie scholastique, serve des preceptes, contraincte soubs l'esperance et la crainte? Je l'aime telle que ~~les~~ loix et religions, non facent mais parfacent, et authorisent: qui se sente dequoy se soustenir sans aide: née en nous de ses propres racines, par la semence de la raison universelle, empreinte en tout homme non desnaturé'. II.12: P 1106–7, V 1059, F 811.

118 [B]'La sagesse a ses excez, et n'a pas moins besoing de moderation que la folie'. III.5: P 882, V 841, F 639. As André Tournon has shown, a similar pattern of thought can be found in *On moderation*. Montaigne here subverts the discourse of continence and restraint by suggesting that moderation itself needs moderating: Tournon 2006, pp. 35–42.

119 [B]'À mesure que les pensemens utiles sont plus pleins, ~~plus graves~~ et solides, ils sont aussi plus empeschans, et plus onereux. Le vice, la mort, la pauvreté, les maladies, sont subjets graves, et qui grevent. Il faut avoir l'ame instruitte des moyens de soustenir et combatre les maux, et instruite des regles de bien vivre, et de bien croire: et souvent l'esveiller et exercer en cette belle estude. Mais à une ame de commune sorte, il faut que ce soit avec relasche et moderation: elle s'affolle, d'estre trop continuellement bandée'. III.5: P 882, V 840–1, F 638.

the chapter itself, which is devoted to a discussion of erotic pleasure and writing.[120]

Crucially, however, these deliberate concessions to pleasure are themselves presented as a form of self-regulation and as a vindication of Montaigne's liberty. His turn to wanton thoughts allows him to free himself from the usurpation of his ageing body, which [B]'rules over' his mind where it had once been ruled by it, 'and more roughly and imperiously', so that it does not 'leave [him] a single hour, sleeping or waking, unoccupied with instruction about death, patience, and penitence'. As he explains: 'I want to be master of myself, in every direction', whether that of pleasure, or of continence; of wisdom, or of folly.[121] Far from jettisoning self-jurisdiction in favour of idle carelessness, Montaigne's point is that true liberty can be achieved only by preserving our will in a condition of judicious equanimity and indifference.

IV

Like *sprezzatura*, nonchalance is to be thought of not merely in aesthetic terms, as a manner or as a pose, but as a disposition of the mind as well as of the body, anchored in the cultivation of a particular temperament or existential attitude. Montaigne's lack of *solicitude* and *curiosité* is to be understood not only as a condition of natural negligence, but as a state of inner equilibrium and detachment, unperturbed by anxiety and distress. The etymology of the term is here revealing: 'chaloir', and thus 'nonchaloir', derive from the Latin *calere*, meaning to be warm or hot. Like *ardere* (to burn), *calere* is frequently used by classical writers, notably Cicero, in a figurative as well as literal sense, to refer to the feverish heat of passion or desire. This meaning is retained in sixteenth-century French through the expressions *peu me chaut* and *il ne me chaut* (it does not matter to me, it does not trouble me). *Mesprizon* and *mespris*, meanwhile, so often paired with *nonchalance* by Castiglione's French translators, both capture *sprezzatura*'s etymological proximity to *disprezzo* or disdain, understood as the literal negation of *prezzo*, as a refusal to prize things. *Sprezzatura*, in this sense, resembles an ethical practice of contempt or disengagement

120 [B]'J'avoy besoing en jeunesse, de m'advertir et solliciter pour me tenir en office: [. . .] Parquoy, je me laisse à cette heure aller un peu à la desbauche, par dessein: et employe ~~par~~ [C]quelque [B]fois l'ame, à des pensemens ~~fols~~ [C]folastres [B]et jeunes, où elle se sejourne: Je ne suis meshuy que trop rassis, trop poisant, et trop meur.'. III.5: P 882, V 841, F 638–9.

121 [C]'Ce corps [. . .] régente à son tour; et plus rudement et imperieusement: Il ne me laisse pas une heure, ny dormant ny veillant, chaumer d'instruction, de mort, de patience, et de pœnitence. [. . .] Or je veux estre maistre de moy, à tout sens'. III.5: P 882, V 841, F 638–9.

(recall the discipline implicit in the image of *affettazione* as a reef which the courtier must avoid at all costs). To be nonchalant, on this reading, is to keep one's cool, to not allow oneself to be inflamed or consumed by the burdens of care.

This dual aspect of *sprezzatura* is captured particularly clearly in a passage from *On the education of children* which alludes unmistakably to Castiglione's work:

> [B]I have willingly imitated that licence which we see in our youth, in the wearing of their clothes. A cloak worn like a scarf, the hood over one shoulder, a loose stocking, which represent a pride disdainful these foreign adornments, and careless of art: but I think it is even better employed in our form of speech. [C]Any affectation, especially in the gaiety and liberty of French, is unbecoming to a courtier. And in a Monarchy, every gentleman should be trained ~~in the manner~~ <in the comportment> of a courtier. Wherefore we do well to lean a little in the direction of naturalness and negligence.[122]

This passage clearly contains an element of self-parody – Montaigne's imitation of these faintly ludicrous youthful fashions is offered to us with more than a touch of irony.[123] Even in the context of something so apparently trivial as the aesthetics of dress, however, the ethical symbolism of *nonchalance* is evident. Affectation is here linked to excessive *care*: carelessness, like self-possession, consists in an attitude of indifference (*desdain*, *mespris*) towards 'foreign adornments' and 'art'. Similarly, when Montaigne writes, in *On vanity*, that [C]'he holds nothing dear [*cher*] but care and trouble' and that he 'seeks [*cherche*] only to make himself nonchalant and slack', the homophony in his phrasing indicates that prizing and striving are inseparably connected.[124] His carelessness, in other words, consists not merely in the absence of strain or effort, but in a refusal to invest value in that which is worthy only of our indifference – a refusal to engage the will to that which is not properly ours.

Montaigne's characterisation of himself as mediocre and useless is designed not merely to attest to his lack of presumption and self-love,

[122] [B]'J'ay volontiers imité cette desbauche qui se voit en nostre jeunesse, au port de leurs vestemens. Un manteau en escharpe, la cape sur une espaule, un bas mal tendu, qui represente une fierté desdaigneuse de ces paremens estrangers, et nonchallante de l'art: mais je la trouve encore mieux employée en la forme du parler. [C]Toute affectation, nommément en la gayeté et liberté Françoise, est mesadvenante au courtisan. Et en une Monarchie, tout gentil'homme doit estre dressé ~~a la façon~~ <au port> d'un courtisan. Parquoy nous faisons bien de gauchir un peu sur le naïf et mesprisant'. I.25: P 178, V 172, F 127.

[123] This point is made by Tetel 1979.

[124] [C]'Je n'ay rien cher que le soucy et la peine: et ne cherche qu'à m'anonchalir et avachir'. III.9: P 998, V 954, F 728.

but to signal his negligent, careless attitude to the empty allure of public reputation and renown, and above all to the attractions of public power. As he writes in *On the incommodity of greatness*:

> [B]I find the effort to bear ills very difficult, but as for being content with a mediocre measure of fortune, and fleeing greatness, I find very little business in that. It is a virtue, it seems to me, which I, who am only a gosling, could attain without much striving. [. . .] When I think of growing, it is in a lowly way: with a constrained and cowardly growth: properly for myself: in resolution, in prudence, in health, in beauty, and even riches.[125]

From the perspective of the world, Montaigne's obscure, private life is a mark of 'lowly' and 'cowardly' weakness; from the vantage point of carelessness, it is ambition and the pursuit of greatness that are deserving of contempt – so much so, that even a mere '*oyson*' like him (a gosling, but also, implicitly, a loafer) can become indifferent to them without effort.[126]

As he indicates in *On presumption*, it is only in the eyes of a decadent age that Montaigne appears so deprived of all qualities and strength. He values himself at nothing, he tells us, because

> [A]even the qualities that are not reproachable in me, I have found useless in this age. The facility of my character would have been called cowardice and weakness; fidelity and conscience would have been thought scrupulous and superstitious; frankness and liberty, irksome, thoughtless, and rash.[127]

His lack of strength and application, in this perspective, is a sign of his contempt for worldly favour, glory and advancement.

> [A]As for ambition, which is neighbour to presumption, or rather daughter, it would have been necessary, to advance me, for fortune to come and take me by the hand: for as for taking pains for the sake of some uncertain hope: and submitting to all the difficulties, that attend those who try to push themselves into favour, at the beginning of their career, I could never have done it.[128]

125 [B]'Je trouve l'effort bien difficile à la souffrance des maux, mais au contentement d'une mediocre mesure de fortune, et fuite de la grandeur, j'y trouve fort peu d'affaire. C'est une vertu, ce me semble, où moy, qui ne suis qu'un oyson, arriverois sans beaucoup de contention. [. . .] Quand je pense à croistre, c'est bassement: d'une accroissance contrainte et couarde: proprement pour moy: en resolution, en prudence, en santé, en beauté, et en richesse encore'. III.7: P 961, V 916, F 699.

126 On the 'contented obscurity' and serene detachment of the retired life in seventeenth-century English poetry, see Røstvig 1954.

127 [A]'Les qualitez mesmes qui sont en moy non reprochables, je les trouvois inutiles en ce siecle. La facilité de mes mœurs, on l'eust nommée lascheté et foiblesse: la foy et la conscience s'y feussent trouvées scrupuleuses et superstitieuses: la franchise et la liberté, importune, inconsidérée et temeraire'. II.17: P 684, V 646, F 490.

128 [A]'Quant à l'ambition, qui est voisine de la presumption, ou fille plustost, il eust fallu pour m'advancer, que la fortune me fust venu querir par le poing: car de me mettre en peine pour

Given his decision to publish his writings and disseminate them across a wide audience, Montaigne's claim in *To the reader* to write with [A]'no goal but a domestic and private one' has tended to be dismissed as purely conventional or disingenuous. Yet the point of this phrase is not merely to insist that the book is 'dedicated to the private convenience' of his 'relatives and friends'. Its deeper meaning is instead provided by the sentence that immediately follows on from it: '[reader,] I have had no thought of your service or my own glory: my powers are not capable of such a design'. His project is 'domestic and private', not merely because it purports to be addressed to a limited circle of intimates, but because it claims to have been written carelessly, without thought to the enhancement of the author's reputation and renown: 'if I had written to seek the world's favour, I should have bedecked myself with borrowed beauties'. This professed indifference to glory, finally, is presented as an affirmation of his liberty: as he tells the reader, 'je n'ay eu nulle consideration de ton service'. His 'powers' are not sufficient for him to be useful, but nor are they adequate to allow him to serve.[129]

Montaigne's nonchalance, in this light, reflects an attitude of ironic detachment from the weakness of the human condition, a stance associated with the laughing figure of Democritus. Whereas Heraclitus [A]'wore a face perpetually sad, and eyes filled with tears', out of 'pity and compassion' for the miserable state of humanity, Democritus chose rather to find it 'vain and ridiculous'. Montaigne prefers this mocking humour, he writes, 'because it is more disdainful, and condemns us more than the other'. 'Pity and commiseration are mingled with some esteem for the thing we pity', whereas the things we laugh at we consider worthless.[130]

This refusal to prize – and thus to engage the will – lies at the heart of his effortless, artless goodness. In *On physiognomy*, [B]'the efforts which [Seneca] gives himself to prepare himself against death, [. . .] sweating from

un' esperance incertaine: et me soubmettre à toutes les difficultez, qui accompaignent ceux qui cherchent à se pousser en credit, sur le commencement de leur progrez, je ne l'eusse sceu faire'. II.17: P 683, V 645, F 489.

[129] [A]'Je n'y ay eu nulle consideration de ton service, ny de ma gloire: mes forces ne sont pas capables d'un tel dessein. [. . .] Si c'eust esté pour rechercher la faveur du monde, je me fusse paré de beautez empruntées'. *Au lecteur*: P 27, V 3, F 2.

[130] [A]'Democritus et Heraclitus ont esté deux philosophes, desquels le premier trouvant vaine et ridicule l'humaine condition, ne sortoit ~~guierre~~ en public, qu'avec un visage moqueur et riant: Heraclitus, ayant pitié et compassion de cette mesme condition nostre, en portoit le visage continuellement ~~atristé~~ <triste>, et les yeux chargez de larmes. [. . .] J'ayme mieux la premiere humeur [. . .] par ce qu'elle est plus desdaigneuse, et qu'elle nous ~~acuse~~ [C]condamne [A]plus que l'autre. [. . .] La plainte et la commiseration ~~elles~~ sont meslées à quelque estimation de la chose qu'on plaint: les choses dequoy on se moque, on les estime sans prix'. I.50: P 323, V 303, F 220.

the exertion of steeling and securing himself' are interpreted as the sign of an 'ardent, and frequent, agitation'. Plutarch's 'manner', by contrast, 'as it is more disdainful and less tense', is 'all the ~~stronger~~ [C]more virile [B]and persuasive'.[131] Socrates' [C]'artless boldness' and '~~puerile~~ <childlike> assurance'[132] are most visible in his [C]'nonchalant and mild way of considering his death',[133] free of any [B]'hatred or horror',[134] like those animals who [C]'cannot fear our killing them', because they do not have 'the faculty of imagining or inferring death'.[135]

It is thus from his own lethargy and negligence that Montaigne draws the ability to face death without fear and without struggle. As he puts it in *That to philosophise is to learn how to die*: [A]'may death find me planting my cabbages, but careless of death, and still more of my imperfect garden'.[136] In *On vanity*, this indolent weakness is recovered as an oblique form of strength and resolution. Tormented by the possibility that he might be killed in his sleep, Montaigne writes that:

> [B]I sometimes derive from nonchalance and laxity a way of strengthening myself against these considerations: They too, to some extent, lend us toward fortitude. It often happens that I imagine, and await mortal dangers with some pleasure. I plunge head down, stupidly into death, without looking at it and recognizing it, as into a silent and dark abyss which swallows me up at one leap, and ~~overwhelms~~ [C]smothers [B]me in an instant, with a heavy sleep, full of insipidity and indolence.[137]

Montaigne's nonchalance here imitates the insensibility and passivity of death itself. His strength is found, not in straining to resist or repel the dangers that oppress him, but in abandoning himself to fortune,[138] and seeking refuge within the heavy dullness of his careless mind.

131 [B]'À veoir les efforts que Seneque se donne pour se preparer contre la mort, à le voir suer d'ahan, pour se roidir et pour s'asseurer [. . .] Son agitation si ardante, si frequente'. 'La façon de Plutarque, d'autant qu'elle est plus desdaigneuse, et plus destendue, elle est selon moy, d'autant plus ~~forte~~ [C]virile [B]et persuasive'. III.12: P 1086, V 1040, F 795.

132 [C]'Une hardiesse inartificielle ~~et niaise~~ [. . .] une securité ~~puerile~~ <enfantine>'. III.12: P 1101, V 1054, F 807.

133 [C]'Une si nonchallante et molle consideration de sa mort'. III.12: P 1101, V 1054, F 807.

134 [B]'La haine et l'horreur'. III.12: P 1102, V 1055, F 808.

135 [C]'Mais que nous les tuions, elles ne le peuvent craindre, ny n'ont la faculté d'imaginer et conclurre la mort'. III.12: P 1102, V 1055, F 808.

136 [A]'Que la mort me treuve plantant mes choux; mais nonchallant d'elle, et encore plus de mon jardin imparfait'. I.19: P 91, V 89, F 62.

137 [B]'Je tire par fois, le moyen de me fermir contre ces considerations, de la nonchalance et lascheté. Elles nous menent aussi aucunement à la resolution. Il m'advient souvent, d'imaginer avec quelque plaisir, les dangers mortels, et les attendre. Je me plonge la teste baissée, stupidement dans la mort, sans la considerer et recognoistre, comme dans une profondeur muette et obscure, qui m'engloutit tout d'un saut, et ~~m'accable~~ [C]m'estouffe [B]en un instant, d'un puissant sommeil, plein d'insipidité et indolence'. III.9: P 1016, V 971, F 742.

138 On this point, see Martin 1977, Giocanti 2001 and Noirot-Maguire 2007.

[B]Not being able to rule events, I rule myself: and adapt myself to them if they do not adapt themselves to me. I have hardly any art to know how to dodge Fortune, and escape her, or force her; and to direct and lead things with prudence to serve my purpose. I have even less ~~patience~~ [C]tolerance [B]to stand the arduous and painful care that is needed for that.[139]

Montaigne's fortitude consists not in a struggle against external events, but in abnegating his power over that which he cannot control, bringing his will to rest within himself: [B]'when things happen, I bear myself like a man; in conducting them, like a child'.[140]

This conception of nonchalance as an experience of careless, indifferent powerlessness akin to death recalls Montaigne's exploration of semi-conscious states in *On practice*.[141] [A]'Those who by some violent accident have fallen into a faint, and lost all sensation', he writes, 'have been very close to seeing death's true and natural face' – a claim which he has himself tested, having been plunged into stupor after being brutally knocked off his horse.[142] His interest here focuses on those movements and thoughts that operate independently of our will and awareness, blurring the boundary separating that which is in our power and that which is not. [A]'While wholly in a faint', he writes, 'I was labouring to rip open my doublet'; 'not only did I make some sort of answer to what was asked me, but also they say I thought of ordering them to give a horse to my wife, whom I saw stumbling and having trouble on the road'. Yet these actions and thoughts did not, in truth, 'come from me'.[143]

Just as in the first [A]'stutter' of sleep, when we 'sense as in a dream what is happening around us, and follow voices with a blurred and uncertain hearing which seems to touch on only the edges of the soul' the 'short and incoherent words and replies' uttered by the dying are not 'evidence that

139 [B]'Ne pouvant regler les evenemens, je me regle moy-mesme: et m'applique à eux, s'ils ne s'appliquent à moy. Je n'ay guere d'art pour sçavoir gauchir la fortune, et luy eschapper, ou la forcer; et pour dresser et conduire par prudence les choses à mon poinct. J'ay encore moins de ~~patience~~ [C]tolerance, [B]pour supporter le soing aspre et penible qu'il faut à cela'. II.17: P 682, V 644, F 488.

140 [B]'Aux evenemens, je me porte virilement, en la conduicte puerilement'. II.17: P 683, V 644, F 489.

141 This point is also made by Naya 2005, according to which Montaigne (in terms similar to Langer 1999) rejects an Aristotelian model of prudent deliberation in favour of a 'prudence naturelle' modeled on the 'action semi-consciente' of *On practice* (p. 216).

142 [A]'Ceux qui sont tombez par quelque violent accident en defaillance de cœur, et qui y ont perdu tous sentimens, ceux là à mon advis ont esté bien près de voir son vray et naturel visage'. II.6: P 390, V 372, F 268.

143 [A]'Car premierement estant tout esvanouy, je me travaillois d'entr'ouvrir mon pourpoinct à ~~belles~~ <beaux> ongles. [. . .] Non seulement je respondois quelque mot à ce qu'on me demandoit, mais encore ils disent que je m'advisay de commander qu'on donnast un cheval à ma femme, que je voyoy s'empestrer et se tracasser dans le chemin. [. . .] Ils ne venoyent pas de chez moy'. II.6: P 394–5, V 375–6, F 271.

they are alive, at least fully alive', for 'there are many movements of ours that do not come from our will', or in which parts of our body 'lend themselves offices, [B]and have agitations aside from our intention'.[144] [A]'These passions which touch only the rind of us cannot be called ours', for 'to make them ours, the whole man must be involved'; these are 'idle thoughts, in the clouds, set in motion by the sensations of the eyes and ears', 'slight effects which the senses produce of themselves, as if by habit'.[145] Yet there is a kind of exquisite pleasure in this deathlike nonchalance:

> [A]It seemed to me that my life was hanging only by the tip of my lips; I closed my eyes in order (it seemed to me) to help push it out, and took pleasure in growing languid and letting myself go. It was an idea that was only floating on the surface of my soul, as delicate and feeble as all the rest, but in truth not only exempt from distress but mingled, with that sweet feeling, that people have who let themselves ~~be carried~~ [C]slide [A]into sleep.[146]

Like his acceptance of the power of fortune in *On presumption* and *On vanity*, this valorisation of langorous disengagement is intimately connected to the ideal of spontaneity and improvisation at the heart of *sprezzatura*. Montaigne's aversion towards effort and strain bears witness to the lingering pleasure and relief that he experiences whenever his will is released from that which lies beyond his power. Liberty here comes to be associated with fortuitousness and a lack of premeditation, as we can see if we examine a further important aspect of his self-presentation: the weakness of his memory.

In *On presumption*, Montaigne claims to be so [A]'entirely lacking' in this faculty that when he has 'a speech of consequence to make, if it is of some length, [he] is reduced to that vile [C]and miserable [A]necessity, of having

[144] [A]'Les vois et responses courtes et descousues [. . .] ce n'est pas tesmoignage qu'ils vivent pourtant, au moins une vie entiere. Il nous advient ainsi sur le beguayement du sommeil, avant qu'il nous ait du tout saisis, de sentir comme en songe, ce qui se faict autour de nous, et suyvre les voix, d'une ouye trouble et incertaine, qui semble ne donner qu'aux bords de l'ame. [. . .] Car il y a plusieurs mouvemens en nous, qui ne partent pas de nostre ordonnance. [. . .] Nos membres se prestent des offices, [B]et ont des agitations à part de nostre discours'. II.6: P 394, V 375–6, F 271.

[145] [A]'Or ces passions qui ne nous touchent que par l'escorse, ne se peuvent dire nostres: Pour les faire nostres, il faut que l'homme y soit engagé tout entier [. . .] c'estoyent des pensemens vains en nue, qui estoyent esmeuz par les sens des yeux et des oreilles [. . .] ce sont de legers effects, que les sens produysoyent d'eux mesmes, comme d'un usage'. II.6: P 394–5, V 376, F 271–2.

[146] [A]'Il me sembloit que ma vie ne me tenoit plus qu'au bout des lèvres: je fermois les yeux pour ayder (ce me sembloit) à la pousser hors, et prenois plaisir à m'alanguir et à me laisser aller. C'estoit une imagination qui ne faisoit que nager superficiellement en mon ame, aussi tendre et aussi foible que tout le reste: mais à la verité non seulement exempte de desplaisir, ains meslée à ceste douceur, que sentent ceux qui se laissent ~~emporter~~ [C]glisser [A]au sommeil'. II.6: P 392, V 374, F 269–70.

to learn by heart [C]word for word [A]what [he] has to say'.[147] Instead of drawing fluently and securely upon a rich storehouse of recollected *topoi* and *exempla*, he must make do with a memory fit only for mechanical repetition. In an addition to the Bordeaux Copy, he contends that even this remedy is of little use to him, partly because it demands so much time from him and partly because [C]'in a work of [~~his~~] <one's> own, the liberty and authority to change the order and alter a word, ever varying the material, makes it harder to keep in the mind of its author'.[148] His memory has, he claims in *On vanity*, of late become so unreliable that [B]'whereas others seek time and opportunity to think over what they have to say', he 'shall have to avoid any preparation, for fear of attaching [him]self to some obligation on which [he] would have to depend'.[149] Freedom and memory are antagonistic forces: to rely on one's memory is to fall into a state of dependency.

Improvisation, Montaigne makes clear, is not an option available to him: [B]'as for throwing [him]self on the mercy of [his] present invention', he would here fare even worse, because this faculty is in him 'heavy and confused' and unable to cope with 'sudden and important necessities'.[150] The polished fluency of a well-rehearsed speech would, in the case of another man, offer a plausible simulacrum of extemporisation. Yet Montaigne's difficulty arises from the weakness of his faltering memory: he struggles to remember what he has prepared, and then struggles to hide his struggle.

> [B]As long as I rely on [my memory], I place myself outside of myself: so much so as to try my countenance. And I have one day found myself at pains to conceal the servitude in which I was bound: Whereas my design is, to represent in speaking a profound carelessness <of accent and of face>, and fortuitous and unpremeditated gestures, as arising from the immediate occasions.[151]

147 [A]'Elle me manque du tout [. . .] Et quand j'ay un propos de consequence à tenir, s'il est de longue haleine, je suis reduit à cette vile [C]et miserable [A]necessité, d'apprendre par cœur [C]mot à mot [A]ce que j'ay a dire'. II.17: P 688, V 649, F 492.

148 [C]'En un ~~mien~~ <propre> ouvrage la liberté et authorité de remuer l'ordre, de changer un mot, variant sans cesse la matiere, la rend plus malaisée à arrester en la memoire de son autheur'. II.17: P 688, V 649, F 493.

149 [B]'Il faudra doresnavant [. . .] qu'au lieu que les autres cherchent temps, et occasion de penser à ce qu'ils ont à dire, je fuye à me preparer, de peur de m'attacher à quelque obligation, de laquelle j'aye à despendre.' III.9: P 1007, V 962, F 735.

150 [B]'Et de me jetter à la mercy de mon invention presente, encore moins: Je l'ay lourde et trouble, qui ne sçauroit fournir aux soudaines necessitez, et importantes'. III.9: P 1008, V 963, F 736.

151 [B]'Autant que je m'en rapporte à elle, je me mets hors de moy: jusques à essayer ma contenance: Et me suis veu quelque jour en peine, de celer la servitude en laquelle j'estois entravé: Là où mon dessein est, de representer en parlant, une profonde nonchalance <d'accent et de visage>, et des mouvemens fortuites et impremeditez, comme naissans des occasions presentes'. III.9: P 1007, V 963, F 735.

In attempting to conceal his 'servitude' (the fact that he is reliant on his memory), Montaigne succeeds only in drawing further attention to his lack of freedom: instead of appearing nonchalant, he merely shows himself to be 'en peine'. His lack of premeditation, paradoxically, is itself a product of 'design': his carelessness can be 'represented' successfully only through some element of deliberate effort and indeed, care.

The ambivalence of such artful artlessness has attracted a great deal of scholarly attention.[152] What has not so clearly been noticed, however, is the contrast between premeditation and slavery, on the one hand, and carelessness and liberty, on the other, implied in this passage. In what sense would having prepared what one has to say amount to an 'obligation' and thus to a form of 'servitude'? In the first instance, Montaigne indicates that he would be at the mercy of his memory: [B]'to be held and bound puts me off my track: and likewise to depend on so feeble an instrument as my memory'.[153] Having [B]'committed and assigned' himself so entirely to his memory, he 'lean[s] so strongly' on it that 'it takes fright at its load', leading him to forget what he was going to say.[154] But he also implies that he would be bound not merely to his memory, but to the very speech that he had undertaken to recite: [B]'the very fact of being bound to what I have to say is enough to break my grip on it'.[155] Finally, he suggests that he would, in addition, be bound by his audience's expectations of eloquence: [B]'to make apparent that one has come prepared to speak well' is [C]'a thing of too great obligation, for one who cannot hold much'.[156]

In *On the force of the imagination*, similarly, Montaigne describes himself as [C]'a sworn enemy of obligation, assiduity, and constancy'. Having been asked by others to write about 'the affairs of my time', he insists that 'even for the glory of Sallust, [he] would not take such pains', there being 'nothing so contrary to [his] style, than an extended narrative'.[157] 'Obligation' is here associated with the pressure of expectation and prescription: premeditation is the enemy of liberty, of that freedom which allows an author to amend

[152] See in particular Posner 1999.

[153] [B]'L'estre tenu et obligé, me fourvoye: et le despendre d'un si foible instrument qu'est ma memoire'. III.9: P 1007, V 962, F 735.

[154] [B]'Quand je me suis commis et assigné entierement à ma memoire, je pends si fort sur elle, que je l'accable: elle s'effraye de sa charge'. III.9: P 1007, V 963, F 735.

[155] [B]'Cela mesme, que je sois lié à ce que j'ay à dire, sert à m'en desprendre'. III.9: P 1007, V 963, F 735.

[156] [B]'De monstrer estre venu preparé pour bien dire [...] [C]chose de trop grande obligation, à qui ne peut beaucoup tenir'. III.9: P 1007, V 963, F 735.

[157] [C]'Aucuns me convient d'escrire les affaires de mon temps [...] Pour la gloire de Salluste je n'en prendoys pas la peine: ennemy juré d'obligation, d'assiduité, de constance: [...] il n'est rien si contraire à mon stile, qu'une narration estendue'. I.20: P 109, V 106, F 76.

and vary his writing, to not be bound by the demands of his subject or by what he has come prepared to say.

Nonchalance – understood as the absence of premeditation or preordinance – here comes to be associated with a form of radical spontaneity, contingency and indeterminacy, to the extent that even self-prescription is a kind of slavery.

> [C]Even in undertakings in which I am alone concerned and wholly free, if I say what I plan to do, it seems to me that I prescribe it for myself, and that to give knowledge of it to another is to impose it upon myself. It seems to me that I promise it when I mention it. Thus I seldom air my plans.[158]

Freedom is here closely identified not merely with indifference and detachment, but with a certain elasticity and versatility – with a liberty to alter one's dispositions and intentions at will. As Montaigne puts it in the opening paragraph of *On three kinds of association*:

> [B]We must not nail ourselves down so firmly to our humours and complexions. [. . .] We are not friends to ourselves, and still less masters; we are slaves to ourselves, if we follow ourselves incessantly and are so caught in our inclinations that we cannot depart from them or twist them about.[159]

Montaigne here deplores his ponderous dullness in favour of a gracious flexibility and suppleness of soul which he claims to lack. In *On experience*, he aligns himself with precisely this kind of elastic changeability: [B]'the best of my bodily qualities is that I am flexible and not very stubborn'. He has 'inclinations that are more proper, customary and agreeable' to him, but 'with very little effort', he is able to 'turn away from them' and to 'easily slip into the opposite habit'.[160] He then reasserts the value of a pliant and protean complexion, unconstrained to any particular inclination or habit:

> [B]A young man should violate his own rules to arouse his vigour and keep it from growing mouldy and lax: And there is no way of life, so stupid and feeble, as that which is conducted by rules and discipline. [. . .] The most unsuitable quality for

158 [C]'Ouy, ès entreprinses toutes miennes et libres, si j'en dy le poinct, il me semble, que je me les prescry: et que, le donner à la science d'autruy, c'est le preordonner à soy. Il me semble que je le promets, quand je le dy. Ainsi j'evente peu mes propositions'. III.9: P 101[illegible]–12, V 967, F 738.

159 [B]'Il ne faut pas se clouer si fort à ses humeurs et complexions. [. . .] Ce n'est pas estre amy de soy, et moins encore maistre; c'est en estre esclave, de se suivre incessamment et estre si pris à ses inclinations, qu'on n'en puisse fourvoyer, qu'on ne les puisse tordre'. III.3: P 85[illegible], V 819, F 621.

160 [B]'La meilleure de mes complexions corporelles, c'est d'estre flexible et peu opiniastre. J'ay des inclinations plus propres et ordinaires, et plus aggreables, que d'autres: Mais avec bien peu d'effort, je m'en destourne, et me coule aisément à la façon contraire'. III.13: P 1130–1, V 1083, F 830.

a gentleman, is overfastidiousness and bondage to certain particular ways. And they are particular if they are not pliable and supple.[161]

As in *On three kinds of association*, however, he immediately qualifies his own flexibility by asserting that, B'although [he] was trained as much as possible for liberty and indifference', he has 'through carelessness, and because [he has] lingered more in certain ways as [he] grow[s] old' allowed 'custom' to 'imprint its character' upon him in such a way that '[he] call[s] it excess to depart from it'.[162]

Freedom is here more particularly contrasted with servitude to habit and custom ('les effects de l'accoustumance'), rather than (as in the case of *On vanity*) with the obligation entailed by premeditation and reliance on one's memory. In both cases, however, Montaigne points to a paradox inherent in his efforts to be careless, a paradox which shall be explored further in Chapter 5. In *On vanity*, as we saw earlier in this chapter, the nonchalance of his manners and speech is itself the product of careful 'design'; in *On experience*, conversely, negligence is identified as the cause of his unwanted subjection to personal habit and inclination. How can carelessness be cultivated? What kind of care is necessary to free ourselves from care?

Instead of relying on his memory and seeking to exert control over it, Montaigne allows it (as he expresses it in *On presumption*) to A'serve [him] by chance encounter [. . .] at its own time, not at [his]'; he has to 'solicit it nonchalantly'.[163] What is true of his memory is true of himself as a whole: in this and A'several other parts', as we noted in Chapter 3, Montaigne 'flee[s] command, obligation, and constraint'.[164] Here too, free agency lies not in control, but in detachment from what one cannot control – in the ability to withdraw the will within the narrow confines of its power. Montaigne's weakness, in this perspective, is not merely compatible with, but an integral component of, his freedom.

161 B'Un jeune homme, doit troubler ses regles, pour esveiller sa vigueur: la garder de moisir et s'apoltronir: Et n'est train de vie, si sot et si debile, que celuy qui se conduict par ordonnance et discipline. [. . .] La plus contraire qualité à un honneste homme, c'est la delicatesse et obligation à certaine façon particuliere. Et elle est particuliere, si elle n'est ployable, et soupple'. III.13: P 1131, V 1083, F 830.

162 B'Quoy que j'aye esté dressé autant qu'on a peu, à la liberté et à l'indifference, si est-ce que par nonchalance, m'estant en vieillisant, plus arresté sur certaines formes [. . .] la coustume a desjà sans y penser, imprimé si bien en moy son charactere, en certaines choses, que j'appelle excez de m'en despartir'. III.13: P 1131, V 1083, F 830.

163 A'Elle me sert mieux par rencontre, il faut que je la solicite nonchalamment. [. . .] Elle me sert à son heure, non pas à la mienne'. II.17: P 688, V 649, F 493.

164 A'Cecy que je sens en la memoire, je le sens en plusieurs autres parties. Je fuis le commandement, l'obligation, et la contrainte'. II.17: P 688, V 650, F 493.

V

This conjunction between liberty and powerlessness is central to Montaigne's claim to speak without guile and without fear, as a man who owns his own speech instead of speaking on behalf of his master. His *franchise* unites a bold and forceful abrasiveness in speech with a trusting and artless weakness, embodying both the independence and the lack of affectation of a man whose natural condition is liberty.

> [A]The speech that I love is a simple, natural speech, the same on paper as in the mouth: a speech succulent and sinewy, brief and compressed, [C]not so much dainty and well-combed as vehement and brusque [. . .]. [A]Rather difficult than boring, remote from affectation: irregular, disconnected, and bold: each bit making a body in itself: not pedantic, not monkish, not lawyer-like, but rather soldierly.[165]

This unpolished, negligent speech draws its potency and vigour precisely from its carelessness, discontinuity and abruptness, lacking in all prudence and affectation, and in particular in knowledge of the art of dissimulation, flattery and manipulation.

Montaigne's frankness, as he explains in *On presumption*, takes on the appearance of insolence and indiscretion, yet he has no skill by which to stop himself from speaking his own mind:

> [B]Displaying to great men the same licence of tongue, and bearing, that I bring from my own house: I feel how much it leans toward indiscretion and incivility: But besides the fact that I am made that way, I have not a supple enough mind to sidestep a sudden question, and escape it by some dodge: neither to feign a truth, nor enough memory to retain it thus feigned: and certainly not enough assurance to maintain it: and I act boldly out of weakness. In this way I abandon myself to naturalness, and to always saying what I think, both by complexion, and by ~~training~~ <design>: leaving it to fortune to conduct the outcome.[166]

As this passage makes clear, Montaigne's careless speech is a fearless speech, undazzled by the power of great men and undaunted by the threat of adverse

165 [A]'Le parler que j'ayme, c'est un parler simple et naïf, tel sur le papier qu'à la bouche: un parler succulent et nerveux, court et serré, [C]non tant delicate et peigné, comme vehement et brusque [. . .] [A]Plutost difficile qu'ennuieux, esloigné d'affectation: desreglé, descousu, et hardy: chaque loppin y face son corps: non pedantesque, non fratesque, non pleideresque, mais plustost soldatesque'. I.25: P 178, V 171–2, F 127.

166 [B]'Presentant aux grands ceste mesme licence de langue, et de contenance, que j'apporte de ma maison: je sens combien elle decline vers l'indiscretion et incivilité: Mais outre ce que je suis ainsi faict, je n'ay pas l'esprit assez souple pour gauchir à une prompte demande, et pour en eschapper par quelque destour: ny pour feindre une verité, ny assez de memoire pour la retenir ainsi feinte: ny certes assez d'asseurance pour la maintenir: et fais le brave par foiblesse. Parquoy je m'abandonne à la nayfveté, et à tousjours dire ce que je pense, et par complexion, et par ~~discours~~ <dessein>: laissant à la fortune d'en conduire l'evenement'. II.17: P 687, V 649, F 492.

consequences, abandoning the outcome to fortune. In *A consideration upon Cicero*, similarly, the ambitious sycophancy of Cicero's carefully polished and self-aggrandizing letters provides a foil for his own disdainful, careless writing:

> [B]I have naturally a familiar and private style: But of a form all my own, inept for public negotiations, as my language is in every way, too compressed, disordered, abrupt, particular. [. . .] That is a far cry from our present practice: for there never was so abject and servile a prostitution of presentations: life, soul, devotion, adoration, serf, slave [. . .] I mortally hate to seem a flatterer. And so I naturally throw myself onto a dry, round and blunt way of speaking, which, to anyone who does not know me otherwise, verges a little on the disdainful.[167]

Montaigne goes on to claim that he write his letters [B]'posthaste', with 'intolerably bad' handwriting, writing 'without a plan; the first remark bringing on the second'. Above all, he has 'accustomed high personages who know [him] to put up with scratchings and crossings-out, and a paper without fold or margin'.[168] This neglect of ceremonial and verbal subjection is a mark of his inborn independence, uncorrupted by any willingness to please or to ingratiate himself with powerful and influential men.

As he puts it in the passage from *On presumption* quoted in the previous paragraph, 'je fais le brave par foiblesse': Montaigne's boldness is a product of his weakness. His frankness is inseparably connected to his trusting, innocent nature (*fiance*), his openness and his loyalty to his word reflecting not only his contempt for dissimulation and deceit, but a certain weakness or vulnerability that earns the trust of others by placing faith in their loyalty in return. The importance of keeping faith is a leading, unifying motif of the *Essais*, established as a central concern from the very outset of the book.[169] The first few chapters are intensely preoccupied with the problem of treachery, subterfuge and breach of faith, and with a concern to establish Montaigne by contrast as a man of his word and his text as 'a book of good faith'.[170] The juxtaposition of a wide range of

[167] [B]'J'ay naturellement un stile comique et privé: Mais c'est d'une forme mienne, inepte aux negotiations publiques, comme en toutes façons est mon langage, trop serré, desordonné, couppé, particulier: [. . .] C'est bien loing de l'usage present: car il ne fut jamais si abjecte et servile prostitution de presentations: la vie, l'ame, devotion, adoration, serf, esclave [. . .] Je hay à mort à sentir le flateur. Qui faict que je me jette naturellement à un parler sec, [C]rond et cru, [B]qui tire à qui ne me cognoit d'ailleurs, un peu vers le desdaigneux'. I.39: P 256–7, V 252–3, F 186.

[168] [B]'En poste, et si precipiteusement'. 'Je peigne insupportablement mal'. 'J'ay accoustumé les grands, qui me cognoissent, à y supporter des litures et des trasseures, et un papier sans plieure et sans marge. [. . .] Je commence volontiers sans project; le premier traict produit le second'. I.39: P 257, V 253, F 186.

[169] Compagnon 1985.

[170] [A]'Un Livre de bonne foy'. *Au lecteur*: P 27, V 3, F 2.

historical and contemporary examples serves as a foil to Montaigne's construction of himself as a man who trusts in others and who can therefore himself be trusted. In this conception, boldness and meekness come to be united within an overarching vision of plain, honourable, and unaffected speech.

Whether the governor of a besieged place should go out to parley examines the use of fraud in the conduct of war, both in ancient and in modern times, in particular the practice of making offers of parley as a cover for surprise offensives. Keeping faith with others and having faith in others, Montaigne suggests, is especially arduous and dangerous in the modern world where deception is held to be an integral aspect of warfare, and where [A]'following Lysander, we say that where the lion's skin will not suffice, we must sew on a bit of the fox's', by pairing ruse with valour.[171] This theme is continued in the next chapter, *Parley time is dangerous*, where he contends that [A]'parties should not trust one another until the last binding seal has been set', and that 'even then there is plenty of room for wariness'.[172]

In a characteristic gesture, Montaigne excepts himself not only from this prudential use of treachery ('finesse', 'subtilité', 'tromperie', 'trahison'), but also from the culture of suspicion and distrust which it fosters and upon which it relies. Whereas [A]'it is a rule in the mouth of all military men of our time, That the governor of a besieged place must ever go out himself to parley',[173] he claims to [B]'entrust [him]self [*me fie*] easily to another man's word [*foy*]', although only 'reluctantly, whenever [he] would give the impression of acting from despair and lack of courage, rather than out of frankness [*franchise*] and faith [*fiance*] in his loyalty'.[174] 'Se fier', 'foy' and 'fiance' all offer variations of *fides* or faith: Montaigne readily entrusts himself to others, but only so long as he may be judged to have done so not out of cowardice or a sense of hopelessness, but out of a frank or free faith in the good faith of others.

In what sense is Montaigne's *fiance* a sign of his *franchise*? In an immediate sense, he simply implies that his trust is voluntary and spontaneous, the product of free choice rather than a lack of alternatives – a deliberate

171 [A]'Après Lysander, disons que, où la peau du Lyon ne peut suffire, il y faut coudre un lopin de celle du Regnard'. I.5: P 48, V 26, F 17.

172 [A]'Ne se doit attendre fiance des uns aux autres, que le dernier seau d'obligation n'y soit passé: encores y a il lors assés affaire'. I.6: P 50, V 28, F 18.

173 [A]'C'est une regle en la bouche de tous les hommes de guerre de nostre temps, Qu'il ne faut jamais que le gouverneur en une place assiegée sorte luy mesmes pour parlementer'. I.5: P 49, V 26, F 17.

174 [B]'Je me fie aysement à la foy d'autruy: mais mal-aysement le feroi-je, lors que je donrois à juger l'avoir plustost faict par desespoir et faute de cœur, que par franchise et fiance de sa loyauté'. I.5: P 49–50, V 27, F 17.

ethical decision rather than a passive response to circumstances. But he also points to a deeper connection between 'franchise' and 'fiance', one that is reinforced by the alliteration between the two terms. Compare his use of 'franchise' in this passage to its appearance at the beginning of the chapter: C'only that man considers himself overcome, who knows he was downed neither by trick nor by luck but by valiance, man to man, in a frank [*franche*] and just war'.[175] In this earlier passage, 'franchise' clearly designates a bold and fearless openness, scornful of trickery and chance – linked to both courage and justice. By associating 'franchise' with 'fiance', Montaigne connects this bold, fearless openness to a simple, trusting disposition, incapable of premeditation and subterfuge.

This pattern of thought can best be illustrated by examining Montaigne's account of his *franchise* in two key chapters: *On the useful and the honourable* and *On physiognomy*. In the first of these, as we saw in Chapter 3, Montaigne refuses to involve himself in treachery, for all its usefulness and necessity in politics, arguing that such commissions should be resigned 'to other more obedient and supple men'. He then proceeds to offer an account of his own dealings with princes, as an alternative to politics as prudent dissimulation:

> BIn what little negotiating I have had to do between our princes, in these divisions and subdivisions that tear our nation apart today, I have carefully avoided letting them be mistaken about me and deceived by my outward appearance. Professional negotiators make every effort within their power to conceal their thoughts and to feign a moderate and conciliatory attitude: as for me, I reveal myself by my most vigorous opinions, presented in my most personal manner, a tender and green negotiator: who would rather fail in his mission than fail to be true to myself. However, up to this time it has been with such good luck (for certainly fortune has the principal share in it) that few men have passed between one party and another with less suspicion and more favour and privacy.[176]

The art of *negotium*, as practised by 'les gens du mestier', is to keep oneself well hidden, by positioning oneself as a moderate and by adapting oneself, chameleon-like, to one's audience. However, simply by offering himself to

175 C'Celuy seul se tient pour surmonté, qui scait l'avoir esté ny par ruse, ny de sort, mais par vaillance, de troupe à troupe, en une franche et juste guerre'. I.5: P 48, V 25, F 16.

176 B'En ce peu que j'ay eu à negocier entre nos Princes, en ces divisions, et subdivisions, qui nous deschirent aujourd'huy: j'ay curieusement evité, qu'ils se mesprinssent en moy, et s'enferrassent en mon masque. Les gens du mestier se tiennent les plus couverts, et se presentent et contrefont les plus moyens, et les plus voysins qu'ils peuvent: moy, je m'offre par mes opinions les plus vives, et par la forme plus mienne: Tendre negotiateur et novice: qui ayme mieux faillir à l'affaire, qu'à moy. Ç'a esté pourtant jusques à cette heure, avec tel heur, (car certes fortune y a la principalle part) que peu ont passé de main à autre, avec moins de soupçon, plus de faveur et de privauté'. III.1: P 831, V 791–2, F 600.

princes in the 'form that is most [his] own' – inexperienced and unschooled, more concerned with himself than with the *affaire* in hand – Montaigne is able to win confidence and trust on all sides, something that eludes these accomplished professionals.

This success is attributed to chance ('for certainly fortune has the principal share in it') rather than to any conscious calculation or effort on Montaigne's part, a good fortune embodied in an easy and open appearance that allows him to give free rein to his 'liberty' without attracting suspicion.

> [B]I have an open way, easy to insinuate itself, and to give itself credit, on first acquaintance. [. . .] Few suspect or find odious the liberty of those who work without any thought for their own interest: And who can truly use the answer of Hyperides to the Athenians when they complained of his harsh way of speaking: Gentlemen, do not consider whether I speak freely, but whether I do so without accepting anything and thereby serving my own affairs.[177]

Liberty is here understood as a quality of speech, a harshness ('aspreté de son parler'). The roughness and fearlessness of Montaigne's parrhesiastic counsel discharges him of any [B]'suspicion of dissimulation' by its 'vigour': he 'does not refrain from saying anything, however grave and burning' and 'could not have said anything worse' in the absence of those whom he addresses so boldly.[178] To be free is to speak without reserve, in the service of truth rather than in one's interest. Yet it is his natural complexion, his 'façon ouverte', that makes such liberty possible, by giving 'credit' to him and leading other men to trust him.

This self-image is not without ambiguity. On the one hand, liberty is upheld as a condition of robust self-sufficiency and self-containment, marked by 'vigueur' and 'aspreté'. The metamorphoses and adaptability of the 'gens du mestier' are here contrasted unfavourably with Montaigne's steadfast loyalty to the truth, and above all to himself, preferring 'to fail in [his] mission rather than to [him]self'. His speech, moreover, has a certain violence or abrasiveness to it, acting as a reproof and as a warning. Yet for all this roughness, his emphasis on 'ease' (he is 'easy to insinuate

[177] [B]'J'ay une façon ouverte, aisée à s'insinuer, et à se donner credit, aux premieres accointances. La naïfveté et la verité pure, en quelque siecle que ce soit, trouvent encore leur opportunité et leur mise. Et puis de ceux-là est la liberté peu suspecte, et peu odieuse, qui besongnent sans aucun leur interest: Et peuvent veritablement employer la reponse de Hipperides aux Atheniens, se plaignans de l'aspreté de son parler: Messieurs, ne considerez pas si je suis libre, mais si je le suis, sans rien prendre, et sans amender par là mes affaires'. III.1: P 831, V 792, F 600.

[178] [B]'Ma liberté m'a aussi aiséement deschargé de soupçon de faintise, par sa vigueur (n'espargnant rien à dire pour poisant et cuisant qu'il fust: je n'eusse peu dire pis absent)'. III.1: P 831, V 792, F 600.

himself', his freedom is 'easily discharged' of suspicion, he passes without obstacle from 'one hand to another') also suggests a supple plasticity and flexibility, rather than enduring stability. He is a '*tender* negotiator and novice', his is [B]'an appearance of obvious simplicity and carelessness'.[179] His liberty is here presented both as a fearless boldness and as an innocent, spontaneous 'naïfveté' – both as a form of courageous virtue, and as a disarming vulnerability.

By offering itself as an alternative to prudent dissimulation, moreover, Montaigne's liberty takes on a crafted or fashioned slant. He has 'curiously' avoided letting other men be deceived by his outward appearance, and yet his success as a negotiator stems precisely from a visible bearing that 'gains credit on first acquaintaince'. He here appeals to his weakness to deflect the accusation that his carelessness is itself a carefully studied pose:

> [B]Those who commonly contradict what I profess, saying that what I call frankness, simplicity, and naturalness, in my conduct, is art and subtlety: and rather prudence, than goodness: industry, than nature: good sense, than good luck: do me more honour than they take away from me. [. . .] I have often seen this counterfeit and artificial liberty in practice, but most often without success. It is apt to smack of Aesop's ass, who, in emulation of the dog, came and threw himself gaily with both feet on his master's shoulders; but for all the petting that the dog received for the same show of affection, the poor ass received twice as many cudgelings. [C]*What most becomes a man is what is most a part of him.*[180]

Counterfeit, artificial liberty, in this passage, is unmasked by its clumsiness, its difficulty, its borrowed nature: Montaigne's liberty, by contrast, is fully a part of himself. His carelessness, as he makes clear in *On physiognomy*, testifies not merely to his artlessness, but to a freedom which protects and secures itself, not by concealing or hiding itself, nor by struggling against those forces that threaten to suppress it, but by trusting in the power of its weakness to win others over to simplicity and carelessness.

179 [B]'Une montre apparente de simplesse et de nonchalance'. III.1: P 831, V 792, F 601.

180 [B]'Ceux qui disent communement contre ma profession, que ce que j'appelle franchise, simplesse, et naïfveté, en mes mœurs, c'est art et finesse: et plustost prudence, que bonté: industrie, que nature: bon sens, que bon heur: me font plus d'honneur qu'ils ne m'en ostent. [. . .] J'ay veu souvent en usage, ces libertez contrefaites, et artificielles, mais le plus souvent, sans succez. Elles sentent volontiers leur asne d'Esope: lequel par emulation du chien, vint à se jetter tout gayement, à deux pieds, sur les espaules de son maistre: mais autant que le chien recevoit de caresses, de pareille feste, le pauvre asne en receut deux fois autant de bastonnades. [C]*Id maximè quemque decet, quod est cuiusque suum maximè* [Cicero, *De officiis*, I.31]'. III.1: P 835, V 795, F 603–4.

The chapter ends by providing an account of two occasions upon which [B]'on the mere credit' of his [C]'presence' and his [B]'air', persons who did not know him 'placed great trust' in him.[181] In the first story, a man arrives in a panic at his house, claiming that he is fleeing from his enemies, and begging for refuge. He is soon joined by increasing numbers of men, thereby alerting Montaigne's suspicions. Instead of seeking to defend himself against this likely threat, however, Montaigne chooses to [B]'let [him]self go the most natural and most simple course', by giving orders for them to come into his house. This gesture of trust unexpectedly leads his aggressors to relent, and to leave him in peace, without pursuing their planned attack. This reversal of fortune he attributes to the conspicuousness of his liberty, his [B]'face' and his 'frankness' disarming his enemies of their treachery.[182]

In the second incident, Montaigne recounts that he was taken prisoner, while away from his estate during a truce in the civil wars, by a band of masked men who confiscated his goods and then debated whether to kill him. Here again, a sudden reversal takes place: without warning, his aggressors decide to return his possessions to him and to set him free. Once again, Montaigne's freedom of countenance and of speech are identified as the cause of his salvation:

> [B]The true cause of so unusual an about-face and change of mind without any apparent motivation, and of such a miraculous repentance, at such a time, in a premeditated and deliberate enterprise [. . .] I truly do not even now well know. The most conspicuous among them, who took off his mask and let me know his name, repeated to me several times that I owed my deliverance to my face, liberty and the firmness of my speech, which made me undeserving of such a misadventure.[183]

Montaigne's characterisation of his liberty as an unstudied, natural disposition, marked by carelessness and vulnerability, rather than the assertion of power and strength, is here offered as a strategy of self-protection,

181 [B]'Sur le simple credit de ~~mon port~~ [C]ma presence, [B]et de mon air, des personnes qui n'avoient aucune cognoissance de moy, s'y sont grandement fiées.' III.12: P 1107, V 1060, F 811–12. On the *franchise* of Montaigne's *visage*, see Posner 1999, ch. 2, sec. iii and Boutcher 1995.

182 [B]'Je me laissay aller au party le plus naturel et le plus simple [. . .] Mon visage, et ma franchise, luy avoient arraché la trahison des poings'. III.12: P 1108, V 1060–1, F 812–3.

183 [B]'La vraye cause d'un changement si nouveau, et de ce ravisement, sans aucune impulsion apparente, et d'un repentir si miraculeux, en tel temps, en une entreprinse pourpensée et deliberée [. . .] certes je ne sçay pas bien encores quelle elle est. ~~Le~~ plus apparent qui se demasqua, et me fit cognoistre son nom, me redist lors plusieurs fois, que je devoy cette delivrance à mon visage, liberté, et fermeté de mes parolles, qui me rendoient indigne d'une telle mesadventure'. III.12: P 1109–1100, V 1062, F 814.

allowing him to exercise his freedom in all boldness and fearlessness, without compromising its lasting preservation:

> [B]If my face did not answer for me, if people did not read in my eyes, and in my voice, the simplicity of my intention, I would not have lasted so long without quarrel and without harm, considering my indiscreet liberty in saying, right or wrong, whatever comes into my head, and in judging things rashly.[184]

Here again, we find that carelessness and self-possession, far from being antagonistic or mutually exclusive, are brought together in a single vision of Montaigne as a free man.

184 [B]'Si mon visage ne respondoit pour moy, si on ne lisoit en mes yeux, et en ma voix, la simplicité de mon intention, je n'eusse pas duré sans querelle, et sans offence, si long temps: avec cette indiscrette liberté, de dire à tort et à droict, ce qui me vient en fantasie, et juger temerairement des choses'. III.12: P 1100, V 1062, F 814.

CHAPTER 5

The art of self-management

I

Self-possession and carelessness, as we saw in Chapter 4, are united in their preoccupation with the protection and detachment of the will. Liberty is to be achieved by handling or disposing of one's will in a particular way – whether (in the case of self-possession) to prevent it from being dominated by the will of another, or (in the case of carelessness) to preserve it from continual strain and distress. This practice of measured disengagement and containment constitutes the self as an object of sustained attention and manipulation. But it also points to an important paradox at the heart of Montaigne's project of self-examination. Freedom cannot be attained by exerting pressure on the will, for that would defeat the purpose of the exercise, which is precisely to release it as much as possible from [B]'inner tension and solicitude'.[1] Yet it is only by studying and working upon ourselves – by [B]'bringing back your mind and your will, which are spending themselves elsewhere, into themselves' – that we are able to detach ourselves from that which lies beyond our power and thus to preserve ourselves in this state of independence and equanimity.[2] Under what conditions might the man who has [C]'declared war to death against all care' and had [A]'neither forced governor nor master to this day' succeed in caring for and governing himself?[3] On what terms must prudence be combined with nonchalance if Montaigne is to safeguard his will from reckless squander and expropriation, and from subjection to an exhausting regimen of self-control?

From the perspective of the *Essais*, self-government consists not in heroic self-overcoming but in an oblique and strategic practice of self-regulation,

[1] [B]'L'attention et sollicitude, de ma volonté au dedans'. III.9: P 1012, V 967, F 739.

[2] [B]'Vostre esprit, et vostre volonté, qui se consomme ailleurs, ramenez la en soy'. III.9: P 1047, V 1001, F 766.

[3] [C]'J'ay denoncé à tout soing guerre capitale'. III.9: P 1015, V 970, F 741. [A]'N'ayant eu jusques à cett' heure ny commandant ny maistre forcé'. II.17: P 681, V 643, F 487.

at once careless and exacting. This 'art of existence' is based partly on discipline, but at the same time on evasion, diversion, ruse and compromise. The model for this practice, I argue in this chapter, is the judicious and generous art of *mesnagerie* or household government. The wise *mesnager*, according to Montaigne, recognises the limits of his power. He rules over his household with calculated indifference and gracious reserve, knowing when to intervene, when to concede and when to turn a blind eye. In governing ourselves, similarly, we should aim not to control ourselves, but to comfort and contain ourselves, without effort, strain or struggle. The aim is not to rule but to regulate oneself – not to master one's will, but rather to manage it.

This parallel between household management and self-management finds root in a close identification, already observed in previous chapters, between freedom and the physical space of the home or estate. The most striking example occurs in the closing pages of *On three kinds of association*, where (as we noted in Chapter 3) Montaigne describes his tower library as his ^C'throne' or 'seat', identifying it as the one corner of the world over which '[he tries] to make [his] dominion pure'. The 'dominion' that the library affords depends partly on the suspension of ^C'all community, conjugal, filial, and civil': it is ^C'a place to belong to oneself: to pay one's court privately to oneself: to hide oneself'.[4] But Montaigne's authority also consists, more immediately, in the exercise of physical oversight and symbolic control over his household:

> ^BWhen at home, I turn aside a little more often to my library, from which at one sweep I command a view of my household: I am over the entrance, and see below me, my garden, my farmyard, my courtyard, and into most of the parts of my house. [. . .] ^CThe shape [of my library] is round, the only flat side being the part needed for my table and chair; and curving round me it presents at a glance all my books, arranged in five rows of shelves on all sides. It offers rich and free views in three directions, and sixteen paces of empty space in diameter.[5]

The library here represents a post of observation and command as well as a place of hiding and retreat. Situated ^C'out of the way', on the third floor of

4 ^C'C'est là mon siege. J'essaye à m'en rendre la domination pure: et à soustraire ce seul coing, à la communauté et conjugale, et filiale, et civile'. ^C'Où estre à soy: où se faire particulierement la cour: où se cacher'. III.3: P 870, V 828, F 629.

5 ^B'Chez moy, je me destourne un peu plus souvent à ma librairie, d'où, tout d'une main, je commande mon mesnage: Je suis sur l'entrée, et vois soubs moy, mon jardin, ma basse cour, ma cour, et dans la plus part des membres de ma maison. [. . .] ^CLa figure en est ronde, et n'a de plat, que ce qu'il faut à ma table et à mon siege: et vient m'offrant en se courbant, d'une veue, tous mes livres, rengez sur des pulpitres à cinq degrez tout à l'environ. Elle a trois veues de riche et libre prospect, et seize pas de vuide en diametre'. III.3: P 869–70, V 828, F 629.

a tower in a house ‘perched on a little hill’, its location combines isolation with elevation.[6] Far from being mutually exclusive, solitary meditation and household authority are inseparably connected: the possibility of seclusion itself depends on the power to admit and exclude others from one’s own space. By placing his study above the entrance to his home, Montaigne is able not only to monitor the activities of his family and servants, but to keep watch over the boundary separating the inside and the outside, the sphere that is his own and that which lies beyond his jurisdiction.

The juxtaposition of lands and books within Montaigne’s field of vision points to a further association between the oversight and management of the estate, on the one hand, and the cultivation of the self through reading and reflection, on the other. The company of books, he writes, is the [B]‘best provision’ he has found ‘for this human journey’. Like the *arriereboutique*, the library is a kind of storehouse in which he surrounds himself with all that he needs to survive: he cannot say [B]‘how much repose and ease’ he finds when he considers that his books are ‘at [his] side to give [him] pleasure at [his] own time’ and ‘how much assistance they bring to [his] life’.[7] His command over the textual materials at his disposal is thus mirrored both in his administration of the household and his jurisdiction over himself.

That dominion, however, is represented in highly circumscribed terms. Far from exercising mastery over his *mesnage* and, by implication, over himself, it is only by retreating within the narrow confines of his study that Montaigne is able to preserve what little power he has from dilution: everywhere else, his [C]‘authority’ is merely ‘verbal’ and ‘in essence, impure’.[8] The library represents a point of stability in the midst of contingency and passivity; its function is one of self-protection rather than self-assertion. Montaigne’s self-management, similarly, takes weakness or ‘impure’ authority as its starting point. As he explains in *On vanity*: [B]‘I have nothing that is mine but myself, and even there my possession is partly defective and borrowed’.[9] As we observed in Chapter 4, his cultivated carelessness leads him (notably in *On practice*) to emphasise the haziness and permeability of the borderline between those parts of his conduct and thinking which are subject to his will and those which are not.

6 [C]‘À l’esquart’. ‘Juchée sur un tertre’. III.3: P 870, V 828, F 629.

7 [B]‘Il ne se peut dire, combien je me repose et sejourne en cette consideration, qu’ils sont à mon costé pour me donner du plaisir à mon heure: et à reconnoistre, combien ils portent de secours à ma vie: C’est la meilleure munition que j’aye trouvé à cet humain voyage’. III.3: P 869, V 827–8, F 628.

8 [C]‘Par tout ailleurs je n’ay qu’une auctorité verbale: en essence, confuse’. III.3: P 870, V 828, F 629. See also Jordan 2004, p. 89.

9 [B]‘Je n’ay rien mien, que moy; et si en est la possession en partie manque et empruntée’. III.9: P 1013, V 968, F 740. See also III.1: P 834, V 794, F 603[B].

Montaigne is thus concerned to stress not only the narrowness of his dominion, but its essential indeterminacy. Crucially, however, this acknowledgement of weakness and 'impurity' does not detract from his refusal to be mastered. To own oneself is not to exercise sovereign power over oneself, but to ensure, as far as possible, that one is not under the power of another. It is perfectly consistent of Montaigne to insist *both* on the importance of being one's own man *and* on the considerable extent to which his 'conditions and humours' lie beyond the scope of his will. The ability to free oneself from the domination of other agents is a necessary but by no means sufficient condition of self-mastery. We may not be able to exercise authority over all parts of ourselves: there is only so much that can be done to control the movements of an untamed or lazy horse. Yet the *handling* of that horse – the decision to tighten or slacken the will according to the demands of the occasion – belongs to ourselves and to ourselves alone.

The passage from *On three kinds of association* also provides some indication of what this judicious handling might look like in practice. Montaigne's description of his library draws attention not only to the limited scope of his authority, but to its oblique, discontinuous and surreptitious quality, both within and without the boundaries of his power. His approach to *mesnagerie* combines watchfulness with aloofness and indirection. Just as he [B]'leaf[s] now through one book, then another, without order and without plan', in a condition suspended somewhere between meditative rumination and restless distraction, he oversees his household at a distance and at a glance, without concern for constant vigilance and inspection.[10] This kind of careless, or at least effortless, administration leaves little space for premeditation and deliberation – like his reading, it is absent-minded, conducted 'without order and without plan'. Yet this very ease itself depends on the institution of a different sort of order, an order associated with regulation and arrangement rather than with preordinance. By positioning his table and chair at the focal point both of his book collection and of the surrounding estate, Montaigne ensures that his resources are always at his disposal, readily accessible and at hand. 'Dominion' here consists not in the exercise of empire and control, but in well-ordered arrangement; not in deliberate premeditation, but in a state of readiness that guarantees ease in action.

Montaigne's account of his library offers just one example of an implicit analogy between the government of the household and that of the self

[10] [B]'Là je feuillette à cette heure un livre, à cette heure un autre, sans ordre et sans dessein'. III.3: P 869, V 828, F 629.

present throughout the *Essais*. This parallel is nowhere confirmed so clearly as in the title of the tenth chapter of the third book, *De mesnager sa volonté* (a phrase translated as 'on husbanding your will' and 'on restraining one's will' by Donald Frame and M. A. Screech, respectively), and in the opening pages of that same chapter, where we are exhorted to [B]'mesnager la liberté de nostre ame, et ne l'hypothequer qu'aux occasions justes' (to 'husband the liberty of our soul, and mortgage it only on just occasions').[11]

What exactly does Montaigne intend the term *mesnager* to convey? Huguet defines the verb in its intransitive form as 's'occuper du ménage, du gouvernment de la maison, du travail domestique' ('to take care of the household, of the government of the house, of domestic tasks'); by extension, its transitive meanings include 'administrer', 'tirer parti de, employer', and 'apprêter, confectionner' ('to administer; to draw upon, to use; to prepare, to fashion').[12] The *mesnage* itself should here be taken to refer not merely to the physical building of the house and the territory that surrounds it, but to the resources, both material and human, which it contains and which sustain it. *Mesnager* one's will or one's liberty is thus to dispose of them with the same prudence and care that one would use in managing one's estates, family, employees and servants.

In the context of III.10, *mesnager* carries a more specific connotation of thrifty and sparing use. We should exercise caution and restraint in investing our will and expending our liberty, just as we should administer our wealth and property with an eye to the dangers of extravagance and insolvency.

> [B]No one distributes his money to others, everyone distributes his time and his life. There is nothing of which we are so prodigal, than of those things, in which alone avarice would be useful to us and laudable.[13]

The phrase 'mesnager sa liberté' is used on two other occasions in the *Essais*, in both cases with the same connotations of parsimony and safekeeping. In *On some verses of Virgil*, Montaigne counsels the reader to avoid submitting to the bond of marriage where possible – [B]'il faut prudemment mesnager sa liberté' – but to follow the 'laws of common duty', or at least make an effort to do so, once one has done so.[14] A similar proscription against

[11] III.10: P 1049, V 1001, F 767–8. Cf. Screech's translation: Montaigne 1991, p. 1135.

[12] Huguet 1925–67.

[13] [B]'Personne ne distribue son argent à autruy, chacun y distribue son temps et sa vie. Il n'est rien dequoy nous soyons si prodigues, que de ces choses là, desquelles seules l'avarice nous seroit utile et louable'. III.10: P 1049, V 1004, F 768.

[14] [B]'Il s'y faut tenir soubs les loix du debvoir commun, aumoins s'en efforcer'. III.5: P 894, V 852, F 648.

the expenditure of liberty is found in *On three kinds of association*, where he writes that women should confine their study of philosophy to the lessons that will train them, among other things, in the task of [B]'mesnager leur liberté'.[15] An apt translation of *mesnager* in this context might be 'to economise' – to hold one's freedom in reserve, to save it, instead of squandering or alienating it. *Mesnagerie*, after all, is the French equivalent of the Greek term *oikonomia* (from *oikos* or household and *nomos*, law or rule), which is in turn the root of the modern word 'economy' and its derivatives.

In *On vanity*, likewise, Montaigne uses the words 'cette mesnagerie' in connection with his habit of [B]'counting as profit' the 'ingratitude, affronts, and indignities' received from those to whom he is indebted by some duty of friendship. These offences, he argues, release him from any obligation of affection and good will beyond [B]'the external civilities that public interest prescribes', thereby 'sparing [him] something of [his] diligence and engagement towards them'. There is some syntactical uncertainty about the intended referent of *mesnagerie* in this passage. One possibility is that it denotes the prudent dispensation of Montaigne's (good) will – an interpretation reinforced by the insertion of a quotation from Cicero's *De amicitia*: [C]'*it is the part of a prudent man to restrain, as he would a chariot, the impulse of good will*'. However, the term could also be taken to refer to the practice of reckoning and record keeping that provides the basis for such self-restraint – a practice echoed elsewhere by Montaigne's description of the *Essais* as an account book or ledger (a 'registre' or 'rolle'). Finally and more simply, the phrase may be interpreted as a reference to the 'great saving' that results from the discharge of Montaigne's debts.[16]

Whatever its exact referent, the intended effect of the term is clear: financial prudence, Montaigne suggests, provides a model for moral probity. The metaphorical scope of *mesnagerie* is not exhausted, however, by the representation of the will as a resource or commodity in need of protection and consolidation. Financial discretion is an important but by no means exhaustive aspect of household management. As the quotation from *De amicitia* suggests, Montaigne's avoidance of profligacy and debt bears

15 III.3: P 864, V 823, F 625.

16 [B]'J'ay parfois compté à profit, les ingratitudes, offences, et indignitez, que j'avois receu de ceux, à qui ou par nature, ou par accident, j'avois quelque devoir d'amitié [. . .]. Je trouve grand espargne pourtant [C]à faire par justice, ce que je faisoy par affection [. . .] [C]*Est prudentis sustinere ut cursum, sic impetum beneuolentiae* [Cicero, *De amicitia*, 17.63]. [. . .] [B]Et me sert cette mesnagerie, de quelque consolation, aux imperfections de ceux qui me touchent. [. . .] J'en espargne [. . .] quelque chose de mon application et engagement envers eux'. III.9: P 1012, V 967, F 739.

witness to his ability to harness the impulses of his will. *Mesnager sa volonté*, accordingly, is not merely to impose limits on the expenditure of one's will, but to attend to, direct and shape it in appropriate and advantageous ways. This more expansive understanding of *mesnagerie* endures in our own use of 'economy' to refer not merely to the sparing and calculating management of our material resources, but to the way in which any complex entity or organism is ordered and arranged.

The metaphor of domestic economy links Montaigne's practice of self-regulation to a wider paradigm of prudent administration and beneficial dispensation, epitomised by but not limited to financial circumspection. A less etymologically accurate but semantically more faithful translation of *mesnager* might therefore be, not 'to economise', but rather 'to manage' – to conduct one's will and handle one's liberty as one would a recalcitrant and unpredictable horse.[17] These wider connotations are evident in Montaigne's deployment of the phrase *mesnager le temps*, a commonplace that echoes Seneca's opening injunction to Lucilius in the *Epistulae* – '*tempus* [. . .] *collige et serva*' – and which may well have provided the model for Montaigne's more idiosyncratic application of the verb to the concepts of will and liberty.[18]

To manage one's time, to handle it well, is in the first instance to have [A]'knowledge of how to seize occasions at the right time', as Montaigne puts it in his *Observations on Julius Caesar's methods of making war*. Caesar's status as [A]'the true and sovereign model of the military art' is here linked to his having been an 'excellent mesnager du temps', a quality exemplified both by the astonishing speed with which he conquered territory after territory and by his mastery of delaying tactics, knowing when to play for time to reinforce his own position.[19] This *mesnagerie* or strategic use of time emerges elsewhere as an ability to make it our own, to shape it to our own ends, even in awareness of the imminence and inevitability of death. In *On practice*, for example, those ancients who tried to [A]'taste and savour'

[17] *Mesnage*, *mesnager*, and *mesnagerie* all derive from the old French verb *manoir* (to remain), which itself stems from the Latin *manere*. The *mesnage*, in this sense, is the *demeure*, the place in which one lives or stays. By contrast, the root of the English term 'manage', like the French *manier*, is the Latin *manus* (hand), via the Italian *maneggiare* ('to handle, to be able to use skilfully, to manage, to direct or exercise a horse'). See, for example, Richard II's lament: 'Down, down I come, like glistr'ing Phaeton, | Wanting the manage of unruly jades' (III.3.180–1). Yet the semantic as well as phonetic proximity of *manage* and *mesnager* meant that the usage of the first came to be influenced by the latter, notably in the now familiar phrase 'household management'.

[18] Seneca 1989, I.1.1, p. 2.

[19] [A]'La science de prendre au poinct les occasions'. 'Le vray et souverain patron de l'art militaire'. II.34: P 772–3, V 736–7, F 556–7.

death even as they were themselves dying, 'to see what this passage was', are (like Caesar) described as 'excellens mesnagers du temps'.[20]

The skill that these individuals display consists partly in the ability to eke out the time accorded to them, by not allowing even their final moments to go to waste, but partly also in a power to turn to their advantage and profit that over which they have only the most tenuous control, by transforming it into an opportunity for reflection and pleasure. As Montaigne explains in *On experience*:

> [B]I have a dictionary all my own: I pass the time, when it is bad and disagreeable; when it is good, I do not want to pass it, I savour it, I cling to it. [. . .] It takes management to enjoy life: I enjoy it twice as much as others: For the measure of enjoyment, depends on the greater or lesser application, that we lend it. Especially at this moment, when I perceive that mine is so brief in time, I try to increase it in weight: I try to arrest the speed of its flight by the speed with which I grasp it, and to compensate for the haste of its ebb, by my vigour in using it. The shorter my possession of life, the deeper and fuller I must make it.[21]

In *On experience* as in *On practice*, the term *mesnage* is explicitly connected with the pleasures of taste and touch (*gouster*, *savourer*, *retaster*), in an echo of the term *essai* itself, with its proximity to the Italian *assaggio*. In contrast to 'those prudent folk' who allow bad time to oppress them and who let good time slip through their hands without utility or profit, Montaigne 'applies' himself to his life in such a way as to deepen and complete his possession of it.[22] This *mesnage* is far removed from any suggestion of miserly hoarding. We should hold fast to time to increase the pleasure of one's life, but may pass over and escape from it when it threatens to crush and overwhelm us. Here again, the language of *mesnagerie* is deployed to suggest the deft manipulation of that which essentially escapes our control. As Montaigne makes clear on the penultimate page of the chapter and indeed of the book, we cannot and should not expect to bend time completely to our profit. Citing Aesop's disbelief at witnessing [B]'his master pissing as he walked', so

20 [A]'Si excellens mesnagers du temps, qu'ils ont essayé en la mort mesme, de la gouster et savourer: [. . .] pour voir que c'estoit de ce passage'. II.6: P 389, V 371, F 267.

21 [B]'J'ay un dictionaire tout à part moy: je passe le temps, quand il est mauvais et incommode; quand il est bon, je ne le veux pas passer, je le retaste, je m'y tiens. [. . .] Il y a du mesnage à la jouyr: je la jouis au double des autres: Car la mesure en la jouissance, depend du plus ou moins d'application, que nous y prestons. Principalement à cette heure, que j'apperçoy la mienne si briefve en temps, je la veux ~~grossir et~~ estendre en poix: Je veux arrester la promptitude de sa fuite par la promptitude de ma saisie: et par la vigueur de l'usage, compenser la hastiveté de son escoulement. À mesure que la possession du vivre est plus courte, il me la faut rendre plus profonde, et plus pleine'. III.13: P 1161–2, V 1111, F 853.

22 [B]'Ces prudentes gens'. III.13: P 1161–2, V 1111, F 853.

anxious was he to save time wherever possible, Montaigne points to the vanity and avarice inherent in such a stance: B'let us manage our time; we shall still have a lot left idle and ill spent'.[23] *Mesnage*, here, is linked not so much to thrift as to the pursuit of present use and enjoyment, to the contribution of considered waste as well as safekeeping to the wisdom of true economy.

II

The appearance of the term *mesnager* in these different contexts is especially striking given that one of the texts that Montaigne included in his 1571 edition of La Boétie's writings was the latter's translation of the archetypal classical treatise on household management, Xenophon's *Oeconomicus*.[24] Montaigne's account of his own approach to the government of his household offers a playful rewriting of this paradigmatic construction of *mesnagerie*. His transposition of this language to the sphere of self-regulation, accordingly, amounts to more than just a casual metaphor: the essayist's self-presentation as a negligent yet exemplary *mesnager* provides not merely an accidental parallel to, but a conscious analogy and template for, his idiosyncratic practice of self-management.

In setting himself the task of translating the *Oeconomicus* into French, La Boétie turned his attention to a text already in wide circulation both in the original Greek and in Latin translation. Between Henri Estienne's 1516 edition of Xenophon and 1561, the year during which La Boétie's version is likely to have been composed, no fewer than eight editions of the dialogue were published.[25] Montaigne himself is known to have owned a copy of *Le mesnagier*, a French translation of the *Oeconomicus* published by François de Ferris in 1562, as well as a 1551 Latin version of the complete works.[26] The proliferation, in the final decades of the sixteenth century, of 'oeconomique' manuals offering practical advice about the running of agricultural estates provides a further indication of the influence and popularity of Xenophon's

[23] B'Ésope Cce grand homme Bvid son maistre qui pissoit en se promenant, Quoy donq, fit-il, nous faudra-il chier en courant? Mesnageons le temps, encore nous en reste-il beaucoup d'oisif, et mal employé'. III.13: P 1166, V 1115, F 856.

[24] La Boétie 1571. *La Mesnagerie de Xenophon* can be found in La Boétie 1991; all references in what follows are to this edition. For a recent edition of the Greek text with parallel English translation and commentary, see Xenophon 1994; in what follows, I have sometimes adopted (and adapted) Pomeroy's formulations in my own translations of the *Mesnagerie* into English. On La Boétie's translation, see O'Brien 2004.

[25] Louis Desgraves, 'Introduction', in La Boétie 1991, p. 36.

[26] Xenophon 1562, Xenophon 1551. See O'Brien 2005, at p. 17.

text.[27] The *Oeconomicus* is well known to modern scholars as one of the central texts discussed by Michel Foucault in *L'usage des plaisirs*, the second volume of his *History of sexuality*. The following account is indebted both to Foucault and to Lorna Hutson's important study of the early-modern English reception of the text.[28]

The work takes the form of a dialogue between Socrates and a wealthy man called Critobulus on the subject of *oikonomia* or *mesnagerie*, which is defined (in La Boétie's rendering) as 'le sçavoir par lequel les hommes peuvent faire les maison[s] [*oikos*] meilleures' ('the knowledge by which men can make their houses better') – or, as the first French translation (published in 1531 by Geoffroy Tory) expressed it in its title, as a 'science, for enriching oneself honestly and easily'.[29] Embedded within this conversation is an account by Socrates of an exchange between himself and Ischomachus, a 'bel et bon homme' or true gentleman, on whose expertise he draws to explain (as Critobulus puts it) 'why it is that some men practise agriculture in such a way, that they draw from it all that they need in great abundance; and others practise it in such a fashion, that it brings no profit to them'.[30]

As this quotation suggests, the art of *mesnagerie*, according to Xenophon, extends not only to the parsimonious management of one's existing resources, but to their increase – to the generation of surplus and profit. Socrates, it is true, accounts himself rich enough for all his modest means, and claims to pity Critobulus for his poverty, even though he acknowledges that the sale of the latter's property 'would bring in a hundred times more money' than that of his own.[31] He does not need to increase his wealth because, as he puts it, 'what I have is sufficient to provide for what I need', whereas Critobulus' reputation for riches means that he is expected to contribute generously and beyond his means to the costs of civic sacrifices, feasts and wars.[32] Ischomachus, however, is unequivocal in his endorsement of enrichment, arguing that 'it is indeed in the power of the husband and wife, by living chastely, to instil such good order, that

[27] Hoffmann 1998, pp. 27–8. See, for example, Estienne 1564, Le Choyselat 1569, Gallo 1571, Gauchet 1583 and Serres 1600.

[28] Foucault 1984a and Hutson 1994. For the English reception of the *Oeconomicus*, see also Xenophon 1994, pp. 75–87.

[29] La Boétie 1991, vol. I, p. 173. 'Science, pour senrichir honestement & facilement' (title), Xenophon 1531.

[30] 'Pourquoy c'est qu'aucuns usent d'agriculture en telle sorte, qu'ils en tirent tout ce qui leur faict mestier, en grande abondance; et les autres en usent de telle façon, qu'elle ne leur vient à aucun profit'. La Boétie 1991, vol. I, p. 174.

[31] 'Sçay bien certainement que de ton bien il s'en feroit d'argent plus de cent fois autant'. La Boétie 1991, vol. I, p. 159.

[32] 'Ce que j'ay est suffisant pour fournir à ce qu'il me fault'. La Boétie 1991, vol. I, p. 160.

the goods which they have already are maintained, and that by honest and just means many more goods arrive besides', and that it is his duty as a citizen to increase his wealth in order to 'honour the gods in a sumptuous manner, help my friends if anyone of them needs me, and to ensure, as far as I can, that my city is never lacking in anything whatsoever which could embellish and adorn it'.[33] This emphasis on the legitimate acquisition of personal wealth echoes Cicero's description of the *Oeconomicus*, both in *De senectute* and in *De officiis*, as an indispensable guide to 'looking after' and 'preserving and increasing' without dishonesty the *res familiaris*, the things of the household or family.[34]

The economic art aims not merely, however, at the preservation and increase of a man's *material* wealth, but at the pursuit and protection of all that is advantageous and of benefit to him. The elision of the economically profitable with the morally beneficial provides one of the leading tropes of Xenophon's text: as Cicero explains in *De officiis*, 'the whole question of seeking and investing money' is directly relevant to the topic under consideration in his own book, that is, the question of *utilitas*.[35] This semantic latitude is established from the very outset of Xenophon's dialogue, where Socrates defines the *oikos*, 'la maison de chacun', not merely as a man's house or estate, or even the sum of his material possessions, but rather as his 'avoir', understood as 'that which is profitable to each man' ('ce qui est profittable à chacun') or 'that which each man has which is good for him' ('ce que chacun a quy luy est bon').[36] A possession cannot properly be

[33] 'Il est bien en la puissance du mary et de la femme, en vivant chastement, de mettre si bon ordre, que les biens qu'ils ont desjà soient bien entretenus, et faire par honnestes et iustes moyens qu'il en vienne encore beaucoup d'ailleurs'. La Boétie 1991, vol. I, p. 177. 'De ma part je prens bien grand plaisir, ô Socrates, d'honorer les Dieux sumptueusement, de secourir mes amis si quelqu'un d'eux a besoing de moy, et faire que ma cité n'aye point faute, que je puisse, d'aucune chose qui soit pour l'embellir et orner'. La Boétie 1991, vol. I, p. 192.

[34] See Cicero 1971, §59 – '. . . in eo libro, qui est de tuenda re familiari, qui Oeconomicus inscribitur' – and Cicero 1968b, 2.87: 'Res autem familiaris quaeri debet iis rebus, a quibus abest turpitudo, conservari autem diligentia et parsimonia, eisdem etiam rebus augeri. Has res commodissime Xenophon Socraticus persecutus est in eo libro, qui Oeconomicus inscribitur' ('personal wealth ought to be pursued by means that are free from dishonourableness, but to be preserved, and also to be increased, by carefulness and thrift. Xenophon the Socratic covered these matters most conveniently in his book entitled *Oeconomicus*'). English translation from Cicero 1991, p. 99.

[35] 'Sed toto hoc de genere, de quaerenda, de collocanda pecunia, (vellem etiam de utenda), commodius a quibusdam optimis viris ad Ianum medium sedentibus quam ab ullis philosophis ulla in schola disputatur. Sunt tamen ea cognoscenda; pertinent enim ad utilitatem, de qua hoc libro disputatum est' ('But the whole question of seeking profit and of investing money [I wish that I could say the same for using it!] is more conveniently discussed by those excellent men who sit at the central gate of Janus than by any philosopher of any school. We must, however, learn about these things, for they are relevant to that which is beneficial, which is the topic of discussion of this book'). Cicero 1968b, 2.87; English translation from Cicero 1991, p. 99.

[36] La Boétie 1991, vol. I, p. 156.

accounted as a 'bien' or good if we use it to our disadvantage: 'if someone used their money in such a way, that he spent it on something, and by that means found himself worse in his person, worse in his mind, and worse in the affairs of his house, how in that case could money be profitable to him?'[37] Even one's enemies, conversely, can be counted as a good, as long as one knows how to make use of (*chrèsthai*) and profit from (*opheleisthai*) them: indeed, 'it is the action of a good householder, to know how to treat his enemies, in such a way that they are useful to him'.[38]

The *sçavoir* disclosed by Xenophon's text, as Hutson has argued, has as much to do with 'the economics of using and ordering a discourse, or the contingencies of a particular situation, as with that of using and ordering a wife and household'. Xenophon's repeated analogies between the art of economy and that of political and military leadership create, in Hutson's apt phrase, 'a space of suspended definition' in which the government of the wife and household function as synecdoches for a wider art of existence, centred around a paradigm of prudent and well-ordered use.[39] This slippage from economics to ethics is also registered by Foucault in his analysis of *oikonomia* as an art of government and command, rather than as a body of technical knowledge. Xenophon's exposition of the 'art de bien mesnager' certainly includes practical guidance on topics such as ordering of the contents of one's house (pp. 184–7) and a discussion of the principles of agronomy (pp. 202–11). However, the *bon mesnager*, as exemplified by Ischomachus, is distinguished above all by his skill in ruling over others and over himself: 'in one respect, [. . .] which is seen in all ways of life, in farming, in the handling of the Republic, in domestic economy, in the practice of arms – that is, in the knowledge of how to command and govern – in this point alone, I say, [. . .] men differ greatly from each other'.[40]

Mesnagerie, according to Xenophon, thus consists not only in the prudent management of one's property and resources, but in the ability to shape the will of one's subordinates – to 'command people in such a way

[37] 'Si quelqu'un usoit de l'argent en telle sorte, qu'il en fist son emploite en une chose, et par ce moyen s'en trouvast mal de sa personne, mal de son esprit, et mal des affaires de sa maison, comment d'ores en là seroit à celuy l'argent profitable?' La Boétie 1991, vol. I, p. 157.

[38] 'C'est le faict d'un bon mesnager, de sçavoir user de ses ennemis, de façon qu'il s'en serve'. La Boétie 1991, vol. I, 157.

[39] Hutson 1994, pp. 31, 35.

[40] 'Mais certes en un point [. . .] qui est cogneu en toutes façons de vivre, à l'agriculture, au maniement de la Republique, à la mesnagerie, au faict des armes, c'est de sçavoir commander & gouverner; en ce point seul, dis-je [. . .] il y a grand'difference des uns aux autres'. La Boétie 1991, vol. I, p. 216.

that it be manifest that it is of their own will'.[41] Cyrus the younger, 'the greatest and most renowned of all known Princes', is introduced early on in the dialogue as an exemplary illustration of this conjunction.[42] His attentive cultivation of his orchard at Sardis (in an influential passage transcribed by Cicero in *De senectute*) mirrors the loyalty that he inspires in his subjects both in life and death.[43] Socrates' questioning of Ischomachus, meanwhile, focuses heavily on the latter's skilful training of his wife in her duty to instil good order within the house. The dialogue also dwells at length on his efforts to teach his foremen to care for his affairs and to 'know how to command', in turn, 'to those who work'.[44] This ability to command willing obedience, Ischomachus argues in the conclusion to the text, is analogous to the power of kings and of God: the man who exercises it has 'something royal in his nature', and it is God 'who saves this good and reserves it for those who have truly devoted themselves to, and made profession of, a pure and chaste life'.[45]

As this last sentence suggests, the *bon mesnager*'s capacity for rule is inextricably bound up with notions of *self*-government and *self*-control: as Foucault argues in *L'usage des plaisirs*, Ischomachus' mastery over his wife and servants offers a parallel and witness to his mastery over himself. Towards the beginning of the *Oeconomicus*, Critobulus observes that some men have 'the knowledge and commodities to greatly increase their household', and yet fail to do so, because 'they have no master to make them do so'.[46] Far from being without a master, Socrates avers, such men are in fact 'serfs' either to 'laziness, weakness of heart and nonchalance' or to 'useless games and company', whereas others are 'under the power of truly terrible mistresses, some [being subject] to greed, others to gluttony, these to drunkeness, those to a foolish ambition and spendthrift magnificence'.[47] Some men cannot provide for themselves and incur debts,

41 'Commander aux personnes de telle sorte qu'il se cognoisse clairement que c'est de leur gré'. La Boétie 1991, vol. I, p. 218.

42 'Le plus grand et le plus renommé Prince qu'on sache'. La Boétie 1991, vol. I, p. 168.

43 See Cicero 1971, pp. 70–2.

44 'Sçavoir commander à ceux qui travaillent'. La Boétie 1991, vol. I, p. 198.

45 'Il a quelque chose de naturel royal. [. . .] C'est luy [Dieu] qui espargne ce bien et le reserve pour ceux qui ont vrayement voué et fait la profession d'une vie pure et chaste'. La Boétie 1991, vol. I, p. 218.

46 'Nous voyons par fois des gents ayant bien le sçavoir et les commoditez pour pouvoir agrandir bien fort leur maison, s'ils y prenoient peine, mais on s'aperçoit bien qu'ils n'en veulent rien faire [. . .] pour ce qu'ils n'ont point de maistre qui leur face faire'. La Boétie 1991, vol. I, p. 158.

47 'La paresse, la lascheté de coeur et la nonchalance [. . .] les jeus, et les compagnies inutiles'. 'Ceux la aussi, [. . .] sont en servage, soubs la puissance de maistresses bien terribles, les uns de la friandise, les autres de la gourmandise, ceux cy de l'yvrongerie, ceux là d'une ambition et magnificence sotte et despensive'. La Boétie 1991, vol. I, p. 158.

whereas others are able to live in plenty and build up reserves. This difference should not, according to Ischomachus, be ascribed to a lack of knowledge about farming, which is easy enough to acquire, but to a lack of 'courage' (*coeur*) and 'care' (*soing*), just as among the leaders of armies, 'clearly it is care and diligence that gives the advantage to one man' over the other.[48] The effective government of the household, resulting in profit and increase, is thus for Xenophon centrally dependent on the ability to master oneself.

III

Montaigne's account of his own approach to *mesnagerie*, as it is presented in the *Essais*, embodies a calculated rejection of those virtues of 'diligence' and 'soing' singled out for praise in the *Oeconomicus*. In *On vanity*, as we observed in Chapter 4, his attitude towards the management of his estate and affairs is described as one of [B]'inexcusable and childish [C]laziness and negligence' in the face of continual frustrations.[49] When at home he tries to [B]'avoid occasions for vexation, and turn away from the knowledge of things that are going badly', although even then he 'cannot contrive well enough not to be constantly bumping into something at home that [he] do[es] not like'.[50] Both in *On vanity* and in *On presumption*, humorous attention is drawn to his [B]'incompetence in household occupations' and his ignorance of the most basic principles of farming, viticulture, and husbandry. We are told that he can barely tell cabbages and lettuces apart, that until recently he had no idea that yeast is needed to make bread, and that he is unable to recognise coins or [A]'reckon, either with counters or with a pen'. Far from exercising self-sufficiency, Montaigne appears content to live at the mercy of his servants: he does not know how to grow or prepare the food he eats, the name and prices of the fabrics he uses to clothe himself, or the fundamental elements of record-keeping and accountancy.[51]

Even more significantly, Montaigne explicitly rejects the idea that *mesnagerie* finds its realization not in the mere preservation of one's *avoir*,

48 'Clairement ce qui donne à l'un l'avantage, c'est le soing et la diligence'. La Boétie 1991, vol. I, p. 212.

49 [C]'Paresse et negligence [B]inexcusable et puerile'. III.9: P 998, V 953, F 727. See also I.38: P 242–3, V 238, F 175[A].

50 [B]'Je me desrobe aux occasions de me fascher: et me destourne de la cognoissance des choses, qui vont mal: Et si ne puis tant faire, qu'à toute heure je ne heurte chez moy, en quelque rencontre, qui me desplaise'. III.9: P 994, V 950, F 725.

51 [B]'Mon insuffisance aux occupations du mesnage'. III.9: P 996, V 952, F 726. [A]'Je ne sçay conter ny à get, ny à plume'. II.17: P 691, V 652, F 495.

but in its increase. His only aim, he writes in *On vanity*, is to honour his obligations to his father by conveying the estate that he has inherited from him without damage or loss. Because he himself has only one surviving daughter to provide for, he has no need to extend his riches to provide for a multitude of heirs. [C]‘The only thing I aspire to acquire’, he writes, ‘is the reputation of having acquired nothing, just as I have squandered nothing, in conformity with the rest of my life, unsuited for doing good or doing evil.’[52] His concern is simply to live ‘comfortably’ and to preserve himself from the wretchedness of poverty (unlike Crates, [B]‘who cast himself into the freedom of poverty to get rid of the indignities and cares of a household’, he claims to ‘hate poverty as much as pain’).[53]

This emphasis on stability and moderation echoes his appeal in *On solitude* for a [A]‘mean’ between the ‘base and vile concern, tense and full of anxiety’ of those men who immerse themselves fully in the management of the household and the ‘profound and extreme negligence, letting everything go with abandon’ seen in others.[54] One should *mesnage* one’s approach to the *mesnage*, by subordinating it to our true advantage and benefit – that is, pleasure: [A]‘in household management’, as ‘in study, in hunting, and in all other pursuits’, we should ‘give up to the utmost limits of pleasure; and beware of engaging ourselves further, where it begins to be mingled with pain’.[55] It is down to us to account the true price of our care, for (as Montaigne explains in *On vanity*) [B]‘a stranger does not understand, how much it costs you and how much you lend, in order to maintain that appearance of order, which people see in your family, and that perhaps you buy too dear’.[56]

The wisdom of the *bon mesnager*, as it is presented in the *Oeconomicus*, centres on the generation of wealth through the elimination of idleness and the fostering of ‘useful’ and productive industry in oneself and one’s subordinates. For Montaigne, by contrast, prudence consists in the

[52] [C]‘Je ne pretens acquerir que la reputation de n’avoir rien acquis, non plus que dissipé: conformément au reste de ma vie, impropre à faire bien et à faire mal qui vaille’. III.9: P 993, V 949, F 724.

[53] [B]‘Crates fit pis, qui se jetta en la franchise de la pauvreté, pour se deffaire des indignitez et cures de la maison. Cela ne ferois-je pas: Je hay la pauvreté à pair de la douleur’. III.9: P 998, V 954, F 728.

[54] [A]‘Un moyen, entre ce bas et vil soing, tendu et plein de solicitude, qu’on voit aux hommes qui s’y plongent du tout; et cette profonde et extreme nonchalance laissant tout aller à l’abandon, qu’on voit en d’autres’. I.38: P 248–9, V 244, F 180.

[55] [A]‘Au mesnage, à l’estude, à la chasse, et tout autre exercice, il faut donner jusques aux dernieres limites du plaisir; et garder de s’engager plus avant, où la peine commence à se mesler parmy’. I.38: P 250, V 246, F 181.

[56] [B]‘L’estranger n’entend pas, combien il vous couste, et combien vous prestez, à maintenir l’apparence de cet ordre, qu’on voit en vostre famille: et qu’à l’avanture l’achetez vous trop cher’. III.9: P 992, V 949, F 723–4.

anticipation of misfortune and distress through the judicious regulation and supple modulation of the soul:

> [B]I have established enough degrees in my soul where I can get along with less than I have. Get along contentedly, I mean. [C]*Not by the calculation of your income, but by your manner of living and your culture, is your wealth truly to be reckoned.* [B]My real need does not so wholly take up all I have that Fortune does not have something of mine to bite on without biting into the flesh.[57]

The best way to ensure that one has enough, Montaigne argues, lies not in augmenting one's resources but in limiting one's expenditure, or rather being prepared to do so. One should use and enjoy one's present wealth in full cognisance of its fragility, always taking care to reserve enough to protect oneself, if necessary, from the depredations of fortune. The key to successful *mesnagerie* lies not so much in the pursuit of frugality and modest living, but rather in the strategic calibration of one's inner dispositions in accordance with the winds of fortune. Paradoxically, it is only by resigning ourselves to the invincible power of fortune that one is able to exercise power over oneself. As he puts it in I.40 (*That the taste of good and evil depends in large part on the opinion we have of them*), [C]'fortune does us neither good nor harm: she only offers us the material and the seed of them: which our soul, more powerful than she, turns and applies as it pleases: sole cause and mistress of its happy or unhappy condition'.[58]

Montaigne's stated aim, in the concluding pages of this earlier chapter, is to demonstrate that [B]'it is not ~~necessity~~ [C]want, [B]but rather abundance, that breeds avarice', by contrasting his present handling of his finances with the carefree prodigality of his youth and the [C]'ridiculous and shameful prudence' of his maturity.[59] In the first instance, he had no income of his own and was thus [B]'dependent on the ordinance and help of others, without certain state or prescription'. However, not only did he derive

57 [B]'J'ay estably [C]au demeurant, [B]en mon ame, assez de degrez, à me passer de moins, que ce que j'ay. Je dis, passer avec contentement. [C]*Non aestimatione census, uerùm uictu atque cultu, terminatur pecuniae modus* [Cicero, *Paradoxa stoicorum*, VI.3.50]. [B]Mon vray besoing n'occupe pas si justement tout mon avoir, que sans venir au vif, fortune n'ait où mordre sur moy.' III.9: P 993, V 949, F 724.

58 [C]'La fortune ne nous fait ny bien ny mal: elle nous en offre seulement la matiere et la semence: laquelle nostre ame, plus puissante qu'elle, tourne et applique comme il luy plaist: seule cause et maistresse de sa condition heureuse ou malheureuse'. I.40: P 276, V 67, F 46.

59 [B]'Ce n'est pas la ~~necessité~~ [C]disette, [B]c'est plustost l'abondance qui produict l'avarice'. I.40: P 272, V 62, F 43. [C]'Ridicule et honteuse prudence'. I.40: P 274, V 64, F 44. This passage is also discussed in some detail in Starobinski 1993, ch. III, sec. 4, as an illustration of the three stages that he posits in Montaigne's understanding of 'la relation à autruy' ('dépendance irraisonnée', 'refus autarcique', 'relation maîtrisée'). See discussion of this argument in Chapter 1, Section V.

[B]'a certain pleasure' from repaying his debts to his friends, as if he were 'unburdening [his] shoulders of a troublesome weight and of that image of slavery', but his 'spending was done the more joyously and carelessly for being all at the hazard of fortune'. In this period, Montaigne contends, he [B]'referred the handling of [his] need more gaily to the stars, and more freely' than he has 'ever referred it since to [his] foresight and sense'.[60]

Most *mesnagers*, he concedes, would be horrified at the [B]'uncertainty' inherent in this first kind of life; and yet, he continues, 'they do not realise that in the first place, most people live thus' – including those 'honest men' who 'have cast away all their security, and do so every day, to pursue the wind of royal favour and of fortune', those merchants who 'begin their traffic by the sale of their farms, which they send to the Indies | *Across so many stormy seas*', and those monks who 'expect every day from the liberality of heaven what they need for dinner'. Not only this, but these *mesnagers* [B]'do not consider that this certainty on which they rely is scarcely less uncertain and chancy than chance itself'.[61]

During the period following his accession to his inheritance, Montaigne fell subject to [B]'vain and pernicious imaginings' of unexpected costs and theft. So convinced was he that, although he [B]'could not provide for all [emergencies], I could for some, and many', that he sought 'to provide by [. . .] superfluous reserve' for all possible eventualities.[62] The third way of life, which Montaigne claims to have adopted following his travels to Italy, offers a synthesis of this dialectic between careless liberty and fearful parsimony. Now, he writes, [B]'I content myself with having enough to meet my present and ordinary needs', having resigned himself to the fact that

60 [B]'Despendant de l'ordonnance et secours d'autruy, sans estat certain et sans prescription. Ma despence se faisoit d'autant plus allegrement et avec moins de soing, qu'elle estoit toute en la temerité de la fortune. [. . .] Je sens naturellement quelque volupté à payer; comme si deschargeois mes espaules d'un ennuyeux poix, et de cette image de servitude. [. . .] Je me remettois de la conduitte de mon besoing plus gayement aux astres, et plus librement que je n'ay faict depuis à ma providence et à mon sens'. I.40: P 272, V 62–3, F 43.

61 [B]'La plus part des mesnagers estiment horrible de vivre ainsin en incertitude; et ne s'advisent pas, premierement, que la plus part du monde vit ainsi. Combien d'honnestes hommes ont rejetté tout leur certain à l'abandon, et le font tous les jours, pour cercher le vent de la faveur des Roys et de la fortune? [. . .] Et combien de marchans commencent leur trafique par la vente de leur metairie, qu'ils envoyent aux Indes. | *Tot per impotentia freta*? [Catullus, IV.18] | En une si grande siccité de devotion, nous avons mille et mille Colleges, qui la passent commodément, attendans tous les jours de la liberalité du Ciel, ce qu'il faut à eux disner. Secondement, ils ne s'advisent pas, que cette certitude, sur laquelle ils se fondent, n'est guere moins incertaine et hazardeuse que le hazard mesme'. I.40: P 272–3, V 63, F 43–4.

62 [B]'Vaines et vitieuses imaginations'. 'Prouvoir par cette superflue reserve à tous inconveniens: [. . .] si ce n'estoit à tous, c'estoit à aucuns et plusieurs'. I.40: P 273–4, V 64, F 44.

'for the extraordinary, all the provision in the world could not suffice'. His aim is simply to [B]'make [his] expense run abreast with [his] receipts', such that 'now one is ahead, now the other, but they are never far apart', with 'neither any real fear that [his] money will run out, nor any desire of increasing it'. Instead of straining against fortune, he seeks rather to imitate its ebb and flow and thereby incorporate it within the flexible patterns of his own life.[63]

Montaigne concludes this discussion of finance management by citing the example of an [C]'old prelate' who has 'given up so completely his purse, his revenue, and his expenses, now to one chosen servant, now to another, that he has let many years flow by, ignorant as a stranger of this sort of household affairs'.[64] He leaves the reader in no doubt as to his approval of this scheme:

> [C]And as regards this prelate, I see no household order run more worthily or with greater constancy than his. Happy the man who has regulated his needs in such just measure that his wealth can satisfy them, without his care and trouble and without the spending or acquiring of it interrupting his pursuit of other occupations better suited to him, more tranquil, and more congenial.[65]

The concepts of regulation and order are central to this revised account of *mesnagerie*. Montaigne's third way of life is [B]'certainly much more pleasant and more regulated' than the others; riches come [C]'rather from order, than from revenue'.[66] This latter sentence could simply be taken to mean that true wealth lies not in the abundance of one's income, but in the 'ordered' balancing of one's revenue, however slight, with one's expenditure. But it also implies that well-regulated finances go hand-in-hand with the 'order' of a well-regulated soul, that is, one that is calibrated in accordance with fortune (in *On managing the will*, similarly, Montaigne speaks of his concern

63 [B]'Je fais courir ma despence quand et quand ma recepte; tantost l'une devance, tantost l'autre: mais c'est de peu qu'elles s'abandonnent. Je vis du jour à la journée, et me contente d'avoir dequoy suffire aux besoings presens et ordinaires: aux extraordinaires toutes les provisions du monde n'y sçauroyent suffire. [. . .] Je n'ay ny guere peur que bien me faille, ny nul desir qu'il m'augmente'. I.40: P 275, V 65–6, F 45–6.

64 [C]'La fortune d'un vieil Prelat, que je voy s'estre si purement demis de sa bourse, et de sa recepte, et de sa mise, tantost à un serviteur choisi, tantost à un autre, qu'il a coulé un long espace d'années, autant ignorant cette sorte d'affaires de son mesnage, comme un estranger'. I.40: P 276, V 66, F 46.

65 [C]'Et pour son regard, je ne voy point d'ordre de maison, ny plus dignement ny plus constamment conduit que le sien. Heureux, qui ait reiglé à si juste mesure son besoin, que ses richesses y puissent suffire sans son soing et empeschement: et sans que leur dispensation ou assemblage, interrompe d'autres occupations, qu'il suit, plus convenables, plus tranquilles, et selon son cœur'. I.40: P 276, V 66, F 46.

66 'Certes plus plaisante beaucoup et plus reglée'. I.40: P 275, V 65, F 45. 'Plus de l'ordre, que de la recepte'. I.40: P 273, V 64, F 44.

to [B]'order and arrange the domestic pressures that oppress [his] entrails and veins').[67]

The notion of 'order' plays an important but very different role in the *Oeconomicus*. Having asked his wife to fetch one of their belongings for him, and seeing her distress at her inability to locate the item in question, Ischomachus explains to her that, like a dramatic chorus, a ship or an army, a household must be ordered, for 'there is nothing in the world [. . .] more easy to use or more beautiful than good order'.[68] Storing each thing in its proper place ensures that 'we will know exactly what we have, and what we have lost [. . .] so that without trouble we will make use of what we have'.[69] This emphasis on static and predetermined arrangement is not entirely absent from Montaigne's concerns, as we saw earlier in this chapter in our analysis of the careful disposition of his library. Montaigne is just as interested, however, in identifying order with the pursuit of 'just measure' within the soul, through a flexible and dynamic practice of self-adjustment and self-regulation.

As the passage about the prelate suggests, this preoccupation with absent-minded order and regulation is fundamentally at odds with the paradigm of self-sufficient mastery and vigilant command at the centre of the *Oeconomicus*. Xenophon, it is true, presents government in terms of persuasive fashioning rather than authoritarian discipline: in some households, the slaves 'are nearly all chained, so to speak', but run away again and again, whereas in others they are free to go and yet stay and work 'freely and willingly'.[70] This characterisation of *mesnagerie* as the art of shaping men's wills to one's advantage is echoed by Montaigne in his own description of Cyrus, in *On coaches*, as a *mesnager* of men's affections, whose liberality towards his subjects has won him [C]'at small cost [. . .] the inestimable treasure of so many friends [. . .] [and] more faithful treasurers than mercenary men without obligation or affection'.[71] In *On the education of children*, similarly, he argues that a young gentleman should learn to observe and judge the value of all those around him, and, like a householder, draw

[67] [B]'Disposer et ranger la presse domestique que j'ay dans mes entrailles, et dans mes veines'. III.10: P 1049, V 1004, F 767.

[68] 'N'y a il au monde [. . .] ny chose plus aisee pour l'usage, ne plus belle que le bon ordre'. La Boétie 1991, vol. I, p. 181.

[69] 'Nous sçaurons sur le doigt ce que nous avons, ou que nous avons perdu [. . .] de sorte que sans peine on se servira de ce qu'on aura'. La Boétie 1991, vol. I, p. 183.

[70] 'Tous attachez, par maniere de dire'. 'Franchement et de bon coeur'. La Boetie 1991, vol. I, p. 163.

[71] [C]'Je ne suis pas moins amoureux des richesses, que les autres princes, et en suis plustost plus mesnager. Vous voyez à combien peu de mise j'ay acquis le thresor inestimable de tant d'amis: et combiens ils me sont plus fideles thresoriers que ne seroient des hommes mercenaires, sans obligation, sans affection'. III.6: P 948–9, V 905, F 690.

profitable instruction from their good or bad example: [A]'he will sound the capacity of each man: a cowherd, a mason, a passer-by; he must put everything to use, and borrow from each man according to his wares, for everything is useful in a household'.[72]

Montaigne takes this anchoring of true authority in persuasion rather than coercion one step further, however, by laying considerable stress on the value of 'mescognoissance' and wilful inattention to the successful conduct of one's servants.

> [B]Whoever has charge of my purse in my travels, has it absolutely and without having to render an account: he could cheat me just as well if I kept accounts. And, unless he is a devil, I oblige him to be honest, by such abandoned trust. [. . .] I lend a hand to ignorance: I purposely keep my knowledge of my money, somewhat hazy and uncertain: Up to a certain measure, I am glad, to be able to be in doubt about it. You have to leave a little room for the dishonesty, or improvidence of your servant: If we have enough left altogether to play our part, let that surplus of fortune's liberality run a little more at her mercy: [C]the gleaner's share.[73]

We have already seen that Montaigne deliberately diverts his attention from the worries and concerns that arise in his household and that he aims to regulate his dispositions in accordance with the flux of fortune. In this passage, the 'abandoned trust' that he places in his servants and purposeful ignorance that he entertains about the exact state of his finances serve both to allow scope for the claims of fortune and to foster a mimetic innocence and honesty in his subordinates. An open and undefended house, similarly, provides the best protection against aggressors and thieves. In an age of civil violence and unrest, Montaigne has made [C]'the conquest of [his] house cowardly and treacherous', by accepting 'no guard or sentinel but that which the stars provide for [him]'. Other houses have been lost precisely because they were guarded, which 'gives the assailant both the desire and the reason' to attack them.[74]

72 [A]'Il sondera la portée d'un chacun: un bouvier, un masson, un passant, il faut tout mettre en besongne, et emprunter chacun selon sa marchandise: car tout sert en mesnage'. I.25: P 161, V 155, F 114.

73 [B]'Qui a la garde de ma bourse de voyage, il l'a pure et sans contrerolle: aussi bien me tromperoit il en comptant. Et si ce n'est un diable, je l'oblige à bien faire, par une si abandonnée confiance. [. . .] Je preste la main à l'ignorance: Je nourris à escient, aucunement trouble et incertaine la science de mon argent: Jusques à certaine mesure, je suis content, d'en pouvoir doubter. Il faut laisser un peu de place à la desloyauté, ou imprudence de vostre valet: S'il nous en reste en gros, dequoy faire nostre effect, cet excez de la liberalité de la fortune, laissons le un peu plus courre à mercy: [C]La portion du glanneur'. III.9: P 997, V 953, F 727.

74 [C]'Je leur rens la conqueste de ma maison lasche et traistresse. [. . .] Je n'ay ny garde ny sentinelle, que celle que les astres font pour moy.' 'Elles se sont perdues de ce, qu'elles estoyent gardées. Cela donne et l'envie et la raison à l'assaillant'. II.15: P 654–5, V 616–17, F 467.

As we have by now come to expect, Montaigne holds that the best *mesnagerie* is (or at least appears) careless and effortless, and that [B]'a gentleman never looks so stupid in his own house as when we see him caught up in the business of governing; whispering in the ear of one servant, threatening another with his eyes', when it 'should flow imperceptibly and seem like an ordinary course'.[75] His point is not merely to castigate the indignity of these strained and ostentatious performances of household authority, but to suggest that, as with fortune, our imperfect power is most effective when we are prepared to concede some, if not most, of our ground. In *On the affection of fathers for their children*, he condemns the tyrannical stance of stern and distant fathers as a [C]'futile farce' that can only lead to their being ridiculed by their children.[76] He cites the example of a man who boasts of his absolute reign over his household when in reality his relatives and servants make a show of obeying and pleasing him while duping him behind his back. He himself does not claim to be immune to such deception, but at least he is aware of it: [C]'if others deceive me, at least I do not deceive myself, either by thinking myself capable of guarding myself against their deception, or by racking my brains to make myself capable'. His art of *mesnagerie* rests not on the assertion of his authority, but rather on the recognition of its limits: [C]'I escape from such betrayals in my own bosom, not by a restless and tumultuous curiosity, but rather by diversion, and resolution'.[77]

This cultivation of strategic indifference and inattention is mirrored in the wise *mesnager*'s concern for economy in intervention. It is better, Montaigne counsels in *On anger*, to relieve our ire by [B]'giving our valet a slap on the cheek a little out of season' than it is to 'strain our inclination' to maintain a 'controlled appearance on the outside', for [B]'we incorporate anger by hiding it'.[78] As David Quint has put it, Montaigne 'lets himself go' instead of seeking to control himself.[79] His own passions 'grow languid when they have vent and expression', and it is always 'better that their point

75 [B]'La plus sotte contenance d'un gentil-homme en sa maison, c'est de le voir empesché ~~de l'ordre~~ [C]du train [B]de sa police; parler à l'oreille d'un valet, en menacer un autre des yeux. Elle doit couler insensiblement, et representer un ~~train~~ [C]cours [B]ordinaire'. III.9: P 999, V 954, F 728.

76 [C]'Farce très-inutile'. II.8: P 412, V 393, F 285.

77 [C]'Si les autres me pippent, aumoins ne me pippé-je pas moy-mesme à m'estimer capable de m'en garder: ny à me ronger la cervelle pour m'en rendre. Je me sauve de telles trahisons en mon propre giron, non par une inquiete et tumultuaire curiosité, mais par diversion plustost, et resolution'. II.8: P 415, V 395, F 287.

78 [B]'On incorpore la cholere en la cachant. [. . .] Je conseille qu'on donne plustost une ~~nazarde~~ [C]buffe à la joue de [B]son valet, un peu hors de saison, que de gehenner sa fantasie, pour representer cette sage contenance'. II.31: P 755, V 718–19, F 543.

79 Quint 2000.

should operate outwardly than be turned against us’.[80] He [B]‘admonish[es]’ those members of his household ‘who have the right to get angry’ to ‘economise’ their anger, expending it with circumspection so as not to undermine ‘its effect and its weight’, and taking care not ‘to get angry in the air’, oblivious to the presence or absence of those whom they have set out to scold.[81] This concern to calibrate one’s passions carefully according to the needs of the situation leads him to sometimes even [B]‘play angry for the governing of my house, without any real emotion’.[82]

The art of *mesnagerie*, according to Montaigne, is thus characterised both by the judicious and sparing use of one’s resources and by the valorisation of calculated inattention and indirection. These two tropes, as we shall now see, emerge elsewhere in the *Essais* as central motifs of his account of self-regulation.

IV

Montaigne’s art of self-management is, in the first instance, an art of evasion and flight. [A]‘The law of resolution and constancy’, he argues in *On constancy*, does not forbid us from fleeing ‘evils and troubles’ as far as ‘it lies in our power’, but binds us only to holding our ground after all honest means of escape have been exhausted: ‘the game of constancy is played principally in bearing troubles steadfastly where there is no remedy’.[83] By linking *constance* and *jeu* in this way, Montaigne subsumes the Stoic moment of patience in the face of evils into a wider counsel of agile versatility in pursuit of self-protection: [A]‘there is neither any suppleness of the body, nor any move with hand weapons, that we should find bad, if it serves to safeguard us from the blow that is struck at us’.[84] This analogy between the avoidance of evils and the improvisatory skill of defensive

80 [B]‘Mes passions [. . .] s’alanguissent en s’esvantant, et en s’exprimant: Il vaut mieux que leur poincte agisse au dehors, que de la plier contre nous’. II.31: P 755, V 718–19, F 543.

81 [B]‘J’advertis ceux, qui ont loy de se pouvoir courroucer en ma famille, premierement qu’ils mesnagerent leur cholere, et ne l’espandent pas à tout prix: car cela en empesche l’effect et le poids. [. . .] Secondement, qu’ils ne se courroussent point en l’air, et regardent que leur reprehension arrive à celuy de qui ils se plaignent’. II.31: P 755–6, V 719, F 543–4.

82 [B]‘Par fois m’advient il aussi, de representer le courroussé, pour le reiglement de ma maison, sans aucune vraye emotion’. II.31: P 757, V 720, F 545.

83 [A]‘La loy de la resolution et de la constance ne porte pas que nous ne nous devions couvrir, autant qu’il est en nostre puissance, des maux et inconveniens qui nous menassent. [. . .] Le jeu de la constance se joue principalement à porter ~~patiemment et~~ de pied ferme, les inconveniens où il n’y a point de remede’. I.12: P 67, V 45, F 30.

84 [A]‘Il n’y a soupplesse de corps, ny mouvement aux armes de main, que nous trouvions mauvais, s’il sert à nous garantir du coup qu’on nous rue’. I.12: P 67, V 45, F 30.

combat is pursued further in the C-text version of this chapter, where Montaigne draws attention to the use of 'flight' by 'many very warlike nations' as a 'principal advantage in their armed encounters', citing the practice of the Scythians, of Aeneas and of the Spartan infantry as examples of how one might 'beat' one's enemy 'by giving ground'.[85]

This emphasis on the tactical use of flight and the importance of 'suppleness' in safeguarding ourselves from evils locates ethical agency in adroit and oblique evasion rather than open resistance to the onslaughts of fortune. The remainder of this short chapter, moreover, casts the *voluntary* nature of even such indirect and responsive self-regulation into doubt, by depicting these evasive movements as the result of accident and chance, set in motion by forces beyond our conscious awareness and control. Montaigne notes that it is thought both unbecoming and futile to flinch under the impact of modern cannon fire, before recounting how both Emperor Charles V and Lorenzo de' Medici successfully dodged blasts aimed at them, as apparent exceptions to this rule. These sudden movements, he insists, are to be attributed to chance and surprise, rather than deliberation: [A]'fortune favoured their fright'.[86] This parodic reversal of the Latin maxim *fortes fortuna adiuvat* (fortune favours the brave) is then elaborated into a wider meditation on human passivity and weakness. Even the Stoics, we are reminded in a C-text addition, do not hold that 'the soul of their sage can resist the first visions and fantasies that come upon him', but rather 'consent that he give in, as to a natural subjection, to the great noise of the heavens or of a falling building, for example, to the point of pallor and contraction'.[87] In the concluding sentences of the chapter, finally, Montaigne distances himself even from this concessive account of Stoic wisdom, arguing that [C]'for the man who is not a sage [. . .] the impression of the passions [. . .] penetrates right to the seat of reason, infecting and corrupting it', and counterposing the Stoic's claim to 'exempt himself from the passions' with the Peripatetic's efforts to 'moderate them'.[88]

85 [C]'Plusieurs nations tresbelliqueuses se servoyent en leurs faits d'armes, de la fuite, pour advantage principal [. . .] seroit ce donc lascheté de les battre en leur faisant place' I.12: P 67, V 45, F 30.

86 [A]'La fortune favorisa leur frayeur'. I.12: P 69, V 46, F 31.

87 [C]'Ny n'entendent les Stoïciens, que l'ame de leur sage puisse resister aux premiers visions et fantaisies qui luy surviennent: ains comme à une subjection naturelle consentent qu'il cede au grand bruit du ciel, ou d'une ruine, pour exemple, jusques à la palleur et contraction'. I.12: P 69, V 46, F 31.

88 [C]'De celuy, qui n'est pas sage [. . .] l'impression des passions ne demeure pas en luy superficielle: ains va penetrant jusques au siege de sa raison, l'infectant et la corrompant. [. . .] Le sage Peripateticien ne s'exempte pas des perturbations, mais il les modere'. I.12: P 69, V 46–7, F 31.

By juxtaposing this vision of ordinary human frailty with the notion that constancy is a ‘gamble’ or ‘game’, Montaigne invites us to reconsider the utility not only of that which appears directly contrary to our advantage (retreating in the face of the enemy), but also of that which may properly be understood only as the action of fortune, rather than ourselves. The Stoic sage [C]‘lends no consent to his fright and suffering’, rendering the involuntary flow of his tears ‘all useless’ (in the words of the quotation from Virgil which he adduces to describe his state of inner imperturbability).[89] But what if we were to consent to, and make use of, these accidental impulses? As the examples of Charles V and Lorenzo de’ Medici suggest, it is precisely because sudden danger startles us into involuntary ‘suppleness’, because fortune takes over from the will, that we are able to elude it. Montaigne is adamant that these interventions of fortune cannot be relied on: [A]‘another time this would be just as good a way to jump into the shot as to avoid it’.[90] His [C]‘science of flight’, however, traces a precarious path between insisting on the possibility of turning our [C]‘natural subjection’ to our advantage, by outmanoeuvring and evading the encroachments of both fortune and passion, and inviting us to surrender ourselves to the direction of these accidental forces, divesting ourselves of any presumption of voluntary agency.[91] This indeterminacy results in a practice of self-regulation that is at turns fortuitous and strategic, and at turns improvisatory and methodical, in keeping with the ‘impure’ status of our authority and agency.

In *On the force of the imagination*, Montaigne dwells at length on the theme of involuntary bodily motion, in reaction not to outward impressions, however, but rather to the powerful influence of our own imaginations or mental representations: [A]‘we drip with sweat, we tremble, we turn pale and turn red at the blows of our imaginations; reclining in our feather beds we feel our bodies agitated by their impact, sometimes to the point of expiring’.[92] Sexual impotence and phantasmic arousal are here analysed as moments of mysterious conjunction and disjunction between the material and the immaterial, testifying to [A]‘the narrow seam between the soul and the body, through which the fortune of one is

89 [C]‘Il ne preste nul consentement à son effroy et souffrance. [. . .] *Mens immota manet, lacrymae uoluuntur inanes* [Virgil, *Aeneid*, IV.449]’. I.12: P 69, V 46–7, F 31.

90 [A]‘Ce seroit moyen une autre fois aussi bien pour se jetter dans le coup, que pour l’eviter’. I.12: P 69, V 46, F 31.

91 [C]‘La science de fuir’. I.12: P 67, V 45, F 30. [C]‘Une subjection naturelle’. I.12: P 69, V 46, F 31.

92 [A]‘Nous tressuons, nous tremblons, nous pallissons, et rougissons aux secousses de nos imaginations; et renversez dans la plume sentons nostre corps agité à leur bransle, quelques-fois jusques à en expirer’. I.20: P 99, V 98, F 69.

communicated to the other', a connection that exceeds the boundaries of voluntary control:

> [A]We are right to notice the indocile liberty of this member, obtruding so importunately when we have no use for it, and failing so importunately when we have the most use for it, and struggling for mastery so imperiously with our will, refusing with so much pride and obstinacy our solicitations, both mental and manual.[93]

The self is here presented as an impure, permeable entity, open to outward impressions that affect and transform it without our permission or even our awareness. In an echo of his reflections on unconscious movement and speech in *On practice* (which we discussed briefly in Chapter 4), Montaigne here argues that there is not one part of our body that does not [C]'often refuse its function to our will and exercise it<self> against our will', moved by 'passions of its own', 'without our leave', 'without our knowledge', 'without the consent, not only of our will, but also of our thoughts'.[94] Even our own will, [C]'on behalf of whose rights we set forth this complaint', is only imperfectly subject to our jurisdiction, being just as guilty as our sexual organs of 'rebellion and sedition' through its 'disorderliness and disobedience': for 'does it always will what we would will it to will? Doesn't it often will what we forbid it to will, and that to our evident disadvantage? Is it any more amenable to the decisions of our reason?'[95]

In this chapter, as in *On constancy*, Montaigne advocates flight rather than opposition as the most effective response to the [C]'piercing impression' of unsettling imaginations: 'my art is to escape it, for lack of strength with which to resist it'.[96] He avoids [C]'the sight of other people's anguish', turning his attention away from distress and other extreme impressions, knowing

[93] [A]'L'estroite cousture de l'esprit et du corps s'entre-communiquants leurs fortunes'. I.20: P 107, V 104, F 74. [C]'On a raison de remarquer l'indocile liberté de ce membre, s'ingerant si importunément lors que nous n'en avons que faire, et defaillant si importunément lors que nous en avons le plus affaire: et contestant de l'authorité, si imperieusement, avec nostre volonté, refusant avec tant de fierté et d'obstination noz solicitations et mentales et manuelles'. I.20: P 104, V 102, F 72.

[94] [C]'Car je vous donne à penser, s'il y a une seule des parties de nostre corps, qui ne refuse à nostre volonté souvent son operation, et qui souvent ne ~~l'exerce~~ <s'exerce> contre nostre volonté. Elles ont chacune des passions propres, qui les esveillent et endorment, sans nostre congé [. . .] sans nostre sceu [. . .] sans l'adveu non seulement de nostre volonté, mais aussi de nostre pensée'. I.20: P 104, V 102, F 72.

[95] [C]'Nostre volonté, pour les droits de qui nous mettons en avant ce reproche, combien plus vraysemblablement la pouvons nous marquer de rebellion et sedition, par son des-reiglement et desobeissance? Veut elle tousjours ce que nous voudrions qu'elle voulsist? Ne veut elle pas souvent ce que nous luy prohibons de vouloir; et à nostre evident dommage? se laisse elle non plus mener aux conclusions de nostre raison?' I.20: P 105, V 103, F 73.

[96] [C]'Son impression me perce: et mon art est de luy eschapper, par faute de force à luy resister'. I.20: P 98, V 97, F 68.

that 'I catch the disease that I study, and lodge it in myself'.[97] *On the force of the imagination* is not limited, however, to these tactics of evasion and diversion: it also offers a blueprint for a practice of strategic self-subterfuge and cognitive manipulation.

Sexual impotence and untimely potency here function as symbols of the body's resistance to the urgent effort of the will, and of the soul's captivity to the tyrannical power of the imagination, in particular the fear of sorcery and enchantment. The way to overcome it, and thus to free ourselves more generally from thraldom to our imaginations, lies not in redoubling one's voluntary resolve and straining against the obstinacy of one's 'indocile member', but in loosening the will and allowing one's mind and body to be lightly teased into cooperation: [C]'before taking possession, the patient should try himself out and offer himself, lightly, by sallies at different times, without priding himself and obstinately insisting on convincing himself definitively'.[98] Montaigne recounts the case of a man for [A]'whom I can answer for as for myself', who, having heard the story of a friend afflicted by 'extraordinary impotence [. . .] at the moment when he needed it least', was 'so struck in his imagination by the horror of this story' that the same disaster befell him on this and several future occasions, so [C]'checked' and 'tyrannised' was he by the 'ugly memory of his mishap'.[99] In such situations, the only solution is to make use of the imagination against itself, by duping ourselves to our own advantage. As Montaigne expresses it:

> [C]He found some remedy for this fancy by another fancy: which was that by admitting this weakness and speaking about it in advance, he relieved the tension of his soul, for when the trouble had been presented as one to be expected, his obligation diminished and weighed upon him less. When he had a chance of his own choosing, with his mind unembroiled and relaxed and his body in good shape, to have his bodily powers first tested, then seized and taken by surprise, with the other party's full knowledge of his problem, he was completely cured in this respect.[100]

97 [C]'La veue des angoisses d'autruy m'angoisse materiellement [. . .] Je saisis le mal, que j'estudie, et le couche en moy'. I.20: P 98–9, V 97–8, F 68.

98 [C]'Avant la possession prinse, le patient se doibt à saillies et divers temps, legerement essayer et offrir, sans se piquer et opiniastrer, à se convaincre definitivement soy-mesme'. I.20: P 104, V 102, F 72.

99 [A]'Tel de qui je puis respondre, comme de moy-mesme'. 'Ayant ouy faire le conte à un sien compagnon d'une defaillance extraordinaire'. 'L'horreur de ce conte luy vint [C]à coup [A]si rudement frapper l'imagination'. [C]'Ce villain souvenir de son inconvenient le gourmandant et tyrannisant'. I.20: P 101, V 99–100, F 70.

100 [C]'Il trouva quelque remede à cette resverie, par une autre resverie. C'est qu'advouant luy mesme, et preschant avant la main, cette sienne subjection, la contention de son ame se soulageoit, sur ce, qu'apportant ce mal comme attendu, son obligation en amoindrissoit, et luy en poisoit moins. Quand il a eu loy, à son chois (sa pensée desbrouillée et desbandée, son corps se trouvant en son deu) de le faire lors premierement tenter, saisir, et surprendre à la cognoissance d'autruy: il s'est guari tout net.' I.20: P 101, V 100, F 70.

Superstitious fears concerning enchantment, similarly, can be undone only by invented incantations, false amulets and other such [C]'monkey tricks', all of which exploit the credulity and susceptibility of the imagination to our advantage.[101]

The idea of self-discipline – that is, of patient habituation or *apprivoisement* to evils through repeated practice and meditation – is far from absent from the *Essais*. Here too, however, emphasis is laid on strategic concession and compromise, rather than steadfast resistance, through the reaping of benefit from those evils that we cannot hope to overcome or avoid. In *On the resemblance of children to their fathers*, Montaigne accounts his kidney stones as a [A]'new acquisition' in the register of his imaginings, and comforts himself with the thought of having [A]'at least this profit' from his illness, 'that it will complete what I have still not been able to accomplish in myself, to reconcile, and familiarise myself completely with death'.[102] This emphasis on advantageous compromise is pursued in Montaigne's description of his condition as a companion with which he has become [A]'acquainted' in the years since he began his text, and to whom he has already [A]'learned to accommodate himself' in the eighteen months or so since it began to manifest itself, 'entering into a truce with this life of the stone' and 'finding in it matter for consolation and hope'.[103]

Montaigne urges us, moreover, to reject the [A]'ceremonious precept' that commands us 'to maintain a good countenance and a ~~grave~~ [C]disdainful [A]and steady comportment, in the suffering of evils', resigning this preoccupation with 'external appearances', rather than 'the living substance and actions', to rhetoricians and actors rather than philosophers. As long as our soul is [A]'able to know itself, to follow its accustomed course, combating the pain and enduring it, rather than prostating itself shamefully at its feet', philosophy ought to [C]'boldly grant to pain' that we should cry out and writhe in our torments, providing that this 'cowardice' lies 'in the voice' and 'neither in the heart nor in the stomach'.[104]

101 [C]'Singeries'. I.20: P 103, V 101, F 71.

102 [A]'Nouvel acquest'. II.37: P 796, V 759, F 574. [A]'J'ay aumoins ce profit de la cholique, que ce que je n'avoy encore peu sur moy, pour me concilier du tout, et m'accointer à la mort, elle le parfera'. II.37: P 798, V 760, F 576.

103 [A]'J'y ay pratiqué la colique, par la liberalité des ans'. II.37: P 796, V 759, F 574. [A]'J'ay desjà appris à m'y accommoder. J'entre desjà en composition de ce vivre coliqueux: j'y trouve dequoy me consoler, et dequoy esperer'. II.37: P 797, V 759, F 575. On this notion of 'composition' and its relationship to Montaigne's *èthos* of nonchalance, see Noirot-Maguire 2007.

104 [A]'Precepte ceremonieux'. 'Tenir bonne contenance et un maintien ~~grave~~ [C]desdaigneux, [A]et posé, à la souffrance des maux'. 'Apparences externes'. 'Le vif, ~~la substance~~ et les effects'. 'Capable de se recognoistre, de suyvre son train accoustumé: combatant la douleur et la soustenant, non se prosternant honteusement à ses pieds'. [C]'Qu'elle condone hardiment au mal, cette lascheté voyelle, si elle n'est ny cordiale, ny stomacale'. II.37: P 798–9, V 760–1, F 576–7.

[A]~~As long as~~ [B]If [A]we play a good game, it ~~makes no difference~~ [B]is a small matter that we make a bad face. ~~It is enough for us to be such as we have accustomed ourselves to being in our reasonings~~ [C]~~thoughts~~ [A]~~and ordinary actions: as for~~ <If> the body ~~if it~~ finds relief in complaining, let it do so: if it likes agitation, let it ~~tremble~~ [C]tumble [A]and toss at its pleasure: if it thinks that the pain evaporates somewhat (as some doctors say that it helps the delivery of women with child) for crying out more violently: or if that distracts its torment, let it shout right out. [C]Let us not command this voice to come out, but permit it to. Epicurus not only permits his sage to cry out in his torments but advises him to. *Even pugilists groan when, flourishing the cestus, they strike, because in throwing out the voice the whole body becomes tense, and the blow becomes harder.*[105]

These bodily motions are explicitly described by Montaigne as [C]'voluntary complaints', even as he urges philosophy to 'assign' them 'to the category of the sighs, sobs, palpitations, and pallors that nature has put out of our control'.[106] It is not that these signs of pain escape us involuntarily, that we are powerless to prevent them; on the contrary, we willingly lend them free rein, whether because they distract us from our suffering, or because they actively help us in the task of preserving our soul from perturbation. Like the analogy of the 'good game', his allusion to the carefully timed cries of pugilists, taken from Cicero's *Tusculanae disputationes*, underlines the deliberate and strategic character of these moments of release. Yet he is equally concerned to emphasise the passivity inherent in our surrender to these motions: 'let us not command this voice to come out, but permit it to'. He himself, we are told, is '<content to groan without shouting out>' – not because [A]'I give myself trouble to do so', but simply because 'I lend the pain as much as it likes'. His moderation is accidental, of uncertain aetiology: he does not know whether his pains 'are less excessive' than those of other people, or whether 'I bring to them more firmness' than most.[107] Here again, Montaigne inhabits a paradoxical space between

105 [A]'~~Pourveu que nous ayons~~ [B]Si nous avons beau jeu, [A]c'est ~~tout un~~ [B]peu [A]que nous ayons mauvaise mine. ~~C'est bien assez que nous soyons tels, que avons nous accoustumé, en nos discours~~ [C]~~pensées~~ [A]~~et actions principales: quant au~~ <Si le> corps ~~qu'il~~ se soulage en se plaignant, qu'il le face: si l'agitation luy plaist, qu'il se ~~tremousse~~ [C]tourneboule [A]et tracasse à sa fantasie: s'il luy semble que le mal s'evapore aucunement (comme aucuns medecins disent que cela aide à la delivrance des femmes enceintes) pour pousser hors la voix avec plus grande violence: ou s'il ~~pense que cela~~ [C]en [A]amuse son tourment, qu'il crie tout à faict. [C]Ne commandons point à ceste voix, qu'elle aille, mais permettons le luy. Epicurus ne pardonne pas seulement à son sage de crier aux tourments, mais il le luy conseille. *Pugiles etiam quum feriunt, in iactandis caestibus ingemiscunt, quia profundenda uoce omne corpus intenditur, uenitque plaga uehementior* [Cicero, *Tusculanae disputationes*, II.23.56]'. II.37: P 799, V 761, F 577.

106 [C]'Et preste ~~ces~~ <ses> pleintes volontaires au genre des souspirs, sanglots, palpitations, pallissements, que nature a mis hors de nostre puissance'. II.37: P 798–9, V 761, F 576.

107 '<Me contente de gemir sans brailler.> [A]Non pourtant que je me mette en peine, pour maintenir ceste decence exterieure: car je fay peu de compte d'un tel advantage: Je preste en cela au mal autant

self-prescription and self-surrender, where the exercise of the will consists precisely in its suspension and withdrawal from action.

Montaigne is keen to emphasise the 'care' that he takes to 'prepare [him]self by reason' for the experience of bodily pain. Quoting Virgil, he claims that no 'toil' is 'new' or 'unexpected' to him, as he has 'forecast' and 'gone through' all of them in his mind. The effect of this practice of premeditation, however, is to trigger immediate and a most impulsive shifts in the disposition of the soul: [A]'in the intervals of [. . .] excessive pain, [C]when my ureters are languid without stinging me too much, [A]I suddenly return to my ordinary condition, ~~I converse, I laugh, I study, without emotion or alteration:~~ since my soul takes no other alarm than that which comes from the senses and the body'.[108] His self-regulation proceeds by jolts and starts, rather than protracted resolution: [C]'I can do anything by a sudden effort; but don't make it last long'.[109] Like those 'voluntary complaints', or indeed those involuntary motions, described elsewhere in the chapter, these sudden efforts and reversals of condition display an uncertain and paradoxical relationship to the will, as evidence both of Montaigne's skill in shaping his own dispositions and of the self-effacement of volition in favour of a studied 'complexion'.

Montaigne's art of self-management does, however, reserve a crucial role for the will as an instrument of diversion, capable of guiding the mind away from present pain, thereby preventing its free movement from becoming tied to the contents of immediate experience.[110] Faced with the agony of the stone, he claims to [C]'test [him]self in the thickest of the pain', confirming to himself that his soul is 'capable of ~~commerce, capable of~~ conversation and other occupation, to a certain degree', 'of speaking, thinking, and answering as sanely as at any other time, but not as steadily'.[111] Self-scrutiny and self-exploration, in this perspective, serve less as instruments of self-discipline

qu'il veut: mais ou mes douleurs ne sont pas si excessives, ou j'y apporte plus de fermeté que le commun'. II.37: P 799, V 762, F 577.

108 [A]'Aux intervalles de ceste douleur excessive [C]lors que mes ureteres languissent sans me ronger, [A]je me remets soudain en ma forme ordinaire: ~~je devise, je ris, j'estudie, sans emotion et alteration:~~ d'autant que mon ame ne prend ~~nulle~~ autre alarme, que la sensible et corporelle. Ce que je doy certainement au soing que j'ay eu à me preparer par ~~estude et par~~ discours à tels accidens: | [B]*laborum | Nulla mihi noua nunc facies inopinâque surgit, | Omnia praecepi, atque animo mecum antè peregi* [Virgil, *Aeneid*, VI, 103–5]'. II.37: P 800, V 762, F 577–8.

109 [C]'Je puis tout par un soudain effort: mais ostez en la durée'. II.37: P 800, V 762, F 577.

110 See Lyons 2005 for an important account of Montaigne's efforts to exercise control over his mental representations.

111 [C]'Je me taste au plus espais du mal: et ay tousjours trouvé que j'estoy capable de dire, de penser, de respondre aussi sainement qu'en une autre heure, mais non si constamment'. 'Capable ~~de commerce, capable~~ d'entretien et d'autre occupation, jusques à certaine mesure'. II.37: P 799–800, V 761–2, F 577.

and self-assessment than as strategies of distraction and relief, allowing us to cope with the experience of extreme, immediate pain by providing an alternative focus for our energies and attention. Here again, however, freedom consists in a practice of dexterous arrangement and judicious manipulation, both of and by the will.

This capacity to redirect our attention and absent ourselves, as it were, from the present experience of evils is explored more fully in the chapter entitled *On diversion*.[112] Montaigne opens with an account of his success in consoling a grieving woman by gradually distracting her from the object of her affliction:

> [B]Very gently deflecting our talk and diverting it bit by bit to subjects nearby, then a little more remote, as she gave me more of her attention, I imperceptibly stole away from her this painful thought [. . .] I made use of diversion.[113]

Diversion, he argues, is [B]'the most ordinary remedy for ailments of the soul' and one which he applies not only to others but to himself.[114] Instead of [B]'making the soul meet the troubles head on' so as to 'withstand or beat down the attack', we 'have it avoid and sidestep them', by '*diverting*' it (in the words of a quotation from Cicero) '*to other interests, preoccupations, cares, business*'.[115] This technique of cognitive evasion can be applied not only to the preservation of the mind from perturbation, but also to the judicious management and moderation of the passions:

> [B]If your passion in love is too powerful, disperse it, they say; and they say true, for I have often tried it with profit. Break it up into various desires, of which one may be ruler and master, if you will; but for fear it may dominate and tyrannise you, weaken it, check it, by dividing and diverting it.[116]

As this passage suggests, diversion is closely connected to ideas of dispersion and dissolution – a range of associations that returns us once more to the idea of 'impure' authority with which we began this chapter:

112 On techniques of mental diversion in the *Essais*, see Giocanti 2001 and Lyons 2005.

113 [B]'Declinant tout mollement noz propos, et les gauchissant peu à peu, aux subjects plus voysins, et puis un peu plus esloignez, selon qu'elle se prestoit plus à moy, je luy desrobay imperceptiblement cette pensée douloureuse [. . .]. J'usay de diversion'. III.4: P 872, V 831, F 631.

114 [B]'La plus ordinaire recepte aux maladies de l'ame'. III.4: P 874, V 832, F 632.

115 [B]'*Abducendus etiam nonnumquam animus est ad alia studia, solicitudines, curas, negotia* [. . .] [Cicero, *Tusculanae disputationes*, IV.34.74]. On luy fait peu choquer les maux de droit fil: on ne luy en fait ny soustenir ny rabatre l'atteinte: on la luy fait decliner et gauchir'. III.4: P 874, V 833, F 632. The term *animus* is inserted by Montaigne into Cicero's text.

116 [B]'Si vostre affection en l'amour est trop puissante, dissipez la, disent-ils: Et disent vray, car je l'ay souvent essayé avec utilité: Rompez la à divers desirs, desquels il y en ayt un regent en un maistre, si vous voulez, mais de peur qu'il ne vous gourmande et tyrannise, affoiblissez-le, sejournez-le, en le divisant et divertissant'. III.4: P 877, V 835, F 634.

[B]A painful notion takes hold of me; I find it quicker to change it than to subdue it. I substitute a contrary one for it, or, if I cannot, at all events a different one. Variation always solaces, dissolves, and dissipates. If I cannot combat it, I escape it; and in fleeing I dodge, I am tricky. By changing place, occupation, and company, I escape into the throng of other occupations and thoughts where it loses my trace and so loses me.[117]

This paragraph reads as a description not merely of a purely cognitive exercise in the manipulation and diversification of one's thought processes, but as an account of Montaigne's specific enterprise in the *Essais* themselves: the written exploration and registration of the wayward movements of the mind.

117 [B]'Une aigre imagination me tient: je trouve plus court, que de la dompter, la changer: je luy en substitue, si je puis une contraire aumoins un'autre: Tousjours la variation soulage, dissout et dissipe: Si je ne puis la combatre, je luy eschappe: et en a fuyant, je fourvoye, je ruse: Muant de lieu, d'occupation, de compagnie, je me sauve dans la presse d'autres amusemens et pensées, où elle perd ma trace, et m'esgare.' III.4: P 877, V 836, F 634–5.

Conclusion

Faced with the arbitrariness of fortune, the extremities of passion and pain, the vicissitudes of personal dependency and the oppressive burdens of care, Montaigne seeks refuge in inward self-containment. His practice of self-study – his introspective fascination with his own 'conditions and humours' – offers an extension of this ethical project. By essaying himself, Montaigne works to distinguish that which properly belongs to him from that which lies beyond his power, to bring his attention, his will, his soul back unto himself, and to apply them without exposing himself to depredation and dispersion. That state of measured engagement and disengagement is a state of liberty – a freedom of which his text is at once an instrument and a witness.

In proposing this analysis, I have contrasted two rival patterns of thinking about selfhood and interiority. The first and more familiar of these frameworks identifies authenticity, or sincerity, as the defining attribute of the self. To have a sense of self, on this understanding, is to imagine oneself as an individual – to experience the gap that separates the subjective, private, solitary realm of inner impulses and dispositions from the outward, public realm constituted by language and social existence. To cleave to oneself, to preserve oneself, is to be true to oneself, to live and write in a manner that reflects one's deepest, most spontaneous and particular intentions, inclinations and affinities; to lose sight of oneself is to adopt a mask, to perform a role, to fall prey (whether strategically or unwittingly) to artifice and falsehood.

This set of concerns has tended to dominate contemporary thinking about inwardness and subjectivity. In analysing Montaigne's reflections, however, I have found it necessary to distinguish this prevalent paradigm from a second, equally significant, but nowadays rather marginal, way of thinking about the self and its boundaries. To have a sense of self, on this latter view, is to constitute oneself, not as an individual, but as an agent: autonomy, rather than identity, defines the limits of our innermost, essential self. To return to oneself, to belong to oneself, is to live within the scope of one's power and thereby free oneself both from the inward compulsion of the passions and from subjection to external objects, forces, and persons. The self, on this understanding, is a moral (rather than a psychological or ontological) category. It names that sphere in which we may be said to act, instead of being acted upon: it is that which remains when all the accidental, contingent qualities conferred upon us by fortune are taken away, that dimension of our lives over which we are able to exercise a degree of power, and in respect of which we may be said to be free.

These two conceptions of the self are by no means incompatible; nor should 'freedom' and 'authenticity' be taken, monolithically and exclusively, to represent uniformly 'classical' and 'modern' approaches to subjectivity. The two paradigms are most usefully thought of as contrasting strands – sometimes found in conjunction with each other, yet always remaining distinct in underlying structure and orientation. The language of essence and appearance, interiority and exteriority, nature and artifice, truth and falsehood, is common to both: the centrality of these distinctions to the *Essais* – which define themselves from the outset in antithesis to 'estude' and 'contention' – is not in doubt. The question at stake concerns the interpretation of these binary oppositions: how and where does Montaigne draw the line between that which is properly part of himself and that which merely appears to be his own?

It is at this juncture that freedom becomes indispensable to a full understanding of Montaigne's text. I am not claiming that there is nothing at all in the *Essais* to suggest a concern with sincerity as opposed to liberty. On closer inspection, however, our own privileged understanding of the self as a form of authentic, individual identity turns out to be much less prominent in Montaigne than has hitherto been assumed. When we recognise that this is not the only way of thinking about the self, it becomes clear that many aspects of the *Essais* conventionally analysed in these terms can also be understood – indeed are better understood – as part of a sustained engagement with the ever-present, ethical problem of dependence.

This analysis has far-reaching consequences for our understanding of the work, even before we consider its implications for its status as an archetype of 'modern' subjectivity. Montaigne's persistent preoccupation with liberty points to the limits of a compelling, but ultimately rather hyperbolic and constraining, assertion: the claim that the *Essais* are a radically uncertain, comprehensively self-subversive text. No credible account of the work, to be sure, can dispense with the fundamental question of its form: the fluid and flexible structure of the *essai*, as I argued in Chapter 1, has profound implications for Montaigne's understanding of freedom. In our concern to rescue the text from reduction to a set of propositions and positions, however, we run the risk of falling into the opposite excess: that of overstating its deconstructive, aporetic qualities. The danger here is not simply that of overlooking significant elements of continuity – of neglecting, as it were, accidental patterns that emerge despite the text's essential design. The problem is rather that, in positing radical noncoherence as its fundamental principle, we unwittingly reduce the *Essais* to its function as epistemological critique, presenting Montaigne's reflections not as searching deliberations on matters of central interest and concern to him, but as manifestos for Pyrrhonian scepticism, designed to expose the ambivalence and confusion of conventional philosophical discourse. As a result, we may end up sidelining the substantive questions explored in the text, and conceiving of Montaigne's enterprise in terms that are at once excessively general and excessively narrow. In particular, as the case of freedom reveals, we may be led to downplay and marginalise the specifically ethical dimensions of the text.

To examine the place of liberty in the *Essais* is certainly to focus attention on Montaigne's handling of a particular theme, as opposed to analysing the formal operations of his thinking and writing in the context of a particular passage, or chapter, or of the work as a whole. It is not, however, to advocate a return to older, often justly discredited attempts to rescue his thought from the outward confusion and disorder of his text, by subordinating its asymmetries and discontinuities to a deductive or sequential logic. The coherence of Montaigne's thinking about freedom lies not in a set of unified, fundamental claims (i.e., in its propositional content), but in the persistence of his engagement with the connected problems of dependency, mental perturbation and self-regulation. His construction of freedom is neither inconsistent nor unitary: its productive suspension between the tensile poles of self-possession and carelessness provides him with space in which to manoeuvre, to explore the contours of the concept, to 'essay' his way towards the flexible and forgiving art of self-management. The *Essais* here emerge as a highly personal exercise in moral thinking – as an undogmatic yet far from incoherent attempt to articulate and enact a certain ordered way of life.

Montaigne's work cannot be reduced to a single enterprise: it encompasses several overlapping projects. These include, to be sure, a sceptical critique of human reason and knowledge, the elaboration of a new literary and philosophical form, an attempt to document the process of thinking rather than its results. As the case of liberty reveals, however, the status of the *Essais* as an exercise of the soul, an art of self-study and self-regulation, is also an indispensable part of this story. Attending to Montaigne's reflections on freedom therefore provides us not only with a new reading of his text, but with a richer and more complete understanding of the character and orientation of the work as a whole.

What light in turn do the *Essais* shed on early modern thinking about liberty more generally? As Quentin Skinner has powerfully demonstrated, our own post-Hobbesian tendency to contrast freedom with interference falters in the face of a much more capacious and exacting 'neo-Roman' understanding of liberty, central to both classical and Renaissance thought, according to which freedom is a status of persons and not merely of actions, subverted not only by forms of coercion and constraint but also, and more fundamentally, by the pure fact of dependency.[1] The distinctive contribution of this way of thinking about liberty to political thought – in particular through its offensive deployment against forms of discretionary or arbitrary power – is now well understood. What has perhaps not always been sufficiently emphasised, however, is the specifically ethical (as opposed to constitutional or juridical) force of this account of freedom as nondomination. As the case of Montaigne makes clear, a preoccupation with independent agency as the defining condition of liberty – with the intrinsic qualities of agents, as opposed to the scope of their outward actions – may find characteristic expression and support not only in the civic vision of the free state, but also in the intensely personal, introspective practice of self-management.

In the first place, certainly, Montaigne identifies liberty with self-possession – with 'belonging to oneself' (estre à soy) in the sense of being one's own person, as opposed to having a master; of living in one's right and under one's own will, rather than being subject to the will of another. Crucially, however, freedom is here constructed in ethical rather than political terms. We are slaves, according to Montaigne, whenever we allow our essential contentment and tranquillity to depend on the favour of fortune or of other men. The free man recognises that the only true and essential goods are those which depend upon himself, and trains his soul, as far as possible, to make do without accidental and external commodities should this become necessary. From the vantage point of carelessness, similarly, freedom is associated with the absence of perturbation and distress, with a

[1] Skinner 2008, p. 2[illegible]1.

state of mental tranquillity and ease, of inner detachment and release from external pressures and burdens.

In examining the impact of Roman moral (as well as political) thought on early modern conceptions of freedom, we may therefore wish to broaden the scope of analysis to include not only the republican strands of thinking excavated by Skinner, but the intersection of that tradition with a different (but, in its origins, equally 'neo-Roman') language of liberty, much less political and juridical in orientation – the ethical, broadly neo-Stoic language of inward disengagement and self-regulation so central to Montaigne's preoccupations. The upshot of my analysis is not merely, then, to bring the *Essais* within the orbit of Skinner's influential interpretation, but to draw attention to the wider, moral context governing early modern discussions of freedom and dependency.

What impact, finally, does my interpretation of Montaigne have on standard accounts of the *Essais* as a canonical episode in the making of the modern self? Its major effect is to complicate, rather than to invalidate, this conventional view, by underlining the insufficiency of these existing interpretations, by drawing attention to the persistence of certain anachronistic frameworks of analysis, and by highlighting their failure to account for dimensions of the text of primordial importance to Montaigne himself. By presenting Montaigne as an idiosyncratic, but not wholly unrepresentative, late Renaissance moralist, I have sought to illuminate (and give special emphasis to) those aspects of his thinking that are less familiar and less well-understood: my purpose has not been to foreclose enquiry into the transformative impact of his reflexive text, but rather to shift the terms of discussion and, I hope, provoke a larger debate about the character of early modern thinking about the self.

This book was conceived not as a contribution to a 'history of the self' in Western thought, but as a study of Montaigne, and in particular as an account of the place of liberty in the *Essais*, its composite sources, its wayward movement, and its complex connection to the project of 'self-study'. In exploring Montaigne's thinking in these areas, I have deliberately avoided larger questions about the emergence of present-day modes of thinking and the place of his text within that story. In advancing freedom, rather than authenticity, as the most appropriate framework within which to consider Montaigne's conception of self, and in drawing attention to the classical antecedents of that conception, my aim has certainly been to put pressure on those accounts of the text that emphasise its proximity to 'modern' preoccupations and presuppositions. The ultimate purpose of this book is not, however, to invite debate about the 'modernity' of Montaigne's text; its effect is rather, I hope, to call the usefulness of that category into question.

The case of the *Essais* exposes the dangers inherent in efforts to trace the origins of our own categories of thought back to a liminal, 'early modern' cultural moment. By enlisting past texts into these retrospective narratives, not only do we obscure much of what their authors were themselves seeking to achieve, but we greatly impoverish the scope of historical enquiry. As the case of Montaigne makes clear, our understanding of these materials will remain skewed and incomplete as long as we consider them to be interesting mainly insofar as they contribute to, and advance, broader processes of change. If we wish to engage with these texts in their own terms, we cannot allow present-day constructions of selfhood to determine our framework of analysis; on the contrary, our first step should be to counteract, or at the very least suspend, these familiar intuitions. These concerns do not disappear, moreover, if we insist that our primary objective is not to analyse these texts in their own right, but to explain how a distinctively modern form of self-awareness has come into being. If we are serious about exploring the historically contingent dimensions of subjectivity, we cannot start by defining selfhood as individuality, or identity, or sincerity as we take ourselves to conceive of them today, and then move back through time in search of these conceptions. To do so is to take for granted precisely that which is in question: we cannot hope to determine the historical boundaries of a phenomenon if we begin by defining it in accordance with our own expectations. Conversely, where these texts are found to resist assimilation to a particular strand of thinking prevailing in our own culture, we cannot conclude by that token that their authors were innocent of any notion of self: we have only shown that they lack the contingent representation that we know as the self.

If we wish to analyse what we now call 'the self' as a cultural construct, rather than as a fundamental, universal aspect of human experience, our starting point cannot be to distil it into a single, identifiable idea (or package of connected ideas) whose development can be traced through time, in relative isolation from the particular contexts and discussions in which these notions appear. To construct our research questions in this way is not only to open the way to proleptic distortion, but to impose an artificial coherence and transparency upon the complex range of concerns – and concepts – invoked in present-day (as well as past) thinking about the self. If we wish to think historically about subjectivity, we must do more than just explain how we have got to where we are today. The task of historical analysis, in this light, involves not only identifying the sources of our own inherited notions of self, but also exploring the shifting contours of interiority and self-awareness across a much wider range of intellectual and linguistic configurations.

To maintain that freedom is essential to Montaigne's concerns is not, therefore, to claim that the *Essais* have no place within a history of Western subjectivity, but that the way in which that broader project is conducted needs to be fundamentally reconceived. It is clear, in particular, that the familiar story about the early modern 'discovery' of interiority and subjectivity, with Montaigne as central protagonist, can be sustained only in a substantially modified and qualified form. In the first instance, we can no longer think of the self as purely and essentially a product of Renaissance culture (a realisation that would scarcely appear controversial to historians of ancient and medieval thought).[2] There is no doubt that, in publishing a book of which he himself is the 'argument' and 'subject', Montaigne is (quite self-consciously) doing things with the self that had not been done before: his concern to register his own thoughts and inclinations, however trivial, eccentric and inconsistent, and to explore the labyrinthine complexity of the mind, represents a fundamental philosophical and literary innovation. In one important sense, however, the introspective activity recorded in the *Essais* is not, in and of itself, new. Montaigne's conception of philosophy as an art of living, in which reading and thinking are undertaken in service not merely of knowledge but of self-knowledge, bears an unmistakable resemblance to ancient (above all Hellenistic) practices of self-awareness and self-regulation (or, as Foucault would term it, self-care). His foregrounding of the self as a space of inner refuge, tranquillity and dominion, contrasted with the illusory nature of external impressions and appearances, rehearses a theme fundamental to ancient ethics, and to Stoic ethics in particular: our true contentment can be found only within ourselves, in those things that are properly ours and subject to our power. Far from being an entirely unprecedented, sui generis phenomenon, his interest in the self represents a re-activation and reworking of a much older set of preoccupations, a contribution to a pre-existing tradition of reflection. The *Essais* – universally acknowledged as a source of privileged insight into early modern notions of self – here provide a vital test case. If Montaigne, of all early modern authors, is to be understood as working within this ancient ethical heritage, and within the broad legacy of Stoic notions of inwardness and freedom in particular, then it becomes impossible to speak

[2] See, for instance, Remes and Sihvola 2008 and Aers 1992.

of the self (at least in an undifferentiated sense) as a distinctively and exclusively modern notion.

Giving due weight to the persistence into the late sixteenth century of ethical conceptions and patterns of language derived from classical antiquity forces us to rethink the contours of the 'modern', without falling into the trap of simply conflating ancient and early modern conceptions. Montaigne's classical inheritance, as we have seen, is always articulated in a heavily refashioned form: the resources furnished by classical moralists such as Plutarch and (above all) Seneca provide a vital context against which to measure his own distinctive presuppositions and preoccupations. His distance from these predecessors is most marked, perhaps, in his emphasis on the limits of human power, his interest in the extreme vulnerability of the will, and his substitution of oblique self-management for studied self-control. This idiosyncratic inflection of Stoicism leads him first to affirm the fragmentation and inconsistency of the self, driving a wedge between the pursuit of independent agency and the classical ethical imperative of constancy, and second to identify the life of freedom with the pursuit of nature, understood not so much, or no longer exclusively, as a set of universal human norms, but as a source of artless, unlearned, unpremeditated goodness. The *Essais* are thus best understood, not as a relic of ancient thinking, but as a witness to a distinctively late sixteenth-century turn of mind – to a moment of transition in which classical understandings and discourses are revived, but also transformed.

This transmutation of ancient notions of self cannot, however, be said to constitute a straightforward, irreversible shift towards more familiar, recognizably 'modern' concerns. Important as it is to mark the distance that separates Montaigne from an author such as Seneca, it is still more vital to emphasise the ways in which his own, historically particular, set of preoccupations resists incorporation into any single narrative of development. The upshot of this shift in perspective is not to dethrone the *Essais*, or any other early modern text, in favour of an earlier, more fundamental moment of discovery, but to underline the shortcomings of any framework of analysis focused on a single, linear path of progression. The question that we should be asking of Montaigne's text is not: 'what can this work tell us about the construction of "modern" subjectivity?' Instead of approaching the work as a decisive landmark or watershed, our aim should rather be to situate it in a much more elastic and extensive historical perspective.

Does this mean that the importance of the *Essais* has been exaggerated? In one sense, certainly, the originality of Montaigne's enterprise stands diminished on my account. Our sense of the significance of the work can be sharpened, however, only by further efforts to contextualise it. Questions about originality cease to appear so important if our aim is no longer to track the emergence of particular ways of thinking, but to reconstruct a much larger, and more pluralistic, complex of redescriptions, reversals and transformations. The historical value of Montaigne's text lies not only in the exceptionally rich and detailed insight which it provides into late sixteenth-century habits of thinking and writing about the self but also in its extraordinary afterlife – in the instrumental role played by this hugely influential text in stimulating further incarnations and transmutations of interiority in the centuries following its publication. The history of Montaigne's self is thus inextricably connected to the history of the text's reception.

That history can in part be understood as a transition from the dominance of one paradigm to that of another, from a broadly neo-Stoic conception of inwardness to what one might describe as a Romantic understanding of interiority – a shift involving a recentring of ethical practices of introspection around notions of emotional self-expression and psychic identity.[3] It could also be told, however, as a story about the enduring role of freedom and dependency in shaping selfhood after the *Essais*, and (more broadly) about the unacknowledged moral dimensions of 'modern' identity. The language of sincerity and authenticity, from this perspective, represents a reincarnation, rather than a complete repudiation, of Montaigne's 'essaying' of liberty.

[3] See Paige 2001.

Bibliography

PRIMARY SOURCES

[Anonymous] (1574a). *Dialogi ab Eusebio Philadelphio cosmopolita, in Gallorum et caeterarum nationum gratiam compositi*, Edinburgh, Basel: ex typographia Iacobi Iamaei.

[Anonymous] (1574b). *Le reveille-matin des François, et de leurs voisins. Composé par Eusebe Philadelphe cosmopolite, en forme de dialogues*, Edinburgh [Basel?]: de l'imprimerie de Iacques Iames.

[Anonymous] (1577). *Vive description de la tyrannie, et des tyrans, avec les moyens de se garentir de leur joug*, Reims: J. Mouchar.

Aristotle (1968). *Nicomachean ethics*, ed. and trans. H. Rackham, Cambridge, MA: Harvard University Press.

Blackwood, Adam (1581). *Aduersus Georgii Buchanani dialogum, de iure regni apud Scotos, pro regibus apologia*, Poitiers: apud Franciscum Pagaeum.

Bodin, Jean (1566). *Methodus ad facilem historiarum cognitionem*, Paris: apud Martinum Iuuenem.

Boissard, Jean Jacques (1593). *Emblematum liber*, Frankfurt: Theodore de Bry.

Buchanan, George (1579). *De iure regni apud Scotos*, Edinburgh: John Ross.

Calvin, Jean (1911). *L'institution de la religion chrestienne: texte de la première édition française (1541)*, eds. A. Lefranc, H. Chatelain and J. Pannier, 2 vols, Paris: Champion.

Castiglione, Baldassare (1537). *Le courtisan nouvellement traduict de langue ytalicque en Francoys*, trans. Jean Chaperon (?) and J[acques?] Colin, Paris: Jehan Longis.

______ (1538). *Le Courtisan de Messire Baltazar de Castillon, nouvellement reveu et corrigé*, trans. J[acques?] Colin, Lyon: François Juste.

______ (1580). *Le parfait courtisan du Comte Baltasar Castillonnois en deux langues*, trans. Gabriel Chapuis, Lyon: Loys Cloquemin.

______ (1981). *Il libro del cortegiano*, eds. A. Quondam and N. Longo, Milan: Garzanti.

______ (2002). *The book of the courtier*, trans. Charles S. Singleton, New York: W. W. Norton.

Cicero (1968a). *Paradoxa stoicorum*, ed. and trans. H. Rackham, Cambridge, MA: Harvard University Press.

——— (1968b). *De officiis*, ed. and trans. W. Miller, Cambridge, MA: Harvard University Press.

——— (1971). *De senectute*, ed. and trans. W. A. Falconer, Cambridge, MA: Harvard University Press.

——— (1991). *On duties*, ed. E. M. Atkins, trans. M. T. Griffin, Cambridge University Press.

Cotgrave, Randall (1611). *Dictionarie of the French and English tongues*, London: Adam Islip.

Erasmus, Desiderius (1969–). *Opera omnia*, Amsterdam: North-Holland.

——— (1974–). *Collected works*, University of Toronto Press.

Estienne, Charles (1564). *Agriculture et maison rustique*, Paris: J. Du Puis.

Gallo, Agostino (1571). *Secrets de la vraye agriculture et honestes plaisirs qu'on reçoit en la mesnagerie des champs*, trans. François de Belle-Forest, Paris: N. Chesneau.

Gauchet, Claude (1583). *Le plaisir des champs, divisé en quatre parties selon les quatre saisons de l'année, . . . où est traicté de la chasse et de tout autre exercice récréatif, honneste et vertueux . . .* , Paris: N. Chesneau.

Goulart, Simon (1577). *Mémoires de l'estat de France, sous Charles Neufiesme*, 3 vols, Meidelburg, Geneva: Henrick Wolf [Eustache Vignon].

La Boétie, Estienne de (1571). *La Mesnagerie de Xenophon. Les Regles de mariage, de Plutarque. Lettre de consolation, de Plutarque à sa femme. Le tout traduict de Grec en François par feu M. Estienne de la Boetie, Conseiller du Roy en sa court de Parlement à Bordeaux. Ensemble quelques Vers Latins & François, de son inuention. Item, un Discours sur la mort dudit Seigneur De la Boëtie, par M. de Montaigne*, Paris: F. Morel.

——— (1987). *Discours de la servitude volontaire, ou contr'un*, ed. Malcolm Smith, Geneva: Droz.

——— (1991). 'La mesnagerie de Xenophon', in Louis Desgraves (ed.), *Oeuvres complètes*, 2 vols, Bordeaux: William Blake and Company, vol. I, pp. 147–218.

Le Choyselat, Prudent (1569). *Discours oeconomique, non moins utile que recreatif: monstrant comment de cinq cens liures . . . l'on peult tirer par an quatre mil cinq cens liuvres de proffict honneste*, Paris: N. Chesneau.

Lipsius, Justus (2004). *Politica: six books of politics or political instruction*, ed. and trans. Jan Waszink, Assen: Royal Van Gorcum.

Locke, John (1975). *An essay concerning humane understanding*, ed. Peter Nidditch, Oxford: Clarendon Press.

Mommsen, Theodor and Krueger, Paul (eds.) (1985). *The Digest of Justinian*, 3 vols, Philadelphia: University of Pennsylvania Press.

Montaigne, Michel de (1580). *Essais de Messire Michel Seigneur de Montaigne, Chevalier de l'Ordre du Roy, et Gentilhomme ordinaire de sa Chambre*, Bordeaux: Simon Millanges.

——— (1588). *Essais de Michel Seigneur de Montaigne: cinquiesme edition, augmentee d'un troisiesme livre et de six cens additions aux deus premiers*, Paris: Abel L'Angelier.

——— (1595). *Les Essais de Michel Seigneur de Montaigne: édition nouvelle, trouvee apres le deceds de l'Autheur, reveuë et augmentee par luy d'un tiers plus qu'aux precedentes Impressions*, Paris: Abel L'Angelier.

——— (1958). *The complete essays of Montaigne*, trans. Donald Frame, Stanford University Press.

——— (1969). *The essayes, or morall, politike and millitarie discourses*, trans. John Florio, Menston: Scholar Press.

——— (1991). *The complete essays*, trans. M. A. Screech, London: Penguin.

——— (2002a). *Reproduction en quadrichrome de l'exemplaire avec notes manuscrites marginales des Essais de Montaigne (Exemplaire de Bordeaux)*, Chicago: Montaigne Studies.

——— (2002b). *The Montaigne project: Villey edition of the Essais with corresponding digital page images from the Bordeaux Copy. Édition Villey-Saulnier avec images digitales correspondantes de l'Exemplaire de Bordeaux*, directed by Philippe Desan, The ARTFL Project / Montaigne Studies, University of Chicago. www.lib.uchicago.edu/efts/ARTFL/projects/montaigne/ [Last accessed 27 October 2011].

——— (2004). *Les Essais*, eds. Pierre Villey and V.-L. Saulnier, Paris: Presses universitaires de France.

——— (2007). *Les Essais*, eds. Jean Balsamo, Michel Magnien and Catherine Magnien-Simonin, Paris: Gallimard.

More, Thomas. (1995). *Utopia: Latin text and English translation*, eds. George M. Logan, Robert M. Adams and Clarence H. Miller, Cambridge University Press.

Pascal, Blaise (2004). *Pensées*, ed. Michel le Guern, Paris: Gallimard.

Plutarch (1560). *Ploutarchou Chaironeos parallèla en biois Ellènonte, kai Romaion. Plutarchi Chaeronei quae vocantur Parallela: hoc est vitae illustrium virorum Graeci nominis ac Latini, prout quaque alteri convenire videbatur accuratius quam ante hac unquam digestae et castigatae*, ed. Simon Grynaeus, Basel: Hieronymus Froben and Eusebius Episcopius.

——— (1565). *Les vies des hommes illustres, grecs & romains, comparees l'une avec l'autre*, trans. Jacques Amyot, 2nd edition, 2 vols, Paris: Michel de Vascosan.

——— (1572). *Les oeuvres morales et meslees de Plutarque*, trans. Jacques Amyot, 2 vols, Paris: Michel de Vascosan.

——— (1951). *Les vies des hommes illustres*, trans. Jacques Amyot, ed. Gérard Walter, Paris: Gallimard.

——— (1962). *Moralia*, eds. and trans. Frank Cole Babbitt, W. C. Helmbold, Phillip H. De Lacy et al., 16 vols, Cambridge, MA: Harvard University Press.

——— (1971). *Les oeuvres morales et meslees de Plutarque*, trans. Jacques Amyot, 2 vols, Paris: Mouton.

Quintilian (2001). *Institutio oratoria*, ed. and trans. Donald A. Russell, 5 vols, Cambridge, MA: Harvard University Press.

Seneca (1557). *L. Annaei Senecae philosophi stoicorum omnium acutissimi opera quae extant omnia*, Basel: per J. Hervagium et B. Brandum.

______ (1582). *Les epistres de L. Annaee Senecque, philosophe tres-excellent*, trans. Geoffroi de La Chassagne, Paris: Guillaume Chaudière.

______ (1585). *L. Annaei Seneca a M. A. Mureto correctus et notis illustratus*, Rome: apud B. Grassium.

______ (1932). *Moral essays*, ed. and trans. John W. Basore, 3 vols, Cambridge, MA: Harvard University Press.

______ (1989). *Ad Lucilium Epistulae Morales*, ed. and trans. Richard M. Gunmere, 3 vols, Cambridge, MA: Harvard University Press.

Serres, Olivier de (1600). *Le théâtre d'agriculture et mesnage des champs*, Paris: Jamet-Métayer.

Vinet, Elie (1886). *Schola aquitanica: programme d'études du collège de Guyenne*, trans. Louis Massebieau, Paris: C. Delagrave.

Xenophon (1531). *Science, pour senrichir honestement & facilement. Intitulé, Leconomic Xenophon*, trans. Geofroy Tory, Paris: Geofroy Tory.

______ (1551). *Xenophontis philosophi et historici . . . opera*, ed. Sébastien Castellion, 2 vols, Basel: apud Isingrinium.

______ (1562). *Le Mesnagier de Xenophon. Plus un discours de l'excellence du mesme Autheur*, trans. François de Ferris, Paris: J. Dalier.

______ (1994). *Xenophon Oeconomicus*, ed. and trans. Sarah B. Pomeroy, Oxford: Clarendon Press.

SECONDARY SOURCES

Abecassis, Jack I. (1995). '"Le maire et Montaigne ont tousjours esté deux, d'une separation bien claire": public necessity and private freedom in Montaigne', *MLN* 110: 1067–89.

Aers, David (1992). 'A whisper in the ear of early modernists; or, reflections on literary critics writing the "history of the subject"', in David Aers (ed.), *Culture and history, 1350–1600: essays on English communities, identities and writing*, Detroit: Wayne State University Press, pp. 177–202.

Albrecht, Michael von (2004). *Wort und Wandlung: Senecas Lebenskunst*, Leiden: Brill.

Atkinson, James B. (1973). 'Montaigne and *naïveté*', *Romanic Review* 64: 245–57.

Auerbach, Erich (1953). *Mimesis: the representation of reality in Western literature*, trans. Willard R. Trask, Princeton University Press.

Aulotte, Robert (1965). *Amyot et Plutarque: la tradition des* Moralia *au XVIè siècle*, Geneva: Droz.

______ (1971). *Plutarque en France au XVIè siècle*, Paris: Klincksieck.

Baldwin, Geoff (2001). 'Individual and self in the late Renaissance', *The Historical Journal* 44: 341–64.

Balsamo, Jean (2001). 'Deux gentilshommes "nécessiteux d'honneur": Montaigne et Pressac', *Montaigne Studies* 13: 141–74.

______ (2006). 'Un gentilhomme et ses patrons: remarques sur la biographie politique de Montaigne', in Philippe Desan (ed.), *Montaigne politique*, Paris: Champion, pp. 223–42.

_____ (2008). 'Montaigne avant Montaigne ou les *scénarios* de Roger Trinquet', *Montaigne Studies* 20: 129–44.

Barker, Francis (1984). *The tremulous private body: essays on subjection*, London: Methuen.

Bartsch, Shadi and Wray, David (2009). 'Introduction: the self in Senecan scholarship', in Shadi Bartsch and David Wray (eds.), *Seneca and the self*, Cambridge University Press, pp. 3–16.

Battista, Anna Maria (1966). *Alle origini del pensiero politico libertino: Montaigne e Charron*, Milan: Giuffrè.

Beaudry, James G. (1976). 'Virtue and nature in the *Essais*', *Kentucky Romance Quarterly* 23: 93–104.

Beaujour, Michel (1980). *Miroirs d'encre: rhétorique de l'auto-portrait*, Paris: Seuil.

Belsey, Catherine (1985). *The subject of tragedy: identity and difference in Renaissance drama*, London: Methuen.

Bencivenga, Ermanno (1990). *The discipline of subjectivity: an essay on Montaigne*, Princeton University Press.

Benson, Edward (1989). 'The historicity of the *Essais*: Montaigne's "registre de durée" and his "contrerolle"', in Marcel Tetel and G. Mallary Masters (eds.), *Le parcours des Essais: Montaigne 1588–1988*, Geneva: Droz, pp. 211–24.

Berger, Harry (2000). *Fictions of the pose: Rembrandt against the Italian Renaissance*, Stanford University Press.

Blinkenberg, Andreas (1974). 'Quel sens Montaigne a-t-il voulu donner au mot *Essais* dans le titre de son oeuvre?', in *Mélanges de linguistique et de littératures Romanes, offerts à Mario Roque*, Geneva: Slatkine, vol. I, pp. 3–14.

Boccassini, Daniela (1993). 'Ruines montaigniennes', *Montaigne Studies* 5: 155–90.

Boutcher, Warren (1995). '"Le moyen de voir ce Senecque escrit à la main": Montaigne's *Journal de voyage* and the politics of science and faveur in the Vatican Library', in John O'Brien (ed.), *(Ré)interprétations: études sur le seizième siècle*, Ann Arbor, MI: Michigan Romance Studies, pp. 177–214.

_____ (2004). 'Awakening the inner man: Montaigne framed for modern intellectual life', *EMF: Studies in Early Modern France* 9: 30–57.

_____ (2005). 'Montaigne's legacy', in Ullrich Langer (ed.), *The Cambridge companion to Montaigne*, Cambridge University Press, pp. 27–52.

Boyle, Marjorie O'Rourke (1997). 'Montaigne's consubstantial book', *Renaissance Quarterly* 50: 723–49.

Brahami, Frédéric (2006). '"Être à soi": la place du politique dans les *Essais*', in Philippe Desan (ed.), *Montaigne politique*, Paris: Champion, pp. 39–56.

Brush, Craig B. (1994). *From the perspective of the self: Montaigne's self-portrait*, New York: Fordham University Press.

Buffum, Imbrie (1957). *Studies in the baroque from Montaigne to Rotrou*, New Haven, CT: Yale University Press.

Burke, Peter (1991). 'Tacitism, scepticism and reason of state', in J. H. Burns and M. Goldie (eds.), *The Cambridge history of political thought, 1450–1750*, Cambridge University Press, pp. 479–98.

——— (1995). *The fortunes of the courtier: the European reception of Castiglione's Cortegiano*, Cambridge University Press.

Cameron, Keith (1968). 'Montaigne and the mask', *L'esprit créateur* 8: 198–207.

Carraud, Vincent and Marion, Jean-Luc (eds.) (2004). *Montaigne: scepticisme, métaphysique, théologie*, Paris: Presses universitaires de France.

Carrithers, Michael, Collins, Steven and Lukes, Steven (eds.) (1985). *The category of the person: anthropology, philosophy, history*, Cambridge University Press.

Cave, Terence (1979). *The cornucopian text: problems of writing in the Renaissance*, Oxford: Clarendon Press.

——— (1982). 'Problems of reading in the *Essays*', in I. D. McFarlane and Ian Maclean (eds.), *Montaigne: essays in memory of Richard Sayce*, Oxford: Clarendon Press, pp. 133–66.

——— (1995). 'Le récit montaignien: un voyage sans repentir', in Zoe Samaras (ed.), *Montaigne: espace, voyage, écriture*, Paris: Champion, pp. 125–35.

——— (1999). *Pré-histoires: textes troublés au seuil de la modernité*, Geneva: Droz.

——— (2007). *How to read Montaigne*, London: Granta Books.

Christodoulou, Kyriaki (1992). 'Sur le grec de Montaigne', *Montaigne Studies* 4: 19–39.

Clark, Carol E. (1968). 'Seneca's *Letters to Lucilius* as a source of some of Montaigne's imagery', *Bibliothèque d'humanisme et Renaissance* 30: 249–66.

Cocula, Anne-Marie (2003). 'L'engagement de Montaigne durant une décennie de périls majeurs pour le royaume de France, 1580–1590', in Françoise Argod-Dutard (ed.), *Des signes au sens: lectures du livre III des Essais*, Paris: Champion, pp. 11–33.

Cohen, G. A. (1995). *Self-ownership, freedom and equality*, Cambridge University Press.

Coleman, Janet (2005). 'Pre-modern property and self-ownership before and after Locke: or, when did common decency become a private rather than a public virtue?', *European Journal of Political Theory* 4: 125–45.

Collins, Robert J. (1992). 'Montaigne's rejection of reason of state in "De l'utile et de l'honneste"', *Sixteenth Century Journal* 23: 71–94.

Compagnon, Antoine (1979). *La seconde main ou le travail de la citation*, Paris: Seuil.

——— (1980). *Nous, Michel de Montaigne*, Paris: Seuil.

——— (1985). 'Montaigne ou la parole donnée', in Frank Lestringant (ed.), *Rhétorique de Montaigne*, Paris: Champion, pp. 9–19.

de Obaldia, Claire (1995). *The essayistic spirit: literature, modern criticism and the essay*, Oxford: Clarendon Press.

Delègue, Yves (1998). *Montaigne et la mauvaise foi: l'écriture de la vérité*, Paris: Champion.

Demonet, Marie-Luce and Legros, Alain (eds.) (2004). *L'écriture du scepticisme chez Montaigne*, Geneva: Droz.

Derrida, Jacques (1967). *L'écriture et la différence*, Paris: Seuil.

Desan, Philippe (1992). *Les commerces de Montaigne: le discours économique des Essais*, Paris: Nizet.

______ (1995). 'La rhétorique comptable des *Essais*', in John O'Brien, Malcolm Quainton, and James Supple (eds.), *Montaigne et la rhétorique*, Paris: Champion, pp. 177–87.

Duff, Tim (1999). *Plutarch's Lives: exploring virtue and vice*, Oxford: Clarendon Press.

Eden, Kathy (2001). *Friends hold all things in common: tradition, intellectual property, and the Adages of Erasmus*. New Haven, CT: Yale University Press.

______ (2008). 'Literary property and the question of style: a prehistory', in Hall Bjørnstad (ed.), *Borrowed feathers: plagiarism and the limits of imitation in early modern Europe*, Oslo: Unipub, pp. 21–38.

Edwards, Catherine (1997). 'Self-scrutiny and self-transformation in Seneca's *Letters*', *Greece and Rome* 44: 23–38.

______ (2009). 'Free yourself! Slavery, freedom and the self in Seneca's *Letters*', in Shadi Bartsch and David Wray (eds.), *Seneca and the self*, Cambridge University Press, pp. 139–59.

Farquhar, Sue W. (1995). 'Irony and the ethics of self-portraiture in Montaigne's *De la praesumption*', *Sixteenth Century Journal* 26: 791–803.

Fontana, Biancamaria (2008). *Montaigne's politics: authority and governance in the Essais*, Princeton University Press.

Force, Pierre (2005). 'Innovation as spiritual exercise: Montaigne and Pascal', *Journal of the History of Ideas* 66: 17–35.

______ (2009). 'Montaigne and the coherence of eclecticism', *Journal of the History of Ideas* 70: 523–54.

Foucault, Michel (1984a). *Histoire de la sexualité 2: L'usage des plaisirs*, Paris: Gallimard.

______ (1984b). *Histoire de la sexualité 3: Le souci de soi*, Paris: Gallimard.

Frame, Donald (1965). *Montaigne: a biography*, London: Hamish Hamilton.

Friedrich, Hugo (1949). *Montaigne*, Bern: Francke.

______ (1991). *Montaigne*, trans. Dawn Eng, Berkeley and Los Angeles, CA: University of California Press.

Fumaroli, Marc (1984). 'Montaigne et l'éloquence du for intérieur', in Jean Lafond (ed.), *Les formes brèves de la prose et le discours discontinu (XVIè – XVIIè siècles)*, Paris: Vrin, pp. 27–50.

Garavini, Fausta (1994). *Monstres et chimères: Montaigne, le texte et le fantasme*, trans. Isabel Picon, Paris: Champion.

______ (1995). 'Voyage du "je" au pays de l'écriture', in Zoe Samaras (ed.), *Montaigne: espace, voyage, écriture*, Paris: Champion, pp. 237–42.

Gaullier, E. (1874). *Histoire du collège de Guyenne* Paris: Sandoz et Fischbacher.

Gill, Christopher (1983). 'The question of character-development: Plutarch and Tacitus', *Classical Quarterly* 33: 469–87.

______ (1996). *Personality in Greek epic, tragedy and philosophy: the self in dialogue*, Oxford: Clarendon Press.

——— (2006). *The structured self in Hellenistic and Roman Thought*, Oxford: Clarendon Press.

Giocanti, Sylvia (2001). *Penser l'irrésolution. Montaigne, Pascal, La Mothe Le Vayer: trois itinéraires sceptiques*, Paris: Champion.

Glidden, Hope (1993). 'The face in the text: Montaigne's emblematic self-portrait', *Renaissance Quarterly* 46: 71–98.

Good, Graham (1988). *The observing self: rediscovering the essay*, London: Routledge.

Gorris Camos, Rosanna (2001). '"Toujours il a frayé avec des hommes de cette farine": André de Gouvéa, principal du Collège de Guyenne et ses "Bordaleses"', *Montaigne Studies* 13: 13–44.

Goyet, Francis (1986–7). 'À propos de "Ces pastissages de lieux communs". (Le rôle des notes de lecture dans la genèse des *Essais*)', *Bulletin de la société des amis de Montaigne*, VII, 5–6: 11–26 and 7–8: 9–30.

Grady, Hugh (2002). *Shakespeare, Machiavelli and Montaigne: power and subjectivity from Richard II to Hamlet*, Oxford: Clarendon Press.

Grafton, Anthony (1997). *Commerce with the classics: ancient texts and Renaissance readers*, Ann Arbor, MI: University of Michigan Press.

Gray, Floyd (1982). *La balance de Montaigne: exagium/essay*, Paris: Nizet.

——— (2004). 'Montaigne et le tombeau de La Boétie', in Marcel Tetel (ed.), *Étienne de la Boétie: sage révolutionnaire et poète périgourdin*, Paris: Champion, pp. 261–77.

Green, Felicity (2009). 'Reading Montaigne in the twenty-first century', *The Historical Journal* 52: 1085–1109.

Greenblatt, Stephen (1980). *Renaissance self-fashioning: from More to Shakespeare*, University of Chicago Press.

——— (2007). 'Psychoanalysis and Renaissance culture', in *Learning to curse: essays in early modern culture*, London: Routledge, pp. 176–95.

Greene, Thomas M. (1986). *The vulnerable text: essays in Renaissance literature*, New York: Columbia University Press.

Grilli, Alberto (1965). 'Su Montaigne e Seneca', in *Studi di letteratura, storia e filosofia in onore di Bruno Revel*, Florence: Olschki, pp. 303–11.

Hadot, Pierre (1987). *Exercices spirituels et philosophie antique*, Paris: Études augustiniennes.

Hallie, Philip (1966). *The scar of Montaigne: an essay in personal philosophy*, Middletown, CT: Wesleyan University Press.

——— (1977). 'The ethics of Montaigne's "De la cruauté"', in Raymond C. La Charité (ed.), *O un amy! Essays on Montaigne in honor of Donald M. Frame*, Lexington, KY: French Forum Publishers, pp. 156–71.

Hampton, Timothy (1990). *Writing from history: the rhetoric of exemplarity in Renaissance literature*, Ithaca, NY: Cornell University Press.

——— (2006). 'Difficult engagements: private passion and public service in Montaigne's *Essais*', in Victoria Kahn, Neil Saccamano and Daniela Coli (eds.), *Politics and the passions, 1500–1850*, Princeton University Press, pp. 30–48.

——— (2009). *Fictions of embassy: literature and diplomacy in early modern Europe*, Ithaca, NY: Cornell University Press.

Hartle, Ann (2003). *Michel de Montaigne: accidental philosopher*, Cambridge University Press.

______ (2006). 'The transformation of virtue in Montaigne's *Essays*', *L'esprit créateur* 46: 3–12.

Hay, Camilla Hill (1938). *Montaigne, lecteur et imitateur de Sénèque*, Poitiers: Société française d'imprimerie et de librairie.

Hillman, David (2007). *Shakespeare's entrails: belief, scepticism and the interior of the body*, Basingstoke: Palgrave Macmillan.

Hoffmann, George (1998). *Montaigne's career*, Oxford: Clarendon Press.

______ (2000). 'Portrayal from life, or to life? The *Essais*'s living effigy', *French Forum* 25: 145–63.

Huguet, Edmond (1925–67). *Dictionnaire de la langue française du seizième siècle*, 7 vols, Paris: Champion.

Huppert, George (1984). *Public schools in Renaissance France*, Urbana and Chicago, IL: University of Illinois Press.

Hutson, Lorna (1994). *The usurer's daughter: male friendship and fictions of women in sixteenth-century England*, London: Routledge.

Inwood, Brad (2005). 'Seneca on freedom and autonomy', in *Reading Seneca: Stoic philosophy at Rome*, Oxford: Clarendon Press, pp. 302–21.

Jordan, Constance (2003). 'Montaigne on property, public service, and political servitude', *Renaissance Quarterly* 56: 408–35.

______ (2004). 'The propriety in an estate: social topography in the *Essais*', *EMF: Studies in Early Modern France* 9: 77–98.

Keohane, Nannerl E. (1977). 'Montaigne's individualism', *Political Theory* 5: 363–90.

Klesczewski, Reinhard (1966). *Die französischen Übersetzungen des Cortegiano von Baldassare Castiglione*, Heidelberg: C. Winter.

Konstantinovic, Isabelle (1989). *Montaigne et Plutarque*, Geneva: Droz.

Krause, Virginia (2000). 'Montaigne's art of idleness', *Viator* 31: 361–80.

Kushner, Eva (1993). 'Intériorité, spatialité, altérité chez Montaigne', in Ilana Zinguer (ed.), *Le lecteur, l'auteur et l'écrivain. Montaigne 1492–1592–1992*, Paris: Champion, pp. 31–40.

Langer, Ullrich (1990). *Divine and poetic freedom in the Renaissance: nominalist theology and literature in France and Italy*, Princeton University Press.

______ (1994). *Perfect friendship: studies in literature and moral philosophy from Boccaccio to Corneille*, Geneva: Droz.

______ (1999). *Vertu du discours, discours de la vertu: littérature et philosophie morale au XVIè siècle en France*, Geneva: Droz.

______ (2005). 'Introduction', in Ullrich Langer (ed.), *The Cambridge companion to Montaigne*, Cambridge University Press, pp. 1–8.

Lapp, John C. (1971). *The esthetics of negligence: La Fontaine's Contes*, Cambridge University Press.

Lee, John (2000). *Shakespeare's Hamlet and the controversies of self*, Oxford: Clarendon Press.

Legros, Alain (1999). 'La main grecque de Montaigne', *Bibliothèque d'humanisme et Renaissance* 61: 461–78.

——— (2000). *Essais sur poutres*, Paris: Klincksieck.

Lévi-Strauss, Claude (1962). *La pensée sauvage*, Paris: Plon.

Levine, Alan (2001). *Sensual philosophy: toleration, skepticism, and Montaigne's politics of the self*, Lanham, MD: Lexington Books.

Lewis, Charlton T. and Charles Short (eds.) (1987). *A Latin dictionary*, Oxford: Clarendon Press.

Long, A. A. (1996). 'Soul and body in Stoicism', in his *Stoic studies*, Cambridge University Press, pp. 224–49.

Lotito, Gianfranco (2001). *Suum esse: forme dell'interiorità senecana*, Bologna: Pàtron.

Lüthy, Herbert (1987). 'Montaigne, or the art of being truthful', in Harold Bloom (ed.), *Michel de Montaigne*, New York: Chelsea House, pp. 11–28.

Lyons, John D. (2005). *Before imagination: embodied thought from Montaigne to Rousseau*, Stanford University Press.

Macpherson, C. B. (1962). *The political theory of possessive individualism: Hobbes to Locke*, Oxford: Clarendon Press.

Martin, Daniel (1977). *Montaigne et la fortune: essai sur le hasard et le langage*, Paris: Champion.

Martin, John Jeffries (1997). 'Inventing sincerity, refashioning prudence: the discovery of the individual in Renaissance Europe', *American Historical Review* 102: 1309–42.

——— (2004). *Myths of Renaissance individualism*, Basingstoke: Palgrave Macmillan.

Martin, Raymond and John Barresi (2006). *The rise and fall of soul and self: an intellectual history of personal identity*, New York: Columbia University Press.

Maskell, D. (1979). 'Montaigne médiateur entre Navarre et Guise', *Bibliothèque d'humanisme et Renaissance* 41: 541–55.

Mathieu-Castellani, G. (1988). *Montaigne: l'écriture de l'essai*, Paris: Presses universitaires de France.

——— (2000). *Montaigne, ou la vérité du mensonge*, Geneva: Droz.

Maus, Katharine Eisman (1995). *Inwardness and theater in the English Renaissance*, University of Chicago Press.

McCrea, Adriana (1997). *Constant minds: political virtue and the Lipsian paradigm in England, 1584–1650*, University of Toronto Press.

McGowan, Margaret (2000). *The vision of Rome in late Renaissance France*, New Haven, CT: Yale University Press.

Meijer, Marianne (1984). 'Mourir lâchement et mollement', in Claude Blum and François Moureau (eds.), *Études montaignistes en hommage à Pierre Michel*, Paris: Champion, pp. 173–82.

Mesnard, Jean (1989). 'Pascal et le "moi haïssable"', in George Craig and Margaret McGowan (eds.), *Moy qui me voy: the writer and the self from Montaigne to Leiris*, Oxford: Clarendon Press, pp. 19–29.

Micha, Alexandre (1956). 'Art et nature dans les *Essais*', *Bulletin de la société des amis de Montaigne* 19: 50–5.

Moss, Ann (2000). *Printed commonplace-books and the structuring of Renaissance thought*, Oxford: Clarendon Press.

Nakam, Géralde (2006). *Montaigne: la matière et la manière*, Paris: Champion.

Naya, Emmanuel (2005). 'De la "médiocrité" à la "mollesse": prudence montaignienne', in Emmanuel Naya and Anne-Pascale Pouey-Mounou (eds.), *Éloge de la médiocrité: le juste milieu à la Renaissance*, Paris: Presses de l'École normale supérieure, pp. 195–216.

Nehamas, Alexander (1998). *The art of living: Socratic reflections from Plato to Foucault*, Berkeley and Los Angeles, CA: University of California Press.

Noirot-Maguire, Corinne (2007). 'Careful carelessness: Montaigne's curious nonchalance', in Corinne Noirot-Maguire and Valérie M. Dionne (eds.), *'Revelations of character': ethos, rhetoric and moral philosophy in Montaigne*, Newcastle: Cambridge Scholars Publishing, pp. 11–30.

Norton, Glyn P. (1975). *Montaigne and the introspective mind*, The Hague: Mouton.

O'Brien, John (2004). 'De l'*Oeconomicus* à *La Mesnagerie*: La Boetie et Xénophon', in Marcel Tetel (ed.), *Étienne de la Boétie: sage révolutionnaire et poète périgourdin*, Paris: Champion, pp. 45–62.

——— (2005). '"Autheur de merveilleux poids": Montaigne et Xénophon', *Montaigne Studies* 17: 17–34.

O'Loughlin, Michael (1978). *The garlands of repose. The literary celebration of civic and retired leisure: the traditions of Homer and Vergil, Horace and Montaigne*, University of Chicago Press.

Paige, Nicholas D. (2001). *Being interior: autobiography and the contradictions of modernity in seventeenth-century France*, Philadelphia, PA: University of Pennsylvania Press.

Parrish, John Michael (1997). 'A new source for More's *Utopia*', *The Historical Journal* 40: 493–8.

Petit, Myriam (1997). 'L'*otium* dans les *Essais* de Michel de Montaigne', *Bulletin de la société des amis de Montaigne* VIII(5–6): 41–61.

Pettit, Philip (1997). *Republicanism: a theory of freedom and government*, Oxford University Press.

——— (2002). 'Keeping republicanism simple: on a difference with Quentin Skinner', *Political Theory* 30: 339–56.

Pigman, G. W. (1980). 'Versions of imitation in the Renaissance', *Renaissance Quarterly* 33: 1–32.

Pieters, Jürgen (2006). *Speaking with the dead: explorations in literature and history*, Edinburgh University Press.

Polachek, Dora E. (1992). 'Imagination, idleness and self-discovery: Montaigne's early voyage inward', in Mario Di Cesare (ed.), *Reconsidering the Renaissance*, Binghamton, NY: Medieval and Renaissance Texts and Studies, pp. 257–69.

Porter, Roy (ed.) (1997). *Rewriting the self: histories from the Renaissance to the present*, London: Routledge.

Posner, David M. (1999). *The performance of nobility in early modern European literature*, Cambridge University Press.

Pouilloux, Jean-Yves (1969). *Lire les Essais de Montaigne*, Paris: Maspero.

______ (1995). *Montaigne: l'éveil de la pensée*, Paris: Champion.

Quint, David (1998). *Montaigne and the quality of mercy: ethical and political themes in the Essais*, Princeton University Press.

______ (2000). 'Letting oneself go: "De la colère" and Montaigne's ethical reflections', *Philosophy and Literature* 24: 126–37.

Regosin, Richard L. (1977). *The matter of my book: Montaigne's* Essais *as the book of the self*, Berkeley and Los Angeles, CA: University of California Press.

Reiss, Timothy J. (1986). 'Montaigne and the subject of polity', in David Quint (ed.), *Literary theory/Renaissance texts*, Baltimore, MD: Johns Hopkins University Press, pp. 115–49.

______ (2005). *Mirages of the selfe: patterns of personhood in ancient and early modern Europe*, Stanford University Press.

Remes, Paulina and Sihvola, Julia (eds.) (2008). *Ancient philosophy of the self*, Dordrecht: Springer.

Rigolot, François (1982). *Le texte de la Renaissance, des rhétoriqueurs à Montaigne*, Geneva: Droz.

______ (1988). *Les métamorphoses de Montaigne*, Paris: Presses universitaires de France.

______ (2005). 'Friendship and voluntary servitude: Plato, Ficino, and Montaigne', *Texas Studies in Literature and Language* 47: 326–44.

Røstvig, Maren-Sofie (1954). *The happy man: studies in the metamorphoses of a classical ideal, 1600–1700*, Oxford: Blackwell.

Saccone, Eduardo (1983). '*Grazia, sprezzatura, affettazione* in the *Courtier*', in Robert W. Hanning and David Rosand (eds.), *Castiglione: the ideal and the real in Renaissance culture*, New Haven, CT: Yale University Press, pp. 45–67.

Sawday, Jonathan (1995). *The body emblazoned: dissection and the human body in Renaissance culture*, London: Routledge.

Sayce, R. A. (1954). 'Baroque elements in Montaigne', *French Studies* 8: 1–16.

______ (1972). *The Essays of Montaigne: a critical exploration*, London: Weidenfeld and Nicolson.

Sayce, R. A. and Maskell, David (1983). *A descriptive bibliography of Montaigne's Essais, 1580–1700*, London Bibliographical Society.

Sayre, Robert (1978). *Solitude in society: a sociological study of French literature*, Cambridge, MA: Harvard University Press.

Schaefer, David Lewis (1990). *The political philosophy of Montaigne*, Ithaca, NY: Cornell University Press.

______ (ed.) (1998). *Freedom over servitude: Montaigne, La Boétie and* On voluntary servitude, Westport and London: Greenwood Press.

Schneider, Bettina (1996). *Nature und art in Montaigne's Essais*, Tübingen: Papers on French Seventeenth-Century Literature.

Schoenfeldt, Michael C. (1999). *Bodies and selves in early-modern England: physiology and inwardness in Spenser, Shakespeare, Herbert, and Milton*, Cambridge University Press.

Scholar, Richard (2006). 'Two cheers for free-thinking', *Paragraph* 29: 40–53.

_______ (2007). 'Friendship and free-thinking in Montaigne', in Corinne Noirot-Maguire and Valérie M. Dionne (eds.), *'Revelations of character': ethos, rhetoric and moral philosophy in Montaigne*, Newcastle: Cambridge Scholars Publishing, pp. 31–46.

_______ (2010). *Montaigne and the art of free-thinking*, Oxford: Peter Lang.

Schwartz, Jerome (2000). 'Reflections on Montaigne's ethical thinking', *Philosophy and Literature* 24: 154–64.

Sedley, David (2005). *Sublimity and skepticism in Montaigne and Milton*, Ann Arbor, MI: University of Michigan Press.

Seigel, Jerrold (2005). *The idea of the self: thought and experience in Western Europe since the seventeenth century*, Cambridge University Press.

Sellevold, Kirsti (2004). *'J'ayme ces mots . . . ': expressions linguistiques de doute dans les Essais de Montaigne*, Paris: Champion.

Shuger, Debora (2000). 'Life-writing in seventeenth-century England', in Patrick Coleman, Jayne Lewis and Jill Kowalik (eds.), *Representations of the self from the Renaissance to Romanticism*, Cambridge University Press, pp. 63–78.

Skinner, Quentin (1998). *Liberty before liberalism*, Cambridge University Press.

_______ (2002a). 'A third concept of liberty', *Proceedings of the British Academy* 117: 237–69.

_______ (2002b). 'Thomas More's *Utopia* and the virtue of true nobility', in *Visions of politics*, 3 vols, Cambridge University Press, vol. II, pp. 213–44.

_______ (2006). 'Rethinking political liberty', *History Workshop Journal* 61: 156–70.

_______ (2008a). 'Freedom as the absence of arbitrary power', in Cécile Laborde and John Maynor (eds.), *Republicanism and political theory*, Oxford: Blackwell, pp. 83–101.

_______ (2008b). *Hobbes and republican liberty*, Cambridge University Press.

Sorabji, Richard (2006). *Self: ancient and modern insights about individuality, life and death*, Oxford: Clarendon Press.

Starobinski, Jean (1985). *Montaigne in motion*, trans. Arthur Goldhammer, University of Chicago Press.

_______ (1993). *Montaigne en mouvement*, 2nd edition, Paris: Gallimard.

Steczowicz, Agnieszka (2007). 'The "know thyself" motif in Montaigne's *De la vanité*', in Corinne Noirot-Maguire and Valerie M. Dionne (eds.), *'Revelations of character': ethos, rhetoric and moral philosophy in Montaigne*, Newcastle: Cambridge Scholars Publishing, pp. 121–32.

Taylor, Charles (1989). *Sources of the self : the making of the modern identity*, Cambridge University Press.

Telle, E. V. (1968). 'À propos du mot 'essai' chez Montaigne', *Bibliothèque d'humanisme et Renaissance* 30: 225–47.

Tetel, Marcel (1979). 'The humanistic situation: Montaigne and Castiglione', *Sixteenth Century Journal* 10: 69–84.

Tournon, André (1990). '"Notre liberté volontaire": le *Contr'un* en marge des *Essais*', *Europe* 58: 72–82.

______ (1996). 'Vacances intérieures: l'essai du loisir', in Jean-Marie André, Jacqueline Dangel and Paul Demont (eds.), *Les loisirs et l'héritage de la culture classique*, Bruxelles: Latomus, pp. 559–66.

______ (2001). *Montaigne: la glose et l'essai*, Paris: Champion.

______ (2006). *'Route par ailleurs': le 'nouveau langage' des Essais*, Paris: Champion.

Traina, A. (1987). *Lo stile 'drammatico' del filosofo Seneca*, 4th edition, Bologna: Pàtron.

Trinquet, Roger (1964). 'Montaigne et la divulgation du *Contr'un*', *Bulletin de la société des amis de Montaigne* III(29): 3–13.

______ (1972). *La jeunesse de Montaigne: ses origines familiales, son enfance et ses études*, Paris: Nizet.

Tuck, Richard (1993). *Philosophy and government, 1572–1651*, Cambridge University Press.

Van Delft, Louis (1990). 'Réflexion morale et économie du moi dans les *Essais*', *Bulletin de la société des amis de Montaigne* VII(19–20): 35–50.

Vickers, Brian (1990). 'Leisure and idleness: the ambivalence of *otium*', *Renaissance Studies* 4: 1–37, 107–54.

Villey, Pierre (1933). *Les sources et l'évolution des Essais de Montaigne*, 2nd edition, 2 vols, Paris: Hachette.

Index

IDEAS IN CONTEXT 101

Edited by David Armitage, Jennifer Pitts, Quentin Skinner and James Tully

1 RICHARD RORTY, J. B. SCHNEEWIND and QUENTIN SKINNER (EDS.)
Philosophy in History
Essays in the historiography of philosophy
pb 978 0 521 27330 5

2 J. G. A. POCOCK
Virtue, Commerce and History
Essays on political thought and history, chiefly in the eighteenth century
pb 978 0 521 27660 3

3 M. M. GOLDSMITH
Private Vices, Public Benefits
Bernard Mandeville's social and political thought
hb 978 0 521 30036 0

4 ANTHONY PAGDEN (ED.)
The Languages of Political Theory in Early Modern Europe
pb 978 0 521 38666 1

5 DAVID SUMMERS
The Judgment of Sense
Renaissance naturalism and the rise of aesthetics
pb 978 0 521 38631 9

6 LAURENCE DICKEY
Hegel: Religion, Economics and the Politics of Spirit, 1770–1807
pb 978 0 521 38912 9

7 MARGO TODD
Christian Humanism and the Puritan Social Order
pb 978 0 521 89228 5

8 LYNN SUMIDA JOY
Gassendi the Atomist
Advocate of history in an age of science
pb 978 0 521 52239 7

9 EDMUND LEITES (ED.)
Conscience and Casuistry in Early Modern Europe
pb 978 0 521 52020 1

10 WOLF LEPENIES and R. J. HOLLINGDALE
Between Literature and Science
The rise of sociology
pb 978 0 521 33810 3

11 TERENCE BALL, JAMES FARR and RUSSELL L. HANSON (EDS.)
Political Innovation and Conceptual Change
pb 978 0 521 35978 8

12 GERD GIGERENZER, ZENO SWIJTINK, THEODORE PORTER and LORRAINE DASTON
The Empire of Chance
How probability changed science and everyday life
pb 978 0 521 39838 1

13 PETER NOVICK
That Noble Dream
The 'objectivity question' and the American historical profession
hb 978 0 521 34328 2 pb 978 0 521 35745 6

14 DAVID LIEBERMAN
The Province of Legislation Determined
Legal theory in eighteenth-century Britain
pb 978 0 521 52854 2

15 DANIEL PICK
Faces of Degeneration
A European disorder, c. 1848–1918
pb 978 0 521 45753 8

16 KEITH MICHAEL BAKER
Inventing the French Revolution
Essays on French political culture in the eighteenth century
pb 978 0 521 38578 7

17 IAN HACKING
The Taming of Chance
hb 978 0 521 38014 0 pb 978 0 521 38884 9

18 GISELA BOCK, QUENTIN SKINNER and MAURIZIO VIROLI (EDS.)
Machiavelli and Republicanism
pb 978 0 521 43589 5

19 DOROTHY ROSS
The Origins of American Social Science
pb 978 0 521 42836 1

20 KLAUS CHRISTIAN KOHNKE, R. J. HOLLINGDALE and LEWIS WHITE BECK
The Rise of Neo-Kantianism
German academic philosophy between idealism and positivism
hb 978 0 521 37336 4

21 IAN MACLEAN
Interpretation and Meaning in the Renaissance
The case of law
hb 978 0 521 41546 0 pb 978 0 521 02027 5

22 MAURIZIO VIROLI
From Politics to Reason of State
The acquisition and transformation of the language of politics 1250–1600
hb 978 0 521 41493 7 pb 978 0 521 67343 3

23 MARTIN VAN GELDEREN
The Political Thought of the Dutch Revolt 1555–1590
hb 978 0 521 39204 4 pb 978 0 521 89163 9

24 NICHOLAS PHILLIPSON and QUENTIN SKINNER (EDS.)
Political Discourse in Early Modern Britain
hb 978 0 521 39242 6

25 JAMES TULLY and QUENTIN SKINNER
An Approach to Political Philosophy
Locke in contexts
hb 978 0 521 43060 9 pb 978 0 521 43638 0

26 RICHARD TUCK
Philosophy and Government 1572–1651
pb 978 0 521 43885 8

27 RICHARD R. YEO
Defining Science
William Whewell, natural knowledge and public debate in early Victorian Britain
hb 978 0 521 43182 8 pb 978 0 521 54116 9

28 MARTIN WARNKE and DAVID MCLINTOCK
The Court Artist
On the ancestry of the modern artist
hb 978 0 521 36375 4

29 PETER N. MILLER
Defining the Common Good
Empire, religion and philosophy in eighteenth-century Britain
hb 978 0 521 44259 6 pb 978 0 521 61712 3

30 CHRISTOPHER J. BERRY
The Idea of Luxury
A conceptual and historical investigation
pb 978 0 521 46691 2

31 E. J. HUNDERT
The Enlightenment's Fable
Bernard Mandeville and the discovery of society
hb 978 0 521 46082 8 pb 978 0 521 61942 4

32 JULIA STAPLETON
Englishness and the Study of Politics
The social and political thought of Ernest Barker
hb 978 0 521 46125 2 pb 978 0 521 02444 0

33 KEITH TRIBE
Strategies of Economic Order
German economic discourse, 1750–1950
hb 978 0 521 46291 4 pb 978 0 521 61943 1

34 SACHIKO KUSUKAWA
The Transformation of Natural Philosophy
The case of Philip Melanchthon
hb 978 0 521 47347 7 pb 978 0 521 03046 5

35 DAVID ARMITAGE, ARMAND HIMY and QUENTIN SKINNER (EDS.)
Milton and Republicanism
hb 978 521 55178 6 pb 978 0 521 64648 2

36 MARKKU PELTONEN
Classical Humanism and Republicanism in English Political Thought 1570–1640
hb 978 0 521 49695 7 pb 978 0 521 61716 1

37 PHILIP IRONSIDE
The Social and Political Thought of Bertrand Russell
The development of an aristocratic liberalism
hb 978 0 521 47383 5 pb 978 0 521 02476 1

38 NANCY CARTWRIGHT, JORDI CAT, LOLA FLECK and THOMAS E. UEBEL
Otto Neurath: Philosophy between Science and Politics
hb 978 0 521 45174 1

39 DONALD WINCH
Riches and Poverty
An intellectual history of political economy in Britain, 1750–1834
pb 978 0 521 55920 1

40 JENNIFER PLATT
A History of Sociological Research Methods in America, 1920–1960
hb 978 0 521 44173 5 pb 978 0 521 64649 9

41 KNUD HAAKONSSEN (ED.)
Enlightenment and Religion
Rational dissent in eighteenth-century Britain
hb 978 0 521 56060 3 pb 978 0 521 02987 2

42 G. E. R. LLOYD
Adversaries and Authorities
Investigations into ancient Greek and Chinese science
hb 978 0 521 55331 5 pb 978 0 521 55695 8

43 ROLF LINDNER, ADRIAN MORRIS, JEREMY GAINES and MARTIN CHALMERS
The Reportage of Urban Culture
Robert Park and the Chicago School
hb 978 0 521 44052 3 pb 978 0 521 02653 6

44 ANNABEL S. BRETT
Liberty, Right and Nature
Individual rights in later scholastic thought
hb 978 0 521 56239 3 pb 978 0 521 54340 8

45 STEWART J. BROWN (ED.)
William Robertson and the Expansion of Empire
hb 978 0 521 57083 1

46 HELENA ROSENBLATT
Rousseau and Geneva
From the first discourse to the social contract, 1749–1762
hb 978 0 521 57004 6 pb 978 0 521 03395 4

47 DAVID RUNCIMAN
Pluralism and the Personality of the State
hb 978 0 521 55191 5 pb 978 0 521 02263 7

48 ANNABEL M. PATTERSON
Early Modern Liberalism
hb 978 0 521 59260 4 pb 978 0 521 02631 4

49 DAVID WEINSTEIN
Equal Freedom and Utility
Herbert Spencer's liberal utilitarianism
hb 978 0 521 62264 6 pb 978 0 521 02686 4

50 YUN LEE TOO and NIALL LIVINGSTONE (EDS.)
Pedagogy and Power
Rhetorics of classical learning
hb 978 0 521 59435 6 pb 978 0 521 03801 0

51 REVIEL NETZ
The Shaping of Deduction in Greek Mathematics
A study in cognitive history
hb 978 0 521 62279 0 pb 978 0 521 54120 6

52 MARY S. MORGAN and MARGARET MORRISON (EDS.)
Models as Mediators
Perspectives on Natural and Social Science
hb 978 0 521 65097 7 pb 978 0 521 65571 2

53 JOEL MICHELL
Measurement in Psychology
A critical history of a methodological concept
hb 978 0 521 62120 5 pb 978 0 521 02151 7

54 RICHARD A. PRIMUS
The American Language of Rights
hb 978 0 521 65250 6 pb 978 0 521 61621 8

55 ROBERT ALUN JONES
The Development of Durkheim's Social Realism
hb 978 0 521 65045 8 pb 978 0 521 02210 1

56 A. N. MCLAREN
Political Culture in the Reign of Elizabeth I
Queen and commonwealth 1558–1585
hb 978 0 521 65144 8 pb 978 0 521 02483 9

57 JAMES HANKINS (ED.)
Renaissance Civic Humanism
Reappraisals and reflections
hb 978 0 521 78090 2 pb 978 0 521 54807 6

58 T. J. HOCHSTRASSER
Natural Law Theories in the Early Enlightenment
hb 978 0 521 66193 5 pb 978 0 521 02787 8

59 DAVID ARMITAGE
The Ideological Origins of the British Empire
hb 978 0 521 59081 5 pb 978 0 521 78978 3

60 IAN HUNTER
Rival Enlightenments
Civil and metaphysical philosophy in early modern Germany
hb 978 0 521 79265 3 pb 978 0 521 02549 2

61 DARIO CASTIGLIONE and IAIN HAMPSHER-MONK (EDS.)
The History of Political Thought in National Context
hb 978 0 521 78234 0

62 IAN MACLEAN
Logic, Signs and Nature in the Renaissance
The case of learned medicine
hb 978 0 521 80648 0

63 PETER MACK
Elizabethan Rhetoric
Theory and practice
hb 978 0 521 812924 pb 978 0 521 02099 2

64 G. E. R. LLOYD
The Ambitions of Curiosity
Understanding the world in ancient Greece and China
hb 978 0 521 81542 0 pb 978 0 521 89461 6

65 MARKKU PELTONEN
The Duel in Early Modern England
Civility, politeness and honour
hb 978 0 521 82062 2 pb 978 0 521 02520 1

66 ADAM SUTCLIFFE
Judaism and Enlightenment
hb 978 0 521 82015 8 pb 978 0 521 67232 0

67 ANDREW FITZMAURICE
Humanism and America
An intellectual history of English colonisation, 1500–1625
hb 978 0 521 82225 1

68 PIERRE FORCE
Self-Interest before Adam Smith
A genealogy of economic science
hb 978 0 521 83060 7 pb 978 0 521 03619 1

69 ERIC NELSON
The Greek Tradition in Republican Thought
hb 978 0 521 83545 9 pb 978 0 521 02428 0

70 HARRO HÖPFL
Jesuit Political Thought
The Society of Jesus and the state, c.1540–1630
hb 978 0 521 83779 8

71 MIKAEL HÖRNQVIST
Machiavelli and Empire
hb 978 0 521 83945 7

72 DAVID COLCLOUGH
Freedom of Speech in Early Stuart England
hb 978 0 521 84748 3

73 JOHN ROBERTSON
The Case for the Enlightenment
Scotland and Naples 1680–1760
hb 978 0 521 84787 2 pb 978 0 521 03572 9

74 DANIEL CAREY
Locke, Shaftesbury, and Hutcheson
Contesting diversity in the enlightenment and beyond
hb 978 0 521 84502 1

75 ALAN CROMARTIE
The Constitutionalist Revolution
An essay on the history of England, 1450–1642
hb 978 0 521 78269 2

76 HANNAH DAWSON
Locke, Language and Early-Modern Philosophy
hb 978 0 521 85271 5

77 CONAL CONDREN, STEPHEN GAUKROGER and IAN HUNTER (EDS.)
The Philosopher in Early Modern Europe
The nature of a contested identity
hb 978 0 521 86646 0

78 ANGUS GOWLAND
The Worlds of Renaissance Melancholy
Robert Burton in context
hb 978 0 521 86768 9

79 PETER STACEY
Roman Monarchy and the Renaissance Prince
hb 978 0 521 86989 8

80 RHODRI LEWIS
Language, Mind and Nature
Artificial languages in England from Bacon to Locke
hb 978 0 521 874750

81 DAVID LEOPOLD
The Young Karl Marx
German philosophy, modern politics, and human flourishing
hb 978 0 521 87477 9

82 JON PARKIN
Taming the Leviathan
The reception of the political and religious ideas of Thomas Hobbes in England 1640–1700
hb 978 0 521 87735 0

83 D. WEINSTEIN
Utilitarianism and the New Liberalism
hb 978 0 521 87528 8

84 LUCY DELAP
The Feminist Avant-Garde
Transatlantic encounters of the early twentieth century
hb 978 0 521 87651 3

85 BORIS WISEMAN
Lévi-Strauss, Anthropology, and Aesthetics
hb 978 0 521 87529 5

86 DUNCAN BELL (ED.)
Victorian Visions of Global Order
Empire and international relations in nineteenth-century political thought
hb 978 0 521 88292 7

97 GREGORY CLAEYS
Imperial Sceptics
British critics of empire 1850–1920
hb 978 0 521 19954 4

98 EDWARD BARING
The Young Derrida and French Philosophy, 1945–1968
hb 9781107009677

99 CAROL PAL
Republic of Women
Rethinking the republic of letters in the seventeenth century
hb 9781107018211

100 C. A. BAYLY
Recovering Liberties
Indian thought in the age of liberalism and empire
hb 9781107013834 pb 9781107601475

101 FELICITY GREEN
Montaigne and the Life of Freedom
hb 9781107024397